An Inn Near Kyoto

Writing by American Women Abroad

AN INN NEAR KYOTO

Writing by American Women Abroad

Edited by
Kathleen Coskran and C.W. Truesdale

A New Rivers Abroad Book

NEW RIVERS PRESS 1998

First Edition
Printed in the United States of America
Library of Congress Catalog Card Number: 97-68817
ISBN: 0-89823-181-7
Edited by Kathleen Coskran and C. W. Truesdale
Copyedited by Sarah Fairchild and Julie Thomson
Book design and typesetting by Steven Canine

New Rivers Press is a nonprofit literary press dedicated to publishing the very best emerging writers in our region, nation, and world.

The publication of *An Inn Near Kyoto* has been made possible by generous grants from the Beim Foundation, the General Mills Foundation, Liberty State Bank, the McKnight Foundation, the Star Tribune/Cowles Media Company, and the contributing members of New Rivers Press.

New Rivers Press
420 North Fifth Street, Suite 910
Minneapolis, MN 55401

www.mtn.org/newrivpr

This book is dedicated to
Bea Exner Liu

(*Remembering China: 1935–1945*,
New Rivers Press, 1996)

Contents

EUROPE

Acknowledgments

Helen Barolini's "Going to Sicily" first appeared in the *Paris Review,* Summer, 1980.

Judith Barrington's "Worlds Apart" is drawn from her memoir *Lifesaving.*

An earlier version of Leslie Brody's "Kyoto" appeared in *Boxcar, A Journal of the Women's Itinerant Hobo's Union.*

Kelly Cherry's "An Underground Hotel in Leningrad" is excerpted from her book, *The Exiled Heart* (Louisiana State University Press, 1991).

Pamela Gullard's "Tourist Zone" is from *Breathe at Every Other Stroke* by Pamela Gullard, © 1996 by Pamela Gullard. Reprinted by permission of Henry Holt & Co., Inc.

Danielle D'Ottavio Harned's "The Light in the Dust" was originally published in *The Abiko Quarterly.*

Marilyn Krysl's "Deeper Darkness" first appeared in *Mãnoa: A Pacific Journal of International Writing,* Summer 1995. Reprinted by permission of the author.

Michelle Dominque Leigh's "An Inn Near Kyoto," "Me Jane: Nagano's Valley of Hell," "Mystic Mountains: The Sacred Path of the *Yamabushi,*" first appeared in *Wingspan: The Inflight Magazine of All Nippon Airways.* Leigh's "The Happy Double Life of Setsuko Tanezawa" originally appeared in *Winds: The Inflight Magazine of Japan Airlines.*

Ann Pancake's "Keeping Clean in Korat" was originally published in *International Quarterly,* Winter 1997.

Simone Poirier-Bures's "Crete, 1966" is excerpted from *That Shining Place* (Oberon Press, 1995).

Lee Sharkey's "Walking with Lena" originally appeared in *Puckerbrush Review,* Summer/Fall 1995.

Joan Silber's "The Dollar in Italy" was originally published in *Global City Review,* Fall 1993.

Carol Spindel's "Marriage Is Very Difficult" originally appeared in her book, *In the Shadow of the Sacred Grove* (Random House, 1989).

Kathleen Coskran

INTRODUCTION

I SPENT A FEW DAYS in a friend's compound in Harar, Ethiopia, this summer. Badria, a middle daughter, was home with her newborn son, Oman. While I was there, she spent her days and nights on a pallet behind a curtain with the infant. When her mother and sisters brought her food or a neighbor visited with her, Badria parted the curtain enough to speak with them, but she never left her child.

"How are you feeling?" I asked her.

"Good," she said. She pulled back the curtain to show me her sleeping infant. I peered at him from what I hoped was a respectful distance. "He is beautiful," I said.

"Yes, you can come in," she said and offered the invitation I was waiting for. I slid behind the curtain and reclined with the two of them in the small, dark space. She was in the twenty-third day of a forty-day confinement. "How long do you do it in America?" she asked.

"Oh, not so long," I said. "Our custom is different." I couldn't bear to be more specific, to tell her that in America new mothers are lucky to spend forty-eight hours alone with their newborns.

I had this conversation behind the curtain with Badria during the time we were preparing *An Inn Near Kyoto* for publication. As I reread these wonderful stories and memoirs against the backdrop of my own recent experiences in Ethiopia, I was struck by the universal desire for the invitation and the ease of accepting it when offered woman to woman. Being born a girl is so radically different from being born a boy in any country that there is scant common ground between the sexes when cultural differences are introduced. Relationships with men are inherently ambiguous, even without sexual overtones. Invitations from men to women across cultures are difficult to read and hard to accept at face value, but women trust each other instinctively because they want to know how other women negotiate their lives.

Elizabeth Mills in "The Hammam" finds common ground when she takes us into the women's baths in Tunisia, an enclave where naked women "of all shapes and sizes moved without embarrassment among the various rooms." The narrator squirms during the shampoo, "unused to the intimate contact and at the same time welcoming the warmth and novelty of it." She discovers her own limits when she pulls back the curtain that shrouds the details of Tunisian women's lives and steps in. Nothing is as it seems; the easy assumption of the passivity of veiled women is contradicted when Mills takes us into the hammam and shows us women who are veiled every hour of their lives except when in the baths. There they shed the protection of their clothes and reveal that their true power is in their own relationships.

In Andrea Benton Rushing's amazing "Living on the Edges: Nigerian Journals," she meets real female power when market women, "those wide-hipped mamas who haven't *seen* the inside of a school," go on strike. The market women literally control *all* the food in Lagos. "I can't believe that, despite its guns and tanks, the military isn't confronting these women! Can't think, despite all the rap about women's liberation, of a U.S. equivalent to the power these women exert with such self-assurance." It is through this intimate, woman-to-woman contact that we see our own situation more clearly.

When I traveled in East Africa for three months, the most frequent question asked of me was, "Where is your husband?" as if I needed a man to explain my presence. A man alone is a man alone; a woman alone is odd at best, easy prey at worst. Many of these writers who travel solo are well aware of the risk of going it alone, but they are out there anyway, making connections.

They are also canny travelers, eyeing the locals for clues of how to behave and then giving over something of themselves in order to fit in gracefully. This relinquishing of control can be terrifying for the reader following the nineteen-year-old narrator in Michelle Blair's story, "Eternal City," on her desperate quest for love and meaning, or oddly satisfying watching Sarah Ventres, a middle-aged Peace Corps volunteer, disrobe in a room full of strangers. "All shreds of my (false?) western modesty fled this weekend; given no real options, I simply observed my hosts' actions and did the same. Lissa and I dressed and undressed in the same room while Mareel conversed with friends. Seemed quite natural!"

In these revealing stories and memoirs, in New Rivers's third anthology of North American women writing about travel, we encounter remarkable women finding the remarkable quite natural. In these stories of travel alone, travel with a partner, romance, adventure, and discovery, the writers show us that life is in the details. It is the points of human contact that reward the woman traveler—the brief exchange with the masseuse, or the kindness of a seat mate on a bus, are the moments these women crossed oceans to experience.

A striking aspect of New Rivers Press's anthologies of North American women abroad—*The House on Via Gombito, Tanzania on Tuesday,* and, now, *An Inn Near Kyoto*—is the focus on relationships, not on monuments. The writers evoke the richness of the detail of life as it's lived in Lagos, in Tokyo, in Leningrad, in Endeber; but, at the same time, they refuse to romanticize life abroad. Andrea Benton Rushing, during her first trip to Nigeria, writes, "Privacy's an alien concept. No one can imagine that you want or need time alone. People read every single piece of paper in sight. Read it and then want to discuss the contents with you. *I am not cut out for this life!*" Yet she goes back to Nigeria a second time and a third.

Savor these stories and memoirs as the writers pull back the curtain and invite you into a world where the smell and shape and pattern of the most ordinary details of life—bathing, dressing, eating, sleeping—are revealing. In the exquisitely noted details of travel in Russia, Italy, Chile, Vietnam, or Nicaragua, these observant women illumine the common ground of human connections everywhere.

C.W. Truesdale

INTRODUCTION

New Rivers Press offers the reader this third anthology in its series of writing by American women living or traveling abroad. The first of these volumes, *The House on Via Gombito,* published in 1991 and subsequently reprinted twice, is our most successful anthology to date. The second of these, *Tanzania on Tuesday,* was published in the spring of 1997. Both *Tanzania on Tuesday* and *An Inn Near Kyoto* were co-edited by Kathleen Coskran and myself.

Our original intention was to bring out just a second anthology, but the quality of submissions was so high, and they were so numerous, it seemed to us a natural choice to bring out yet a third volume in this series. Even so, we found ourselves having to leave out a great deal of superb material. (Almost all of the pieces in *An Inn Near Kyoto* were originally submitted for what came to be called *Tanzania on Tuesday.*)

The title of this third anthology comes from one of the pieces by Michelle Dominique Leigh. This is very fitting, since the whole idea for the original volume grew out of a conversation many years ago that the two of us had at a New York Small Press Book Fair in the Loeb Center at New York University. Ms. Leigh had a number of short pieces on Africa in *The House on Via Gombito,* and four, now, in *An Inn Near Kyoto*—all about Japan (where she lived for a number of years) as seen through the eyes of an American woman.

I've made an admittedly random selection of examples from among the many writers included in this far-ranging and interconnected collection. All of them, in one way or another, turn the physical environments they write about into a kind of "home"—a psychological state. Sometimes, as in the work of Michelle Leigh and Rhiannon Paine, these writers explore how manners and customs (very different from what they are used to) help define a place as home. Faylene De Vries (writing about rural Ireland) and Judith Azrael (writing about Southeast Asia) show us how the sheer beauty of our surroundings can turn a foreign place into home—though that beauty itself can be a kind of distraction.

Rhiannon Paine, like Michelle Leigh, was also represented in *The House on Via Gombito*—by some very amusing pieces on traveling in England. They were so funny and so professionally written, I was very surprised to hear from her afterward that these were her first published pieces—a real discovery for us. The five pieces of Paine's in *An Inn Near Kyoto* are, like Leigh's, about Japan. They are taken from an unpublished book-length manuscript of hers called *Too Late for the Festival: An American Salary Woman in Japan,* an account—in her characteristically humorous style—of the eighteen months she spent in Japan working for an American computer company. We could have picked any number of selections from it but decided to use four related pieces dealing with some close Japanese friends she made while living and working there. A fifth piece, from the introductory chapter, explains what Paine was doing in Japan. She ends this chapter of her book with an interesting comparison of her feelings about living in two foreign countries, England and Japan, and what it took to make each place feel like home:

> Living in England I had tried hard to be English. I'd worn tweedy clothes, drunk endless cups of tea, adopted an English accent, cultivated reserve, and disdained money (this was easy to do since I didn't have any). I had become English—the accent never fooled anyone but Americans—but I had changed, inside and out. "How do you feel about getting divorced?" my best friend asked me when I moved back to America. I fixed her with the look that English people give you when you ask "impertinent" questions and changed the subject. If I proved similarly susceptible in Japan, I could end up in a Buddhist monastery with all my hair shaved off. Of course, Japan wouldn't accept me the way that Britain had. Britain had held out her arms and said, "Welcome home, I remember your dear grandparents, would you like to see the family albums?" Japan had greeted me with a nicely judged bow, the kind you give to female foreigners of relatively low socioeconomic status. Japan would treat me with respect but would never let me forget that I was

> *gaijin,* an other-person, ineradicably different.
>
> I wasn't sure what frightened me more: the thought of being different for a year or finding out that I didn't feel different at all.
>
> Either way, I thought, as I fell back into jet-lagged sleep, I'm going to be shaken, and by a lot more than a minor earthquake.

The book as a whole deals in great and often amusing detail with Paine's often futile efforts to assimilate herself into Japanese society. She writes about her efforts to buy furniture for her new apartment, the fact that she lives as a single woman in large, sumptuous (by Japanese standards) lodgings, her efforts to get along with her fellow workers (most of whom are Japanese), her efforts to purchase food, and a thousand other things. All these pieces not only illuminate, vividly, her own American attitudes but Japanese society as well.

One early chapter in her book deals with shopping around Tokyo for her new apartment. At one point she goes into a particular store to buy a new vacuum cleaner. She points to the model she wants:

> The shopkeepers, a husband and wife, offered it to me in pale blue or burgundy, but I insisted on white [to match her refrigerator], like the one on display outside the shop. They tried to explain that they had no vacuum cleaner in white, only the display model, but I didn't understand them. Finally, instead of doing the sensible thing—hitting me over the head with an attachment—they brought the display model, spent fifteen minutes cleaning it and another fifteen minutes demonstrating its functions, and then gave me a twenty percent discount off the price I'd already agreed to pay. All this with as many bows and smiles as if they actually wanted to see me again, instead of hoping that the first time I used the vacuum cleaner I'd suck myself up the nozzle.

The other selections deal with her two friends, Yasuhiro Nakamura and Miyuki-san. Yasuhiro, "Yas" as he insists she call him, is a true Japanese eccentric who would not be at all unusual in an American context but is truly a rare phenomenon in Japan. Because Yas is so different from the stereotypical Japanese male, Paine uses him to bring out those stereotypes by contrast. Miyuki-san, who knows English well and frequently serves Paine as a translator, is someone usually treated as most Japanese women are—she is, though immensely qualified for some high-level technical job, forced to be a secretary in a dominantly male environment. She is tough, smart, and for the most part, loyal if not quite obsequious. In other words, she is, from Paine's point of view, immensely admirable. The account of her "rebellion" against Establishment values—with another woman named Mikiko-san—is given in the third of these four selections. Mikiko-san is a Japanese-American woman "who had gone to American schools in Switzerland. . . . She was not only qualified to be an engineer, she was also fully bilingual in two of the world's most difficult languages." The rebellion is their excessively polite refusal to serve morning and afternoon tea to the males in the office.

Like Michelle Leigh and Rhiannon Paine, Faylene De Vries spends much of her time abroad. Every summer (and sometimes longer, when she and her husband have sabbaticals or leaves from their teaching positions in the States) De Vries lives in a small cottage they own in the Irish countryside in County Clare about thirty miles from Shannon Airport. The two pieces we have included here are evocative of that country environment, to be sure (especially her description of her kitchen in that cottage in the second), but she constantly reminds us of her other life—the one she lives in America. In "And How's the Missus?" her main subject is really how difficult it is for her to adjust, as her husband's second wife, to life in Ireland. Lincoln, who had lived in that same village for some time with his first wife and the mother of De Vries's two stepsons, has been accepted—and even venerated—by the locals. These same people, however, give De Vries "the Look" (something like the "evil eye," I suppose) and make her acutely self-conscious: "In the next few days, I was to hear the 'welcome home' greeting many times. I heard it, but was not its recipient. The words, warm and familiar, were for Lincoln; looks, curious and suspicious, were reserved for me. I felt assaulted by the Small Town Look." She details this galling sense of estrangement in recounting many incidents—which, in effect, seem to be ruining her life in Kilnadoon. It is not until several years later that her stepson, Andrew, asks her why she doesn't "give them [the local villagers] time to know you?" She and Lincoln arrive in the village the next summer and decide to go to the local Market Day in Carrigfeale—which she lovingly describes—before going on to open up the cottage. She is thoroughly delighted when a brother and sister, selling vegetables there, greet her with a statement that, simple as it is, has an exhilarating effect on her: "Welcome home, Missus."

In the second of these two sketches, "Views from the Kitchen," De Vries concentrates more on what she actually views from the two windows in her kitchen. What we get is a wonderful description of the cottage itself and its setting in the Irish countryside near the sea. But we also get a strong sense of her life beyond the cottage and the effect of that place on her rounds of teaching:

> To be truthful, this essay surfaced during an afternoon mopping spree. Down on all fours, grinding my boney knees against the tiled cement, I was also listening to an R.T.E. interview with Marilyn French, whose *The Woman's Room* had been receiving attention in Ireland. Caught up in that discussion, the drudgery of the task seemed less oppressive since I was reminded that women's work is also done outside the kitchen. However, that transformation is only possible if I, the kitchen worker, also have access to that outside world. I am happy in my Kilnadoon kitchen because I am not trapped here. My identity is not shaped in its confines. I can look beyond the windows into a classroom where I find satisfaction (most of the time) developing basic skills and, even more, challenging my students to think beyond stereotypes. At the same time, I assert that I teach better and enjoy it more because of my kitchen's reflection.
>
> Luckily for me, two windows open our Kilnadoon kitchen to light.

In Judith Azrael's "Sketch Book"—about her solitary travels in Southeast Asia—we come across an utterly unique style. These "sketches" (as she calls them) of her stays in Bali, Bangkok, and elsewhere consist of tiny images of each place that read more like series of prose poems than anything else. Of Bali, she writes, "Always somewhere a gamelon is playing, relentless and full of sorrow and of joy, a clear stream of melody moving through the slow afternoons." Later, in the same Bali sketches, she writes beautifully of the mountains, the ritual processions, and the children:

> In the mountains the air is cool and moist. Bright splashes of blue morning glories amidst a jungle of greenery. Monkeys with small tufts on their heads are sitting in the road.

> I stand in the crowd and watch giant statues of gods carried aloft on frames. It takes many men to support them. Orchestras pass with gamelons and drums and resounding gongs. The

> women are dressed in sarongs and temple scarves. They carry tall intricate arrangements of fruit on their heads.

> The village boys are filled with longing. Ketut wants a bag to carry his books. Wayan wants a watch he can wear into the sea. They want my scuffed sandals and my sweater and my daughter's photograph. We have nothing, they tell me. I gesture toward the fringe of shining white sand and the sea. We have nothing, they say again.

> At dawn I run down to the beach where a boat is waiting. It is long and narrow, carved from a mango tree. We motor far out to sea until we find the dolphins. The sun is rising and dolphins are leaping all around us.

Azrael has also spent much time in Greece, particularly on the Greek islands, which she writes about with equal intensity. Her close attention to details of place helps anchor her to her surroundings—wherever she might find herself.

These three writers—all very different from one another—are typical of the range and variety of women writing here about traveling or staying for long periods abroad. I could easily have chosen other pieces to write about: Kelly Cherry's "An Underground Hotel in Leningrad" is a memoir, really, but reads like a short story, about her near marriage to a Latvian composer named Imant. More than anything else, she tells this story in the context of the grotesque rules, regulations, and environment of the Soviet Union in the days before its collapse. Pamela Gullard's "Tourist Zone" is a story about a man and a woman visiting Puerto Rico and trying to decide whether to become more or less permanent partners and not just occasional vacationers. In "Wearing the Good Red Earth, Down Under," Judy Rosen describes the encounter of an American park ranger on leave in Australia to work for the Queensland National Parks and Wildlife Service. She manages to open up to us a region in that country few have ever heard of. Simone Poirier-Bures, in "Crete, 1966," describes in vivid detail her experiences as a teacher in that country thirty-two years ago. Among many other things, she talks about class differences in the Greek island community of Chania and the difficulties she, as a young and very independent American woman, encounters there. In Mary Ellen Fieweger's "Teresa," the author tells the story of an Ecuadorian servant she employed there who becomes unexpectedly pregnant. This challenges American attitudes in foreign cultures. Nor Hall's contribution, "Aphrodite in Avignon," details a sojourn she and her daughter had at a seminar/conference for women in France two or three years ago. Finally, Margaret Todd Maitland's piece, "The Days of the Dead," describes a trip she made to Oaxaca in Mexico, mainly to deal with the loss of her son. (Maitland is the only writer represented in all three New Rivers Press anthologies of writing by American women traveling or living abroad.)

All of these stories and essays, including the many not mentioned here, describe, in rich, vivid detail, the encounters of these remarkable and highly individual writers with cultures from which they learn in many surprising ways what it means to be at home in the world and what it means to be American in an often strange, sometimes exotic, sometimes ordinary place.

AFRICA

Elizabeth Mills

THE HAMMAM

The night before I had ridden through the streets on the back of someone's moped. I had seen cows standing in the streets with cats, feeding on the leftovers that had been put out for them. It had been so hot that day that people had moved their pallets onto the sidewalks to sleep. Golden light streamed over their reclining forms from arched, cobalt blue doorways, open to the night. Their low white adobe houses seemed to hunker protectively over them as they lay chatting softly to each other, propped languidly on elbows.

In Kairouan we awoke every morning to fervent calls to prayer from the minarets and to the sounds of drumbeats. The stench of raw sewage was everywhere; somehow we had gotten accustomed even to that. The sweet pungency of jasmine, equally pervasive, seemed to cut through it.

A man wore jasmine blossoms behind his left or right ear, depending on whether he wanted a wife or whether he was married. Abdul had been wearing one behind his right ear, a detail that registered later, when he and Latfi picked us up for dinner at his mother's house. Abdul was married.

We made a little parade, the two guys in front, as we walked through the streets lined with men. There wasn't a woman to be seen in any café here except when we went.

"Betsey, do you realize we're walking two steps behind?" Kim said. We broke up laughing, and I felt a pang: in two days we'd be walking side by side with American men who loved our questing natures, men whom we loved.

At dinner Latfi had pulled out all the stops. "I want you to feel how white-hot my heart is," he said.

"I have no doubt," I said, "but I am leaving tomorrow."

He massaged mint essence into my forehead and read my palm, and he placed sprigs of mint and basil in the pockets of my shirt. He drew a baton of kohl between the sweeps of his long lashes and showed me photographs of himself with and without. A country where the men are beautiful and wear makeup; I was moved.

"If you see a pretty carpet, you buy it, don't you? " he said.

"I don't buy carpets," I said, an easy lie.

"If you sleep with me," he said, "you will take all of Tunisia with you: the earth, the trees, the sky. It is not I who says it, but Allah who decrees it."

"Where I live a man and woman must be friends first," I said, "and in your country I don't think friendship between a man and woman is possible."

"Oh, no," he said. "Men are for friendship, women are for love."

"There you are," I said, "and it would crush my spirit. Anyway, I'm leaving tomorrow."

The men were trying to get us drunk, and when it didn't work the women embraced us. Abdul had been singing paeans to Kim's eyebrows, and when she made it clear she would not sleep with him, in a fit of temper he tore up the address he had given her.

She handed him a lighter and said, "Why don't you torch it, while you're at it? " which he could not resist doing as he made a dramatic exit, repeating the words, "I am free man, I am free."

As soon as he was gone, the courtyard burst into laughter, and Mahgouba, the matriarch, moved from her cushion to our side of the table, plopped herself down and threw an arm around each of us in a gesture that said, *There's my girl.*

Men were always proposing things, and it was exhausting to be with them sometimes. "Aren't you scared," they would ask, "two women traveling alone?"

"We're not alone," we would tell them. "We're together." You could see them sit up and take notice.

The next morning, as promised, Mahgouba's daughter Latifah marched us through the sandy streets to the hammam, the Turkish bath. The men had fetched us in a car for the occasion, and they seemed excited, anticipating what we were about to experience. They had a proprietary and hopeful air about them, as if they were getting an early start this time, and today's efforts might yield a more favorable outcome.

They told us about the masseur and the strong friction of his glove, but he would not do us, they said, laughing. They explained that there was a men's side and a women's at the bath. They talked about the betel nut that would color our gums and lips, and about the next time, when they hoped to mark our feet and hands with henna.

"This brings happiness to women," they said.

Inside the hammam, the smells of musky soap and dampness rose from the floor. The guttural sounds of Arabic, which I had come to love, echoed off the tile walls of the entry room. We were both amazed and terrified by the scene; we wanted to stay and we wanted to bolt. Dark faces stared at us with open curiosity, and to us the place had the look and feel of harems we'd seen in the movies. Women in traditional Berber dress sat on a ledge among columns spaced around the room, their red and black plaids reverberating against the bright green and blue mosaic tiles. This was an enclave for women; Latifah got her news here, and this was where she had swapped a scarf for her new earrings. Women of all shapes and sizes moved without embarrassment among the various rooms. Islam required one to wear panties, they had told us, so we wore lycra bathing suits that could be rolled down around our hips.

Latifah spoke with the masseuse and motioned us into the next room for our massages. Kim went first. As soon as I sat down to watch, another woman shoved some betel nut under my upper lip. She motioned me to move it to the lower gum too, I supposed to stain my mouth evenly and activate the tranquilizing drug. It had a roughness and acidity that hurt my gums, a deep green color and bitter taste.

The masseuse was a massive Berber woman with fishbone tattoos on her chin and forehead, graying hair pulled into a cotton scarf, and enormous great breasts under a thin yellow nightie, clinging wet to her skin. Sitting on the green tile floor of the main washroom, she motioned for me to lie with my head in her lap. For a second I wondered about it, but the thought passed. I found courage. I wouldn't miss this for anything.

There was water slushing everywhere, and things floating in it, like hair. Kim said, "Hey Bets, what would your mother think of this?"

"She'd be horrified by the hygiene of it," I said, and we laughed giddily. Maybe the betel nut was starting to work. It hurt, like holding a piece of bark in my mouth, but sucking on it gave me focus while the masseuse's powerful scrub rocked me against her thighs. She twirled me around and turned me over with one finger, then with the French words *"haut, haut"* ordered me to stand so she could do my legs. I watched a lifetime of silt along with a Mediterranean tan disappear, as the skin sloughed off under her glove.

In a muddle, I crossed the floor into one of the little stalls that lined the main washroom, where Kim and Latifah and a beautiful young girl with big black hair were shampooing and rinsing each other. In each stall there were women working shampoo into each other's hair and pouring buckets of water over each other's heads to rinse. Kim and Latifah finished and went to dry off. The young girl stayed.

"You are beautiful," she said. She looked directly and sweetly into my face.

"We think *you* are beautiful," I said, hiding behind the royal *we.*

"Your skin is beautiful," she said, "the whiteness." She seemed to be fascinated with my skin as we stood naked, facing each other. She watched me shampoo and then poured one bucket after another of water over my head from the streaming faucet. I squirmed, unused to the intimate contact and at the same time welcoming the warmth and novelty of it.

"We tan ourselves in the sun so we can have coffee-colored skin like yours," I said. "Do you see many Americans in the *hammam?*"

"Oh yes," she said, "professors who teach at the university, and I love to speak with them. I would love to visit America."

She asked if we were friends, and whether I would give her my address. I wrote it out for her and thanked her for her kindness.

I dried off, and dressed, and looked around to record the place in my mind. The room with the columns was now packed with women in Berber dress gossiping and merchandising, trading personal possessions. There were handshakes all around, with the masseuse, who was sitting cross-legged on the floor, now, eating couscous, with the woman who sat at the cash box, and with others who wanted to meet us.

Later, at the hotel, I sat in the lobby and wrote some about the hammam. Even in this hundred-degree heat, the massage had improved my spirit. My skin was new skin, and my gums were humming from the betel nut. I thought about the men and the women we had met in Kairouan, how we could not seem to find a happy encounter with the men, yet we felt such solidarity with the women, such warmth and intimacy. With the men we were always on guard, aware that more was wanted of us; with the women alone, we could be ourselves and laugh openly. Among women, our company was enough.

Laurel Berger

MOROCCAN JOURNAL

SUMMER, 1992. The distinguished Koranic scholar Fatima Mernissi invites me to Rabat. Everything about her is larger-than-life: her aquiline nose, her enormous brown eyes lined with smudgy kohl, her majestic bearing.

"I will open doors for you," she says in her slow, precise, ever-so-slightly autocratic French. Last time I went to Morocco the doors were shut tight. No chance of meeting the women who dashed across the open squares in birdlike formation, nylon *djellabas* aflutter. Or anyone else, for that matter.

Fatima is blunt about what she wants from me. "Write about what's going on here. Talk to people. Ask questions." And then, sounding like the women's activist she is, she adds, "The printed word is our most powerful weapon."

I hesitate. I'm no expert on things Islamic, nor, in all honesty, do I believe anything I write will further the feminist cause. Even so, I wangle a magazine assignment and block out two weeks on my calendar.

In the stories of my childhood, Morocco was a place where women disappeared at market; where they were bought and sold like old mutton; where even the flies in the medina would lead you astray, if you let them. At first, when I moved to Spain eight years ago, I resisted Morocco. Then I discovered Tahar Ben Jelloun, whose stories unfurl in a mythical North African landscape, and after that I couldn't keep away. Maybe it was the idea of crossing into forbidden territory that pleased me, I don't know. But when the jagged-toothed men approach me in the medina now, I improvise a past. "I am the wife of Mohamed from Zarf el Safar," I say. With my dark hair and Mediterranean complexion I might be from anywhere. I give myself a Muslim name: Khadija, the most beloved of the Prophet's wives.

RABAT. Fatima's assistant, Myriam, telephones to invite me to a dinner party on the edge of town. Some fifty or so guests mill about the brilliant white villa, chatting over the percussive strains of Berber folk music, while a stream of domestics in billowy white robes shuffle into the dining room, balancing heavy platters of food. They range heaps of couscous, spiced carrots on silver trays, and a huge grilled fish on the long walnut table. It is the end of summer. Through the open windows seeps the narcotic odor of rain and sandalwood leaves, headier than kef.

I find Fatima sitting against the wall, on a cushioned banquette, near a window; she's splendidly attired in flowing pants shot with gold, her henna-red hair wrapped in a turban. Taking my hand, she propels me around the room and introduces me to her fellow activists: writers, teachers, artists, lawyers, students.

Mohamed Abderrahman Tazi, the party's host, shambles over to me. "So you're the journalist?" he says without preamble, drawing on his pipe. A salt-and-pepper bearded man with bright amber eyes, skin the color of sandstone, and a certain aura of inscrutability, Tazi is a filmmaker in a country that produces three films a year. He tells me that Fatima conscripted him to do a series of short, jokey, down-with-machismo video clips for national television—a powerful medium of communication in a land of widespread illiteracy. When I ask about *Badis,* his first and only feature film, he promises to screen it for me.

Long before I knew Fatima Mernissi, I knew her work. It had enthralled me ever since I came across *The Forgotten Queens of Islam,* a marvelous piece of detective work in which she convincingly demonstrates that women—shrewd courtesans and enterprising slaves—once ruled in ancient Islam. From the start I was taken by the clarity of her voice, her meticulous research, and her intriguing subject matter. All her books advance the argument that Islam is basically an egalitarian religion whose true spirit has been distorted for centuries by the male elite.

But I only met her recently, when I attended a talk she gave at the stuffy, down-at-the-heels Ateneo Club in Madrid. Afterwards, Fatima was swept away by a group of young Spaniards for beer and *tapas*—and I tagged along. Storm clouds hung low in the sky, throwing the crumbling, once-elegant buildings into relief. As we walked along the quiet street, we got into conversation. Fatima was swathed in her usual riot of color—the most fantastic shades of orange and purple and pink. She talked a bit about the women's movement in Morocco, and when she paused for breath I asked the obvious: How active was it? And miraculously, or so it seemed to me at the time, she replied, "Why don't you come and see for yourself?"

Fatima is editing an anthology about the place of women in postcolonial North Africa. All this week she'll be leading a workshop, a kind of extended editorial meeting, for the book's contributors. Their talks, which I've been invited to observe, will take place at the headquarters of the organization underwriting the project, the Ebert Foundation.

The non-Moroccans, who have journeyed from Tunisia and Algeria for the event, are staying at the Hotel les Oudayas, a tatty little place behind the flower market. It's not too bad, really, except that when I checked in last night the bed linens beneath the orange coverlet were rumpled and there was a condom floating in the toilet bowl. By coincidence or design, the men have been given rooms at the far end of the hall. Next door to me is Rachida, a thirty-nine-year-old Tunisian journalist who is lively and quick-witted and full of good cheer. She and another woman here, a school teacher named Amel, are in the process of founding a women's college, the first in North Africa.

"Our legislation is relatively evolved," Rachida tells me, seated on a rickety chair in her bare room. She is a large-boned woman with a handsome face and close-cropped hair. "In Tunisia women make up twenty percent of the working population, so we have certain rights, certainly more than in any other country in North Africa." She frowns at my awkward attempt to peel an apple without a knife. "And yet," she goes on, "when it comes to giving an opinion, or expressing our sexuality, we simply don't exist. Convenient, is it not?"

The Ebert Foundation is housed in a cube-shaped structure perched high above the city. Mornings I sit in on Fatima's workshop, which she rules like a sultana, to little effect. After the first half hour, the discussion invariably disintegrates into a shouting match, and I find myself watching the door for the woman who brings lovely mint tea and sweet cakes.

My scratchpad is littered with Fatima's *aperçus.* On the North African women's movement: "We must become as organized as the Mafia." On women who take the veil: "They think we're contemptuous of them. We are. But we have to work with them anyway." On Islamic law: "Because the Prophet left no instructions on how to run the place after his death, his followers had to improvise as they went along. As a result, political Islam has turned out to be one of the most ruthless, most despotic systems ever known to humanity."

All day long I walk, stopping for mint tea at one café, then another, and another. The sky is clear and bright, the sun feels good on my arms, even in the sultry heat. Rabat, Morocco's capital, lies on the Atlantic coast, in the north of the country. In the twelfth century it was the stomping grounds of the Almohad conqueror, Yacoub el Mansour, who established his capital here. Today it's home to both King Hassan II and the Moroccan intelligentsia. The new town is a mix of dismal concrete buildings and French colonial architecture, but in the old quarter it's easy to lose oneself among high lime-rinsed walls that smell of freshly laundered clothes.

At dusk I meet up with Mohamed Tazi in the city center. He arrives with two heartbreakingly beautiful girls and a composer called Nouman, a rangy young man with hooded eyes. We stand there for awhile, talking in the half-light, as a stream of people curve around us. Mouna, impish and spritelike, with nut-brown skin and stylishly bobbed hair, is the eighteen-year-old star of his latest film, *In Search of My Wife's Husband,* a sort of tragicomedy about a polygamist who impulsively repudiates his favorite wife (played by the winsome Mouna).

We pile into Mohamed's white van, a mud-splattered tumbledown affair, and head for the suburbs. At times Mohamed seems so grave, as if he bears some heavy burden, but right now he's laughing and joking in Arabic with the girls like a kid. I don't quite know what to make of him. My mind drifts to the landscape beyond the window, to the plain boxlike houses strung along the wayside. Mohamed lives farther down the road, in a posh if charmless sub-division. When we finally reach the house, night has fallen and ink-blue clouds are scudding across the sky. Like some magical thing, the sandalwood tree glows silver in the vespertine light, scenting the air with its astringent tang. We follow Mohamed down the flagstone path to the heavy cedarwood portal and make our way inside. While the others settle in to the living room, I install myself in Mohamed's study to watch *Badis.*

The narrative unfolds with all the languor of a public storyteller's tale. A motherless girl falls in love with a Spanish soldier who is stationed in her remote northern village. When her father learns of their romance, he (falsely) accuses the young man of pissing in the local water supply, and the soldier is removed from his post. The girl tries to flee with her tutor, an outsider who longs to escape her tyrannical husband, but the villagers pick up their scent and stone both of them to death. The film eloquently conveys the tedium and suffocating insularity of village life as well as its spare beauty. And it does so with a uniquely Moroccan sensibility.

Later that evening, Mohamed, with a tumbler of scotch in one hand, tells me that when he presented the film in Algiers last year, the theater was packed. Four hundred people in all, only two women: "Khalida," he says, gesturing to his house guest, Khalida Messaoudi (a thirty-four-year old mathematics teacher who happens to be Algeria's preeminent feminist) and the wife of the French vice-consul. He stood at the front of the theater and said to the audience, "I'm very pleased to be here this evening but I'm surprised to see so few women. . . ." To his delight every man in the house applauded. At first he flattered himself that they agreed with him. But as their cheers and shouts grew louder he realized it was the very absence of women they were applauding.

He laughs as he tells the story, laughs at his own foolishness. When I try to draw him out about his background, he pours himself another finger of scotch and tells me that his forebears were polygamists. The youngest son of a prominent Fès family, he was reared in a harem and educated at the Sorbonne and Syracuse University. His father was an astronomer, "a great sage," who cast astrology charts for diversion. "He was a myth to me," Mohamed says, tapping the bowl of his pipe against an ashtray. "He commanded respect," he continues. "Demanded it." But it was the women—his mothers, sisters, aunts, concubines—who formed him. "They were the ones who shaped my beliefs, the ones who educated me, the ones who made me what I am."

We move into the dining room, where the old cook serves *kefta,* balls of minced lamb seasoned with cumin, and salad. To my left sits Khalida, a delicate-looking woman with a mop of red curls and milky skin. Dangling from a chain around her neck is a small gold hand of Fatima, a talisman.

For months, she tells me, she's led an unrelenting crusade to overturn Algeria's family code, a set of laws rooted in seventh century Islamic sharia. Under its provisions, women are prohibited from marrying without the permission of a male guardian (as in Morocco) or working without their husband's consent. Yet the greater threat to Algerian women is the Islamic Salvation Front, or FIS, who, in December of 1991, won the first round of voting in the country's first free elections since 1962, the year in which Algeria attained its independence from France. The FIS call for a totally segregated society, an Islamic nation in which women would be required to take the veil and adulterers would be stoned.

After dinner, Khalida says, "In 1984, when the family code was adopted, we waited for Amnesty International to speak out. They were silent. We waited for a reaction from the International League of Human Rights. *Rien.* Then, last year, when the militants began setting light to unveiled women, we thought, oh, at last your Western decision-makers will do something. But suddenly, when the army refused to deliver the country into the hands of the FIS, the international community discovered that human rights in my country don't exist. They say we're violating the terrorists' civil liberties, but never once do they mention the situation of women. Frankly, I find their interest in us just a *little* suspicious."

She delivers this extraordinary philippic in the manner of an angry prophetess, softly, evenly, bitterly. As well she should. In January of 1991, the army suspended the electoral process and declared a state of emergency. In June of 1992, the president of Algeria, Mohamed Boudiaf, a nationalist hero, was assassinated by a member of his security force, a mere five-and-a-half months after taking office. His death, Khalida says, was a devastating blow for Algerian women, one from which she herself is still reeling. She, too, has received her share of death threats, which she shrugs off. "I am too well known," she says, not very convincingly.

When Nouman starts playing Algerian folk songs on his oud, Khalida, who knows these plaintive tunes well, sings along in a mellifluous soprano. As she gives herself to the music, her face becomes less masklike, more luminous, like a glass bead dropped in water.

The party breaks up at midnight as Mouna has a curfew. Mohamed can't hide his disappointment. No one wants a nightcap? He's enjoying the music, the talk; his cheeks are flushed from drink. But Mouna really has to leave, so off we go, careering down the now-empty city streets. Turning on to a residential block, we pull up before a dilapidated French colonial house; Mouna jumps out and flits down the gravel drive, turning once to wave good-bye. Mohamed, a little vexed, shakes his head.

"It's crazy," he says. "Her parents let her run off to Casa for ten days. But at home she's got to be in bed by twelve!"

Back at the hotel, Rachida pulls me next door as I'm turning my key in the lock. Her friend, Amel, and a woman named Zineb, also from Tunisia, are lolling on the queen-sized bed, chattering away. We talk about small things, foolish things. With great patience, in lilting voices, they teach me an Arabic folk song about a spurned woman who offers her eyes to her beloved. But when I ask about their personal relations with men, they let out peals of laughter. "But my dear," Rachida cries as she struggles to collect herself, her face streaked with tears, "We don't have any!"

Tea at the home of the freshly minted British press attaché. I met him in the hallway of the Ebert Foundation yesterday afternoon, eavesdropping on the discussion in the smoky conference room.

"When are you going back to Madrid?" he whispered.

"Day after tomorrow."

"Too bad!"

Nicholas lives in the Casbah, in a many-leveled house of somewhat faded grandeur. His writing table overlooks the brackish waters of the Bou Regreg.

Young and extremely good-looking, he's lonely at his new post, terribly so. "Whenever I invite anyone to dinner, I have to remind him to bring his wife," he says glumly.

To a birthday party with Nouman, the composer. It's for a friend of his, a well-known young chanteuse whom I'll call Amina. Amina lives in Agdal, the tree-lined university quarter, in a modern building of reinforced concrete. Her parents have set her up in a ground-floor apartment furnished with red velvet banquettes, lots of mirrors, and little else. They live upstairs. Because she comes from a clan of musicians, Nouman explains on the ride over, she and her sisters can pretty much do as they please. He himself is something of a teen idol in Morocco—probably the first to pursue a doctorate.

Our entrance is attended by the whole family. The girls are wearing embroidered robes of silk brocade and the older women, fancy European dresses with full bodices, their faces bathed in the chiaroscuro glow of small brass lamps. Nouman excuses himself to work the room, entrusting me to the care of his sister, a willowy girl in a short ivory dress who wouldn't look out of place at some trendy Paris club (it turns out she's an agricultural engineer). As we weave our way to the back of the room, a woman puts a glass in my hand: a shake of some sort, milk with mashed avocado, sweet but good. Later, after midnight, there will be food, lots of it, but for now there is only drink. Except for the musicians and Amina's three dancing sisters, nearly everyone is sitting against the wall.

A plump, heavily made-up twenty-three year old, Amina runs off to change her dress each time the musicians finish a song. When I see her next, she's trying to snatch the microphone from Nouman, who is showing definite signs of star quality (his birthday present to Amina was a magnificently framed photograph of . . . himself). In the midst of this extemporaneous floor show, Amina's fifteen-year-old cousin, a lithe girl with long dark hair and bewitching eyes, wraps her shawl around her hips and begins to dance. Gazing downward, she moves this way, now that way, turning her head slightly from side to side, like a swaying tree. A sandalwood tree.

"She moves rather well," Nouman's sister murmurs in condescending tones. Then, all of a sudden, the girl stops dancing. Gliding across the room almost somnambulistically, she kisses me on both cheeks and disappears from sight. By now Amina has reemerged in a black bodysuit and skimpy fringe skirt. She plants herself in front of her father, a mild, graying man, and gyrates her pelvis. "I'd be shot if I danced in front of my father like that," my minder whispers in my ear with barely suppressed glee. A moment later, she turns to me again. "The difference between my brother and Amina," she remarks, divining my thoughts, "is that my brother is educated. Our father was a learned man. Amina is just a singer."

Long talk with the elusive Fatima. Much to my chagrin, like some spirit guide from *Thousand and One Nights,* she brought me to this place and vanished. Today, finally, after a sumptuous lunch in the gardens of the foundation, she sits for an interview.

It is no coincidence, she tells me, that the Islamist movement first gathered momentum in the eighties, when Europe closed its doors to immigrants. King Hassan II, as constitutional monarch and Commander of the Faithful, has managed to contain Islamic extremism in his Morocco. Even so, the civil unrest in Algeria directly affects Europe and the rest of North Africa.

It's a class war, Fatima says, between traditionally-educated Arabs and Western-educated ones. The fundamentalist leaders are no different than terrorists, she explains. They crave power and will kill anyone who doesn't share their ideas. But at bottom, she says, they fear they have no place in the world.

"What about women?" I ask. "Why so many adherents?"

She shrugs. "There's no mystery to it. Remember that women were the biggest supporters of fascism in Europe. You're lost and looking for someone to take care of you. The leftist parties don't offer what the fundamentalist groups do: an organization that will resolve all your problems from marriage to transportation to health care to death."

Fatima Mernissi's mother and grandmother were both illiterate. Born in 1941 into a family of landed aristocrats, Fatima broke with tradition at the age of three, when her father sent her to Koranic school. There she learned the word of God through rote recitation, a discipline to which she attributes her prodigious memory. She attended the Sorbonne and was awarded a doctorate in sociology from Brandeis University. "Before these last few decades," she has written, "women in our Muslim societies were not allowed a future. They only grew old." She speaks with all the authority of experience, for she passed her childhood in one of the last harems in the imperial city of Fès, where her mother remained in seclusion until Independence, in 1956.

The Western media, no doubt envisioning some kind of orientalist seraglio, have an almost tabloid fascination with this fact. Last year, she tells me, she was interviewed by a French women's magazine. She had not yet written her memoir, *Dreams of Trespass.* The first thing the reporter said to her was, "So, Mme. Mernissi, tell us about your childhood in the harem." No Arab journalist would ever talk to her that way, she says, drawing a veil over the subject. Nonetheless, because of her upbringing, Mernissi and others of her generation lay stress on involving men in the women's movement. "When I'm working with a group of women I feel like I'm back in the harem," she says. "And since I escaped from one I'm always glad when men are around. It reminds me that the days of the harem are over."

✧ ✧ ✧

Last day in Morocco. I spend the afternoon at Mohamed Tazi's. Also there is Nourredine Saadi, an Algerian professor of law and the co-founder of a women's press. Against all of my expectations, I find myself gravitating to the men in Fatima's milieu, partly because I genuinely like them, partly because they've undermined my preconceptions about them.

Sunday is the cook's day off so Mohamed goes into the kitchen to make coffee. While he potters about, Nourredine and I talk in the fading light. Slight of build with fine white hair and gray eyes set into a narrow face, he has an ethereal, faintly bohemian air.

Earlier he'd told me how he feared for his teenaged daughters, who would only be safe in his benighted country if they were veiled. Now I ask him if there was any particular moment when he became aware of the gulf between the sexes. He looks away and grows very still. Then, with his eyes still averted, he tells me about a signal event in his life, a rite of passage whose imprint upon him was "as indelible as circumcision."

"Like most North African boys," he begins, "I went with my mother once a week to the public bath house. I felt secure there. I had a sense of belonging. And then one day—I suppose I must have been about five or six—the bath matron told my mother that I was too old to come in with her anymore."

Mohamed, who has been listening quietly, narrows his eyes and says, "I shall never forget the pain and sorrow of being refused entrance to the hammam. You can't imagine the shock of it." From that day on, at social gatherings and family celebrations, he was herded off with the men. "You'd listen to their talk," he says, "but whenever you tried to join in they'd tell you to shut the hell up. And that is how you became a man, whether you were ready or not."

Nourredine then remarks on the bloodshed and violence of the marriage ritual. He says, "It's a form of rape, yes, but it's traumatic for the groom as well. Imagine being thrown into the bridal chamber with a strange woman and expected to prove your manhood."

"Our relationships with women are often *disastrous!*" says Mohamed, who has been married no less than three times. "But you mustn't get the wrong idea. We're not feminists or militants or anything of the sort. And this is not a battle of the sexes. If anything, it's about redressing a terrible injustice."

"And yet, even so," says Nourredine, "many of us do have pleasurable relationships with women, normal erotic relationships. . . ."

"But it's important to demystify this idea of woman-as-object-of-desire or dangerous creature who's best kept out of sight, secluded, and concealed," interjected Mohamed.

"From the outside world," I say.

"Yeah."

The afternoon has shaded into night, and outside the rain is falling in sheets. We've been talking for hours, but still there is something I want to know. Have they ever been tempted to leave?

"I have," Mohamed admits. "I tried to make my life elsewhere." For nearly four years, he tells me, he lived in Madrid, grinding out documentaries for Spanish television, but he felt utterly deracinated. Morocco, he says, is the deepest source of his work, and his identity is bound up in its culture.

A pained look flickers across Nourredine's face. It would be easy to leave, he says, sighing; he'd often thought of it. But he won't be made to feel like a foreigner in his own country. Unless his personal safety is threatened he'll stay, although he doesn't blame the ones who choose to leave.

At that moment a young Moroccan woman, slender with dark eyes, noiselessly enters the room flinging droplets from her shoulder-length hair. "The door was open," she says.

"We're talking about men in the women's movement," Nourredine tells her as she sits down on the sofa, curling her legs around her.

She says in a mocking voice, "Oh, you mean *male chauvinism* in the women's movement!" We look at each other with complicity and laugh.

I ask Mohamed if he will take me to the bus stop, about a mile from his house. As we draw near, he offers to drive me halfway to town. We trundle along the darkened rain-slicked road in companionable silence. Finally I ask him, "Did you ever go to Koranic school?"

He smiles but doesn't answer right away. Then he says that indeed he did, but briefly.

On his first day of school, Mohamed's teacher showed him a wooden crate that was roughly the size of a small boy. It was filled with rats. Or at least that is what the teacher told him. If Mohamed were to fall behind in his studies, he threatened, he and the rodents would soon be keeping company.

As we approach my drop-off point, the bus rears into view. Mohamed floors it and stops short, beeping his horn. *"Filez!"* he shouts. I clamber out, but the bus pulls away before I reach the stop. I get back in the van, and he resumes his tale.

That night, Mohamed took ill with fever. He dreamed that rats were eating away at his flesh. He wept and wailed and flailed about. All that night his mother remained at his bedside, daubing his forehead.

Another stop, the same bus. We go through the same routine, but this time, however, I contrive to miss the bus. I'm drenched to the skin, and besides, I want to know how the story ends.

When his father came home that evening, Mohamed continues, his mother had composed herself. Very quietly she told him, "Unless you take my son out of that school you will never take another meal in this house again." He never went back.

Postscript

I crossed paths with Mohamed twice after that. The following year we ran into each other at a film festival in France. *In Search of My Wife's Husband* was having its European premiere. This time, a good number of Muslim women were in the audience and they broke into applause at the end.

Later, over a meal at a crêperie, he told me that Nourredine and his family had fled Algeria for France. Tens of thousands of "infidels" had been killed by Islamic militants, and intellectuals were especially vulnerable. As for Khalida, she'd left her teaching post and gone into hiding. I read somewhere that every few days she moved to another safe house. And still she refused to quit Algeria.

A month later I chanced upon Mohamed once more, this time in Madrid. He was having dinner with his young son and daughter at a restaurant on my street. As I walked by, I happened to look in, and there they were. I never saw him or any of the others again.

Nancy Von Rosk

IN AND OUT OF THE LABYRINTH: A JOURNEY THROUGH FÈS

Undeniably Fès gives the impression of a city folded in upon itself, intent on hiding whatever it contains from the inquisitive gaze of the outsider.

—PAUL BOWLES

Each evening I would keep my ritual and leave the throbbing confusion of Fès's medina for the outlying hills where I waited for nightfall; it was then that the horizon burned into a red and purple haze and the lights of Fès magically appeared like shimmering stars in the distance. There, among the faded tiled tombstones of the Merenid hills, while the colors faded into darkness, I listened. The hush of sunset, the soft hum of distant noise: a rush of swallows' wings, the faint barking of dogs in the valley, and the cries of the city's many mosques echoing, calling the faithful to prayer. The chaos of the medina seemed so far away then, and I could see how Fès was perfectly contained in the valley—how the city appeared to be a natural outgrowth, spreading along the valley's slopes, nearly reaching the Merenid cemeteries, that circle of hillsides covered in ponderous beds of stone. The weight of the past seems to enclose Fès, to perhaps protect it and sustain it—even after a thousand years, this ancient city is still in so many ways unchanged, untouched—seeming to exist in its own time, under its own terms.

I spent my days in the valley—in Fès el Bali—the medina, the most ancient part of Fès, and began my journey at the giant Moorish archway, Bab Boujeloud, a ceremonial gate that marks the entrance to the medina—a gate that seems designed to draw you in. It is covered in tiles that shine with an unreal brilliance: swirling Arabic calligraphy and geometric shapes glistening against a background of cobalt blue. In ancient Moroccan cities, arches and gateways always mark entrances, creating a startling, almost hypnotic effect. The moment of arrival is framed. And this intensifies the scene—captures it—concentrates it, focuses the eye and mind, draws you in and forces you to pause, to take in the scene, to look around you. With that magnificent gateway outlining the donkeys, the veiled women, the turbaned men, the minarets in the distance, everything is thrown into relief; colors suddenly seem so much brighter.

Yet soon after I walk under those tremendous arches and down into the maze of the medina, I am far away from the bright blinding glare of the sun and below a roof of rushes where shafts of hazy sunlight filter in, faintly illuminating the swirling dust. It is cool under the rushes, even with the crowds of people hurrying by, especially in the butcher's section where the cobblestone path is slimy and slippery. The fragrance of mint and cedar also cools and refreshes the air, and when my eyes adjust to the darkness, I notice a man walking past with two hens in each fist—bouquets of russet, black, and ivory feathers swinging by his side. Older women rush by me, clutching their veils tightly around their mouths, their hands stained a burnt orange with henna. A woman in front of me has hennaed her feet and each time her gold-threaded velvet-black slippers click the ground, I glimpse her heel: a flash of intricate arabesques looking like dark burgundy doilies. At every corner there is a decrepit tiled fountain—wet blues and yellows glistening against battered, crumbling stone. I hear a rooster call and see the flame of a red beak poking out of a decaying window, and when I turn a corner, I hear singing. I stop to look through a window in the wall, a hole covered with a dusty wrought iron grill, and again my eyes adjust to the deeper darkness within as I make out a small room filled with children. On the blackboard there are fractions, and each child has a slate. All the children are clapping, chanting in unison while an old man, bearded and turbaned, smiles and nods, keeping time with his stick.

While these children are singing in school, I see so many other children working: selling cigarettes, carrying raw leather, directing donkeys, hammering away on brass. Children are essential to the business of life here; they do not have to wait to grow up nor play make-believe games to feel important. It is usually young girls who have infants strapped to their backs, and it is usually young boys who must move the animal hides to and from the tanneries. Always, it is the children who rush off to the communal ovens, balancing trays of dough on their heads, dodging all the alley obstacles in their path. Even though these children have such responsibility, such a sense of purpose, and walk with such pride and determination, they still have a playful enthusiasm, and it is usually the children who take a keen interest in the stranger passing through. Their bright eyes watch from the dark wooden doorways, and they whisper, *"bonjour."* Some of them yell *"batika,"* reminding me to watch out for a passing donkey.

The constant traffic of donkeys keeps things moving in the medina. Saddled with wool, rubble, leather, wood shavings, or crates of empty Pepsi bottles, they move slowly, wobbling along, sometimes knocking into people and often getting stuck in the alleyways. Around tiny bends and blind corners, there are often donkey traffic jams and men arguing over who is going to back up or move to the side. Whether it be a donkey tottering under its load in a narrow alley or a shoemaker working away in his little closet of a shop, this city's use of all conceivable space astounds me.

Home crowds upon home: cave-like homes—tiny doorways—tiny cell-like windows. In a city such as this, space is not only rare, it is sacred. It is the mosques that have luxurious space for contemplating, and walking into the mosque is literally walking into the light: one steps onto enormous marble-white courtyards open to the skies and the blue-tiled fountains overflow with cool, clear water. Since I am not Muslim, I must take in this splendor from a dark and distant doorway. I notice a young girl playfully splashing water from one of the fountains; she hides behind the mosque's massive wooden doors and stares at me with a shy smile. From the darkness of the alley, I smile back, dazzled by the sun, the brilliance of tile and marble.

And the sacred space of the tomb of Moulay Idriss, the founder of Fès, must also be taken in from a distance. As the narrow dark alley ends near this sanctuary, a thick wooden bar juts out at me, blocking the entrance—a reminder that only Muslims are allowed. I stand next to the stalls outside this holy place, stalls where sacred candles are sold—candles as tall as a child with swirling golden ribbons whirling around them—and I look beyond these holy wares to the inside of the sanctuary where all is color and motion and passionate prayers. Crowds of people are frantically gesticulating, touching the tomb, weeping, moaning; there are rich red oriental carpets covering the floors, geometric designs of tile lining the walls and an enormous, ornate chandelier is hanging down heavily. Struggling for a glimpse from my dark corner, I am reminded again that I am an intruder.

Yet there is space open to all in this city. Out of the rush and push of the crowd, I am able to enter an open, sunlit courtyard—the calm emptiness of a seven-hundred-year-old *medersa.* The *medersas*—ancient universities once affiliated with the mosques—are architectural wonders from the golden days of the Islamic empire. Inside, there are quiet, empty, maze-like hallways that somehow always find a circular way back to the center. Tiny rooms—dormitories of students long ago—are all grouped around a main marble courtyard. The doorways are of carved cedar wood, framed by elaborate stucco arabesques and swirls—plasterwork of intricate detail and symmetry. Adorning the walls are tiles of green, yellow, blue, and black, mosaics of endless geometric repetition. Indeed, from the medersa's architectural layout to a single piece of tile on the medersa's wall, there is always this attention to geometry, to balance, to creating a soothing, harmonious effect.

Fès's mosques and medersas are of a startling beauty, yet with the city's concentration of so much life in so little space, other unrelenting forces inevitably crowd around you: the dizzying heat, the pushing crowds, the haunting visions of devastation. In these dark alleys, I pass crippled, deformed men wearing slippers on their hands so they can crawl through the mud. A woman dressed in rags with a rope around her neck, talks to herself while the children follow her and laugh. A man rushes past me in his heavy hooded robe or *jellabah,* his head down and his nose nearly gone, raw and bloody, decaying, as if something had been gnawing on it. And I hear the rhythmic cries of "Aaaah La" reverberate in the darkness—blind beggars hovering around the mosque doors—hands suspended, open palmed—calling God's name all day long. At the edge of the medina, I watch the river Fès, a powerful rush of muddy brown water, a river of flowing garbage, the orange peels bobbing along with the plastic bottles, the tattered cardboard, the pieces of ancient worn tires. The river rages on while the little boys laugh, alternating between washing their brass pots and pelting each other with orange skins. As they play, I see the garbage being thrown from the bridge. I notice the trail of human feces alongside the walls.

Fès is a city I cannot fully understand; yet, for all its strangeness, it is a city so familiar to me that whenever I come here, I experience a curious sort of homecoming. It is here, more than anywhere else, that I have been confronted with the gritty, earthy aspect of life—the sweat, the toil, the dirt, the sickness. Yet, at the same time, it is here that I am reminded of the spiritual, the sacred, the music; it is here that I have been overwhelmed by beauty. Each time I come to Fès, I am somehow compelled to see it whole, to go beyond its monuments, to see all that Fès is, and always I am left weary and exhilarated.

Before I leave its dark labyrinth, I climb up to the rooftop terrace of the café next to the Karouine mosque. The Karouine, reputed to be the oldest university in the world, is Fès's symbol, its most sacred place of all. Once up on the café terrace, the green-tiled roof of the Karouine spreads out beyond me—shimmering in the burning sun while all the city's decaying rooftops, clotheslines and minarets crowd round it. From the terrace, I am able to see inside the mosque; I can see that there is space to sit alone and many men are reclining; some are kneeling and I hear chanting, prayers carried along the breeze, prayers reaching up to the rooftops. Swallows are flying so close to the mosque now, and as they make their tremendous arcs against green tile, their flight seems a rising and falling to the rhythm of those sacred songs. On the dusty rooftops next door, an old woman beats at the piles of wool slung over her clothesline, and a younger, stout, tattooed Berber woman bends over her washtub, meditatively moving the clothing back and forth. Once more, I look down at this city and listen to the ecstatic rush of swallow's wings, to the defiant and persistent beating of wool, to the splashing of water. To the endless chanting of prayers.

Kathleen Moore

RETURNING

Genbot (May 1993)

Lifetimes have gone by in the twenty-seven years since I left Ethiopia. I had returned often, but only in my thoughts and my dreams. Then one May evening when I collected my mail from the rusted tin box on my front porch, there was a paper-thin, blue aerogram with the name Wondimu Woldesenbet and a return address in Addis Ababa. I stood there for a long time unable to move. I could see Wondimu as he looks in the last photograph I took of him, packing up my bed, hand-carved by the Guragi people, a silly grin on his teen-age face because he thought his Peace Corps teachers were crazy to send their beds back to America. How relieved I was to know that he was alive! All these years of knowing only about famine and revolution and bloody terror in the streets, I had never had the nerve to find out about my former students. Like rain after a long, dry summer, this letter brought relief and joy.

I was so sure that they had forgotten all about me, but Wondimu's letter began with "Dear *Etiye*" and that told me everything, that he remembered, that it had all been as important to him as it was to me.

> *Ter (January 1965)*
>
> Names are ways to caress each other, to honor each other, to recognize the quality of the other. *Etiye* was the name my students finally decided to call me. They couldn't translate it exactly so they showed me examples of it, like my landlord's oldest daughter who did everything for her family—cooked, watched over the younger children, cleaned the house, brought water from the river, washed the clothes, ground the coffee beans, and took care of me. She was

considerably more *Etiye* than I wanted to be, but I got the idea. "Older sister who loves you, and wants to take care of you and you should listen to me and do as I say but we can be friends and play together, too, because I'm not all that much older." Words. There are no easy translations. . . .

Yekatit (February 1965)

Using the words of the people with whom you live is as necessary as drinking their water, breathing their air, walking on their earth. *Saar-bet* literally means grass house, but the ones built by the Guragi people in the little village of Emdeber, where I lived, are too extraordinary for that simple translation. They begin with a tree, two stories high and six feet around, as the center post. One huge round wall is built of eucalyptus wood, the rough hewn boards placed tightly together and cemented with mud. Long thin poles are lashed to the top of the center post, slanting down to the top edge of the wall, making a giant pointed cap. Strips of bark are woven over and under, layer after layer, as tightly as thin threads in a piece of cloth. Not a dot of light comes through the roof after the layers of grass are lashed on. Inside the old village houses, aged with the breath of family members dead and present, with smoke from the constant fire, with pungent aromas of cattle and sheep, the wood becomes ebony and shines in the soft light from the fire circle before the door is closed against the night, the hyenas, and the cold.

Supper was late in the evening. After dark as I walked down the road to my *saar-bet*, I saw through the open doorways the gold-red flames burning against the blackness, scattered over the hillsides and valley like giant fireflies, too big to catch and put in Mason jars, but as magical and entrancing as those flickering lights were in my aunt's backyard in Pittsburgh on summer nights.

From my *saar-bet* I could see Emdeber's only road, with women carrying enormous packs of pottery or baskets or live chickens on their backs to trade in the market. Their bodies were hues of color from pale beige to ochre to deep black. They fit with the place, blended with the trees and the earth, seemingly sprung from the ground, the soil just extending upward into a human form that moved and spoke. I saw little children running to school carrying scraps of paper and tiny stubs of pencils, their frayed tunics blowing out behind them revealing caramel-colored bare bottoms. I saw teenage girls in bright blue plastic shoes walking slowly and looking out of the corners of their eyes as they passed my house, giggling when the boys called out to them. How can I say "grass hut" when *saar-bet* means all this?

Sene (June 1993)

Wondimu and I exchanged only two letters. My second one told him when I would arrive in Addis Ababa and asked him to make a reservation for me at a hotel. No need of that, he wrote back, startled but delighted that I was coming to visit. Debero had a villa near the airport and I was to stay there in his extra house. Debero? The one who didn't pass ninth grade and had to leave school? That Debero? He was now a lawyer and worked for the government. Why was I surprised? Wasn't this the same Debero who could charm the old women at the market into giving him their precious bananas? So now our lives would come full circle. I would stay in a house Debero had built and he would take care of me, just as he and Wondimu and the other boys had lived in the little house I had built so many years ago for them.

Megahbit (March 1965)

A thin, dark-skinned boy with big, excited eyes stood in my doorway. He was wearing a plaid shirt, dark blue pants and no shoes. I could tell he had just bathed and his clothes had been washed and ironed. He wanted something from me, no doubt. Debero was a ninth grade student, not one of mine. I invited him in and we asked each other about the health and well-being of our parents and all other family members. Debero was nervous. It must be something big he wanted.

"I am a poor from Hosanna," he began. "It is far and I have no money, but I desire education. My father is a poor, also, and I have many brothers. I must have education or I will surely die."

I'd heard this story before. At first, it upset me that children should be in such dire straits, but one gets used to anything, even hard-luck stories from children. I looked skeptical, and Debero said quickly, "Oh, *Etiye*. I do not want you to give me money. I want only to live with you and work as your servant. I will work hardly. I will do everything—bring water, cook, wash your clothes."

I did need someone to do chores for me, and Debero was so earnest and enthusiastic. He and a dozen other boys who came from Hosanna, a village that was more than a hundred kilometers away but had no secondary school, really did need help. They had no relatives in Emdeber to live with, so they scraped together what money they could to rent an old, rat-infested shack and ate cheap, stale bread. I told Debero he could start work the next day.

By the end of the week, I had three Hosanna boys working for me, and by the end of the month, they and my landlord had built a small hut, about the size of a garage, for them just outside my compound fence. They only slept there. They spent most of their time in my house eating and studying. For ten *birr* (Ethiopian dollars) a month each, they brought water from the river and boiled it to kill the invisible germs that they didn't believe existed, washed the dishes, cleaned the water filter, split wood, made coffee twice a day, went shopping at the Tuesday and Friday markets, killed the chickens and slaughtered the lambs they bought there, ground the beef when we could get any, and every Saturday they filled the bucket in the out-house with hot water and tied it to the inside of the roof so I could take a shower. They read all my books and my letters from home, ate all my *ferengi* (foreign) food, coveted my red jeans (which I could never wear because women just didn't wear pants), insisted that I take endless photos of them, played chess and checkers with me, told stories and sang songs into my tape recorder, asked me a thousand questions, and answered all of mine. They cried and laughed, were sick, got well, were homesick, and loved me.

Debero was an energetic entrepreneur. I came home from school one day and found he had set up a barber shop in my compound. Black curly hair was flying from the head of one boy while half a dozen others lounged around my garden, joking with each other like men in any barber shop anywhere in the world. "*Etiye,* you want your hair cut? You must wait your turn," Debero said before I could utter a word of objection to his using my compound, my scissors, and my one and only chair without asking.

Debero had an understanding with the barren, iron-filled soil of Emdeber. He knew its limitations but refused to accept them. He spoke to it harshly, like an angry parent to a recalcitrant child, as he planted the vegetable and flower seeds my father sent me. "You must grow these seeds for *Etiye.* She is *ferengi* and needs this food. And she is Peace Corpse," he whispered to the red dirt, dropping the seeds in one by one and patting the earth over them, promising them a drink of soapy dish water later that night.

Debero was the essence of the boys' favorite word, *gobuz.* There is no good English translation for *gobuz.* The children said it meant brave or clever. If you could figure out what the *ferengis* meant when they spoke English too fast, you were *gobuz.* If you walked through town in the dark and didn't get eaten by hyenas, you were *gobuz.* If you got good grades in school, you were *gobuz.* Debero was *gobuz* in all respects but that last one. He couldn't pass ninth grade. I helped him every night with his homework, but I couldn't take his tests for him, and as much as everyone loved him, the other Peace Corps teachers who taught ninth grade could not pass him. I was heartbroken. He had become woven into the daily fabric of my life, and I could not imagine what it would be like without him. I wanted him to stay on and work for me, and I would continue to teach him in the evenings. But being idle was not for Debero. He got a job teaching in a mission school back in Hosanna and asked me if he should take it. What could I say? I was leaving in another year anyway. What good was I to him? I wanted to say, "Stay with me, Debero. You will take away the laughter and joy you brought to my life." But I didn't. I watched him walk down the road away from Emdeber and waved when he turned to look back at me. I knew we were both crying.

Miazia (April 1965)

Life became routine in that tiny village in Ethiopia that had no road and was not on any map, that was hidden by huge green "false banana" trees, and that had become my home. I would wake every morning to the rhythmic thud, thud, thud of roasted coffee beans being pounded in a wooden mortar and pestle—a soft, comforting sound, the morning sound I loved. There was comfort in the sameness, in the routine that changed into boredom what would otherwise have been too exotic and incomprehensible to be endured.

In the village of Emdeber, just living from moment to moment took a concentrated effort. Drinking a glass of water, for example, was not something one did hastily. Standing by the back door looking out at my would-be garden (planted against all odds, as my landlord told me seeds sown by a woman wouldn't grow), I held the glass under the tiny spigot of the water filter while it slowly filled with liquid, the color a pale orange or deep rust-red depending on how long it had been since the filter had been cleaned. But there was more than color in the water; there was sediment that had to settle to the bottom of the glass. So I waited, looking out the back door at the sky or hills in the distance thinking about how to teach the passive voice to my first hour class. Finally, I sipped the water slowly so as not to stir up the little pile of whatever that was lying on the bottom of the glass. When I got close to it, I stopped drinking, went out to the garden and poured the remaining drops on a struggling carrot plant. Everything was connected: the garden, the students, the river, and drinking a glass of water. When it became time for me to leave this life where every action required thought and intention and had consequences, it would not be easy. I had become accustomed to the complex routines of living in that grass house, and I did not want a life that would require less of me.

I threw on my clothes, not noticing which cotton shirtwaist dress I was wearing. They all seemed the same, all becoming the same shade of brownish red from the river water and faded from the bright sun. I wore once-white cotton socks and tennis shoes, now also turned a deep sienna. I spread some jelly that my father had sent from home on a chunk of bread and ate it as I walked to school with my fellow Peace Corps volunteers. On the way, the children who didn't attend school screamed at us, "*ferengi, ferengi*," so incessantly that I would have done anything to shut them up. If I had my *dula*, my walking stick, I would chase them with it but they scampered just far enough away that I couldn't reach them. There were other children, though, who didn't speak at all. Hardly more than infants, they sat on the ground in front of their *saar-bets*, dirt clutched in their little fists. Their black eyes stared at me but all I could see were the flies crawling in and out of the corners of their eyes, around their nostrils, into their mouths. These children never brushed the flies away. Did they no longer feel the insect legs crawling over their skin, sticking to their eyelashes?

Sometimes we passed a funeral procession wending its way to the mission church. There were so many funerals, I stopped noticing them. But I never forgot the first funeral I experienced in Emdeber a few days after I arrived. I was living at the mission while I waited for my *saar-bet* to be built. My tiny, cell-like room had no windows or furniture. I stood one of my trunks on end next to the bed so I could put a candle on it to see at night. I hated to let that candle go out. When the door was closed and the candle out, it felt like a tomb.

One day, walking back to the mission after school, I stopped at my *saar-bet* to check on its progress. "How I wish they'd hurry," I complained, as I did every day. I wanted so much to move in and be on my own. When I heard a carpenter pounding, I hoped someone was working on my house. But when I went in to see, he was only making some kind of wooden box. One of my students told me, "*Etiye,* it is a baby's box—to bury it in."

Death was so intricately bound with life, with birth itself, that I wondered if there was joy at a baby's birth here. With such a great possibility that it would die, how attached could a mother become to her baby? Later that day, as the church bells were ringing, I saw a crowd of people coming up the path from the woods. The women had black scarves on their hair instead of the brightly colored ones they usually wore and one woman was being supported by two others as they walked back to the steps of the church. She must be the mother of the dead baby, I thought. But she looked too old, like a grandmother. Is this what having so many children does to women, makes them as old as grandmothers when they are burying their own babies? How many other babies had this mother lost? How many more would she have—or lose—before she died herself?

When they had all gone into the church, I went down the path through the woods to find the graves. I looked for a new one with fresh dirt on it. There it was. My God, it was tiny! I wanted to dig away the dirt and bring out the box that the carpenter had made in *my* house, to take out the baby and hold it next to my heart and make it live again. I wanted to hear it cry and take it to its mother and say, "Here is your baby. It isn't really dead. See, he breathes, he cries, he wants you," and the tearful mother would smile and hold her baby and everyone would be happy and go home. I felt close to that baby because its coffin was made in my *saar-bet.* But I could only stand there and look at the grave. When I returned up the path it was almost dark and the funeral party had left to get home before the hyenas came out. The little orphan boys who lived at the mission were playing and laughing. One was sitting on the church steps singing in a clear, high voice, and the others sang the response after each verse, "*Ubay, caramella.*" It was a song about candy.

Nehase (August, 1993)
I was anxious about seeing Alemnesh, one of the few girl students I had had at Emdeber. When Wondimu told her I was coming, he said she began to cry. That surprised me. I thought I had been, at most, a passing oddity in her youth. Wondimu and Debero met me at the airport with their children and great bouquets of flowers, but Alemnesh was not there. She telephoned later and said she would come to Debero's house as soon as she could. She couldn't be very excited about seeing me, I thought. When her car drove into the compound, I went outside and stood there wondering how to react, trying to stay composed. She stepped out of the car, and we didn't, couldn't speak. We put our arms around each other and wept. Finally, Debero came out and led us back into the house where we sat on the sofa, holding hands and smiling at each other like two little girls who were best friends.

Hedar (November 1965)
"My name is Alemnesh Haile Mariam. I am 13 years old. I am in eighth form at Emdeber school. I am a very goo student, I must say so myself. Maths and science are best subjects. I am happy to have Peace Corps for teachers now. I wish they will not go away from Emdeber."

I couldn't believe this essay, stuck in the middle of my stack of eighth grade English papers, most of which were incomprehensible. Those I could decipher consisted of two sentences: "I am Gebre. I must be student to be civilized."

Those who knew no English would copy from the student sitting next to them, name and all! Alemnesh was by far the best student in the entire school. Not only could she read and write English, she could think in it. She never had to study, she just absorbed everything like a sponge. In class, her hand shot up to answer every question, and outside of class, she asked me questions I couldn't answer.

Alemnesh would have been my favorite even if she had not been so intelligent. She was too tall and thin for a proper Ethiopian girl. She was like a young gazelle with unbounded energy and an adolescent gangliness that made it awkward for her to sit in the small desks or walk slowly home with us after school. Alemnesh was a happy child. She was curious about everything. She was completely optimistic about her future and the world's. Her name meant "You are the world."

I had dreams of taking Alemnesh home with me. She could live with me, finish high school, and then go to college. I imagined her as a doctor, coming back to Ethiopia, back even to Emdeber, setting up clinics, training local villagers. Alemnesh would be *the* woman of Ethiopia, and I would help her become it. On Parents' Day at school, I sought out her family to tell them how brilliant she was. "I hope she can continue her studies in America as her brothers have," I hinted. Her father nodded his head with obvious pleasure and pride. His wife stood a little behind him, smiling at me but not speaking. I wondered what she wanted for her daughter, for that skinny tomboy who still romped over the hills with the sheep but had a cracker-jack mind as quick and bright as her lawyer brother. Did she have a vision for her little girl as I did, or was living in a *saar-bet* in Emdeber and being a mother the only reality she could imagine?

Tahsas (December 1966)

When my two years ended and I was about to leave Emdeber, Alemnesh invited me to her home for a farewell dinner. I walked with her over hills green from the "big rains," past old *saar-bets* falling to ruin and new ones being built. Little boys left the cattle they were tending to walk behind us as far as they dared. They still laughed and called me *ferengi,* and I still hated it.

In their *saar-bet*, I sat on a straw mat next to her mother in the sunlight streaming through the front door. We were silent most of the time since we had no common language. What we did have in common was Alemnesh, but I didn't know how to tell her that. Alemnesh's father came in with a live lamb that I realized was to be our dinner. Twice the boys had bought a lamb at the market and slaughtered it for me, but I'd not seen it alive and kicking before I cooked it. Alemnesh laughed at my obvious discomfort. This was a great honor they were doing me because I was *ferengi* and because I was leaving. Usually an animal was slaughtered and cooked only for special religious holidays, and even then most Emdeber families couldn't afford it. The lamb was finally reduced to a peppery stew, and we ate until they were satisfied that I really couldn't take another bite and let me wash the *berberay* sauce from my hands. While her mother made coffee, I had Alemnesh tell her father about my plan to have her come to America after I got home. She lowered her eyes and almost whispered it to him. He agreed, for now, that she should go to Addis Ababa to live with her older married sister and finish high school there. That would be a big first step and I was hopeful that the rest would come.

Pagume (between August and September 1993)

Debero, Wondimu, Alemnesh and I sat around telling "Do you remember" stories about those days in Emdeber, and one that Alemnesh told greatly surprised me. She said one day the headmaster had a loud argument with me about a test I had given. He wanted me to give it over, but I had refused. Later that day, he called her into his office and slapped her repeatedly, although she had done nothing to deserve punishment. She knew it was because he could not hit me, she said, and knowing how much I loved her, he used her as a way to make me suffer. Painful as the story was, it made me realize that Alemnesh had always known, then and now, how much I loved her.

I told Alemnesh I had wanted to take her to America to live with me and go to college and that I thought she might have become a doctor. "My family is disappointed in me, I think, and I am disappointed in myself that I have not done more with my life. I married too soon," she said with a quiet sadness that puzzled me. Her husband was well educated and had an important position in the new government, and they had four children whom she obviously adored. I wouldn't have thought she was unhappy. "I was alone here in Addis Ababa during the revolution," she said, "and it was dangerous for girls who had no protector. The soldiers, you know, were everywhere. They would catch girls who were alone." I understood.

Maskaram (September 1993)

It was almost Meskal, a holy day that comes at the end of the rainy season when the countryside is covered with bright yellow daisy-like flowers that grow only in Ethiopia. The Guragi people, who come from Emdeber and the nearby villages, trek home at Meskal just as Americans go home for Christmas. I had never been in Emdeber at Meskal. When I was in the Peace Corps we had to leave the village before the rain washed out the little dirt path and the river flooded. When I asked Alemnesh if I could go home with her for the holiday, she was willing to take me but worried about the "accommodations" for me. They would all be staying at her mother's *saar-bet* with no bathroom, no beds, no running water. "Just like Emdeber always was?" I asked.

"Yes," she answered.

"And after I lived there for two years, do you think I can't do it for a weekend?"

"But *Etiye,*" she said, "you are old now."

There were eleven of us tightly packed into the borrowed Land Cruiser. Even though the road to Emdeber is now raised and graded and worthy to be called a real road, it is not paved and not very wide. We bumped and jostled over the lumps and swerved around slower moving buses and honked our horn at the cattle and sheep, making little boys and old men and women selling chickens leap out of our way. It was still a long and nauseating trip, as it had always been, but the four little girls in the back sang spirited songs, and we stopped to pick Meskal flowers, and only Alemnesh's littlest son actually did get sick.

We were close to Emdeber, near the river, when I saw the bridge. Its strong, steel beams were painted the same rust-red as the Emdeber earth. The river roared and foamed beneath it. For the first time, I could see how wide and deep the Emdeber river really was; I could stand on that solid, wonderful bridge and look through its beams at the red, rushing water below. Girls with baskets of bananas balanced on their heads ran to me, hoping for a sale. I took their photographs, but first I took pictures of the bridge alone. These girls were too young to know that there had been a time when there was no bridge, a time when Emdeber was cut off from the rest of the world, a time when no one got into or out of that village for three months or more out of every year, a time when if you got very sick, you simply died. If there was no food, you went hungry. I stood there, realizing the real meaning of the word *bridge,* the joining of two places that had been separate, making into one what had been different and apart. I loved and hated that bridge. It would allow me to go back to Emdeber, but it would also allow the old Emdeber to ooze and seep out of the area that had been assigned to it by God and be absorbed into a very different world.

We stayed in the *saar-bet* where Alemnesh grew up, where I had had my farewell dinner of lamb stew the last time I was in Emdeber. It was full of relatives and neighbors, old men and women who gathered here daily for coffee and gossip with Alemnesh's mother. Those sitting on the little three-legged wooden stools along the wall got up to give us seats. *"Wehay wareem,"* (Are you well?) was asked over and over of each person. *"Wehay. Wehay."* The Guragi greeting. You couldn't say it often enough. It was like a chant, a sweet-sounding, soothing mantra.

There were no "facilities" as Alemnesh had told me with regret over and over. We went for a walk on the slippery-wet grass into a secluded pasture. "Find a place," she said and went away to give me privacy. I didn't go too far. I have no sense of direction and usually find my way around by noticing landmarks. With every bush and blade of grass looking like every other, I spent a lot of time wandering around looking for the narrow path out of the trees. Finally, one of the little girls found me and led me back out. I slid on the muddy path and caught my skirt on the thorns of the leafless shrubbery. "I am not too old for this," I kept repeating to myself.

There are no separate rooms in a *saar-bet;* it is one big round space. The family all sleep on the floor together on thin woven mats. I thought of it as camping out. At least there weren't any cattle and sheep in the *saar-bet* with us at night. Only one forlorn baby chick tried to keep itself warm in the fireplace. The children loved this part of visiting their grandmother the best, undressing by the weak glow of a flashlight and sleeping on the floor all together. When bedtime came, they rolled into a heap, arms and legs plopped around each other like one round body with many heads attached. We adults arranged ourselves around the edges of the children, the men on one side and the women on the other but everyone very close, touching whoever was nearest. The *saar-bet* is huge and there was more than enough room to spread out and claim one's own space as we would have done in America. I wondered why this closeness. Perhaps for warmth, perhaps because in most houses the animals would take up much of the space leaving little for the humans, perhaps tradition. Whatever the reason, I liked it.

Alemnesh and her brother, Yakob, talked about their father, now dead for almost ten years. Even though others in the village thought it foolish, he had insisted that all his children, including the girls, go to school. He told Yakob repeatedly, "You must go as far as you can in school. What do you call it, the highest you can go?" And Yakob would tell him again, "A degree, *abba*, a university degree." "Yes," Haile Mariam would say, "a degree. You must get that." And they all did. Their father was also the first to dig a well, and it was from that same well that the servants were drawing water for us now to wash and from which the neighbors also drew their water. I had been wrong about this man so many years ago, I realized, thinking he did not want Alemnesh to go to college or to come to the United States. I had thought he was like most of the others who believed girls should marry young and have children. He had wanted more for her than I ever imagined.

Everyone had tall bunches of dry branches propped up in front of their house to be burned at sunset on the day of Meskal. In the late afternoon, children gathered outside to sing and dance. They were led by a young woman playing a small hand-held drum just like the one my students had used when they stopped at my *saar-bet* to get out of the rain and sang songs for me, the one my landlord's daughter had given me and that now lay gathering dust in my attic. Now they danced in a circle going from house to house like old-fashioned Christmas carolers. The circle swelled, and I joined it, holding hands with Alemnesh's daughters. As it got darker, families came outside to light their Meskal fires. Yakob was the oldest male family member in his mother's home, so he lit the branches standing outside her compound. It reminded me of autumns years ago when we raked billions of elm leaves into huge piles in the street in front of our houses and our fathers set them ablaze. The smell of dry leaves burning in the almost-cold night air, the smoke wrapping itself around the bare tree branches, the great orange flames dancing. It was a mystical rite that I relived watching the Meskal fire. Young and old men joined us now as their own Meskal fires burned out. Stools were brought out for the old men to sit on and bottles of the local liquor were produced from under the warm *gabis* (blankets) in which the men were wrapped. As the singers became more rowdy, Alemnesh and her sister took their children inside. I stayed outside in the cold air, listening to the Guragi songs I hadn't heard for twenty-seven years.

We had to leave Emdeber the day after Meskal so Alemnesh and her husband could get back to their jobs in Addis Ababa and I could get ready to go back to the States. Wondimu took me to the great outdoor market in Addis to buy souvenirs for my friends back home. One shop was stuffed from floor to roof with baskets of every color, size, and shape. A little basket lying by itself, tossed off in a corner, attached itself to me, and I held on to it as I chose bigger, prettier, more unusual ones for gifts. It was a Guragi basket and there weren't many like that here. It was small and plain and I had spent all my money, so I reluctantly left it, giving it a loving pat as I set it back in its corner.

Tekempt (October 1993)

The next night was my departure and my former students and their families gathered for a farewell party. Everyone brought me gifts, a traditional Ethiopian dress, a gold ring, a carving of a woman pounding coffee with a mortar and pestle, a *meskal* (cross) like the priests carry. Alemnesh came with a small gift-wrapped package that I opened as she straightened the *netala* (shawl) that kept slipping off my new dress. It was a little Guragi basket just like the one I hadn't bought for myself at the market the day before. When I told her how much I had wanted that basket, she said, "When two hearts are the same, they know each other without telling."

Andrea Benton Rushing

LIVING ON THE EDGES: NIGERIAN JOURNALS

23 November '83

When Osula, Yvonne, and I land, it will be 2:00 A.M. in NYC and 9:00 A.M. in Nigeria. FINALLY going to the continent I've been reading and teaching about since the '70s. Fulbright senior lectureship, teaching, though I've no idea what, in the Department of Literature in English at the University of Ife.

25 November '83

Thanksgiving Day. Just up from the nap jet-lag mandated. Haven't kissed the ground yet. Lost one of our twelve suitcases in the suffocating Babel of Murtala Muhammed Airport—have never (and I'm from New York City) heard so much noise in so many different languages (English, Yoruba, Hausa, Igbo, pidgin) in my life. We're 7,000 miles from home and a mere seventeen degrees from the equator. Been to Antigua, the Bahamas, Barbados, Gaudeloupe, Jamaica, and Trinidad. Like the U.S., they have echoes and traces of our origin. Africa is the source.

26 November '83

In Ile-Ife—center of the Yoruba world—I'm glad I came. Feel the temptation—untested—to stay. Coming here is one of my best decisions ever. Adventuring Andrea, forty-three and determined not to rut, makes a middle-aged pilgrimage to the "motherland."

29 November '83

Arrived in Ile-Ife with two stunned children and eleven pieces of luggage. No room at the campus center inn, and managers of grungy motels in town sneered at my American Express traveler's checks. Later, snug in the VIP guest house, I began to expect that the problems of housing, transportation, teaching in a department whose head is outraged to see me because he wanted to hire two Africans instead, would soon be solved. Not so. . . .

3 December '83

Department of Literature in English. No sign of the acting head of department, a tall, skinny, scowling Marxist with an AfAm (African American) wife. Secretaries, all men, talk on the phone a lot. Students, most in Western dress, pick up mimeoed hand-outs (foreign exchange problems make books scarce). No paper clips or staples. Stacks of browning papers on shelves along one wall, and a lazy ceiling fan. Electricity went off ("NEPA took light" is how folk say it here) while I waited, but all the typewriters are ancient manuals, so work continued. Hope the head of department answers the urgent note I left. His signature's required on a couple of forms before I can get on the salary list and move from the guest house into campus housing.

6 December '83, P.M.

So much for the vaunted importance of greetings in the elaborate etiquette of Yoruba culture! When we pass folk on campus, they don't speak or even nod. When we ask for directions, we get gruff, inaccurate answers. Our skin color, hair length and texture, and body language mark us as strangers, and people point us out as if we couldn't see them. No "brother" and "sister" rap here. Even our neighbors don't greet us. The capital city of Lagos might be more accustomed to foreigners—or maybe just more insincere.

9 December '83

Have lived out of a suitcase since 21 November, without a shampoo, shower, or tub bath since Thanksgiving. Bouts of stomach trouble seem to come from tension rather than foreign water or food. EVERYTHING moves much more slowly than C.P.T. ("colored people's time") in the U.S., or even Jamaica-time (in the Caribbean). White people live *on* time, Africans live *in* time. Spend hours waiting for various officials to sign dog-eared "documents," only to learn that "he has traveled" or "he is not on seat." Though Nigeria's official language is English, Yoruba seems to be spoken all the time and everywhere in Ile-Ife. Folk have unfamiliar accents, cadence, syntax, and grammar when they speak English. And, colonized by the British, they don't understand U.S. accents, let alone

Black English. Besides, they *think* in Yoruba, a tonal language where—according to a Jamaican who's been married to a Nigerian for twenty or thirty years—folk can think one thing, intend another, and say something different. . . . And not consider themselves lying.

15 December '83

Road 7B, House 9 is L-shaped so there's a cross-breeze. . . . Trees full of papaya outside the front door. Unlike a house in Ife town, this one has running water because the university has its own dam. Four bedrooms, two toilets, shower, and bathtub. We have, courtesy of the Oluyedes who insist we need one, Emmanuel, an Igbo steward (folk always mention ethnic groups here) who has worked for other *oyingbo*—as they call foreigners. Living room, dining room, and bedroom furniture come with the place. Since all I brought from the U.S., besides clothes, medicine, books, etc., was a pair of rubber gloves, a potato peeler, and two knives, we desperately need goods. We're going to try to buy kitchenware from tumultuous Leslie (she bit her head of department at the staff club—in front of lots of Nigerian men!), the Hampton graduate, who is leaving after six or eight years.

28 December '83

Furious at the way culture-shocked Yvonne and Osula, who ignored all my advice about reading up on Nigeria before we came, cling to the house, insist they're not hot while dressing like it's autumn in Maine, and guzzle up stories of my nerve-wracking daily forays into Yoruba life. Wish I had the missing suitcase's sneakers, contact lenses, nail polish, and lipstick; the key to the pantry and refrigerator; trouble-free toilets; Osula and Yvonne registered at Moremi secondary school; a church home; an idea of my rainy season teaching load; relief from muscle spasms which vise-clamp my left side; more AfAm music; and that good man who is so very hard to find.

29 December '83

The chilly quiet of 8 A.M. Gray sky a stark contrast to postcards of tropical Africa. Feels like the day is taffy—waiting for me to mold. . . .

1 January '84

A Sunday. Faith (my guide here in Nigeria, like I was hers when her husband was a visiting professor at Amherst College) and I were to go to Ife market. Arriving and greeting me in Yoruba, she says the government has fallen. I, certain she's talking about some faraway place like Bolivia, ask where and am amazed when she says, "In this our Nigeria. Didn't you hear the drums talk?" Heard them all night but, illiterate in their language, thought students were celebrating the New Year. The military has replaced Shagari's civilian government (recently elected with weeks of glowing reports in the *New York Times*) and charged it with rampant corruption. Borders have been sealed and Faith's husband, the vice-chancellor, doesn't think it safe for us to go out yet. Hours later, Faith returns, saying it's safe to shop. Though military broadcasts urge citizens to keep calm and observe the 7:00 P.M. to 6:00 A.M. curfew, there's no military presence on the streets, and no one in the market seems worried about the coup. "Compliments of the season" is the common greeting. Since folk confuse *s* and *sh* the response often sounds like "Wiss you the shame." And they add, "Happy new government!"

3 January '84

Spiders scurrying though speckled cotton leaves; lizards splayed on cement walls. Squat dwarf goats chomping banana leaves. A ping-pong game in a dusty front yard along the back road between the university and the market. Shopkeepers dozing on battered plastic chairs in the afternoon's relentless heat and waking *slowly* when potential customers come to price goods.

6 January '84

Today's the Feast of Epiphany, a showing forth, a manifestation of God. Look where God's brought me from! Two years ago, I was under the hysterectomy knife. A year ago, I was defending my doctoral thesis on women characters in contemporary African and African American novels. Now I'm here seeing connections between their lives and ours—for myself.

18 January '84

Women aren't in purdah here and even the Muslims don't veil their faces, but this is the kind of sex-segregated society where girls and boys can't socialize in secondary school, where women and men buying Omo detergent wait on separate lines. But, unlike U.S. culture, which prescribes pink for baby girls and blue for baby boys, which markets disposable diapers by gender, etc., Yoruba (including those with non-African spouses) routinely confuse *he* and *she* when speaking English because Yoruba language doesn't make this distinction. And, although given names reveal whether one is an *ibeji* twin—highly valued in Yorubaland, whether one is *Idowu,* the first child after twins, what your parents were praying for when you were born, that you've been named

Iyabo or Babutunde after a recently dead grandmother or grandfather, etc., they don't usually tell whether you're female or male.

21 January '84

Though Faith and I arrive at markets in a Peugeot or a Mercedes, she is never too expensively dressed. Throughout transactions she's relaxed and her glowing teak face smiles. She marvels at the size of the seller's children (and gives them *kobo*-coins) and asks about the rest of her family. While she studies yams (or vegetables or beans), I take mind-photos of the art in women's arrangement of their wares. Hair-plaiting, nursing toddlers, uniformed children doing schoolwork or eating snacks of rice and stew on banana leaves. When she consults me, I mask my ignorance of Yoruba by pouting, shrugging my shoulders, and walking away looking for a better bargain elsewhere. Which usually makes the seller reduce her asking price.

23 January '84

My University of Ife students can't believe that race kept Richard Wright's Bigger Thomas from being a pilot or that in my own hundreds of thousands of miles on U.S. planes, I've never had a Black pilot. . . . Folk are surprised that I know anything about respecting my elders, sucking my teeth, dancing with my hips, or getting caught up in the Holy Spirit. And can't believe I grew up eating sugar cane, avocado, black-eyed peas, okra, and hot sauce, and sucking meat off bones.

27 January '84

Never occurred to me that there'd already be AfAm women on this Nigerian campus, but, once I saw them, I expected sisterhood. And had my feelings hurt. The AfAm wives of Yoruba faculty are aloof—as if visiting me would taint their loyalty to their African husbands and in-laws. Maybe it has nothing to do with me. . . . Perhaps the sisters are just worn down working, running extended family households, keeping foodstuff and cooking gas in store in an economy where scarcity's an everyday occurence, and keeping polygamy at bay.

2 February '84

On the verge of losing my mind. There is entirely too much togetherness here. Not only are Yvonne, Osula, and I together all the time because they hate almost everything about being in Nigeria, people visit daily (customary visiting hours are from 7:00 A.M. to 10:00 P.M.). There's a special Yoruba greeting (*'E-ku jo metta*) that apologizes for not having seen someone in three days, and, strange but true, powerful grown men have prostrated themselves in our threshold doing it! *And.* . . . Privacy's an alien concept. No one can imagine that you want or need time alone. People read every single piece of paper in sight. Read it and then want to discuss the contents with you. *I am not cut out for this life!*

13 February '84

This February heat is beating up on me. A cool breeze just blew across the room, but my Express Salon basket-style cornrows are soaking wet though the scorching sun went down five hours ago. Even when I'm absolutely still my body's covered with sweat. In 1969 I wondered how Jamaican women could wear pantyhose in August. Now it's how can Nigerian women wear *gèlè* (headwrap), *bubu* (blouse), *iro* (skirt), and *iborun* (shawl) in such relentlessly steaming weather?

27 February '84

One of the things I like best about my veterinarian suitor is how self-confident he is, but Osula and Yvonne call him brash and arrogant. Here's the deal: he's grown up in a country where his race doesn't mean his career will be stopped by the glass ceiling beyond which no Black person can go, or where he'll be killed by a police officer who either confused him with someone else or thought he was reaching for a weapon. Unlike brothers at home, he doesn't talk about how he's oppressed by Mr. Whitefolks and needs me to be super-understanding. No rap about how he came up the fatherless-mother-scrubbing-floors hard way and/or feels guilty about the neighborhood boys he's left behind. Exhausted by all the variations of that whine, I'm savoring the difference.

4 March '84

Back, late night, from the vice-chancellor's spaciously elegant lodge. Just saw another slice of African women's lives. At first I relax over a Maltina (*Ugh* . . . but the strongest drink polite Yoruba society offers to women) in one of the informal sitting rooms. As usual the children and stewards come to greet me with soft smiles, lowered eyes, and hushed voices. Faith—a radiant and relaxed attitude that belies her six children and full-time secretarial job in the university's Department of Nursing, presides over the sitting room's guests. . . . Chat with V.-C. and his male guests. After a while, "Let's go discuss women's business." When we're in the formal dining room, she closes the door. The topic is not recipes, child care, cosmetics, how to keep your man, ob-gyn, y'all. She talks money. Buying and selling cloth and beads. Wanting a machine so she can pierce baby girls' ears. Using her earnings to travel to Brazil, London, the U.S. Money as women's business. On the surface, in public, women defer to men, "Let me discuss with my husband if I can come to the U.S.," but the most important ties a woman has are to the family she was born into, the children she has, and the same sex friends she came of age with. And that's not all. Men are afraid of women's coolness and calm and their formidable spiritual power, and they say so.

27 March '84

I am late, *even* by Nigerian standards, for a Department of Literature in English meeting, driving back from the bank. Folk honk and point at me, so I pull over at the first service station. Not just *one*, y'all, but *two* flat tires. Yoruba classes haven't taught me how to discuss car problems and (despite the chart I show them) my Nigerian brothers have no idea how to get the tires off the car. I'm, seemingly resigned, sitting on a wood bench when my vet honey drives up and insists that I get out of the midday sun. He talks to the workers about what needs to be done, pays them, and says he'll stop by "Madame's" this evening to check the car and, if it isn't perfectly fixed, he'll look for them tomorrow. If liberation means handling all this by my feminist self, I *elect* to be oppressed.

10 April '84

Constantly stunned (and exasperated) by how nothing—not even knowing Africans in the U.S. or having read and taught about Africa for a decade—prepared me for the taboos about women going to a nightclub alone, being at the university staff club at night, or wearing bathing suits. No advance warning about lethal highways or a servant who barely understands the basics of food storage. Achebe, Armah, Emecheta, Nwapa, and Soyinka, I've read and taught you since the early '70s, but you didn't describe the Africa I'd find. Maybe there's no written way to do so.

17 April '84

More convinced than ever that the fabled (and vilified) strength of AfAm women came not from slavery, but from the roles—as workers, wives, mothers—in pre-colonial Africa. Not so much that chattel slavery made us strong, as that our improvisations on traditional African patterns made us survivors and, sometimes, transcenders.

18 April '84

For all the self-possession women show in their sphere of market and home, the more traditional still curtsy to men and almost all women speak more softly when addressing men. Those who are Western-educated and work are still expected to soothe and wait on their husbands. The concept of friendship between men and women is snickered at. Sex is imagined to be behind, above, under, around everything. The mere idea of joint checking accounts stuns women here into speechlessness. People marry to have children; families marry each other. Romantic love seems as much of a supersition to the Yoruba as the idea that children inevitably have fall-out-on-the-floor temper tantrums when they're two-years old. And despite AfAms brothers' rap about how African women are more submissive, subservient, etc. than we are, I haven't met one who married, or even considered, marrying a man who didn't have more money than she had. Underneath the public deference women display iron wills.

19 April '84

Just met my first African feminist! Dr. (Mrs.) Shola Osofian. ("We all have our own confusion.". . . She's a Christian Scientist. . . .) Lecturer in Modern European languages. She describes an egalitarian marriage, with three daughters and a son, to the man who heads the university's Mechanical Engineering Department. We have a 9:00 A.M. appointment next week to talk more, and I'm counting the days!

Easter Tuesday, '84

First storm of rainy season finally rinsing all the grainy ocher dust from the faraway Sahel off the house louvers and broad tree leaves. By God's great grace storm didn't meet us—as they say here—on the deadly highway between Ibadan and Ile-Ife. Once safe inside the house, Osula and I improvised a Thanksgiving dance for another safe journey and for this sweet change in the weather.

27 April '84

Military government's announced that Nigeria will have new currency "as from tomorrow." Ostensible purpose is to stop counterfeiters and flush out folk who have more than the allowed NN 5,000 at home, but I suspect closet acceptance of IMF and World Bank's acid austerity plans. Program to change old money for new, which sounds sane, was probably devised in some Japanese or Swiss boardroom. Can't imagine it working in this chaotic country where part of the military's "war against indiscipline" is to get people to stand on lines ("queue up" is how they say it here). Ready to be wrong, though.

29 April '84
Hard to believe, but true all the same. Market women, those wide-hipped Mamas who haven't *seen* the inside of a school, have decided they're too busy to waste time standing on lines to turn old money in at the bank so they can collect new money later. In the self-same university city where arm-chair radicals docilely line up for *naira*, explaining that protesting government policy will give the new regime an excuse to jail them, unlettered women have sucked their teeth at military power. Their decision wouldn't matter if all they sold was cigarettes and snacks. But, aside from fresh meat, they control all the food—tomatoes, oranges, pineapples, maize, *pepe*, onion, okra, red palm oil, beans, cassava, rice, stockfish, and yam-the-staple. I can't believe that, despite its guns and tanks, the military isn't confronting these women! Can't think, despite all the rap about women's liberation, of a U.S. equivalent to the power these women exert with such self-assurance.

10 May '84
Osula and I talk about when she and Yvonne started Moremi, the select school I had to lobby ("walk on long legs") to get them admitted to, where folk said they'd be happy, where I thought they'd make friends—they hated it daily and fiercely. (Someone urinated on the plant for Osula's science project, classmates laughed when—at recess—she was inept at cutting grass with a machete. . . . Yvonne had to carry her chair daily, had a teacher correct her for leaving the "e" off of salt, and vomited when—common practice here—a teacher beat a student with a metal ruler.

18 May '84
Last night Osula and Folake went to a movie at Oduduwa Hall. Delayed by a Scrabble game, I got there late. No sign of them there and didn't see them on the drive home either. About an hour after F. B. and I got back to the house, they sauntered in. F. B. berated them for disobeying me and not waiting until I arrived. It's this morning when I realize that, despite the insatiable libidos of Nigerian men, he and I weren't afraid they'd be raped.

23 May '84
Haven't, despite my intentions and efforts, met any African women, besides Faith, to become friends with. (The rap is that they're afraid I have designs on their husbands—I know that scenario from the U.S.—and/or think I'll snicker at their English, menu, attire, manners—and so stay clear of me.)

3 June '84
So much tension caused by the men in our Ile-Ife life. My idea (scoffed at by Mom and Osula) was to pretend to be married and expecting my husband within the month. Then he'd be delayed by responsibilities at work and in his family. As it is, we're single female foreigners—a combo that attracts men to us like F. B.'s letters on a Scrabble board call for other words to join them. (Besides, though I didn't know this before I got here, AfAms have reputations as loose women.)

5 June '84
Talkin' about hospitality! Dr. (Mrs.) Shola Osofian, the feminist, had invited us—and her best friend—to dinner at her house. Had to cancel because her friend's husband had been killed on the fatal Ibadan-Ife road and folk didn't want to tell the new widow unless Shola herself was there. In the midst of all that, she brought the planned meal to us—mangoes, *egusi* and vegetable, corn and coconut (to be eaten together), a stew of chicken, goat, and liver, made sure that F. B. would show us how to eat everything, AND said she'd come back to collect the dirty containers she brought the food in!

14 June '84
Bulletin. Hard work under the hot sun wasn't a new experience for enslaved Africans. This week watching construction on the largest campus in Africa, I saw woman after woman excavating building sites with wash basins and then head-load carrying the basins to dumping sites. West African women's "place" was never in the home. They planted and reaped and ran markets all across West Africa. Being ripped away from place of origin, family, and culture probably traumatized them much, much more.

23 June '84
What has me interested in the deity Osun isn't that she gives children to those who have lost all hope. (My child-bearing years are behind me.) Impressed with how she is mother-warrior-indigo dyer-lover-healer. I like the praise *oriki* that declares: Where medicine is impotent, she cures with clear water. And the creation story about how, as the only female among the seventeen deities the High God brought into being, the male *orisa* ignored her when they made their plans. But when they took their designs to Oludumare, the High God, they were refused because Osun hadn't been consulted. Nothing they intended could occur unless she agreed. Sixteen of them and one of her. What a

contrast to Pandora opening a forbidden box and sinful Eve undoing poor Adam in Eden.

27 June '84
Finally got to Osun's Osogbo shrine. Awed to be in such a large nature shrine and captivated by Taiwo's descriptions of the acrobatics and miracles at Osun's annual August rainy season festival. Too much—on a continent where measles and diarrhea kill a million children annually—about the *orisa's* granting fertility to desperate women. Not enough about her owning the beaded comb that attests to harmony in the cosmos—embodied in women's artistically patterned cornrows—or using clear water as effective medicine when everything has failed. (I love a metaphor!)

2 July '84
Malaria surprised me! Back—you know God's good!—after F. B. found me shivering and cold-sweating, dressed me, took me first to the University Health Center and then, since no doctor was on duty, to the doctor's house. The hospital didn't have the medicine I needed, so my veterinarian suitor, more shaken than I thought this oh-so-macho-man would ever be, drove to a pharmacy in Ife-town for it. Spent nine hours being fed intravenously in a room where a bold rat strutted across the floor and the smell of the toilet (why are Nigerian toilets *so* filthy?) made my empty stomach retch and dry heave.

5 July '84
Currency exchange has Nigeria snarled. Not enough new money to replace the old, so banks—believe it or not—*ration money!* No matter how much you had in the bank before the currency exchange, you're only allowed to withdraw N25 a day (and that's on days when the bank has money). Have money and can't buy salt! Rumor—which we live on since we have neither phone, radio, nor television—has the crisis easing. Long after this ordeal is over, I'll remember having to send to the vice-chancellor's lodge to borrow salt.

13 August '84
Family and friends didn't believe that, wasted away to ninety-seven pounds, I'd be able to survive Nigeria's rigors. Only my chiropractor insisted that going would help my health. . . . Left knee keeps locking in painful and crippling way. Sprained my left ankle twice. Lots of stomach

trouble. Scary malaria. *But*, my blood pressure, high since my Ph.D days, went down to 90/70. (The AfAm nurse at the U.S. Embassy—an unmilitant soul married to a big time AfAm Eastman Kodak official—stunned me by saying that even with all the salty food and daily tensions in Nigeria, I'm more relaxed now because "there aren't any white people here.") And, though far from the robust size they love in adult women here—I've gained *some* weight.

19 August '84
Want to go—and want to come back. Couldn't go if I wasn't sure I could, when Osula's finished high school, come back and spend years here. Go "home" so I can smell like something besides the insect repellent that takes the top coat off both leather and red nail polish, drink water from a tap instead of a water filter, escape the rainy season smell of camphor balls in closets to stave off mildew. Want a solid month of Aretha Franklin, Nina Simone, Sweet Honey in the Rock, James Cleveland, Joe Williams, Otis Redding, Johnny Hartman. . . . Want mounds of liverwurst, salami, fried porgies, steamed crabs, turnip and mustard greens, beets, nectarines, peaches, yogurt, tofu. . . . Long for St. Paul A.M.E.; easy phone calls and reliable mail; magazine subscriptions and stocked bookstores; and the textures, cadences, and riffs of my Black English mother tongue.

8 January '86
Had to come back and would have been here even sooner, except for January's knee surgery last year. Remember how low my blood pressure was when I left here? Two weeks in Amherst, Massachusetts BEFORE the semester had even started, both the bottom and top numbers had doubled! Being here will put me back in touch with African artists and intellectuals I can't have mail or phone contact with in the U.S. This time I'll take photos of Yoruba women at work so folk in the U.S., part of Africa's diaspora, will have visual images of African women who are usually invisible, primitive, subordinate, Other. Have missed Nigeria, and not just the hot weather in January. . . . The spider web of connections. . . . When you stub your toe or sneeze here, folk say, *"pele,"* sorry. Being here's a reprieve from the U.S. obsession with racial politics. Since I've lugged an entire suitcase of supplies for the University of Ife's new day care center and the Department of Literature in English, I get to share our obscene (considering how few MATERIAL things most people of African descent in the world have) U.S. wealth with sisters and brothers here.

9 January '86

Disoriented by jet-lag, raking the crowd to see who'd come to pick me up, and worrying that if no one came I'd have to negotiate a cab to the University's guest house, I—of all seasoned travelers—*lost* $500 to an airport tout who ran a "the-new-military-government-requires-everyone-to-exchange-that-much-before-leaving-the-airport" rap on me. Must have *looked* as distressed as I felt, because a *real* airport official rescued me from staring into space and convinced a taxi driver to take me to Ikeja for one third what it usually costs.

10 January '86

At the Akinlade's in Ikeja. "My enemies," the Bible says, "meant it for evil, but my God meant it for good." Decided to come here because it's near the University guest house where I'm to meet F. B. to travel to Ile-Ife, and this house has—a luxury in this weak-infrastructured nation—a working telephone. The famous, fifty-ish architect Katie introduced me to in '84, invites me in, dispatches someone to collect my luggage from the cab, asks if I want to eat, and directs a quarter of his nieces and daughters to prepare evening meal for me. While I sip palm wine and I tell my airport trials, he "pets" me. "It's only money." I'm safe. "This problem can be solved." I surprise (and impress) him by eating with the natural fork of my hand. Before he goes to work this A.M., he arranges transportation for me and gives me *naira* to spend. Then, as a sort of afterthought, he asks my name. Where in the U.S.—even in the deepest South—could I possibly see this kind of courtesy? *He didn't even know my name!* And this house has a swimming pool! A few lazy laps on my back and my cares—in the U.S. and in Nigeria—slip off like a silk dress.

8 January '87

Counting on Yvonne and Osula who both had two cameras back in '83–'84, I, a wordsmith, didn't take a single photo during the nine months we lived here. Showed last January's photos to students in a literature class. As always, I'd been insisting on this: "There is no text without context" (and no reader without context, either). When my students, whose images of Africans had been limited to violence in South Africa and starvation in Ethiopia and Somalia, were astonished that, though Wanikin village has no running water or electricity and my visit was unannounced, girls and women in this "underdeveloped country" were dressed up in a way the students rarely got, I *understood* that my nine months in Nigeria taught me to see so many things through Yoruba lenses (I had worse culture shock when I got back to Amherst, Massachusetts, than I had when I landed in the Babel of Murtala Muhammed Airport). I knew how to "read" Yoruba women's attire, translate its language for outsiders, and speak it in the way I dress in Nigeria and back "home" in the U.S.

9 January '87
Spent the entire day trying to get the lens on the Nikon 2000—with no success. Reject the veterinarian's exasperated suggestion about hiring a professional photographer—and press on. I am, after all, an heir of Phillis Wheatley, Sojourner Truth, and Fannie Lou Hamer.

11 January '87
At Ede cloth market with Kemi—which is, I finally learn—Faith's Yoruba name. Her usual long shopping. Astounding fabric patterns: skulls, umbrellas, random alphabet letters. Taking photos in this hive of women would drive the cost of fabrics Kemi's bargaining on *way* up. Watching a market woman at work, I rethink how, though enslaved African women took their spiritual powers to and through the Middle Passage with them, they lost their awesome economic power in the Americas, colonized by sexist Euro-Americans who *knew* "a woman's place was in the home."

16 January '87
Back, for the second time, to Osun's Osogbo. This visit I get to see the *Iya-Osun's* quarters in the *Oba* of Osogbo's palace. Led by Kemi's gentle brother, Wole (who tried to teach Osula and me Yoruba in '84), we pay homage to the *orisa* by taking our shoes off and kneeling until her "priestess" invites us to sit. Present bananas, honey, sugar cane, oranges, pineapples, and *naira* (this is Wole's idea because the *orisa* likes sweet things and yellow and orange are her favorite colors). Seeing the photos Wole and I took last January and hearing his testimony about how I've been interested in Osun for years and always give people copies of my photos of them (he shows the priestess photos of him—and Osun's grotto—I took last year), she allows me to take her picture.

25 January '87
Bola, the senior Akinlade daughter, took me to a Christian Yoruba wedding yesterday, and I took rolls and rolls of photos—even got to use the telephoto lenses. Bride and groom were the only people (besides Bola and her pharmacist friend, Yemi) in Western dress. You could tell all the

family groups present because they were "*aso-ebi*" (in ensembles of identical cloth). Learning more and more about this complicated culture. Anxious to see these photos.

26 January '87
Unbelievable, but true all the same, in a few hours, I'll be battered by New England's cruel winter and single parenthood and—which no one here believes or understands—bombarded by billboards, television, newspapers, and magazines full of folk who don't look at all like me. No more wall-to-wall suitors. The respect and deference my age, motherhood, and professor-status assures here will sink under the U.S. racial politics. And I will be light years away from the centers of spiritual, cultural, economic, and political power to which life in Nigeria gives me such easy access.

3 January '88
Back by God's great grace, for the third time in three years. Have been robbed in Nigeria *again!* "Managed," as they say here. Besides, now, I "belong" to three separate Yoruba families—Odeyale, Akinlade, and Olusola. (Relatives in the States think I make these trips to see a man. Can't *even* imagine the way my "kinfolk" here take care of me. And how family is more than wealth in "this our Nigeria.")

14 January '88
In '83 I thought I'd learn to speak enough Yoruba to get by, amass a wardrobe of fabulous cloth and jewelry, add Yoruba cooking to my repertoire, make friends with Yoruba women, become—after years of wearing them—skilled at plaiting cornrows. Which goes to show you that I (despite my caul) don't have periscopic vision. So many other things happened. Taught in a department where, unlike anything I know in the U.S., outspoken Marxists prevail. Learned to match my pronunciation, idioms, tone of voice, speech rhythms to Nigeria's own brand of English. Lived almost absolutely free from housework. Grew accustomed to easy access to people in power because, no matter how high I go, the person in charge is *Black* (except in the U.S. Embassy, which is a slice of Mississippi in '57). And ever since my first trip, I write more here than I ever do in the U.S.

15 January '88
Every time I go "home" to the States, it's exactly as hard to tell people what I miss when I'm away from this difficult country ("if you can live

with us, you can live anywhere, even Antarctica" is how they put it). Crave red palm oil stews; *egusi*; prawns; cassava; yam roasted, ground into flour, or pounded. Long for this world where the sacred and secular overlap even more than at "home" where Al Green, Sam Cooke, Aretha Franklin, and company glide between gospel and soul singing. Everything is art here. Hand-painted signs on the sides of *molue* buses ("covered by the blood" is my favorite), home shrines full of sculptures Western collectors would drool over. Women's easy curtsies, little way of shifting their back-carried babies around to nurse, and hip-swinging walks ("backyard" is what they called our buttocks here, and women are routinely said to have gotten something through "bottom power"). Women's art demonstrated in market arrangements of produce, hairstyles, and stunningly wrapped cloth ensembles.

17 January '88

Andrea, who didn't bring a camera here in '83, has had a mid-life career blessing. Last August she curated and mounted "A Language of Their Own," an exhibit at Amherst College of the cloth and jewelry from her collection of wearable art and the color photographs she took in '86 and '87. Absolutely ignorant in '83, over the years I have mastered wearing Yoruba attire so appropriately other Yoruba think I am, despite my slight body and "light" skin, and mostly un-Yoruba body language, one of them. I can now read age, class, place of origin, and ideas about gender from Yoruba women's hair-styles, *gèlè*, cloth, and jewelry. A folded *iborun* shawl draped on a woman's left shoulder indicates marriage and motherhood; *gèlè* head-ties are the province of adult/married women; gray, white, and beige are the colors for those who follow *orisa* deity Obatala; many Yoruba Muslim women wear white cloth (green and white are Islam's colors) atop their *gèlè*; the more cloth one wears, the more decoration on that cloth, the more *naira* money one is perceived to have; deeply dyed indigo cloth, the kind that stains one's hands, is another such sign. For special occasions, families often come in ensembles of identical cloth; when you see women in identical cloth, you don't know exactly how they're related: sisters? co-wives? women who married into the same family? close friends? members of the same market association? Their attire masks the differences, like who is rich and who is poor; instead it announces the group solidarity the Yorubas prize much more than individuality.

19 January '88

Back, for the third time, in the Osobgo center of Osun worship. Impressed the guards at the *oba's* palace by flashing last January's photos of the *Iya-Osun*, and was led to her door by praise-singers. She and two stern post-menopausal associates were just back from the grove I first went to in '84 and got sand-fly stung in last January. Don't think she'd ever seen a photo of herself before. . . . Children afoot, afternoon meal cooking. Though I got to photograph the mystery of a sixteen cowrie divination, no goose pimples this time. Kemi translated the *Iya-Osun's* directions for me to take a one *naira* note and whisper whatever I wanted. Worried about too many things (in Nigeria and the U.S.) to choose just one.

22 January '88

Water's been a hassle this trip. Washing my feet in a bucket at Unife's VIP guesthouse means getting another one to "flush" the toilet, and I realize that the metal pail here is so much heavier than the plastic one at the Akinlade's upscale Ikeja home. Brand-new sympathy for women the world over who have water-hauling as one of their tedious daily tasks.

25 January '88

Ever since '84, I've thought I'd settle here when Osula started college. Can't do it, and feel like Nigeria's betrayed me. Explaining to folk here, I start with how I already have so much research material, I shouldn't come back until I've written it up. But there's this, too. . . . It's painful to live in an oil-rich nation where there are so many political, economic, and social things corrupt and horribly wrong. My private sector friends are flush with their polo horses, luxurious homes, full pantries, overseas bank accounts, five car stables, and overseas shopping trips; devout nationalist university colleagues are driving battered cars with bald tires and begging for jobs in the States; and small-small people like my former steward are scraping the bottom of bare barrels. Tons of arm-chair radicalism. No organized opposition to the government, so I couldn't make money here and donate it to progressive causes and speaking out myself would get me deported. I miss having women friends whose lives are as unconventional as my own. And, honest here if nowhere else, can't (even with my relaxed attitude about polygamy) imagine a harmonious, satisfying relationship with a man here. (AfAm women are perceived as sexually available, so Nigerian women worry that I have eyes for their men). Hysterectomy behind me, I can't be a biological mother again; since the Yoruba boggle at the idea of friendships between women and men, men display an intense jealousy I find incredible, silly, and exasperating.

28 January '88

You've heard me go on and on about how people-centered this world is: visiting, borrowing and lending, gift-giving, family responsibilities—rather than job and career—as *the* reason folk can't do things. Love all that, but soul-sapping is what you call this visit where three different women—one each in the Odeyale, Akinlade, and Osundare families—confide about their pain. The unmarried senior sister running her father's household chomps her nails, has a rainbow of allergies, and an ulcer. The AfAm married to a Yoruba is, despite her four children, thin enough to be anorexic. She "reports" his failures to me, and, since this is Nigeria, twenty-four hours later, he complains to me about her. On center stage I'm up in the middle of Faith/Kemi's polygamy argument with her husband. Yes, I'm impressed by the way, in a culture that can't conceive a problem without a solution, folk involve themselves (and me) in what would, in the States, be a painfully private matter. No, I don't like the way all the formal conferring and advising has yanked energy from me.

30 January '88

This country has been, despite a zillion hassles and a hundred crises, so good to me. Living here has changed my life. I'm a cultural translator now—and don't just mean I can explain AfAms and E/Ams (European Americans) to each other. Always, whether in the States, the Carribean, or Nigeria, aware of two other Black worlds, never altogether at home in any one. Couldn't leave this time if I didn't know I can come back. Couldn't bear landing in a rich, arrogant, racist, sexist, wintry, oh-so materialistic place if I had to stay there. I'm liminal now, living on the edges.

Carol Spindel

BLESSINGS

Before Adama became our interpreter, the constant exchange of blessings made me a little uneasy. After all, the one I received most frequently was "May Allah give you children." In Berkeley, having a child was a weighty personal decision, something one pondered for years and went to therapy to resolve, not something one wished lightly on others like, "Have a good day." When the blessing was given in Senufo, the deity was Kolotyolo, and so I could translate it, "May Ancient Mother give you children." I preferred the Senufo version because I thought that Ancient Mother was more likely to understand my feelings on the matter: children were desirable, but there were better and worse times to receive them. As far as Allah was concerned, I imagined him to be the Grand Old Patriarch with a white beard who had never actually carried a baby on his back or wiped a runny nose, and I figured that his main concern in the matter was the production of more little Muslims. If this were true, an infidel like me was probably safe from his schemes for the grand design of things. Nevertheless, the constant collective desire of sixteen hundred people to see me become pregnant as expressed through frequent fervent blessings gave me pause for thought.

Whenever I gained a few pounds or was sick to my stomach, I could see their eyes light up hopefully. Against this strong collective desire, I worried that my diaphragm would prove too weak. After all, it was designed to repel mere matter. Could it really stand up against something as powerful as the collective faith of an entire village who daily invoked two different deities to aid them in their desire to see me bear a child? Did a man-made scrap of rubber, an upstart human invention, have a chance against a desire that strong and that ancient? This is what I asked myself uneasily as I muttered *"amina"* to their blessings.

Whenever Adama translated the blessings, he always used the French word *Dieu* for God, and this also made me feel uneasy. I wasn't sure I believed in one. Certainly I believed in vague "forces" or "powers" in the universe, but I felt more comfortable if I left my forces in an unnamed state of spiritual ambiguity. Like many people I knew, I claimed to believe in Something. I just didn't want that Something defined too clearly.

But the forces I felt in the universe were not something I invoked as personally and specifically as the people of Kalikaha invoked theirs. When Sita prayed at dawn, she seemed to open her heart to Allah in a way I had never considered doing. And when my neighbors gave me blessings, they were always concrete and specific. They asked God to give me a good afternoon or a peaceful night or to help with my work that day, to give me a child, a harmonious marriage, a safe trip back from Korhogo, and a long life. At first, I tapped my forehead to help the blessing sink in and muttered *"amina"* as a matter of course. I was pleased that I was able to catch the first word, *Allah*, and that I could respond appropriately by saying "amen."

Being around Adama changed me. When we went into the village to do interviews, Adama gave out blessings to everyone. This was something Yardjuma had never done. If someone told Adama of a death or an illness, he immediately responded with a heartfelt blessing. "*Alla ka nagoya kay*. May God make it better. *Allah ka hinara*. May this person go to heaven." The blessings soothed the roughness of the moment. This did not mean that Adama did not try to help. He did. But first, he always invoked God's aid.

"May God give your children life," Adama said fervently to every mother. And they all, no matter how young and hopeful or how old and wizened, whispered intently, *"amina"* and their eyes thanked Adama for expressing the concern that they lived with daily in their hearts.

This giving out of blessings was more than polite utterance. It was a way of sharing hope, for people in Kalikaha needed hope to survive. No abstract relationship with deities who lived far above, this was a gritty daily contact with two deities who seemed, through people's words, to be always present in the village with us. Nor were the deities themselves estranged in enmity. Sometimes Adama spoke in Senufo of Ancient Mother, sometimes in Dyula of Allah; to us he spoke in French of *Dieu*. When I questioned him about distinctions, he said it didn't matter, that God was always the same.

Tom and I, at the end of interviews and conversations, found ourselves making up our own blessings and asking Adama to translate and deliver them for us. I didn't do this unconsciously, the way I sometimes picked up new words. Rather, I found myself wanting to hand out blessings and feeling sincerely touched and, in the most appropriate word, *blessed*, when I received them.

I started a page in my Dyula notebook for blessings and began to learn hundreds of different ones that applied to particular situations. "I need a blessing to help the potters in their work," I would say to Adama. "One that says, 'May the firing turn out well.'"

"Allah an jayma," replied Adama instantly. "May Allah help us in our work."

Adama regarded my new relationship to blessings with obvious approval, and the page of blessings in my dog-eared Dyula notebook was quickly filled. There was a blessing for the young Dyula girls who wandered through the village selling bits of soap or bouillon cubes. "God help the alleyways to please you." When someone bought a new piece of cloth in the market, you said, "May it wear out before you do," a pragmatic blessing if ever there was one. At about three-thirty, I could bring smiles to stoney faces of even the most proper Dyuna elders by saying as I passed them on their way to the mosque, "May the afternoon prayers be good."

When I gave out my favorite blessing, I could never keep a totally straight face—a certain irrepressible delight in the phrase itself always came out with it. It was so idiomatic, so absolutely, essentially Dyula in character, that villagers crowed with delight at the absurdity of hearing it from me. I could astonish Dyula guests in the village by casually saying as I told them good night, *"Allah yan kelen kelen wuli."* Literally it means, "May everyone here wake up one at a time."

"Do you know the value of waking up one at a time?" the Dyula man who taught me this blesssing asked me. I had to admit that I had no idea.

"If there is some disaster in the night," he replied, "like a fire or a death or a war, someone will call out, and we will all wake up at once. But if the night passes in peace, each of us will wake up in the morning at our own moment, one at a time."

When someone gave a gift, everyone present showered the giver with blessings. The most frequent was, *"Allah i baraji."* "May God give you something even greater than what you have given me." This blessing represents most clearly the sense in traditional African thought of the communal good. For it will probably not be me who will repay you. Life is not that neat, and Africans do not pretend that it is. To assume the responsibility for equity yourself is a form of arrogance in Kalikaha. You receive from those more fortunate than you—older, wiser, or wealthier. You give to those less fortunate. The age-class system is based on these precepts. Somehow, the gift will be returned. It will not come back in the same form. Nor will it come back from the same hand. Years may pass.

It was not only knowing the blessing which was important but also saying it at the proper time, with (of utmost importance) the proper pauses. If I blurted out a blessing at the wrong moment, no one understood. They didn't say *"amina,"* even though I was sure I had gotten the words right.

Not only did I need to know the right words. I needed to know the appropriate situations in which blessings were given and the appropriate moments at which to give them. Once Tom and I had mastered that, we progressed to multiple blessings. Blessings flowed nicely when they came in three's. "May God heal you. May God grant you happiness. May God give you a long life." We learned to pronounce them one after another with just the right pause between. Then we were rewarded with a long chorus of head-tapping and the soft sound of *"amina, amina, amina here be."* The best reward of all was seeing the soft look of appreciation, that moment of *blessedness* that came over people when they received a string of heartfelt blessings.

The sound of the three blessings reminded me of services when I was a girl and how, at the end, the rabbi always raised his arms. We were supposed to bow our heads, but I always looked up to see his black, bell-shaped sleeves stretched out like wings as he gave three singsong blessings in Hebrew and English, with a long pause between each one—the same long pause they used in Kalikaha. But in Kalikaha, I didn't need to be a rabbi, and I didn't need a long black robe.

I do not feel nearly so powerful nor so rational as I did before I went to Kalikaha. There, I saw my good intentions go awry too many times. In Kalikaha, I tried to save a child, a month-old baby. I failed. The baby died. And when Adama said, "It is God's will. May the child go to heaven," I felt a little bit comforted.

Not everything is within our will or understanding. Not everything can be harnessed by our rational powers. In Kalikaha, I felt a spirituality that was threaded through every small encounter. I no longer hesitate to call on the help of other powers and to wish that help on my friends. When I speak to myself, I call these blessings what they truly are: prayers.

Carol Spindel

MARRIAGE IS VERY DIFFICULT

For weeks, the Dyula women had been talking about the wedding. For the past two days, guests had streamed into the Dyula part of the village, arriving on foot from small villages in the bush, tired and dusty, their heads loaded with food and bundles, or grandly, swathed in expensive cloth as they stepped out of taxis from the city. Others came on mopeds, the women sidesaddle on the back, miraculously not falling off without appearing to hold on. On every cooking fire a thirty-gallon pot of rice simmered. Mariam, who had to count each franc with care, had bought twice as many spices as usual just to feed her guests. As for me, I walked the long way around to the potters' quarter, going twice as far in the afternoon sun, just so that I could pass through Dyulaso and observe the bustle.

"Come and cook with us!" the women called. "There's lots to do."

"I can't today," I called back. "I'm going to make pots."

"All you do these days is make pots. But we haven't seen you at the market selling them. You must be selling them in other towns and getting very rich. When are you going to give us some of your pots?"

"Soon," I promised vaguely, as I went on my way. When I was put on the spot, the important thing was to give an answer; any answer was better than none.

The next day was the first day of the week-long Muslim wedding. Three brides were being married at once, two from my adopted family, the Traores, and a third girl who was a Silla from Sillera.

As soon as we heard the drums start up in the afternoon, Adama and I walked over to watch. A large crowd had gathered. In the middle of the crowd were the three brides. Matching cloths were twisted around their waists to form long skirts, but to my surprise, they were bare-breasted.

They wore necklaces of brightly-colored plastic beads and on their heads, like crowns, were hats made of origami-folded foil, as if they were going to a New Year's ball. They also wore sunglasses with heavy black frames. I hadn't expected white eyelet, but this outfit took me completely aback.

"Why don't they wear shirts?" I asked Adama. "I thought Muslim women always wore shirts."

"Not on their wedding day," replied Adama. "It's to prove they're virgins."

"How can we tell?" I asked.

"Because their breasts are small," he said, giving me an odd look. "They aren't pregnant."

"What are the glasses for?" I persisted.

"To make them beautiful," he replied solemnly, gazing at the brides with rapt satisfaction.

Behind each bride danced a supporting chorus of her younger sisters and friends. They carried towels to wipe away the sweat and the tears, both of which were shed copiously as the afternoon progressed. Some held aloft full-length portraits of the brides's boyfriends, large black-and-white photographs about sixteen inches tall, framed in glass with red tape on the edges, taken by a photographer who came to Kalikaha sometimes on market days.

The institution of boyfriends and girlfriends is a traditional custom in Dyula society. When a girl has accepted a boy, he goes to her parents and presents them with a gift of kola nuts. If the kola nuts are accepted, he is officially recognized as her boyfriend. She is allowed to spend nights with him in his house at the edge of the quarter. Sexual intimacy is encouraged, but intercourse is strictly forbidden. The boy must protect the girl from other boys and men and if, on her wedding night, she is found to be a virgin, this is held up as a credit not only to her family but also as a sign of the good character of her *petit ami*. It is his reputation that is on the line, not her's. One day, perhaps with very short notice, she must forget this young lover that she chose and marry the man her family chooses for her, a man who is often twenty or thirty years older than she is.

Several young men played drums and the older women shook gourd rattles but the bulk of the music came from the three brides, as they sang continuously in a repeating rhythm that rose and fell. The young men swarmed around them with jumbo-sized bottles of baby powder and toilet water, dumping both on their bare shoulders. Admirers ran up and attached thousand franc notes to their foil crowns. The women who followed the brides had on their best outfits and the giant, brightly-colored designs seemed to swim through the village, as if they moved independently of the women who wore them. Multi-colored butterflies and flowers, black and yellow television sets with rabbit ears, alphabets and inkpots, papaya trees, cotton bolls and huge geometric motifs striped and dotted and x'ed their way along the paths in red, purple, black, and orange. If I had thought that this part of the wedding had anything to do with the solemnity of marriage or their future husbands, I was totally mistaken. At midnight, the girls would be given to their grooms, dressed in white from head to toe, prayed over and blessed with solemn chanting. But this afternoon was the final fling, the last revelry of youth. It reminded me of a parade at a New Orleans Mardi Gras.

The three brides sang their way from quarter to quarter and I followed in the crowd, feeling like a sparrow who has wandered into a flock of peacocks. The girl from Sillera, who was cross-eyed, didn't sing with the same gusto as the other two, yet she hung onto a picture of her boyfriend, sang as best she could and cried constantly. I did not know her name, but the two Traore girls were named Biba and Jiata. Biba was to marry the tailor, a young man of twenty-five. Jiata would be given to a man in his fifties, a cousin, who already had two wives. Cross-cousins are a preferred marriage among the Dyula.

Many of the women stared at me with odd, curious, even distrustful looks, and I realized that these were the guests from other villages. I had already forgotten how it had been when I first came to Kalikaha and was regarded like that by everyone. For gradually, I and the villagers had drifted into a mutual acceptance, and my presence was now more or less taken for granted. "She lives here with us. She speaks Dyula," I heard the women from Kalikaha whisper over and over with a proud, proprietary air that surprised me.

From quarter to quarter we paraded, the brides singing the same tune over and over, the crowd following after, the young men sprinkling baby powder and toilet water until the brides turned white. The young men handed out candy and cigarettes to the spectators and when something especially pleased them, they threw handfuls of candy into the air, and all the children scrambled after it. Young girls meandered through the crowd selling fried dough balls and paper cones of peanuts.

One of the brides pulled a young man out of the group and danced sensually in front of him, flipping the hair whisk she carried across his face playfully. Everyone laughed, candy flew into the air, and Mariam told me that he was the girl's boyfriend.

The older women, dressed in flowing robes and scarves, formed a benevolent chorus on the steps of the mosque. The young girls came to them and asked for blessings, which the women chanted softly in unison. I stood near Mariam, who looked saint-like in flowing white, and let the soft chants of the choir roll over me.

From time to time, one of the brides would go up to a woman and sing to her, standing very close, their faces nearly touching. Then, inevitably, the older woman would break down and cry. Tears, in odd contrast to the carnival atmosphere, flowed everywhere. The brides cried often. Everyone cried except the young men who were having their last day of fun before their childhood friends left them to become wives and mothers. Adama and I had become separated in the crowds, and so I couldn't ask him what it all meant. I thought that they cried because, as one traditional song went, "marriage is very difficult" and because the brides did not want to leave their boyfriends for husbands they had not chosen.

Finally, in the dusky light of evening, Biba and Jiata broke off and headed for the house of the elder of their family, El Hadji Traore. Everyone must have known this was coming because the cement terrace of his house had emptied of people and he was seated there alone, as if on a throne, an enormous man bedecked in white robes and red hat, holding his prayer beads in his plump hands.

The two brides made their way toward him singing and waving their black whisks. What remained of their voices was hoarse and strained. They had started singing at one in the afternoon and it was now after six. They could barely get out the words, but they sang on determinedly, supported by the young girls behind them. They sang sadly, their tired voices raspy and broken. I couldn't understand the words, but I imagined that they were pleading with him not to marry them off to strangers, not to send them away from the tight circle of the family. They went down on their knees in front of him, swaying and brushing him with their whisks, chanting the same refrain over and over. El Hadji's face was pained; he didn't look directly at them; it was as if he could not bear to. He kept his eyes fixed on the prayer beads in his lap. Finally, he raised his hands slightly, his palms toward them, as if to say, "Enough. Please, no more."

But they kept on, their hoarse voices rising and falling. Finally, I saw one single tear flow out of his eye and roll down his cheek, and it fell on his hands, bedecked with silver rings, where he wiped at it. At this, Biba and Jiata turned and danced, tired but triumphant, down the steps. All of the old women and many of the young ones were crying freely.

I stood not far away from the corner of his terrace and stared at El Hadji. It was a strangely moving sight, the old patriarch who wields so much power over the lives of his family, who could, by a word, marry these girls to whomever he chose, brought to shed a tear by the pleas of the hoarse, sweating young women with supple shoulders and dark, ripe breasts. I couldn't take my eyes off the old man, although everyone was leaving the quarter and I knew that I would soon be conspicuous, staring at him like that. He pushed back his heavy sleeve, glanced at his watch, and then bent his head and stared intensely once again at his prayer beads. He looked strangely satisfied, although why this should be I had no idea.

Adama and I walked home with Noupka, who had been in the crowd. Wherever there was music and dancing, you could be sure Noupka would be there, no matter when the event. "You should be ashamed," Adama admonished her, "to come to the wedding without a shirt. It isn't right. You were the only one." Noupka shrugged and handed me Mama, who was trying to jump off Noupka's back into my arms. Mama had spent the afternoon tied onto Noupka's back, being jogged up and down, and she was ready for a change. As for me, I was sweaty and tired, and my T-shirt and my hair were coated with baby powder, sprinkled on me by way of salute from the young men.

The next day, I went to see Mariam to ask what it all meant. Each bride makes up her own songs, improvising on the spot, Mariam told me. When she sees the young men, she sings, "Come and dance! Today is my great day!" When she sings before the chorus of elder women, she asks them to give her blessings, to ask Allah to give her health, children, and a harmonious marriage.

When she sees a woman she knows, she sings of the woman's sorrows, the children she has lost, for example. That is why all the women cry when the brides sing to them. Then the brides give blessings to comfort the women. Through the brides' songs, the tragic events of the past year are brought forward and remembered. On that afternoon, when they are no longer children and not quite women, the brides have the power to bring forth tears. After the tears have been spilled, they give blessings for solace.

When the brides want to end, they sing before the elder of their family. It seemed to me that they pleaded with him not to marry them away, but I was wrong. They sang to him of his life and of the tragedies of the last year, the wife who died, the babies that were lost. And then they gave him benedictions to console him. "It is Allah's will," they sang. "Be comforted." And that is why he cried.

AMERICAS

Joan Lindgren

WEARING THE CHILEAN GREEN

Esta campaña rota
quiere sin embargo cantar.

This broken bell
still wants to sing.

— PABLO NERUDA
The Sea and the Bells

In the Frank O'Connor story, "The American Wife," the expatriate bride receives great sympathy from her mother-in-law, who has herself undergone the pain of emigration, from North Cork to South Cork. Sojourners are apparently in constant need of hearkening back to the departure point to chart the eternal return. In my case it is not the New York suburb where I grew up, but more the Ireland of my immigrant grandmother's dreams that remains that point of emotional grounding.

And so I should have known from reading and breathing the poetry of Pablo Neruda that Chile would immediately become the Ireland of Latin America for me. Not the mountains and the green so much as the people's attachment to the land; not the people themselves, who tend to be small and neat, slightly oriental in appearance with the Indian strain their blood continues, but their lace-curtain decency and earnestness. Storytellers in love with their own history and folklore, Chileños are intensely political and reluctant to come to a quorum. The presence of an old oppressor looms heavily in Santiago, as real as the great white mystical Andes Range in the distance. The huge statue of a forgiving Virgin Mother high on the *cerro* of San Cristobal, the vast but comfortable and well-worn churches that dominate the city and the lives of their parishioners, the dampness and mist rising off the river—all these would make a Dubliner feel right at home.

I spent ten days in Chile in the autumn of 1989, hardly enough to make judgments. But I knew the history and the people's suffering under Pinochet. I had essentially come in mourning, on a pilgrimage. The government palace, for example, La Moneda, a building of uncommon pristine beauty—in spite of the stories disenchanted friends told of Allende, his philandering and boozing, abuse of power—I could not pass the place without seeing Allende's body slumped at a desk within. His ghost would reappear on a balcony for me each time I passed that palace with its guard, uniformed, booted, and rifled to SS standards.

For my first visit to the famous cemetery, we stocked up on red flowers. First stop was the tomb of Violeta Para who composed the song, *"Gracias a la vida,"* among others. Because she ended her life before the Pinochet regime, she enjoys an honorable grave. María and I, two battle-scarred survivors on the late cusp of middle age, tenderly loaded her stone with red carnations, gave *"Gracias a la vida,"* and took each other's pictures in the company of our brilliant but fragile *comadre.* (The legend of the great singer-songwriter who resurrected the rich folk-music heritage of Chile is that she ended her life when abandoned by the young lover of her middle years.) We moved on then to the common graves, no more than niches in a wall, and stopped to talk to Victor Jara, the guitarist-folk singer whose hands were cut off by the Junta. Many had preceded us here with their red flowers and scribbled messages. Our ultimate visit, of course, was to Neruda himself, also housed in a niche from which spilled forth a profusion of flowers and messages, mostly in verse, dog-eared bits of the apparently endless yearning and hope of the Chilean people. An old woman wrapped in a new blanket, which trailed in the mud puddles, haunted the Nobel Prize winner's grave and recited long passages of Neruda's poems. Slight and gentle of manner, she appeared somehow girlish; and when I questioned her, she recited a litany of her lineage to identify herself. Ironically, several generals were included. Neruda's beloved wife Matilde was permitted placement not next to but near her husband. The family of the stranger buried—thanks to random statistics—beneath Neruda had written on that grave: *"un nicho abajo te escucha, Neruda, con los oidos de dolor."* (One niche down, Neruda, the ears of grief are listening to you.)

Later during our visit to Neruda's house by the sea at Isla Negra, we found millions of messages penciled on the fence which at that time closed off the property (now a public museum) to the public. Perhaps the most tender was, *"Todo pasa y todo muere como la espuma deshace la ola—menos tu obra, Pablo."* (Everything passes and dies as the spray undoes the wave—except your poems, Pablo.) NERUDA was written on the great rocks at the edge of the sea with more testimony, *"Cuando muere un poeta, nace una estrella."* (When a poet dies, a star is born.) In Chile, as in Ireland, poetry is irrepressible, and the people are its caretakers.

Santiago has many more early Colonial buildings and narrow passages than Buenos Aires, but it has as many graceful turn-of-the-century European buildings and similar statuary in its gracious parks. It is smaller and more prim than Buenos Aires, with even more ugly, modern office and apartment buildings. Excellent transportation, including a splendid Metro system, is available. Street vendors abound as well as musicians and corner orators. I saw Indians, come into town with their huge drums on their backs, dancing and playing. A tiny child was too tired to shoulder his drum any longer and rested limply. There were Born-agains (*halelujos*) in groups, singing, saving souls, and threatening where they could in parks. Prices paralleled U.S. prices, though money is in short supply for most. An old avenue was renamed—to my horror—*"Once de septiembre,"* the date of the brutal and deadly Pinochet coup. It is home to lots of tall glass buildings and yuppie-looking shops. But in a supermarket close to the central bus terminal you could buy *chicha,* a popular raw liquor, from a wooden barrel with a ladle. I avoided the rich suburbs. But I did visit an old Colonial building that Señora Pinochet had fitted out as a craft center.

But the place to buy crafts was the Vicaría, a rambling ancient building next to the old cathedral, where the Human Rights Organization has its headquarters. Here you can buy *arpilleras*, the little tapestries made by the families of the "disappeared," which depict children jumping rope outside the jails or other such insistences on bearing witness. The Vicaría is a place of miracles; it is testament to the nature and power of the Church in Chile that the Pinochet regime has permitted it to continue its work. I left messages there for my friend Berta Castro, who had come to my city the previous year to raise support for political prisoners and their families. Berta had told me, tearlessly, how all her sons were losing their teeth in their twenties, thanks to the electric prods of the torturers. All that struggling to feed them well in their early years. And when there were no jobs, how could a mother keep her sons from political demonstrations?

Would it be possible to visit Santiago and not be heavy-hearted, even now with the elections coming? I found the burden of oppression exhausting. My friend María kept me in her home as if I were, in fact, her daughter (my dear friend at home). I was hardly permitted to go out alone. Since María works, her sister Aida came and escorted me everywhere, took me home to her house for lunch. A son of friends, Marcos, who was finishing his degree in economics, accompanied me to a symphony concert at the University. He was hungry for dialogue with the outside world. María's friends invited us to be among them. One family—a couple with two daughters living in one room without running water (the two rickety iron bedsteads, each with its crucifix above, remain engraved on my memory)—received us for cake. It was the older girl's fifteenth birthday celebration. Send the photos, was their request everywhere. Marcos's family invited us. Two young granddaughters played guitar and sang for us all the lovely New Songs of political optimism in code. To survive in retirement, Marcos's father was obliged to turn his living room into a tiny store. Neighbors came in for provisions during the visit. His playing the role of storekeeper in no way diminished his dignity. On the contrary, it enlarged our community.

Nothing could have prepared me for the deprivation these people experience nor for the impact of their coping strategies, love, and community. They nurtured me—only because I knew their story—as one nurtures a spark from tinder, cupping the hands in hopes of starting a flame. They gave me small souvenir gifts as I left. It was a solemn departure, I felt, more, by far, than I had earned. That night the streets were thronged with youth peacefully demonstrating the Brazilian violence against their soccer team in Rio for the America's Cup Match. It seemed to me an unbearable indignity that these young people, groomed in emotional restraint uncommon in adolescence, should have to suffer that public hysteria. But unbearable indignity had become bearable to them.

The little I saw of the countryside had the power to take my breath away. It was the Chilean spring, and fruit trees were in bloom everywhere. Green and fresh and hilly or mountainous, the land manifested the people's pleasure in it. There was visible a dedicated husbandry and the economy of masterful survivors, an economy not overwhelmed by the shame and confusion of waste. The sea is magnificent, the cypress and vegetation at its edge not unlike that of the Monterey Peninsula. Except for Viña del Mar, there was little tourist-type development. Across from Neruda's house, a saturnine old woman, tiny and brisk in her printed apron, cooked a fish lunch for us; we ate it in her dining room under her wedding portrait. She had helped care for Neruda as he lay dying his mysterious heart-break death in the weeks following the coup, while soldiers were burning his books.

María and her sister both received in middle age the gift of sons. *"Tía"* (aunt) the boys called me, and because of the snow in the pass, I was their prisoner for an extra day, they said. It was hard to say good-bye to those who wanted me so much to stay—I was a breath of new air they would like to have bottled. But at last the weather broke and I bid farewell to them and to Moby Dick, as I had come to think of the great white cordillera that towers over the city and comes in or goes out of view capriciously. The bus to Buenos Aires wound up through the mines and farming villages and sawmills into the frozen white silence of the Andes. I wrote half of Neruda's poems second-hand, sipping Pisco against the altitude, and suddenly Chile was gone, the other side of the mountain, *no más*—as if the little people had sprinkled their sand in my eyes.

Joan Lindgren

BUENOS AIRES: THE QUEEN OF THE PLATE

"What gives value to travel is fear."
—ALBERT CAMUS

And who would argue with Camus? Yet here in a borrowed apartment, unheated and with the barest amenities, in a working-class city neighborhood of a bankrupt third-world nation, thousands of miles from family and familiars, I am registering no fear. I think I am thrilled. Maybe that's close enough.

It must be because I have paid the bills and boarded the cat, filed away my identity, and survived twenty hours of flight, because I have found the building and discovered the key, and because I have navigated the strange elevator, the stares of the permanent residents, and the tricky corridor light switches. I have tracked down the place to buy milk, there next to the green grocer with his outdoor art exhibit; the woman selling fragrant coffee beans; the bakery with its succulent *medias lunas*; the *kiosco* where matches are sold. I think this is probably the exhilaration of a lizard shedding an old tail, a crab its shell.

Reflection can wait, but not Buenos Aires, a city of ten million, the Paris of Latin America, the home of the tango and gaucho myths, the womb of a brilliant and enigmatic literary tradition, the bloody battleground of an overweening military mentality versus a swelling populism. My new neighborhood lacks chic but not history. One of the numerous cafés in my block is the café Hómero Manzi, named for a famous tango composer. Its mosaic floor and dark woodwork, its massive bar and hissing espresso machine, its regulars—retired men with workman's caps, cardigans, woolen mufflers, and drooping tobacco-stained mustaches—I will come to know well, for the Hómero Manzi houses a public telephone. Seventy years ago it was partitioned off into private-party booths, privy to who knows what scenes of seduction, all to the pulsing strains of melancholy, no, tragic, tango. Today, housewives with string shopping bags drink bitter brew and we wait our turn to connect with the outside world.

¡Gracias a Dios! the tango is still here. The record store blasts it out into the street between rock and roll. It comes over the radio of the butcher's stall in the turn-of-the-century public market, where pigeons nest high in the chilly rafters, where the butcher wears a cap and a bloodstained apron wrapped over his vintage sweater. It is comforting to be in a city that is not forever erasing its social past.

After dark those grandfathers who've exhausted their coffee money listen to tango with their cronies on car radios. The night before I leave Buenos Aires my friend's teen-age son will teach me the tango in the street to car radios—he does not mind that I am "old." He loves his grandmother—she is older than I am—and I watched him finger her gold crucifix at her throat as they conversed. Such intimacy between the young and the old is not common in my culture.

As one who has molted, I can go on and choose my next identity, but here there is the question of language. I speak the language well enough to ask questions but not to understand, infallibly, the answers in this strange sibilant Spanish with its archaic intimate pronouns. All the vital vocabulary is transformed—the Mexican terms carry no peso here. One starts from scratch.

And these are tough city people. But since I arrive without menfolk, grandchildren, or standard-bearer, ultimately the Porteños, residents of this great port city, feel sorry for me in my powerlessness; they become patient. My friend will write me after I have left that they inquire about me, "*¿Cuando vuelve, la señora norteamericana, la profesora?*" I bring a fresh breeze to them, a taste of the unimaginable. At the same time I am happy in their city, I read their newspapers, drink their coffee—it's the best, they all know that—I ride their *subte* (subways) and buses, *con respeto* (with respect). And they melt. They forgive me my plastic raincoat and my Rockport shoes—how would I know better who wasn't trained here? They become my teachers. The tables are turned and I am free to seem foolish. Soon it is clear that I am disarmed and therefore disarming, *tonta* (I was born on April Fool's Day), a strange but pleasant enough person to be. But I am smart enough to like their city. Their chests swell slightly.

Quickly one establishes a routine. The English language newspaper puts me in touch with a young Irish woman who recommends a language tutor and would have given me work teaching English for a negligible wage. My tutor lives in a luxury apartment house with a handsome view of the city, the River Plate, and a suggestion of Uruguay beyond the horizon—Uruguay is important to Argentineans because they can slip across the river and redeem dollars there when their own government, to stabilize the economy, disallows this.

Cristina is the wife of a banker, mother of two university sons, daughter of parents who lived Argentina's heyday to the hilt. She lives in perennial nostalgia for the might-have-been and assigns me the autobiography of Victoria Ocampo, daughter of local aristocracy, Evita Perón's antithesis or nemesis. I bring her articles from *Pagina 12*, the leftist radical newspaper, to explain. When the water becomes too muddied by our differences, we work on the subjunctive.

I love my sorties into Cristina's neighborhood, which is near to the grand Libertador Avenue, skirted by expansive tree-shaded parks. There are joggers and cyclists and especially there are the dog-walkers. My favorite, a dashing boy in sweatshirt, jeans, and leather gloves, generally has sixteen canines on leashes, plus an afghan in the lead, tail on high like a plumed standard, and a German shepherd to bring up the rear.

The dogs do not fight, ever. "Why should they?" Cristina remarks. But the people do—we are reminded of this periodically when the newspaper prints the photo of a student on the anniversary of his disappearance during the Dirty War. Whatever it is that Porteños resolve on the psychiatrist's couch—the rate of per capita psychoanalysis is the highest in the world and most of Spain's analysts are trained there—it isn't their impulse to resort to physical violence, as Argentina's bloody history reminds us.

Walking to the center of the city from Cristina's neighborhood, you can pass by the necropolis, the Recoleta, one of Buenos Aires's grandest monuments and not at all ghoulish. Each mausoleum is a masterpiece of black marble and bronze—in many are polished brass candlesticks, starched linen tablecloths, and fresh flowers. There are bas reliefs depicting headmistresses surrounded by their girl students—Victoria Ocampo? There is a statue of a boxer in gloves and robe. Evita is here, irretrievably buried beneath a simple but final black casket-shaped marble, definitely lonely among the elite—but wasn't loneliness her destiny?

A friend at home told me that when his father died, the key to the mausoleum was held by another branch of the family, who, hoarding the remaining space, refused to relinquish it. I wonder if that is when my friend decided to emigrate. But I love this cemetery, the massive trees with sun slanting through to cast shadows upon the marble, the statues, the tombs a little girl would love to play house in, an occasional abandoned ruin of a tomb that opens on to a mystery of its own. A lot of personal history reposes here, a lot of love and respect for tradition. On the walls a sign reminding us to keep decorum tells us balefully that here lie those who have preceded us on life's path. And I think of my father, buried far from his home or mine—in the family plot of his third wife—and how my brothers and I nervously flare up when the subject is a suitable place for Mama's ashes.

Still, it must be all that respect at the root of Argentina's political problems, never individuating, never telling your old man off and going your own way. *"Falta de respeto,"* people say on the bus if someone, even a child, is out of line.

I have come here to test the lifestyle, to understand the inconsistencies of Argentina. I admit to feeling comfortable, even safe, among the respectful, with their tasteful, but not individualistic clothing, neatly shod and combed—except, of course, in the heart of the city, where the punks, the whores, the sharks, the pickpockets rule. The jostle and bustle is completely Latin American here. Even the juxtaposition of names is seductive to a stranger—imagine a convergence of Ayacucho, Boulogne, Suipacha, and Avenida Juan D. Perón (never Avenida Perón).

Since downtown is definitely where it's at, everybody in the city seems to come to the center for his daily energy fix. The president's Casa Rosada is here, the grand old national cathedral, the majestic Colón Opera House. Beautiful Colonial buildings rub elbows with steel and glass skyscrapers. The Mothers march on Thursdays in their Plaza Mayo among pigeons, bench-sitters, and bus queues.

The ubiquitous cafés with their terraces, glassed in at this time of year, are grand for coffee and newspapers or meeting a friend. There are free concerts regularly of excellent quality on Wednesdays at the Teatro Opera and, in the Sala de Oro of the Colón, small chamber concerts at six. An institutional seediness prevails here due to shortage of government funds, but numerous people are dressed in furs, leather, and a glitz of general enthusiasm, and their presence in restaurants and shops belies, as well, the national poverty.

And since the glue of humanity holds better here than in the more secular world, there are few homeless, less crime. I hug my purse as in any large city, but lovely leather bags sway seductively at the hips of most women. An occasional male behind me will quicken his gait to catch up—deceived by the rear-view—then look away quickly, seeing the time-etched face. Then, since his hair is tinted, he seems a little pathetic to me, vulnerable, human, in other words. Maybe he is molting, too.

The ultimate lessons to be learned here are from the children. Never has one seen such precious children, children content with the knowledge that when their parents got them, they ceased longing. A child is the ultimate gift. The father playing word games with his small daughter on the bus—"I see something red"—time has stopped for him. The tender expectancy on the faces of the grandparents waiting outside the kindergartens at noon. Glory is about to materialize—this is the high point of their day. Grandfathers, too, are pressed into willing service as baby-sitters and dress for the occasion. In their snappy camel hair coats and jaunty fedoras, they stroll in the parks, treat their progeny to pony rides, and *garapiñada* (the street vendor's sugar-roasted peanuts). The walls of the buildings, alive with graffiti, say DIVORCIO ¡NO! FAMILIA ¡SI! This is the message of MODEFA, the League for the Defense of the Family. And I beg off thinking about how the restrictions of their agenda would offend my radical feminist position, which I somehow forgot to pack. In Argentina, we who have floundered in the wreckage of the American family, part and parcel of progress, want to bask in the positives of this enigmatic society, in the tender self-abnegating attentions of adults, the warm security of children whose minds seem never to have been crossed by the possibility of lovelessness. Here it is uncommon to hire sitters, for children participate. And they go to bed when they are tired, not when the parents are tired of them.

Porteños revere the traditions they brought from the old country a hundred years ago; the plaza and monuments, parks and wide boulevards, fin-de-siècle architecture, the plane trees, pruned and gnarled—an occasional man wears the shawl of Verdi or Unamuno. Buenos Aires is more the Paris of my student years than Paris today. Sitting on an art-nouveau bench under a huge Palo Boracho tree in the Plaza San Martin, feeding the pigeons, I permit myself the rose-colored glasses of shameless nostalgia. And removing them, I suddenly see the perverse nature of this old monarchy. All this respect may protect privilege. To protect democracy, you need law and accountability. Can these tough and unforgiving commodities flourish out here at the south-most edge of the world?

In all this good air?

Would they suit a queen?

Barbara Abel

THE MOMENT OF FALLING AWAY

Baños, Ecuador, lies in a narrow valley, a gateway to the Amazon jungle. The deep surrounding green of the mountains is a strong and constant presence. With their tips hidden in clouds, the bases of the mountains envelop the town in masses of growing range, lava-cooled and shifted not too long ago, and in motion still. Giants with masked faces, they leave no doubt whose crevice of earth this valley belongs to.

In a small store-front shop with a black silhouette of a backpacker painted on the front, a rugged, muscular man with a weathered face slumps, dozing on a bench against the wall. He startles, blinks at me with a bewildered gaze. I wait until his eyes clear, and explain to him that I have little Spanish, am alone, and would like to go into the mountains. His face brightens, he kindly compliments my broken Spanish, and proclaims this situation good. His son speaks some English. He steps into the street and bellows a directive with a force and voice that easily outweigh the wind. I have a fleeting concern that his son might be angry, might be formed by a childhood full of that voice, and wonder what sort of person I am about to meet.

Into the shop comes a tall young man, lithe and smooth-skinned, with deep black eyes and a shock of raven hair that falls to one side of his face. But far more striking is the palpable calm of him, the sense of solid self-acceptance. There is nothing unusual in his movements or behavior, or even in his eyes. It is simply a quiet but extremely clear strength of presence, and whatever fear I may have harbored about walking into the Andes with a stranger whose language I speak little of is gone.

He unrolls a worn map of the surrounding terrain and runs an elegant finger along the trail to a village that he says will enjoy a visitor. It looks so simple on the map, hand-drawn with pen and ink, so flat, the mountains so contained and managed. Nothing like the spirited appendages of earth that sprawl outside in every direction.

Concerned with rain, he suggests a pair of boots from a shelf against the wall, but they all fit poorly. I say I'll wear my shoes. He is irritated with me. His eyes grow darker and narrow, his shoulders tighten. But the calm he exudes remains. He says firmly that he will bring boots if he thinks they're needed, and water. I could bring some chocolate if I like. He will come to the *cabañas* at nine.

Lying in bed that night, I think of miracles. As the wind rips through the valley in fitful bursts, I think of the basilica in town. Lining the thick stone walls was a series of paintings. In one a man has fallen from his horse while crossing the bridge in a storm. Below the painting is the man's name, the date and location, and an explanation that as he fell toward the torrents below he called out to the Virgin and was saved. Other paintings show people in transit accidents, burning hotels, and exploding volcanoes, all saved by the Virgin.

The wind is steady now, and the iron roof resumes an odd, grieving cry. The little oil figures in the paintings run through my mind in flight from the river and volcanoes. My body feels apart from me, I think because I do not want to note the way my heart and chest, legs and arms are half-cocked with awareness of the volcano outside. Tungurahua erupts far less frequently than volcanoes I've slept on in Hawaii, yet it seems wilder and less predictable—perhaps because there are no instruments visible, geologists' and seismologists' stations, or films shown twice nightly to visitors. In the stronger gusts of wind the door rattles in its frame. Buildings are clearly temporary in this rich volcanic corridor. Things shake on their foundations. The land can toss, raze, or bury all this whenever it is ready.

The climb grows harder again, the trail slick with rocks and ruts and washouts, the view more and more expansive. I stop frequently and gaze at the chain of the Andes to the north and south of Tungurahua, an endless succession of massive arms crossing the belly of the valley. Fabian seems more interested in the occasional dog, pig, or rooster we pass loose along the trail, addressing each of them. When the animals growl or scatter, he turns to me and says, "It does not love me," his voice forlorn, face sad, and eyes laughing.

We come around a sharp bend to a startling absence of trail. A portion of the mountain has fallen away with the heavy rains. All that remain are the raw insides of the rich earth, the torn roots of trees reaching blindly into the chasm. We are in no danger, and it's likely that someone along the way has warned Fabian, yet the sight of it shakes me. I stand staring down the deadly drop, for a moment unwilling to move. Fabian rests a hand on my shoulder and says with mild sarcasm, "This is why you should wear boots."

The new trail, if it is one at all, is the steepest climb yet, cutting across a hill perpendicular to the valley basin and entering a field of tall, dry corn, that with any respect at all for the force of gravity should not be standing. Fabian crashes into it headlong. Based on his pace this morning just prior to the grassy precipice, I figure we're getting close to something, and push hard to keep up with the illusive sight of his red pack and black hair weaving through the maze of stalks. He never pauses or checks his breakneck speed through this vertical, disorienting field, but only glances back. I don't mention stopping; between the wind at this angle and the noise he's making in the corn, he wouldn't hear me anyway. Suddenly he slows a bit, allows me to catch up, and a few yards later we burst from the corn onto a mercifully level dirt path. The trail curves abruptly, and three mammoth dogs converge upon us in a snarling pack. We have arrived.

Two young men come out of a shack much like the one we visited this morning. Their faces brighten with surprise and pleasure when they see Fabian, and the dogs fall off at once, without command. The young men both have striking features, strong, flat cheekbones, and deep-set, dark-brown eyes. They seem shy of me, and somewhat careful, but with an energy of spirit that makes me like them immediately. When we shake hands their touch has the same juxtaposition of qualities, their grasps quick and light, but warm. They speak briefly with Fabian and return to the room they came out of.

We go in the other room, which is cold upon entry, the moment I step out of the sun. A wooden bench is placed against one wall, a rusted iron bed and old dresser on another, with a small TV set on the dresser. The floor is dirt and there are no windows, but the wall along the bed had been painted sky blue a long time ago, and even cracked and peeling signifies a special place. The bed is just big enough for one, and I wonder who it is that sleeps here.

I'm content to sit in the cool air and rest, and don't try to make conversation. Fabian leaves for a while, then returns and sits very close beside me on the bench and says the family would like us to eat here. This is exactly the wrong place for an unaccustomed traveler to eat: there is no running water, livestock come in and out of the house, and everything is very damp. But I am honored, and accept the invitation. He looks pleased, goes out, comes back again, and starts in on the repetition of my name, which I ignore. He sighs, puts his hands on my shoulders, and says in English, "Come, there is a thing I have to show you."

We go outside and he points out how the land plunges severely just inches beyond the knee-high line of growth that frames the small yard. I am amazed to realize that the house sits like an eagle's nest on a jagged precipice of sickening height. Miles below, the river winds in a tiny, silent brook, the canyon a few inches deep. The buildings along the road to Quito are simply bits of white or pink among a hundred shades of green. Only the hulking base of the volcano directly across the canyon maw has any real proportion to this spot.

The young men emerge from the shadowed opening of the other room. They lean long legs against the concrete rain catch, talk to Fabian, and cast slow, quiet glances in my direction. They both wear thick wool sweaters the color of moist earth and sand, and I wonder how they can be comfortable in the intensity of the intermittent sun. Their curiosity is nearly palpable, but then so is what I assume to be their shyness.

All at once Fabian stops talking, grabs my shoulders, turns me away from the brothers and into the sudden, high wind blowing across the canyon, and points toward Tungurahua. The clouds have broken, so that the upper sections far above the timberline are revealed in thick, metallic limbs, steely blue, reflecting the equatorial sun with a wholly different quality than any part of the surrounding landscape. We all stand facing the volcano, hushed and expectant. I look at that cold, metallic hue and recall that Tungurahua means "Little Hell" in Quechua, and against all rationality or reason I am afraid to see its peak. But the wind shifts then, the clouds thicken toward the top, and the sudden change in light and air reaches across the intervening canyon with a sigh. Fabian is visibly disappointed, the air of possibility disperses, and the young men resume their conversation.

It is difficult to see when we enter the other room to eat, in spite of the fire crackling in one corner. We sit at a table of gray, weathered wood on a single bench placed against the wall. From where I'm asked to sit, I look directly out the doorframe, which has no door, across the valley to the volcano. Again I am aware of how intense the sun is here, even through the clouds, of how fully the shadows obscure. It takes a few moments before I see the woman standing in the corner near the fire, and the heavy caldron she tends. In contrast to the angular faces and lanky limbs of her sons, she is wide and solid and round. She wears several layers of skirts in materials of varied texture, each hem a few inches shorter than the one beneath, so that her fullness is emphasized further. Her sweater is the same coarse, moist-looking wool as her boys', but hers is the color of red wine poured on soil.

A mass of salty hair is pulled back from her fine, wide face into a braid wrapped in cloth that falls to her waist. The motion of her arm as she stirs the contents of the caldron is something entirely apart from linear or measured time. With a gesture akin to the turning earth, she slowly draws her heavy spoon around the perimeter of the pot, oblivious to the flames that race up its thick black sides from time to time and leap toward the roof. The rafters above are nothing more than the charred remains of beams, and the slats of the roof, for several feet around the tin frame of the smoke hole, have burned away completely.

She walks over to Fabian and kisses him. When he asks how she is, she places her hands on various parts of her body in a series of wonderful dramatic gestures, and speaks at length in a plaintive, keening voice. He seems quite irritated by this, but I am fascinated and sympathetic. As she turns toward me, he says something I don't understand, but which cuts her off and turns her away. I ask her name but she seems not to hear. I ask him what her name is, but when I say, "Hello, Susana," she does not respond. It is only a few minutes later when she sets a bowl before me and I can make certain eye contact with her, that she seems to hear. She smiles then, and her smile makes me grin. She smiles wider, and I am completely taken by the sheer breadth of her face.

I open my mouth to speak to her but am interrupted by the sudden ferocious clamor of the dogs, which she doesn't seem to register. It's then I'm finally sure she's deaf, confirmed by her friends, two women and a man, who enter and touch her arm before she shows an awareness of their presence. The women are dressed much like Susana, the man like her sons but with a long, single braid. They smile and nod and whisk her off into the other room.

The enameled tin bowl is filled with rice, corn, carrots, peppers, and several kinds of beans. A boiled egg, still hot and in the shell, rests on the bowl's edge. The young men move about the fire, making order of the food and utensils that lie about, their movements light years from their mother's. One of them sings the refrain of a Christmas carol over and over again, and when he next turns one of those shy glances toward me,

I catch his eye and hold it, and I ask him with mock ignorance if Christmas is in April. I thank whatever deity the ever-present volcano is beginning to represent to me that he understands my attempts to tease him, and likes it. He watches me a bit more openly then, still carefully, but intently. He asks my name, and when I answer he grins. I say, "Yes, I know it's crazy," and he laughs openly. He is named Pablo, his brother Pedro, and they have lived on this precipice since birth. The disciples' names make me think again of miracles. Pedro asks how old I am, but all other questions and comments regarding me they direct to Fabian.

The food is more satisfying than anything I've eaten in a long time, anywhere. It seems like months since breakfast, since my last drink of water, since my teeth and tongue and stomach have had the pleasure of taking something in. After the first few mouthfuls I look up, about to say how good this is, and see the three of them watching me, the brothers with curiosity, Fabian with satisfaction, as if he'd just accomplished something. He looks at the bowl, at me, and his eyes contain the smile that has not moved a muscle in his face, an expression that in less than a day has become something familiar. "It is good, no? It is better than meals you eat in any of the restaurants in town." I agree, and thank the brothers. Then, his eyes serious, he asks if I've eaten in the countryside before. I tell him yes, in Mexico, but not with a family. "Ah," he nods, "in a restaurant," and I know by the slight drop in his voice and the way he angles his chin just a bit that this does not count.

A big russet hen scratches and pecks her way across the floor and settles under the bench behind my feet, followed by her brood. The largest of the dogs lies sprawled across the doorway, a more pragmatic barrier than any door, looks up at me, and whines from time to time. Susana comes in and out with dishes for her company, kicks and cusses at the dog rather wickedly each time, then turns and smiles charmingly. The sudden gusts of wind that cross the canyon shake and rattle the slats of the outer walls.

About to peel the egg, I remember that my hands are covered with sweat and dirt and dog's tongue, and ask if I might wash them. Pablo, still singing, grabs a greasy looking rag off a nail on the wall and pitches it across the room. All at once I feel very happy, accepted somehow by the ease and normalcy of the gesture. But the rag never reaches me. Fabian jumps to intercept it, nearly knocking the bowls from the table, and whips it back at him, speaking rapidly. He slows then, tells me to come outside. Pablo follows, having grabbed a bar of soap from somewhere, draws water from the rain catch with a plastic cup, and indicates the waste catch beside it filled with clothes. I thank him profusely, and use as little as possible of both soap and water.

When I sit down again by Fabian I realize I am angry, in spite of knowing that he's right about the rag. His intervening leap has re-established the distance between us, and I am fully relegated to my place as the outsider. I peel and cut the egg, aware of him watching me. As soon as I've finished he reaches across me, his face deeply serious, and points out the rich red-orange of the yolk like it's the rightful center of the universe. With calm pride, he announces in English, "It is more natural that way." His voice has this centered, unshakable quality, akin to the way he had cupped both hands to his heart to illustrate a breast. He watches me bite into it and waits, the moment suspended in silence since he's stopped his conversation with his brothers to tell me this. I take my time tasting it, then turn and look him in the eye, say it's very good. He nods, the little smile sparkling in his eyes, and then continues talking. I wonder what he must look like when something large and wonderful enters his life, like falling in love or the birth of a child. His pleasure makes me think again of how removed from the land my culture is.

The inside of the hut seems warmer now, with the fire burning hot and the food fueling my body. The conversation of Fabian and the brothers grows heated over something. I listen hard to pick out, identify, and piece together at least some of what they say. But I'm too tired and content, and drift quickly from the effort, allowing myself instead the pleasure of their sounds, lulled by their voices even as they argue.

As I lift the other half of the egg to my mouth I look up and out the door, across the sky-filled miles to the glint of dazzling light on the peak of Tungurahua, and for a moment I am blinded. I want to turn to Fabian, to say, "Look, the volcano!" but I can't move or speak. Something has me gently by the throat, held midair thousands of feet up the mountain side, ever so lightly, like a seed, like some small, silent thing of potential. Through the door of earth and wood, the world lies gleaming. I am deeply aware of the tremendous falling away of land just yards from where we sit. Something in me shifts and cracks, and I cannot tear my gaze from the volcano. *Little Hell*, I hear my own voice whisper in my mind, and though I don't know what that means to me, I feel a cleaving, instantaneous departure of much of what I'm used to in my outlook on the world.

A learned, acquired covering crumbles all at once, a tightly woven veil between myself and the natural world. Its fibers are a mix of class, sex, family, and the lifestyle of acquisition that is trumpeted from nearly every aspect of living in the dominant culture of my country. I am painfully aware of the stringent boundaries of my culture, and of the contrasting presence here of all the things we keep so hidden from view: the crippled, old, and poor. The boundaries between inside and out, people and animals, hands and food. The cutting boundary between reality and "not" that feeds our persistent disbelief in other ways of seeing, and thus the myth that we have an ear to The God and an unerring eye for what is "real." I think of how this conviction leaves us room for little else, not miracle or mystery or even the fantastic, not vision, magic, or quest.

Gone, for the moment, is this constricted way of seeing, perception trained and tethered until choked in its ability to envision the world as whole. The veil splits and falls like the absent jut of land we came upon this morning where the trail was no more. In its wake is a moment of electrical clarity. I can feel the featherlight step of the chicks through the leather and cotton of my shoes and socks, smell the damp fur of the huge dog sprawled across the door and the damp llama wool on Susana's boys. I can feel the slight heat of Fabian on the bench beside me, and the warmth of the brothers leaning against the slats a few feet away. I'm aware of the current of air drawn in through the buttressed doorframe, up to the flame of the cooking fire, and out through the roof, passing between the velvet texture of charred timber. Much of what I mistakenly think of as life slides through this door that has no closure, falls sharply with the land, away from the yard and the shack, the fire and the corn, and plummets to the canyon bed, to the depths of the Pastaza that births the mighty Amazon, and onward, out to sea.

The inside of the hut is dark, the world outside on fire, the door of earth and wood and dog both dangerous and protective in the moment it so eloquently frames. I hear the young men's voices, the open vowels of their language, feel the energy of their kinship with each other and this place. This is all like water in the darkness, like some nutrient-rich fluid so the moment does not burn. I am grateful to these young men grounded in the mountain. The brothers have known this land all their lives. Fabian has been up and down the volcano, has dug in spikes and crampons, and slept in Tungurahua's snows. Their closeness to the land is like a lightning rod to the crackling energy that courses all around the buttressed door. The dog twitches and whines in his sleep, and the chicks again cross over my feet with tiny, weightless steps that punctuate the hurtling rush of all that is falling away.

This is not just from altitude, not from the water loss or from the hard pounding of the heart it took to get here. I have been high that way enough before to know that this is something else. I feel entirely wide open, and aware of something light and round and solid in the center of my chest, a repository for this moment. It reminds me of the long-forgotten Host in the Catholic Mass of my childhood, of the stunning little gold box on the center of the altar, its double doors opened together, with great ceremony, the gesture always meticulous. The doors to the center of one's being, I suppose, which the Church made obscure for me, grace that could come only through another, infinitely more Godlike than ourselves. But in this moment the little doors fly, the opening is crazy, unceremonial, compelled by sight of "Little Hell," by the contrasting light within and outside the hut, by the heat that emanates from all of us, by the fire that licks the rafters, and the bright orange yolk in the center of the egg.

With that image the falling stops, the clouds thicken, the moment passes without any sense of time. The dog in the doorway lifts his bearlike head and stares at me, steadily, until even the young men notice and begin to smile. We eat more rice, boiled to a mush, heavy with brown sugar.

In the yard the sun is warm, the day grown ripe and full, miles above sea level, within a hundred of the equator. The brothers show me their hutches of glossy furred rabbits, and one crammed with plump guinea pigs to be sold for *cuyo*, a delicacy, the small pigs roasted whole like Cornish hens. I tell them that the pigs are common pets in the U.S., especially for children, and immediately regret saying so. The way they look at me with narrowed eyes, their usually curious expressions darkened, makes me think they find this wasteful, perhaps bizarrely so. I feel increasingly aware of the waste in my country anyway, not just as a citizen informed of an essential issue, but in the knowledge of the body that I find heightened here.

I lean against the rain catch and look out across the canyon to the flanks of Tungurahua, its upper portions clothed solidly in cloud. The cement is warm on my legs, the water reflects the sun on this side of the canyon to my back. The brothers lean against the split rails of the fence across from me, and I am amazed by their confidence in these propped pieces of wood that border the drop. Fabian walks off toward the cornfield, the dogs sniffing at his heels. Once he has disappeared from view, the brothers openly examine me. Pedro, the bolder, steps forward and lightly touches the tag sewn into the pocket of my denim jacket. "Ah, *Levi*," he says, and his brother steps closer with interest. He nods as he pronounces the word, one they are clearly familiar with, and that appears to mean to them exactly what the ads intend: quality, desirability, worth the effort to acquire. He asks how much the jacket costs, and, confronted with a specific of my relative wealth, I feel uneasy.

I tell them twenty dollars used, forty new. They look disappointed, wistful, as they eye the jacket more closely and Pablo asks the cost of round trip airfare from the U.S. to Ecuador. I cringe, wanting terribly to lie, and force myself to say five hundred dollars and to look at them directly as I speak. They are visibly taken aback, their eyes still clear, but fiery deep inside the pupils, little sparks of anger dancing in the black. Although I have worked hard, taken on extra jobs, and budgeted tightly to make this trip, the justice of their anger strikes me with some weight. Economically marginal in my own country, my advantages here are blatant. I force myself to keep eye contact; they do not look away. We stand facing what we see in one another, and I am forced to face the ugliness of at least some of what I present them with.

They move on to the camera. I thank Tungurahua that it isn't mine, not another possession that I wouldn't mind disowning at this moment. I explain that it's my friend's and I've borrowed it for this trip, give them prices for new and used 35mm cameras, mid-range. Moved by sheer discomfort, I say I can't afford this camera, as if my position in my country must somehow be made known to them, as if my lower than average wages, my renter's status, or my non-professional standing would matter one bit to the reality they know, or to what they see in me.

Soon the limits of my Spanish have us stuck. They want to know an amount, but it is not of something they can point out, or that I can guess. I say, "Ask your friend," meaning Fabian, who has not returned from the field. They look at each other, and their eyes light with silent laughter. They cup their hands to their mouths and both call out at once, the word "guide," long and drawn out like a farmer to the pigs. *"Gyiiiiii,a! Ay! Guiiiii, a!"* He comes around the corner of the house, chagrined, and they look so delighted to have ribbed his position and disturbed that lovely calm of his, that I can't help but laugh, which clearly adds to their pleasure.

Fabian takes a quick, sharp look at the sky and announces our departure. He hauls his pack out of the room where Susana and her company remain and distributes the weight of corn, tomatoes, beans, and jars of some dark liquid he's been given to haul to town. I go to thank Susana for the food and say good-bye. She is completely engrossed in the TV and doesn't notice that I enter or speak to her. The women smile and nod and say a few *"de nada's,"* and spread their fingers wide in waving, protective gestures, and I understand that I should not disturb her. She sits on the rusted metal bed against the wall long ago painted blue, deeply absorbed in what appears to be a Latin American "General Hospital." Her entire body leans into the drama, her neck elongated, craned toward the grayish light that is caught and held by the silver of her hair. The way she trains her attention so completely, the sharp curve and hook of her nose, forehead, and chin against the peeling sky blue wall *is* startling. All of her roundness is diminished, and she appears as some magnificent hawk-like creature perched on the end of the iron bed, whose strength ensured the adulthood of the fine young men now leaning at the edge of the precipice outside her door.

Back outside, her sons return to the question that had us stuck a few minutes ago. They want to know my salary. The prickling discomfort washes over me again as I tell them not much, at least in the United States not much, but even to myself my words ring hollow. They look at me skeptically, all of us aware of the camera, the jacket, the ticket. There is no shyness or reserve in the way they watch me roll and stuff my jacket into Fabian's pack, tighten the laces of my shoes, roll down my sleeves, and turn my collar up to protect against the now harsh sun for the long walk down.

I feel foolish giving them the chocolate that Fabian suggested I bring, but it is good, and I want to give them something. When I tell them to make sure their mother gets some, they look surprised and laugh, then grin at me as though they'd been found out. I am moved, as we say goodbye, by the eagerness and warmth with which they grasp my hands, and the solidity of their touch leaves an impression I continue to feel a long way down the mountain's side.

Later I will miss them. I will remember the sight of them in their home, their faces, their voices, and the greeting of their hands. I will realize again the integrity of their presence to that blazing moment, and the dignity of their being who they are.

Mary Ellen Fieweger

TERESA

For years after coming to live here, I did without a maid, something almost unheard of in Ecuador's gringo community. I knew only one other person in like circumstances. Nancy's reasons for doing without were political. One Sunday morning I found her enveloped in the cloud of dust she was raising as she swept the wall-to-wall carpet that covered every floor in the massive apartment she and her husband sublet in one of Quito's exclusive neighborhoods. "Did you know that there isn't a single vacuum cleaner factory in Ecuador?" Nancy yelled by way of greeting. "And you know why? Because there are armies of women who have no choice but to work themselves ragged cleaning up after the privileged few, for which they are paid a pittance, but at least their children don't starve."

My own reasons were personal—based on years of upbringing. This was in the seventies, before anyone had made a connection between the personal and the political. "You make a mess," my mother used to say, "you clean it up." There was a corollary to that rule, understood rather than stated. It went something like this: "Unless you are male, in which case your sister will clean it up for you." I grew up with four brothers.

I also had a practical reason for remaining maidless: my apartment was small, two rooms, not counting the closet-sized kitchen and bath; no refrigerator to defrost, no oven to scrub.

Then one day, while I sat at the small round table that filled half the living/dining area of my apartment, a little cottage perched on top of a two-story building, Teresa came to the door. Teresa was the landlady's full-time, live-in maid. The landlady and her children, Jorge and Paulina, lived on the second floor. Teresa lived on the ground floor, in a dark, dank concrete block box only slightly roomier than the closet that was my kitchen. For several months, and with the landlady's permission, she had been supplementing her salary—1,200 sucres a month, about fifteen U.S. dollars at the time—by working one afternoon a week for my first floor neighbor, Michael. Michael was also paying her 1,200 sucres a month, a sum that delighted Teresa and seemed criminal to the two of us, but then gringos are infamous for spoiling the help here. Because my apartment was so much smaller than Michael's, Teresa proposed to clean it once a week for half the wage he was paying, but I had to promise not to tell the landlady, and to say, if she asked, that I was paying 200 sucres a month.

I hesitated.

"That includes laundry," said Teresa.

To this day women who live in rural areas in Ecuador do their laundry in a time-honored fashion: they haul it down to the banks of the nearest river and beat it clean against the rocks. Women in urban areas, not counting those few who have automatic washing machines, do something similar, the only difference being that they wash the family clothes at a *lavandería*, a concrete affair with a tank for soaking, a scrub board for beating, and a single tap that delivers water as icy as the country's snow-fed mountain streams. Since there was an automatic washer and dryer in Nancy's apartment, I'll never know if her political convictions would have withstood torture on a weekly basis at the *lavandería*. My years of upbringing did not. I hired Teresa on the spot.

My apartment was over the landlady's kitchen. Due to an acoustical quirk, sounds produced by pots and pans banging, a glass breaking, the blender whirring, seemed to come from above, as did the voices of Teresa and the Señora shouting at one another. This they usually did on Saturday nights between seven and eight. Then the Señora left with her children to visit relatives. As soon as she was alone, Teresa turned the radio on, the volume full blast, and sang at the top of her lungs. I also heard a lot of frenetic knocking and pounding more or less in time to the music. Michael and I decided that she was dancing, bursting with the euphoria that had come to fill the space left by resentments and complaints just aired.

The resentments and complaints were legion I discovered when Teresa, after testing the waters with some guarded remarks, decided that mine was a sympathetic ear. She began visiting at night, tip-toeing up the stairs once or twice a week after the Señora and her children had retired to the master bedroom where they watched television. As we sat at the round table drinking a cup of tea, Teresa told me in whispers about her many *penas*, past and present. Past *penas* were mostly associated with growing up in Ibarra, a town to the north, between Quito and the Colombian border. Teresa was the oldest of six living siblings—two died before celebrating their first birthdays. Her mother had been cleaning other people's houses since the age of twelve. Her father was a bricklayer when there was work and he was sober, which, according to Teresa, wasn't often. He beat his wife and children, and that was the main reason Teresa left home at fourteen to look for work in Quito.

Present *penas* all had to do with the Señora, her first employer. Things hadn't been so bad in the beginning, Teresa said. But then tragedy struck. Twice. First the landlady's youngest, a ten-year-old son, climbed up to the roof when they were building my apartment. He slipped and fell two stories, hitting his head on a pile of concrete blocks below, and died instantly. Then the Señora's husband had a routine prostate operation a few months later. The surgeon left a sponge or two inside when he sewed the patient up. After her husband died of peritonitis, the landlady began to vent her grief and rage on Teresa, who from then on could do nothing right: the toilet wasn't scrubbed enough; the rice was sticky; the windows were streaky; the faucets and floors didn't shine. According to the Señora, Teresa was lazy, sloppy, stupid, and, worst of all, a liar and a thief. Teresa said that at first she ignored the criticisms and accusations because the Señora was in mourning, after all, and these things must be respected. But a year after the second death, she reached the end of her tether. Now, said Teresa, she gave as good as she got.

Sometimes Teresa dreamed out loud about a future free of *penas*. She wanted to enroll in an adult education program, get her elementary school diploma—she had dropped out of school before finishing third grade to take care of the brothers and sisters that didn't stop coming—and then take a course in sewing or cosmetology, and open her own shop. Marriage did not figure in Teresa's plans for the future. Until the day Angel appeared.

The landlady decided to see to a series of minor problems that had developed in the plumbing, electrical wiring, and so on, in all three apartments. A family friend, an architect, brought one of the men from a construction site he was working on, Angel, jack of all trades. Michael saw Angel first.

"He's gorgeous," Michael said.

I didn't meet Angel until about a week after he arrived. Nor did I see Teresa during that period. Then I came home late one night and there they were, locked in a tight embrace under a tree opposite the house. Teresa disengaged herself to introduce her companion, Angel. He *was* gorgeous.

Angel came after work every day for about three weeks. He fixed faucets that leaked, toilets that ran, switches that threw sparks. Afterwards, he and Teresa rendezvoused on the street under the tree opposite the house. Angel also came during the day on weekends. Then he finished the repairs and Teresa's visits resumed.

The first night she was back, Teresa, stars in her eyes, a blush on her cheeks, announced that she had revised her plans for the future.

"We're going to get married," she said.

"But Teresa, you hardly know him," I said. I went on to tell her what experience and observation had taught me about men in general and Latin men in particular. The latter, I told her, were notorious for their tendency to declare eternal and undying love five minutes after meeting a woman.

"They probably mean it at the time," I said, "but then they meet someone else, a day or two later, and promise the same thing. They have very poor memories, Teresa. Some of them even forget that they have a wife at home, the woman they've been married to for ten years, and three kids."

Teresa smiled. "Angel's different," she said.

For a month or so after finishing repairs for the Señora, Angel came back to visit Teresa. Sometimes I found them out on the street, holding hands, embracing, talking quietly as they gazed into one another's eyes. Then Angel stopped coming altogether, and Teresa came more often to visit me. When I asked about Angel, she alluded to problems he might be having, a death or an illness in the family, or maybe another job on a site so far away he couldn't visit after work.

"Why don't you ask around, at the site where he was working?" I suggested.

"He never told me where he worked," Teresa said. Then, straightening up in her chair, she added, "Besides, women who want to be respected don't chase after men."

I stopped asking about Angel after that. Instead, we talked about her *penas* again, past and present. To the latter list she added a new one. Rubbing her abdomen, Teresa said she was having a serious *malestar*, a complaint, in that area.

If there's one thing gringos who spend any time in the Third World know about, it's intestinal *malestares*. Even the lucky few, like me, with hearty viscera, become experts on the subject because whenever two or more gringos are gathered it comes up, without fail. Symptoms are discussed, along with treatment for problems caused by the myriad parasites, bacteria, and viruses that wreak havoc on the delicate First-World digestive apparatus. People compare notes: the best labs, the most effective remedies, the ideal moment in the course of a bowel movement to collect a sample likely to be seething with the critters. Interest in the topic is obsessive, almost morbid. I remember a morning years ago when I was sitting in the teachers's room with some colleagues, having a cup of coffee before facing my first hour class. Suddenly, the special education teacher, Carol, burst in. "I shat a worm! I shat a worm! It's this long!" she howled, holding her hands about two feet apart. My colleagues bolted from their chairs and raced behind her to the toilet to see the worm. Not being in any shape to handle something quite so spectacular so early in the morning, I stayed where I was, staring into my cup of coffee. Nevertheless, having been a party to countless conversations on the subject, I shared my wisdom with Teresa.

"You have to take a stool sample to a lab, Teresa. You mustn't let these things go. It's probably parasites. They can be very serious. They multiply and divide and burrow into all your organs if you don't get rid of them. They go to the lungs, Teresa, and the heart and the brain."

Teresa listened politely and nodded, and said it couldn't possibly be parasites. The subject came up again and again. Each time the *malestar* was worse. Her stomach was beginning to swell, she said.

"That's gas, Teresa. Parasites cause gas. You bloat up. Take a sample to a lab, Teresa, please."

But she wasn't convinced by my diagnosis. Nor was I surprised by Teresa's denials. Ecuadorians associate parasites with the poor, the beggars, the rabble. Decent people simply don't get parasites, excepting gringos, who, due to some curious twist of logic, are not considered any less decent as a result. But I was getting impatient with Teresa and her stubborn denials. And she with me and my dramatic anecdotes.

"A friend of mine, Richard, got cysts, Teresa, because he did exactly what you're doing: absolutely nothing. And his symptoms were very similar to yours. They had to operate, Teresa. They cut out great chunks of his liver."

Teresa nodded and yawned.

On a Saturday morning, at 7:30, a month after Teresa had seen Angel last, I was jerked from a deep sleep by the doorbell, a device designed to be heard throughout a seventy-five room mansion. It sounded three more times before I managed to find my bathrobe and stumble to the door. There he was, Angel, on the landing, carrying a bag of tools, and flanked by the landlady and her son Jorge, who explained that they had come to fix a leaky faucet in the bathroom. I invited them in, pointed Angel to the bathroom, and asked the others if they would like a cup of coffee. The three of us sat at the round table, less than a yard from the open bathroom door through which I could see Angel, his muscles rippling under that splendid, taut, brown skin as he changed the gasket. He truly was gorgeous. Teresa's name came up early in the conversation.

"She's *mal, muy mal,*" said the Señora as she patted her stomach, shook her head, and looked thoroughly disgusted in general. Judging this a less than sympathetic attitude toward Teresa, whose work was no doubt suffering in the landlady's view as a result of her ailment, I rushed to the defense.

"Oh, I know, Señora. I've talked to her about how serious parasites can be. You really should see that she gets some lab tests done and begins treatment as soon as possible."

The landlady and her son stared at one another, amazed. And appalled, too, I subsequently realized, that a woman my age could be so shockingly innocent. In a stage whisper she said, "Teresa is pregnant," and nodded toward the bathroom. Angel didn't bat those lovely long eyelashes. After they left, I went to the bathroom to brush my teeth. I couldn't open the tap; the faucets had been sealed.

That night Teresa told me that the Señora had had a chat with Angel, in the course of which he admitted that he had a wife and three children. Nevertheless, after being bullied for more than an hour by the landlady, Angel agreed to go with Teresa after the child was born to the *Registro Civil* to sign the birth certificate. Teresa was sad, but relieved that her child would not be a bastard after all in this nation where a child born out of wedlock is automatically designated *hijo/a de puta*—son/daughter of a whore—and where everyone knows about his or her illegitimate status as the law requires that citizens carry at all times an official identity card which lists the surnames of both parents. When the father is unknown or, as is most often the case, refuses to come forward, the mother's last name is listed twice on this document. To carry a card that says "José Miguel Bolaños Bolaños," or "María Dolores Chiliquinga Chiliquinga" is equivalent to going through life with a scarlet letter dangling from one's neck. It is difficult to get a job, to find a husband or wife. And heaven forbid that one should be stopped by the police who routinely look for any excuse at all to beat so-called suspects to a bloody pulp.

The weeks and months went by. As Teresa's pregnancy advanced, her worries grew apace: there was no word from Angel.

The Señora was also worried. She confided in Michael, first, because he was the only mature adult male on the premises, now that her husband was gone, and the landlady would never ever have questioned whether this particular situation required mature adult male counsel. And, second, because Michael inspired in the landlady what struck me as an inordinate degree of trust and admiration. But, then, most Ecuadorian women strike me as displaying an inordinate degree of respect and admiration for North American males, unless and until they marry one. This is due to a rumor somebody—probably a North American male—started about how, without exception, gringos work hard, pay the bills, seldom if ever drink to excess, do not cheat on their wives, and, best of all, cook and clean and wash and scrub daily, without being asked.

"My house is an honorable one," the landlady said to Michael, time and again. He listened, all the while nodding and murmuring. But he was at a loss when she begged him to come up with a solution.

Teresa's time came. She went to Ibarra to have the baby. There she stayed with her mother for the two months of maternity leave prescribed by law, the one shining light in an otherwise antediluvian legal firmament, as regards women, one that until recently allowed a man to murder with virtual impunity a wife, sister, mother, or daughter caught *in flagrante delicto* with another man.

When Teresa returned, the landlady did not allow her to have María Angélica in the house with her while she worked. Thus, the infant spent most of the day alone on the cot in the dark, dank, closet-sized maid's room. Because she had so little time to spend with her baby during the day, and because she feared her crying might alert the Señora to her nighttime visits with me, Teresa seldom came upstairs after the birth. But when she did she had a new *pena* to tell me about: the Señora was complaining bitterly that Teresa neglected her duties under the pretext of feeding the baby. Teresa, for her part, claimed that the landlady invented new tasks every day to keep her away from María Angélica.

The landlady, in the meantime, was desperate to find a way to restore the family's lost honor. As a result of weeks of inquiries, she discovered where Angel lived. Then she asked Michael to go with her, to confront him in the presence of his family, to shame him into recognizing Teresa's child as his own. Michael, she just knew, would add that dollop of gringo credibility needed to guarantee the success of the undertaking.

And so, one morning the Señora and Teresa in their Sunday best, Michael in suit and tie, and María Angélica smothered in lace and ruffles that must have cost her mother a half-year's wages, got into a cab and headed for Mena II, one of Quito's outlying *suburbios*. The suburbs of Latin American cities have nothing in common with those in northern, developed climes. They are also known as *barrios periféricos*, slums where the poor and working class masses live, usually without light, sewage services, or paved streets. Such were the conditions in Angel's barrio the day the Señora arrived, with Michael, Teresa, and María Angélica in tow. Because it was the middle of the rainy season, the taxi driver refused to take his passengers up the side of the mountain; they walked the last half-kilometer, the landlady's high heels sinking deep into the mud every step of the way.

When they got to Angel's house, a small, two-room concrete block box, a woman answered the door. Michael said that she stared at the strangers, standing there in all their mud-splattered finery. They stared back. The woman, Angel's wife, finally broke the silence.

"*¿Sí?*" she said.

The landlady, dispensing with the niceties, pushed Teresa forward, babe in arms, and launched into a speech informing Angel's wife that her husband was the father of this girl's child, and that she, a respectable and respected woman, was there to see to it that he shouldered his legal and moral responsibilities, because her house was an honorable one and she would not have illegitimate children on the premises. The woman was literally taken aback by those words, and as she retreated into the house the landlady followed. When the visitors were inside, and the landlady's speech over, there was another silence. Three small children stood in the doorway to the adjoining room, staring at the strangers. The woman sent the oldest one off to find his father and bring him home. Then, her manners beyond reproach, Angel's wife invited her callers to sit down, and offered them coffee. No one spoke while the coffee was prepared and served. Though she avoided looking at María Angélica, who slept the entire time, Angel's wife, worn and unkempt, studied her younger, still lovely rival. Teresa blushed, and fixed her gaze on her daughter. The older woman's face remained expressionless. They sat there without saying a word for twenty minutes at least, said Michael, the longest twenty minutes of his entire life. He couldn't think of a thing to say to break that awful silence. He spent those long minutes taking a discreet inventory of the furnishings: three benches, a small unfinished table in the center; another, similar table against the wall with a gas cooker on top, along with a bag of rice, a few onions, a small collection of tin plates and cups; on one wall, a faded, curling print of the Virgin of the Holy Water with the Christ Child on her lap. That was all.

While the callers sat in silence, first one woman, then a second and a third slipped in and stood near the door. Angel's wife acknowledged them with a nod as they arrived, but made no introductions. The little boy came back with news that his father was at the *salón* up the hill, drinking with members of the neighborhood soccer team. His mother sent him off again: "Get him," she said, *"now."* The second time he returned, still alone, to report that his father promised to be along *ya mismo*—an expression that can mean anything from within the next five minutes to sometime before the speaker's demise—the child's mother raised her hand and told him to bring Angel back "this instant, or else." He didn't return, most likely because his father received his mother's message with a similar gesture, bringing the little boy to conclude, wisely, that this was going to be a no-win situation as far as he was concerned.

By now the landlady's patience had run out. She broke the silence with a new version of her opening speech, adding that not only her house, but her entire family, and the family of her late husband—"may he rest in peace"—and every last one of her ancestors going back for generations, they were all honorable, and she would *not* have all those good names dragged through the mud, and so on.

Michael, beginning to feel very nervous—now there were seven strange women crowded into that small room and they had formed a tight phalanx behind Angel's wife—interrupted the speech. He addressed the entire group of women, assuring them that he understood how unexpected, how painful this must be for Angel's wife, how neither the Señora nor Teresa wanted to upset her home, her family, how all they were asking was that Angel do the right thing, that is, give Teresa's child his last name.

Angel's wife was outraged by the suggestion. *She* had three children of her own, she said. *They* had Angel's name, and rightly so; if she were to give it away to a stranger's child, what would *her* children do?

The soul of reason, Michael explained that it didn't work like that, that her children wouldn't lose Angel's name when he gave it to Teresa's child, that *everyone* could have that name, and live happily ever after, or at least more happily than they would have without a paternal surname to carry through life.

Michael said that Angel's wife seemed to be seriously considering his words when the Señora piped up yet again with that speech about her honorable family and her honorable house. Angel's wife cut her off.

"If your house is so all-fired honorable," she said, "how is it that your maid got knocked up there?" Her backers murmured words of assent. Michael said that, given the way the landlady insisted on framing her argument, Angel's wife had a very good point.

The discussion was closed. The Señora, Michael, and Teresa—who hadn't said a word the entire time—holding María Angélica tightly, trudged down the mountain through the mud.

Teresa stayed on for another month, and then the landlady fired her. Michael and I were sad to see her go. In my case the sadness was increased immeasurably, I admit, by the prospect of spending Saturday mornings out back again, bent over the *lavandería*. We wished Teresa luck, gave her an envelope with money to tide her over until she could find another job, and invited her to visit.

Teresa did visit, once, about a year later. She brought María Angélica, dressed in a new outfit of ruffles and lace, and a picture hat festooned with ribbons and flowers, an outfit that must have cost Teresa a half-year's wages. We chatted over a cup of tea, just like in the old days, while María Angélica sat in Teresa's lap eating a plateful of cookies.

Teresa talked about her present *penas*. She had a new job, she said, with a family. Both parents worked outside the home and their four children were in school, and this was good since María Angélica could be with her in the house when everyone was out. Besides, the new Señora wasn't there much to look over her shoulder and criticize. But the house was huge, and there was a lot of laundry and no automatic washing machine.

She also dreamed out loud about a future free of *penas*, not for herself any longer, but for María Angélica. Teresa was going to send her to school, all the way through twelfth grade, she said. Then, tentatively, shyly, she asked what I thought about María Angélica going to the university, studying to be a teacher, maybe, or an accountant. I thought that a fine idea, a wonderful idea.

A few months later I moved to a bigger apartment, on the other side of Quito, and I hired someone else, Mercedes, to clean up after me once a week. That was twelve years ago. To this day, Mercedes cleans for me, and washes my clothes at the *lavandería* out back.

Margaret Todd Maitland

THE DAYS OF THE DEAD

I.

Driving down the valley of Oaxaca, between the Sierra Madre of the north and of the south, the two great mothers, I see yellow flowers growing in ditches, shooting up among corn stalks, taking over fields.

"What is the name of that flower?" I ask. Pedro can't hear above the roar of the bus, so I shout. He still can't hear, so I shout again, then everyone in the seats in front of me chants, "What is the name of that flower?"

Pedro laughs. Our guide from the Oaxaca Cultural Center, he is a young Zapotec man who must have gone to university somewhere. He raises the tour bus microphone to his lips, but the mike doesn't work. He tries to say the name over the noise, then shakes the mike and frowns at the bus driver who apparently is in charge of the bus and all its accoutrements. The driver peers more intently at the road.

Pedro unscrews the microphone handle, sticks a ballpoint pen into the bottom, and holding the pen there says through the crackle, "It is called *'socheeteel,'* the death flower."

I already had my notebook out. Pedro sees me trying to write the name of the flower. He laughs and stumbles down the aisle, the yellow flowers streaking by on both sides of the bus, some six feet tall, a blur of color. He takes the notebook out of my hand and writes *"xochitl"* and *"semposuchitl,"* two names as everything has—the original Nahuatl name, from the ancient people, and the Zapotec name, and sometimes a third, the Spanish name affixed by Cortés.

"Yellow is the color of the fields in November. The *xochitl* bloom every year for the Days of the Dead."

I sit back, let my head rest against the cushions, and watch the fields. This pilgrimage, which I have longed for and anxiously avoided, will begin with the *xochitl.*

It is odd that I have come alone, odd that for this celebration, which draws families together, I have had to leave mine. It was wrenching to kiss my small son in his bed and surprisingly painful, regular traveler though I used to be, to say good-bye to my husband.

But for some years, the *Días de los Muertos* has intrigued me. During the days surrounding November 1 (elsewhere Halloween, All Saints Day, All Souls Day), many in Mexico prepare to welcome the souls of those who have died, making beautiful home altars of fruit and flowers, setting out favorite foods of a deceased father or sister or child to invite their spirits to return. In the corner of a house, over the sprays of *xochitl* and offerings of tangerines, *pan de muertos, chocolate, mole,* two worlds meet. What if the notion of family included the living and the dead?

The day I bought my ticket to Oaxaca a friend told me that when you ask a Mexican woman how many children she has, she will answer, "Six, four living," or, "Three, one living." That, I knew, was why I had longed to travel to Mexico, to be among people who think that way.

The mountains move slowly past, blue in their nearness, and I turn toward the window. I have come a long way with my own grief. After seven years, I thought I would no longer carry the son and daughter, born prematurely, each dying at birth. I thought time and distance would absorb them, as the invisible wind disperses small clouds at the horizon. But they do not disappear, the lost children, the twins of birth and death.

Now I am on a bus, riding down the Valley of Oaxaca. The mountains hold villages and rainstorms in their pockets. The radiant fields zigzag away from the road.

"The *xochitl,*" says Pedro. "You do not have to plant them. They spring up everywhere."

2.

Our tour bus steams along the Pan American Highway, which may or may not ribbon down the continents; a marvel, someone said, an illusion, said another. We stop unexpectedly at a little shop in the middle of nowhere. The new cement-block building, with its red tile roof alone among scrub and cactus, seems a surprising outcropping of prosperity. Stranger still, we are stopping for mescal.

Mescal is a clear and fiery liquor of the type many cultures produce from unlikely products of nature. In northern Italy, I had encountered grappa, made from the tough stems and bark of grape vines. After the grapes have gone into the light, fragrant wines, the rejected material finds a use. Nothing is wasted. In another unimaginable transformation, mescal is made from the agave cactus, whose many-spiked clusters burst from the ground like bristling knives. I do not like strong liquor, but I can appreciate explosive energy. The night we arrived at our hotel, the Calesa Real, the manager treated us with small cocktails, melon-colored juice spiked with mescal—an exotic, unidentifiable fruit with a hot undertone of smoke.

The group meanders into the shop, willing, though not eager, to try any new treat arranged for us. The mescal would be free—there are many kinds to sample, and we can buy some if we like. A mescal outlet store in the middle of this forlorn landscape seems bizarre. I can't imagine drinking anything strong before lunch. Already I feel the lethargic and slightly sullen mood that settles over adults for whom everything has been planned, who have paid to be amused.

I hustle away from the group, into the scrubby brush surrounding the building, to investigate the *xochitl* that appear everywhere here, too. It is my first chance to see them up close. There are several types: small, feathery-petalled, pungent marigolds; wild zinnias; tall daisies with yellow eyes.

A white horse grazes among the flowers. I am glad to be away from the others. I pick some flowers, feel my chest suddenly filling with emotion. I wind the stems together and say prayers for my children.

Americans are supposed to recover from grief, to bury the dead, smooth over feelings, and move on. We have time-tables for this: the so-called stages of grief. Miscarriages, stillbirths, premature births—there is no proper name in our language for these glimmers of life. They are numerous as the *xochitl,* spread across the history of most families, but unlike the flowers, named and renamed in wonderment by successive generations, the lost children sink nameless into the past. There is no word that carries both the image of what was and what might have been, that, like the stones of a ruin, lets you hold possibility and emptiness together in your hand.

Several people sipping from small plastic cups step out onto the veranda of the shop, so I head further back, past rows of agave. A large turkey with a brilliant head and turquoise nose hides with chicks in a bush. In the back building a man gloomily stirs something in a large blue barrel. The cement floor is slick; a pile of dark husks lies rotting in the center of a stone circle. A smell like burning rubber and fresh celery drifts out the open door.

Pedro and a few others wander toward me. I want to know how mescal is made. "The agave produces a fruit, like a pineapple. Here they are roasted." Pedro points to a small pit lined with rocks, next to it a pyramid of stones, and a pile of firewood. "They build a fire in the pit to heat the stones, pile in the agave, then cover with more hot stones." Pedro leads us into the building where the man still silently pokes into the barrel with a stick.

"Here the cactus are crushed." A thick wheel of stone, four feet tall, stands above the pile of damp husks.

"The horse is yoked to the stone. He walks around the circle," (Pedro must be talking about the white horse I saw in the flowers) "and the stone grinds the juice from the agave—over and over, as long as it takes."

Rocks, wood, horse, a man stirring. I can see each part of the process. I can feel the weight of the work, the energy it would take to gather more wood (not a tree in sight), to stack and unstack hot rocks in the sun, to persuade the horse to trudge around the circle.

Suddenly I want to drink the drink of this cactus, which angrily asserts its life against the sand. I want to taste the smoke from this particular fire, to feel the burning in my throat of someone's energy and exhaustion the day the wood is gathered.

What is grief? A blind trudging, wearing grooves in the dirt floor of loss? Who can withstand an experience that produces nothing?

In recent years, a new anger has replaced the old one. If death cheated me of two children at first, something else has robbed me ever since. I never had their lives, but now I resent the disappearance of their deaths. As events in the life of my family, they are like the agave, painfully bristling out of the past, events no one wants to touch. But I want more from them, not just the right to remember them. Anger has scorched my grief, scraped up the husks, and offered them to the grinding wheel. What if I said I want some distillation of beauty, of power, some blessing from these rejected lives?

I ask for a cup of mescal and carry it into the blazing sun. It burns all the way down.

3.

A year or two after we lost the children, my husband, Dan, brought home from school a collection of origin stories from around the world. I read through this book eagerly, fascinated to see how each culture imagined itself to have come into being, how the first humans sprang from the marriage of a tiger and a river, or how dewdrops grew into babies. I especially liked the stories that produced infants rather than adults like Adam and Eve, because I needed to contemplate the question of where babies come from.

I felt a strong connection to the ancient peoples who grappled with this mystery, who used every poetic and imaginative tool at their disposal to make some relationship to the question. It seemed to me absurd that my culture offered only the findings of biology—mother's egg and father's sperm—as an explanation for what was psychologically, spiritually, and metaphysically much more complicated.

The Mixtec people of Oaxaca tell this story: An enormous tree grew at the edge of a vast lake. Its branches came together, entwined, and produced blossoms which fell into the water. Carried gently by the lake, the blossoms were transformed into infants, and at the proper time washed into the joyful arms of the waiting shore. These were the first Mixtec people.

Hearing this story, my attention focused on the miracle of the transformation, from blossom to child, just as the pregnancy books focus on the unbelievable changes by which the fertilized egg grows itself a heart and hands. But in my case, at the end of the process the child was not delivered safely to the shore. When the child suddenly vanishes, there is the grief of loss, but there is also the thunderous turmoil of the lake, the energy and readiness of the lake, the fury of the waiting shore.

At the hospital in Minneapolis, they were ready for me. I had been suffering premature labor and had been in bed for four days. It was the fourth month of my first pregnancy. They were ready for the ambulance, for my distraught husband, and for the stretcher that carried me and the tiny child, born in our apartment, into the emergency room where a doctor cut the umbilical cord. All I knew was that the excruciating pains were over, and I didn't have to do anything except lie very still.

I was on my back on a rolling table, watching the ceiling lights pass as a nurse rolled me into an elevator and maneuvered through the elevator door, which bumped and banged against the sides of the table. Dan walked along next to me. We came to an empty room, and the nurse left us.

Dan held my hand.

The nurse came and asked if we would like to spend some time with our baby. We said yes, and she returned with a small bundle wrapped in a piece of blue-and-white flannel. Dan reached out, and she placed the bundle in his hands. I sat up and held out mine, and we passed the tiny baby between us from one cradle of hands to the other.

The nurse returned, and we were ready for her to take the little body. The room was quiet and dim. Then a doctor appeared and asked how we were feeling. I wasn't sad yet, but shocked, outraged, and guilty.

"Why did this happen?" I asked.

"It could be many things. You may never find out. Sometimes where the placenta implants itself makes a difference. The inside of the uterus, the lining, is like the surface of the earth. It can be very irregular, hills and valleys, some places more or less fertile for the embryo to attach itself. Maybe it was not a good place, not a rich enough supply of blood vessels to sustain the growth of the fetus."

I had another idea. "I have been working too hard, late at night, not getting enough sleep." I had a terrible desire to go back and undo the past months. Also, Dan and I had been having bad arguments, but I didn't mention that.

"Can stress cause a miscarriage?" I asked.

He smiled a very gentle smile.

"No, not the kind you're talking about. We know that in concentration camps and in times of war—when people are starving or under siege—fertility rates drop. Women miscarry or stop conceiving. Their bodies are too overwhelmed with survival. But you are healthy, and nothing you could have done caused your child to be born too soon."

For the moment I believed him. I felt more than anything the relief of his attention. He sat with us, did not seem in a hurry, and the quietness of his body in the chair felt like acceptance. He was not afraid of what had happened.

Someone came and wheeled me into a room where another woman sat propped up in her bed watching a small television. Dan pulled the curtain around my bed, a silly, circular thing like a shower curtain. Very gently he lay next to me on the bed. After a while—it was dark by now—a nurse came and told Dan it was time for him to leave.

"Can't you find a way for me to stay the night?" he asked.

"I know what you mean," said the nurse. "It is a hard time to be separated. I'll see what I can do."

In the end he found a plastic couch in a waiting room down the hall, and I lay in the eerie green hospital light, the invisible woman next to me whispering in low complaining tones into the telephone far into the night.

I couldn't sleep. On one of her visits, the nurse had given me a book called *Empty Arms,* written by a woman who had lost a stillborn son. "Do you want to name your child?" it asked. "Do you want to bury your child?" She said the worst moment of her ordeal came when she and her husband left the hospital without the child. Her arms physically ached with unused readiness.

In the next weeks, the storm of feelings I lived with grew sharper and clearer. My body, the lake, had failed, had been unable to carry the blossom through its transformation. My efforts to find out what went wrong all met dead ends. But my body was both inner lake and waiting shore, and a fury possessed me.

How do we prepare for a child? Perhaps blossom is not a good metaphor for the beginnings of life—fragile, yes, but failing to suggest the fierce process by which a child digs its way into the awareness of the human beings whose life it enters. A tiny glacier, scooping and digging up the virgin soil of its parents' psyches, deepening the lake every day. Parents of living children do not contemplate this lake—they draw on its waters for the energy to care for the child. When a child dies, you stumble into this lake at every turn. The inner space—this preparedness we call love—stretches to the horizon, vastly empty, painfully full. The amount a person can cry does nothing to diminish the size of the lake.

4.

One morning the tour bus takes us to the market town of Xaachila. Everything is in motion, stirred by the coming Days of the Dead. The Mexican women, hurrying children at their skirts, stride toward the market, a mixture of panic and determination in their shoulders. I recognize their mood across the cultures: this is the day of preparation, the day to make ready for the holiday, when how much money you have strikes up against what you had hoped for, and the energy for extra work must be carved out of days that already consume all you have.

This is the day the altar must be constructed, the chocolate stirred, the chiles ground and simmered. This is the hour to find and haggle over the turkey, to buy sugarcane stalks to weave for the altar (if they aren't too expensive this year) and the cigarettes and rum that will please your father's spirit. You are preparing to receive the living and the dead—both have their requirements.

We leave our bus and slip into the stream of people surging along the road, the market's energy pulling us like a vortex. Xaachila is not a tourist town. It is simply lucky this year. The regular Thursday market, to which people from all the outlying villages bring their produce, means great business the day before the Days of the Dead.

We turn the corner, and the market appears like an incredible congregation of barges. It seems to be rigged with hundreds of sails, which turn out to be bed sheets, flowered and plain, white and pink, strung between ropes in a crazy pattern of awnings, shade for the vendors and their wares. Our group marches on, but I stop to look: giant yellow marigolds are piled on straw mats, the mats layered atop one another; brilliant, furry purple cockscomb lie in mounds as high as my shoulder. Two boys sit among squashes the size of steamer trunks. Cheeses and chocolate, tomatoes, grapefruit, pineapple. It is as if the earth has erupted with abundance for the *Días de los Muertos.* Next to some huge white radishes I see purple wooden chairs, three tiny ones for children. I stop to take a picture of the children's chairs, kneel down, then look up, and the tour group is gone.

I run between vendors in what seems like the most likely path, though fruit and vegetables cover the ground everywhere, and do not see my friends. I branch off in another direction. I can't believe they could have vanished so quickly. I retrace my steps. I try to ask two women selling avocados if they have seen any North Americans, but from their vague smiles I can tell I have not said it correctly. Some men selling wrenches and screwdrivers seem to know what I am asking and point toward another block filled with sheets and food. I hurry in that direction, afraid to lose my bearings in the zigzag side streets. No sign of the tall pale ones. I find my way back to the main street to look for the bus, and it, too, is gone. Then I panic.

I don't have much money with me, but worse, I have no idea where we are. I wasn't paying attention to how we got here or how long we were planning to stay or whether there was something else we were to see in this village whose name I cannot remember. What is the word for taxi? Would a place like this have one, and what would it cost to get back to Oaxaca? I can't imagine how to call the hotel to leave a message about what has happened to me. I feel furious with myself for falling into the same passive state as the others in the group, letting the bus take me wherever it would. I stand at the edge of the market for quite a while wondering what to do.

Across the road, broad steps lead to a high plaza in the middle of which sits a church. Stalls with embroidered blouses and woven blankets cover the steps, but as I stand there, an old metal sign swims into focus amongst the confusion. It reads *Zona Archeológica* and has an arrow pointing away from the church. I am saved. There must be a ruin nearby and the tour must have gone there. The sign gives me the clue I need and the words to follow the clue. I approach an old woman selling sugarcane, and pronounce *"zona archeológica?"* as best I can, as if it were a question. Archeology is undoubtedly not uppermost in this woman's mind, but the blank look passes from her face, and she gesticulates toward a road up the hill behind the church.

I follow the cobblestone road, then scramble up a gully between thorny bushes. At the top of the hill I see Pedro. He is standing in the shade of a lone tree. Several others from the group, looking spent, sit on rocks. I rush toward them, overjoyed.

"I was lost!" But in the crowd and confusion of the market they hadn't noticed I was missing. Winded and perspiring, they seem overcome with lethargy. "I'm so glad to see you!" Then I, too, sit on a rock to catch my breath.

Soon it is time to return to the center of the village—the archeological site is a single underground tomb, all that remains of a large Zapotec temple. Xaachila had been the central city of the Zapotec culture. It is hard going back down the hill to the market—now clumps of people head for home laden with supplies: a hefty man strides purposefully with an enormous round basket on his shoulder from which bob hundreds of *xochitl* flowers; two girls carry armloads of flowers and balance flat bread-filled baskets on their heads; a man in a straw hat hoists twenty-foot sugarcane stalks over his shoulder; a woman lugs a turkey by its neck, black and white feathers puffing in the breeze, its wings flopping and dragging in the road.

I want flowers. Everyone is carrying them; baskets, horse carts, bicycles, pick-up trucks, everything is full of flowers. Back in the maze of the market, I ask a man sitting on the ground between mounds of flowers if I may buy a small bunch—yellow and pale lavender. He picks them out.

"¿Cuanto?" I ask. How much?

"No!" he exclaims, smiling. A gift. From a woman I buy purple cockscomb. I want to carry my own unmanageable profusion, a tangle of procreation, these bizarre and gentle blossoms whose only purpose is to gleam, to attract, to receive a shower of pollen, to swell with seeds that drop and burrow and burst, that rot and sprout and cry out again for life. I want to carry an armful of flowers, to feel them heavy and awkward, to have to wrap my arms around them.

Diane Lefer

TROPIGÓTICO

The Zapotec women of the isthmus are liberated by Mexican standards, and that's what drew me to Tehuantepec: I expected to feel more at home there than anywhere else in the country. Even young girls travel around unchaperoned, selling hammocks and *totopos* and dried shrimp; my own traveling wouldn't seem so strange. I soon found that, like independent women everywhere, the Tehuanas get slandered. The usual stuff: they've emasculated the local men who've turned in unprecedented numbers to an involuntary and despairing homosexuality. And the extraordinary: they keep secret rooms on the top floor of the enclosed market where they torture young men who interfere with their business affairs. Supposedly, you can hear muffled cries of agony emanating from the building all day and night, except at sundown when hundreds of blackbirds rise in whirling agitation in the plaza and their shrill chatter drowns out the sound.

I never heard any cries, and, the way I remember it, in 1970, Tehuantepec was a mournfully beautiful town with red-tiled roofs and palm trees, a slight odor of decay from the marshes, and fat proud women who put their bare feet down on the earth with such confidence you'd have thought they owned every inch.

One Saturday afternoon in December, a woman approached me in the plaza and offered to tell my fortune. Witchcraft and magic were what I'd come to Mexico to find, and so I agreed. We had begun to discuss terms when a teenaged girl—of the new and modern generation, therefore slender in jeans—came swooping down on us, waving her arms and shouting like someone trying to scatter chickens. The fortune teller chose to retreat.

"Gringa," the girl told me, "that was a Gypsy," and she pulled down the corner of one eye, meaning *watch out*. The Zapotec women wear

long flowered petticoats as skirts, embroidered velvet tops, and earrings and necklaces made of gold-colored coins. The fortune teller had looked the same, except for bright lipstick and darkly outlined eyes. "Hungarians," said the girl. "They're bad people. Thieves."

"I'm sure they're not all bad," I said, with kneejerk tolerance and self-righteousness.

"They look at your cards and tell you something terrible is going to happen unless you give them your cow."

"Well then, I don't have anything to worry about. I don't own a cow."

Reyna—that was her name—laughed. "Maybe not," she said, "but you're a *gringa*. I'm sure you've got something they'd want."

The upshot of it was that Reyna decided to take charge of me, and I decided to forgive her interference. An hour later, a rattling second class bus dropped us and two giggling cousins off at cliffside, and we were scrambling down a rough descent to the Pacific Ocean beach. The setting sun was tropical Gothic: thrashing palms, and winds that whipped our hair and drowned out our voices, that teased threads of foam up from the whitecapped waves and blew them into rainbow nets. Most unsettling of all, the gulls were fixed, stationary in the sky, beating their wings wildly just to keep from being blown away. The flying sand cut like bits of glass.

We ran into the surf fully clothed and fought the undertow, then let the high hot winds dry us, leaving salt and sand caked on our clothes and skin. We were not quite presentable, but who cared? We were liberated and, anyway, entirely alone on the desolate beach. Until Acho came along.

He seemed to come out of nowhere. His huge belly protruded from a dirty undershirt; the belt on his baggy pants flapped open. Every now and then, he let out a cry and jiggled for an instant. On one shoulder he had placed a carefully folded, though filthy, towel and, on it, a large block of ice. As the cargo melted, the towel absorbed some of the water; the rest trickled its icy way down Acho's back. A friend of his had opened a restaurant at a cove further down the beach, he told us, and he was doing him a favor. We should follow along and have something to eat.

Acho made an unpleasant first impression, but his deep voice—like his bulk—commanded attention and—unlike his body—respect. We followed. The block of ice steadily diminished as we walked; by the time we reached our destination it would be almost gone. I drew close to Reyna and, shouting above the wind, told her the story of Sisyphus, hoping, I think, for a trade: I would tell her our myths, she would tell me hers.

The restaurant turned out to be a primitive shelter, bamboo walls on three sides, open in the direction of the sea. A single card table with four folding chairs, all bearing advertisements for Corona beer; a palm-frond overhang to offer shade; some sturdy wooden posts sunk deep enough in the sand to support hammocks and the weight of customers (even Acho?) who might lie in them. We were the only customers and took the table. Acho delivered what was left of his burden to the ice chest and chose a hammock. The Cokes we were served were, not surprisingly, warm. Reyna's cousins asked for shrimp cocktails and complained, when they came, that there was a fly in the shrimp. The owner solemnly assured us that the fly was not in the shrimp but in the sauce and therefore of no consequence.

"That's no way to treat your customers!" bellowed Acho. Since our arrival, he had not said a word, but now, having taken our part, he felt free to join us. He lurched up from his reclining position and came to stand by the table. "Not enough chairs," he remarked, and smiled at me. "Perhaps you should sit on my lap." I said I was uncomfortable, though his lips were pursed in a way that seemed to contradict his flirtatiousness: prissy rather than lewd. When I didn't answer, he laughed good-naturedly and apologized for his friend's ignorance. He told us of his plans to build a small hotel in the area and develop a little tourist business. "In a few years, you'll come back and find a real restaurant here," he told us, "not this shit." Acho stayed by us, standing and leaning forward, his hands out on our table, bringing the smell of fish and beer and dried sweat that the winds failed to blow away.

"I'm always interested to talk to *gringos,*" he said suddenly, raising his hand and pointing at me. "You are people with a lot of brain. At least that's what they tell us. Lots of brain. We have some people here, some Mexicans, like the President of the Republic, who have brains, too. That's okay." He shrugged but he wasn't finished. "I'm an ignorant man. Not as ignorant as he is," he indicated his friend, "Ignorant, yes, but I've seen a lot and who do I have to talk to?" He cleared his throat and spat in the sand. "No one. But today I want to talk to you, *gringa,*" he said. "You see, living by the sea, even the most ignorant, uncivilized person must think thoughts and meditate on the lessons life has taught him. I would like us to exchange ideas."

"Well, yes. I would like that," I said, pleased by the high seriousness of his speech. But uncomfortable at his proximity, I added, "I'm going to try out one of the hammocks," and left the table.

The ropes creaked like the rigging of a ship; the wooden posts creaked; the palm fronds above creaked and rustled. "Have you ever slept in one of these?" asked the restaurant owner. "Much much better than a bed."

"I'd like to," I answered. "It's like being suspended between heaven and earth. I'd like to be right here, swaying and watching the sun go down, and then the stars. . . ."

For a small fee, the man told me, he let people stay in the hammocks all night. Then he smiled as Acho drew up a chair. "I think you have conquered a heart," he said.

Acho was staring directly into my face. Beyond him, the sun was beginning to go down over the sea, and, though the sky had not yet changed colors, the wet sand reflected light and glistened in overlapping rounds of pink and gold and blue-green. The hammock swung, drawing me close to him, then away. "Señorita," he said quietly, "I respect your countrymen very much. But sometimes you will find that my people know things that would surprise even the wisest men of your land, things that you great *gringos* cannot even dream of." Throughout my journeys in Mexico, I had been looking for some sort of *brujo* or shaman. A typical American traveler of that era, I expected the Third World to provide primitive rites and mystic revelations. I had lost my fortune teller, but maybe Acho was the real thing—the worker of magic I'd hoped to meet.

The cousins began to insist that we leave; if we didn't hurry, we would miss the last bus back. Only minutes earlier, I'd been ready to go, but that was before I realized Acho might be more than he seemed. "We can sleep in the hammocks," I suggested. The idea got the young girls nervous, but Reyna was willing. "Tell my mother I won't be home tonight," she instructed the cousins. I was impressed: I could not have sent my parents that message at her age.

Acho's friend served us a dinner of saltine crackers and minced shark, which we ate hungrily; it was getting too dark to spot any strange flies. Then Reyna and I threw ourselves happily into hammocks, watching the sunset and—even when clouds blew in to obscure the anticipated stars—congratulating ourselves for having stayed. Now, I thought, Acho would begin to speak as promised; he would talk to us of myth and magic in the dark. Instead he called out, "*Gringa!* You have a boyfriend?"

At the time, I did believe myself to be madly and deeply in love. "Yes, and we're getting married when I return home." Most Mexicans suspected this alleged fiancé was an invention; others expressed amazement and admiration that he could be so understanding and let me travel around alone. I shivered. The winds had begun to grow cold.

"And I suppose you think you can't live without him," said Acho.

True enough, I could hardly imagine spending my life without the man, but Acho's tone made me cautious. "Oh, I *can* live without him. We'd just *prefer* to be together."

"But why?"

"We love each other. Of course."

Acho was drinking beer. He swallowed, one, two, three great gulps, then belched, then laughed. "Ay, *gringa!* There's only one reason to get married, and it has nothing to do with love. You marry to make your life better. That's all. And I've been married three times—not counting the ones I wasn't really married to—so I should know."

"Our marriage," I said primly, "is going to last." I stood and asked for the bathroom. Our forlorn host stepped out of the shadows and pointed the way, muttering about how yes, it was time for us to go, it was closing time.

"We're sleeping in your hammocks," Reyna reminded him. But no, we had misunderstood. He didn't let people spend the night in December—it was too windy and cold—and as for unchaperoned girls—impossible at any time.

Acho came to the rescue so quickly, Reyna and I exchanged glances: had it been planned? He had a *cabaña* not far away, on a rise over the beach. No, he didn't live there himself. It was a model room, a small start for the hotel he hoped to build. And we were welcome to stay there free of charge. *"Gringa,"* he added, "maybe later I will tell you about my wives."

The horizon line was still fiery but the air around us was dark. Acho produced a flashlight and handed it to me and I headed off in the direction I'd been shown. The bathroom proved to be a small area closed off from view, a square yard of sand where women could squat in peace and men could urinate against a concrete wall. Even in this isolated place, graffiti artists had been at work: drawings of male organs (labeled with Acho's name) and scrawled messages accusing him of a variety of obscene and unnatural acts. It would all have been invisible without the flashlight Acho had given me: he must have wanted me to see.

He was comparing genealogies with Reyna when I returned. I placed his flashlight on the table and calmly suggested to Reyna that we walk back to the bus stop. We'd seen a number of shacks up there. Surely we could find a family—a place with a mother and respectable daughters—and they would give us shelter for the night. But Reyna had learned that she and Acho were related. The thought amused her and she insisted that his *cabaña* would be okay.

We followed him back along the beach, then inland where a footpath crossed the dunes. He swept the sand with his light, showing us a shadowy cactus plant and, once, the skull of a horned cow, glowing for a moment, half-covered by sand, then lost as we passed in the dark.

The promised *cabaña* was a single room. Inside there was nothing but a cot. Acho didn't try to linger. We thanked him for his hospitality. He refused our money and left in a gentlemanly way after wishing us goodnight.

Reyna and I lay side by side on the cot, talking about life until she fell asleep in the middle of a phrase. It wasn't so easy for me. My head was light, and I felt slightly nauseated from too much sun. The sand and grit in my clothes had become more irritating than toast crumbs in bed. So I was awake when the knocking on the door began, and I heard Acho's drunken voice: "*Gringa!* Let me in! I want to tell you about my wives!"

If there was a lock or latch on the door, I hadn't noticed, and didn't think Reyna had used it. Sure enough, Acho's voice was soon coming to me from close by, though the room was so dark I had not seen him come in. I touched Reyna, nudged her, shook her, but she continued (or pretended) to sleep. Acho's eyes saw better in the dark than mine; my movement let him know I was awake.

"Don't be afraid," he said, still invisible, but apparently squatting on the floor at the side of the cot. "I just want to talk to you, a *gringa*, a North American. I just want to tell you about my wives. . . ."

"We can talk in the morning," I said firmly. "I'm tired now. It's late. . . ."

But Acho could not be dissuaded. Through the night, he told me his story. At first I blamed my imperfect Spanish for what I was hearing: he could not have said what I'd heard. Then I listened, intrigued by his imagination—or better, as I hoped—by what he, himself, seemed to believe.

"My home was in the dry, dusty valley where people try to make a living planting corn. And that's where I married the first one. I was young, and still believed in love, like you do, *gringa*. I married her because I was young and impulsive and it was time to get started. Life is all in stages, in laps. And at each stage, you need something else. You get married to improve your life, and you get unmarried for the same reason. To make your life better. That's what life and marriage and death are all about. But I didn't know that at the time.

"So there we were in the valley with nothing to eat, and I had more responsibilities than ever because of Epidilia. Marriage had not improved things for me, and I soon stopped thinking about love. That's what I'm trying to tell you, *gringa*. So in the end, I sold my wife to the Devil for a herd of cattle.

"The Devil kept his word and my life improved. I only had one problem. People guessed where my fine herd had come from and where my Epidilia had gone, and so no other woman would have me. Now, I'm a man who wants women, so what could I do? It was clear that the stage of my life in that little town had come to an end. I moved to the coast where no one knew me and married Serafina.

"She was pretty, Serafina. Of all my wives, the prettiest of all. But as the years went by, she kept having babies and the babies kept dying and she became sad and fat and sloppy. So my journey together with Sera had to end. One year, the catch was bad for weeks. There just weren't any fish in the sea. Finally, I called to the Devil again and offered to sell Serafina. But he refused. He said by the time he got Epidilia, she was so tired and worn out from working for me, she was no longer good for much at all. This was a severe and unexpected blow: if the Devil wouldn't take my wives, where was I supposed to turn in times of trouble or emergency?

"Finally, I left Serafina. Of course, I couldn't marry again in the church as long as she was alive, but I am a little intelligent in spite of being an ignorant man, and so I took no action to have her killed until I no longer had any choice.

"Well, I wasn't married then, but I was living for awhile with Elda who was lovely and only fourteen. So now she's only thirty-four and who knows how many stages she's passed through and how many more she'll know. I should have started so young myself. Now I'm practically an old man. But twenty years ago . . . twenty years ago I was still a good looking fellow. So good looking that even after I'd left her, Serafina was still in love with me. She would come to see me and that would make Elda feel so bad. Serafina would tell me she'd seen my name and hers written in gold letters in the sky. That was really a miracle, because Sera couldn't read. She'd say she couldn't go on without me, that she couldn't stand it anymore. But I knew that stage was over and I'd just tell her to go away.

"That's when the trouble started. You see, Sera, it turns out, had a friend who was a witch, and this Doña Lupe went and showed her how to get me back.

"One morning, I was taking my nets out to sea, when suddenly, everything went black around me. I started to pray loudly because I thought it was an eclipse, but then I felt something very strange. I don't know what to call it—an impulse, a compulsion—that guided my legs. I didn't know where I was going because I couldn't see a thing. At last, I felt my hand opening a door, and in some mysterious way I knew that on the other side of the door I would find the woman I loved more than life itself. Sure enough, she was waiting. I took her in my arms, and she was naked. She led me to a hammock, and we made love. It was wonderful, *gringa*. It was like making love to the sea. When we finished, my vision cleared, and I saw the woman's face. 'So it's you, Sera,' I said, and I got up and left.

"Of course, Sera was very disappointed that the effects of the magic wore off so fast. I found out what Doña Lupe taught her: to catch a toad in the night of the full moon, then sew its eyelids together with a white silk thread, thinking of me. The result of this was I was unable to see the light of day until I'd gone to her and loved her. But after I did it, the spell had no power to make me stay.

"Poor Sera. She must have loved me a lot, because it happened again and again. Every full moon I think she filled a bucket full with toads, because I was blinded almost every morning and there I was, stumbling to where she was waiting for me in the hammock. And Elda moved out.

"I didn't want to hurt Sera, but I started to see I had to do something to stop her. I was beginning to worry. This thing with sewing up the toad has to be done very carefully. I knew if she was careless enough to let the needle pass through the pupil, I'd be blinded forever and no lovemaking, no matter how many times or with how much passion, would bring back my sight.

"One day she had a fight with Hector, my *compadre*, and I saw my chance. That night, I threw poison to Hector's chickens. In the morning, the whole flock was dead. Everyone knew how Sera had been bewitching me, and now everyone could see she'd used those powers for evil. The village wouldn't interfere in matters of love, you understand, but once they thought Sera was a chicken-killer, something had to be done.

"The police went to get her, and we all gathered and burned her. Yes, we burned her, though some people still say that she walked out of the flames and went to live in Mexico City, but I know that isn't true. I know she died, though I didn't actually see the burning.

"I didn't actually see her die, because . . . *gringa,* imagine how I felt when I awakened the morning they went to get her and found I could not see! I prayed they had not killed her yet. Unless I could make love to her, I would never see again. My steps were drawn along the path to the center of town by the same strange force as always. Hector grabbed me and had to hold me back to prevent me from throwing myself upon the flaming body. He held me until the burning was over and seawater had been thrown on the bones and they had cooled. Then he let me go.

"You may think I did it just to get my vision back, but believe me, I enjoyed it. Of course, in my normal state, the idea makes me sick. But she had bewitched me just before she died, and bewitched as I was, sexual relations with her remains brought me pleasure. Her skeleton held me, *gringa*, but at the same time, it didn't hold me. I was powerful and manly, entering and whipping about, above the earth, like the wind in a tree.

"Well, once that was over, I was free to take another wife. Elda was gone and didn't come back, but I found a girl named Altagracia who married me in the church. She had a bad disposition, so that didn't last, and I came to live here. Now I don't get married anymore. I've reached the stage where you don't bother with formalities."

That was Acho's story, just as I'd wanted and expected it to be, full of brutal machismo, witchcraft, and sex. I'd listened silently, in fascination, trying to remember every detail for my journal. But once it was over, Acho both frightened and sickened me, and I wanted him to leave.

"Gringa," he whispered hoarsely, "I'm an old man now, *gringa*, but I still appreciate a pretty girl. I'm so glad I met you on the beach. You don't have to be afraid. I was very careful when I sewed up the toad. There was no damage to the pupils. I guarantee it."

I burst out laughing and then silenced myself, afraid to give offense. I wasn't scared of sewn-up toads, but of Acho, yes. . . .

"It's noon, *gringa*, and the sun is shining on the beach, the light is pouring through the window, but you can't see it. The magic is working, *gringa*. Listen to your heart. It's beating quickly, quickly, and even though I'm an old man, you're beginning to want me. You want me very much. I was very careful, *gringa*, very careful with the toad, just sewed the little eyelids together. I didn't damage the little eyes at all. . . ."

I couldn't laugh or speak or move any more than I could make out figures in the thick and total dark. And he was right: my heart was still beating, frantic, though I was frozen and fixed in place. The door rattled and banged on its rough frame and Reyna, at last, sat bolt upright beside me. "Girls!" called Acho, outside and knocking. "Girls, let me in!"

"Go away, you dirty old pimp and let us sleep!" Reyna cried.

"Girls, please!"

"Old man, I know all about you. I know your mother!" And then the door and windows kept rattling and the wind howled all night, but we didn't hear from Acho again.

✧ ✧ ✧

Before I ever went to Mexico, many years ago, I used to write tales about men like Acho and about primitive powers strong enough to confound the rational American mind. While I lived there, I never encountered anything of the sort—the story of Acho's wives is an invention—and so I should know better now. But here I am again, still insistent on spreading falsehood, blind to everything true I might have found.

I turn to my old travel journals—What did I really see? What did I learn?—and find pages copied from occult manuals. I used to buy them in the marketplace: *El libro de San Cipriano*; *La sabiduria del rey Salomón.*

Reyna still sends me letters. She was—is—entirely real. She did have cousins—at least I think so—though their names never made it into my notes. And yes, we once found an empty *cabaña* on the beach. We stayed the night, though I didn't bother to record what we talked about. Men, I believe, though the betrayals she told me about were the ordinary man/woman kind, without resort to supernatural trickery. We talked about the Mexican economy, what she was studying in school, how the oil industry was likely to ruin the beach. My journal says, "Fabulous sunset," and I wrote a few lines in the morning, when we woke.

Sunlight poured through the windows and I was about to step down from the cot.

"Scorpion!" Reyna warned, "Don't move."

It was the especially poisonous kind, she said. She could tell by its color, though now I don't remember what color it was. She took her sandal and dispatched it with a quick, efficient blow, and I remember—though now I cannot call it up in my mind—that before she did, I sat up eagerly, and watched it swing its tail slowly, slowly, over the concrete floor.

Sarah Ventres

LIFE AND DEATH IN THE ARTIBONITE VALLEY

On the day after we met in Miami, we seventeen Peace Corps recruits were flown to the Caribbean island of Hispaniola. Two nights later, I lay trying to sleep in a tiny room, door and window tightly closed to keep out the evil spirits that otherwise might invade the rural home of my Haitian "family"—five people with whom I was unable to communicate except in sign language and with whom I was to live for the next three months. To me, it was unbearably hot and humid. Just days before, I had left Minnesota in the midst of a blizzard. I had taken early retirement, sold my house, stored my worldly goods, and embarked on what I hoped would be a great experience. Now I lay, bathed in perspiration and feeling claustrophobic, listening to the grunts of the family pig, the flapping of bats, and the buzzing of hordes of mosquitoes. I kept saying to myself, like The Little Engine That Could, "I can do it . . . I *can* do it . . . I *will* do it!"

We met daily at a house that had been rented as a training center and absorbed steady infusions of language, cross-cultural, and technical studies. Midway through training, we were fanned out through the countryside for a three-day visit to Haitian families. Totally on our own for the first time, and with only limited facility in Creole, the spoken language, we were given written instructions detailing how to travel to our destinations. From then on we were left each to our own devices.

My destination was St. Marc, roughly 100 kilometers north of Port-au-Prince. But that is as the crow flies. To arrive there by midafternoon,

I first had to ride a *tap-tap* south into Port-au-Prince, walk a mile to the "bus station" near the waterfront, then board a bus headed for St. Marc. This turned out not to be possible, for although I had set out at daybreak, all of the buses headed north were filled—not only the seats, but the aisles and the rooftops as well. A bus station in Haiti can best be described as an open-air wrestling match. There is no building. Buses headed for each destination simply have a particular street corner that is known to be their site of origin. Haitian buses closely resemble American school buses—and may well once have been such. The seats are equally uncomfortable, and the springs are likewise nonexistent. Ninety passengers can be squeezed into a bus whose capacity, written in English above the driver, is forty-eight. At each station, a flock of buses, each with its own hawker and pusher, is surrounded by hundreds of aspirant travelers—all carrying boxes and bags of food, often including live chickens and goats, all shouting and shoving and elbowing to gain a place on a bus.

My whiteness did rather stand out in this sea of black, and one extraordinarily kind gentleman, recognizing my plight, explained that a friend of his was about to leave for the north and would take me aboard—whereupon he pointed across the road to a *camión* (a slat-sided open truck) already nearly full of produce and people. I decided without hesitation that if that were the only way I was going to get to St. Marc, I would take it. So he escorted me to the driver and negotiated a substantial "white man's" fee. I joined about thirty Haitians and an equal number of hundred-pound sacks of ConAgra flour on the flatbed of the truck, successfully finding a spot to sit, using my small duffel as a cushion.

Once out of the city, our driver rocketed northward at breakneck speed along *Route Nationale*, creating a stream of wind that quenched the sting of the blistering sun beating down on us in the open truck. We passed through Bon Répos, where Michelle Duvalier, Baby Doc's extravagant wife, had erected a hospital for the people of Haiti, but which now stood empty and unused; through Cabaret, the model town Papa Doc built to prove to the world he was helping his people, but which he populated with his *Macoute* henchmen. He named it Duvalierville, but after the fall of the Duvaliers, it resumed the name of the old village it had replaced, Cabaret. *Route Nationale* from Port-au-Prince to St. Marc follows the coastline of the *Golfe de la Gonâve*. Through the wide-spaced slats of the truck, I could see the cerulean blue waters of the gulf when the view was not obstructed by the walled summer homes of the wealthy.

Near Montrouis we passed the former vacation estate of Baby Doc, Papa Doc Duvalier's profligate son and successor, whose overthrow in

1986 ended the grotesque thirty-year dictatorship of the Duvalier family. When he was in residence, and particularly when he wanted to sport along the coastline in his speedboat, Baby Doc would often have *Route Nationale* closed to traffic so no oppositionist could take a potshot at him. He was unconcerned that this closed all traffic from Haiti's breadbasket, the Artibonite River Valley, to Port-au-Prince. *Route Nationale,* amusingly called Route #1, was the only road providing a through connection from the north to south of the island. Once, it is told, an American agricultural consultant helped farmers in the Artibonite Valley develop an export crop of lush tomatoes—to be shipped by air to the U.S. Everything went superbly—in a country where almost nothing goes well. The tomatoes flourished and were picked ripe and beautiful, packing boxes were filled, trucks were loaded and sent on their way to the airport in Port-au-Prince, where a cargo plane waited on the tarmac. But the trucks were stopped at Montrouis by the Army roadblock protecting Baby Doc Duvalier at his play. No traffic was permitted to proceed for three days. The tomatoes rotted in the hot sun. That, the anecdote ends, is "the story of Haiti."

We arrived in St. Marc in the early afternoon, and I located the mortuary where I was to meet my weekend host. He turned out to be the photographer of the dead and manager of the establishment, a tall and handsome young man of about thirty years named Marcel. All of the employees came out to meet me. One of them, a strong, emphatic young woman who served as "dresser of the dead," upon learning I had had nothing to eat all day, took me in hand. We bought melons from a street vendor, split them open and ate them while perched on a railing under the trees lining the city square. These few trees were remnants of many that had once helped make St. Marc a lovely city. Now, however, it is crumbling and decrepit. Once-handsome turn-of-the-century commercial buildings lined the main street, baking in a dusty gray haze that permeated everything.

At four o'clock closing time, Marcel locked the mortuary door, and we started off on foot to his home. The route turned out to be long and circuitous—away from the main street and waterfront, along denuded and dusty side streets flanked by helpless little houses crammed together side by side on the barren, scorched earth. After walking about a mile, Marcel stopped in front of a tiny one-room house built of concrete block topped by a tin roof. *"Bien,"* he said, "We will rest here. I want you to meet my girlfriend." He led me in and ceremoniously introduced not only his girlfriend, but the thirteen-month-old child she was tending, who, he proudly announced, was his daughter.

It was clear that this was not Marcel's home, and I was beginning to wonder about the situation I would find myself in this weekend. Perhaps, I thought, Marcel lived with his mother?

After a Coke and some pleasantries—difficult, at best, because no one spoke English and my Creole was still no better than rudimentary—Marcel and I proceeded on, sharing the weight of my duffel, hung by its strap between us. Beyond the depressing slum we emerged, finally, onto a broad street of once-beautiful Victorian villas. Threadbare and weatherbeaten now, their shutters hung askew, their trees were gone, and their terraced gardens had been untended for decades. Squatter shanties spawned like mushrooms along both sides of the walls guarding the perimeters of the old estates. It was nevertheless apparent that one hundred years ago these had been magnificent properties. We turned into a wide, curving driveway, through an ornate but rusted and broken gate suspended from a five-foot stuccoed wall, on which stood sentinel remnants of marble statuary. Inside, the grounds were strewn with at least a dozen old Cadillac hearses in various stages of cannibalization. Several young men were working on them in a desultory fashion. Marcel introduced me to them, indicating that they, too, worked for the mortuary and lived here.

This, then, was Marcel's house. The whole structure was of horizontal tongue-and-groove board, long ago painted yellow. A wide gallery, its roof supported by white pillars, undulated around the house. There were no windows, but a series of huge, black, double doors opened onto the gallery on all sides. Cement forms that once held massive beds of flowers still circled the house, rising to a crescendo beside the fifteen-foot-wide curved steps leading to the front entrance. Today, the former flower beds were the resting places of dozens of unfinished wooden caskets.

We deposited my duffel in the first huge room—which must once have been the parlor and turned out to be Marcel's home. It was nearly thirty feet square with a fifteen foot ceiling. French doors on three sides opened onto the gallery. The doors, all double, were ten feet high and three inches thick. The floor was a stunning parquet in a diamond pattern; the design met in a sunburst in the center of the room—but it was worn to a silvery gray and obviously had not been varnished in decades.

Furnishings consisted of one bed, a table, three wooden chairs, and open shelving in one corner for cooking equipment and food supplies. A charcoal brazier stood on the gallery outside. Clothing was suspended from hooks on the wall behind the bed and included, I noticed, some dresses. Did Marcel's mother sleep in another room, I wondered?

But Marcel gave me a tour of the whole house and there was no other room for Mother. There were six huge rooms. All but the hexagonal room in the center had doors on three sides, those on the outside opening onto the gallery. No windows needed! Just open the doors and air flows through the entire building.

The six other young men who lived in the house bunked on the floor of one of the smaller rooms in the back. The entire estate housed a vertically-integrated mortuary industry: in the back yard, sawing of wood for caskets; on the back gallery, construction of caskets; in the center room, fabrication and spray-painting of *tôle* funereal wreaths; another room served as an equipment repair shop. In the front yard, in addition to the work on all the hearses, was sanding and spray painting of the coffins. (When finished, the painted wooden caskets closely resembled polished steel.) The house had no electricity and no plumbing. Portable diesel generators provided electricity for the spraying equipment. In the back of the property, there was a well with an outhouse perched nearby.

Back in his room, Marcel removed his shirt and loosened his pants, then unrolled a rush mat and lay down on the floor. I was becoming a bit more nervous about what the arrangements for this weekend were going to be. Then another young man, Claude, arrived and the two of them worked over their lesson for church that evening, reading from a fundamentalist tract published in Tennessee entitled *L'Unité des Croyants La Lumière Éternelle.* This week's study was Ephesians 1:3-4 and concentrated on the need for followers of Christ to be "holy and without blemish." Claude read the French tract haltingly, and Marcel paraphrased in Creole. I realized that Marcel either could not read or, at least, could not read French.

At five o'clock, we three, Claude, Marcel, and I, walked about a mile to their church, a small and austere rectangular structure newly built by the congregation. Marcel and Claude appeared to be the leaders of the congregation. They faced a dozen young men and put them through a grilling on Ephesians. Much was discussed about the need to respect the "thou shalt not's" of *Les Dix Commandements.* At the same time, on the other side of the center aisle, several young women were practicing hymns. And in the back, two men were hammering together some new church benches.

The lessons finished, Marcel introduced me to one of the singing women: his wife, Lissa. She was very pretty, affecting American style with straightened hair and modish dress. But I was somewhat taken aback after all the exhortation about the Ten Commandments to find that Marcel had a wife in addition to his girlfriend and their daughter.

Claude, Marcel, and I walked then to Lissa's mother's home, where we had a rice and bean supper with her parents. There, I met Lissa and Marcel's two children, a boy of five and a girl of about three. Marcel explained that their children lived with Lissa's parents, but that they usually saw them every day. Lissa's parents, her children, and her brother, his wife, and child all lived in two tiny rooms connected to a patchwork warren of similar plaster shanties built behind the walls of an old manse near the center of town. When we arrived, the neighbor women who had been tending their cookpots on their doorsteps and the dozens of happy children playing in the dirt lane between them all crowded around to greet me.

Back at Marcel's house, several friends gathered in what appeared to be a regular Saturday night event. I asked Lissa if there were somewhere nearby where I could buy a beer, for I was very thirsty. (I did not say that I dared not drink the water from the well, it being so close to the latrine.) Lissa snapped her fingers and out from a dark corner came an urchin whom she sent out with my five-*gourde* note. I asked who the boy was. Marcel's son, she said. He was a *timoun-kay* (house boy), and although I knew that a Haitian man may require *timoun-kay* services of his illegitimate offspring, removing them from the mother's house to work for his legitimate wife, I had not come across one before. This little boy, who seemed to have no name, was totally meek and submissive, without smile or any spark in his eye. He fetched water, food, washed dishes, did any and all errands and services demanded by Lissa. Marcel, his father, appeared to ignore him. The boy seemed intelligent, but it seemed that all initiative had been beaten out of him. He slept on a straw mat on the floor under the table in the only shirt and pants he owned. Later, I slipped him some cookies I had brought with me. He glanced up and whispered, *"Méci."* His name, he told me in a whisper and in answer to my question, was Renauld.

When it came time to retire, Marcel and Lissa (actually at my insistence) slept on their bed, Renauld and I on rush mats on the floor. This was after bathing on the gallery while the men wandered in and out. They seemed to pay no attention to us, so I just proceeded. I used the last of the beer to brush my teeth. All shreds of my (false?) western modesty fled this weekend; given no real options, I simply observed my hosts' actions and did the same. Lissa and I dressed and undressed in the same room while Marcel conversed with friends. Seemed quite natural!

Church service on Sunday was interesting, if long: it lasted from 8:00 to 1:00. Mostly, it sounded to me like Bedlam. The congregants' individual prayers were shouted simultaneously. Four *professeurs*, two being Marcel and Claude, divided up the congregation and exhorted their sections, again simultaneously, on Ephesians. Over the yelling of the *professeurs,* constant oral response was required—all rendered at a shout.

The exhortation completed, a group of older women, all dressed completely in white, donned dark blue overseas caps and tied blue sashes embroidered with cryptic lettering across their chests. Stepping to the altar, they stood facing the congregation and, accompanied by a *tambou* (drum), sang in rousing harmony with Haitian beat. Their performance produced cries of accord from the congregation, as well as three "possessions"—a telling manifestation of the vestigial practice of Voodoo. I mused about this adherence to ancient African traditions. As far as I could tell, Marcel perceived no conflict between the message he so vehemently preached this Sunday and his own distinctly nonmonogamous personal life.

Marcel introduced me to the congregation. I was asked to say a few words, which somehow I managed to do in Creole. Marcel then spoke at length about me: why I was in Haiti, my children, my age—at which there was an audible intake of collective breath. I was then asked to sit on the altar with the elders, facing the congregation, for the last segment of the service, the hymns. I sang audibly, reading from a much-thumbed and moth-eaten French hymnal. I could see the congregation watching me. I think they were surprised I could read French. Although all of them proudly held hymnals, it is doubtful that many could read any language, much less music. But they knew the hymns and sang passionately.

There was a funeral that afternoon. Marcel was in charge of it. Lissa told me I would have to change my clothes if I wished to go with them. She said the red dress I was wearing would signify my responsibility for the death. So she and I dashed back to their house. She looked over the few other pieces of clothing I had brought with me and selected a white T-shirt and denim skirt as the most appropriate.

Another mad dash back to the mortuary, where a hired *tap-tap* already full of fifteen people, all dressed in their funereal best, was waiting for us. Scrunching ourselves in, we drove far out into the countryside, across the Artibonite River and over the coastal range of mountains, to a wide arable plateau. All this on gravel and dirt roads. The wheezing white Cadillac hearse preceded us. I conversed on the way with the grandson of the deceased, who sat next to me. He said he was a Baptist pastor with a Haitian congregation in Ft. Lauderdale, Florida. He returned to Haiti periodically because he had founded a small school in the village we were heading for. Marcel had once been a teacher in this school, he said, adding that he had been a very good one.

There were at least 150 people at the funeral in this very small village—I counted ten houses. A tarpaulin was propped between two of the houses, which were all cockeyed, one-room, daub-and-wattle structures with thatched roofs. Pallbearers placed the coffin out of the sun under the tarp. Marcel led the service and the singing, which was sadly melodic and syncopated. Cool soft drinks were served from a cement box filled with ice. The ice had been brought up from St. Marc with the deceased, and the container looked suspiciously like an animal watering trough. Everyone passed by the coffin to look at the body—although I didn't, because I, possibly the first white woman to have come to this village, had already caused enough of a sensation by just being there and was trying to remain inconspicuous in the background. This may have been a mistake, for I was quickly surrounded by a score of small boys, many of whom were stark naked. Why they were not involved in the funeral, I didn't know: perhaps they did not have appropriate clothes, or perhaps their clothes were being worn by immediate relatives participating in the funeral. The boys were intensely curious and somewhat afraid of this strange white woman in their midst. Several summoned courage to dart up to me, touch my arm, then bolt back beside their friends encircling me. They were precious, finally all smiles with white, white teeth and huge black eyes. They just stood there, smiling and staring.

The people of this isolated village at the foot of the mountains had a common appearance that was quite different from that of other Haitians I had known. The villagers tended to be very tall and thin, their faces long and narrow, their noses aquiline. Their skin was pure ebony, even the inside of their mouths and the palms of their hands. I wondered if they were descendants of slaves from East Africa, perhaps Sudan? Most of the slaves brought to Haiti by the French were from West African tribes, the Fon and Yoruba primarily. But, of course, slavery existed also in Africa, and Africans commonly sold to traders their own slaves that had been taken in battle.

These women were astounding, all dressed in their best funeral finery. Those who had come up from St. Marc wore silk-like polyester jacquard dresses of many colors—all colors except red and yellow. They wore black patent leather shoes and black Panama hats adorned with wired tulle flowers. Even the poorest women in Haiti have black Panama hats to wear at funerals.

With the hearse leading, everyone started off on foot across the fields to the dirt road leading to the cemetery in a larger village about ten kilometers away. This was primarily rice country. The fields were surrounded by irrigation berms and ditches. The hearse got hung up on its undercarriage on a narrow dirt bridge over one of the ditches. A dozen strong men threw their jackets on the ground and, with great effort, finally lifted it off, but considerable damage was done, as we were to discover later.

The *tap-tap* made a couple of trips between the village and the cemetery to transport the elderly. The driver wanted me to ride in the *tap-tap,* but since I was quite hale, even though elderly by Haitian standards, I felt it appropriate to walk with the other sturdy mourners. This also gave me an opportunity to talk with them. One young man became most attentive and appointed himself my escort, taking my arm to help me over the irrigation ditches. Much of his conversation concerned questions about life in the U.S. Of course, he wanted to go to the U.S. Just as we arrived at the cemetery, he asked if I would marry him so he could get there.

By the time we got to the cemetery, the walking women were exhausted; it was beastly hot and humid and their feet were killing them from their funeral shoes: cheap, high-heeled, black patent leather ones. I asked why they did not wear flat shoes, as I did. Because much *honneur,* they said, is thus paid to the dead. Dress is very important to Haitians.

Only the immediate family of the deceased entered the cemetery for the interment. The rest of us stood outside along the road, waiting and listening to the wails of the bereaved.

The sun had set by the time the interment was over. Some of the guests, most of whom were from St. Marc, but obviously originated in the village of the deceased, hailed passing *camions* to return to the city. Others returned in the hired *tap-tap* in which we had come. Marcel's little group, about fifteen of us, were to return in the hearse, the ancient white Cadillac, now empty of its coffin. But it wouldn't start! After much tinkering and discussion, the men decided it was the battery cable, but it was by now pitch dark and they couldn't see and, besides, they bemoaned, they had no tools. More discussion ensued. When I produced from my knapsack my flashlight and Swiss Army knife, there was great whooping and clapping. *"L'Américan gen tout ki nou bezwen!"* (The American has everything we need!) My offering was the main topic of conversation all the way home. The knife was painstakingly inspected by every passenger; each of its many tools was pulled out and retracted with awe.

However, the poor Cadillac was still severely damaged. At any speed faster than fifteen miles per hour, some rather frightening combustion trailed from the undercarriage. I confess I was more than a bit concerned. There were flames erupting, and it occurred to me that very likely the gas tank on this wreck had a hole or two in it. But hours later, we arrived safely in St. Marc. Depositing the ailing hearse outside the mortuary, we walked the mile or so back to the house.

The next morning I was to leave St. Marc. Several of Marcel's friends came by the house to say good-bye and to escort me to the bus stop. Once again, there was no room on the first bus, nor on the second. We waited for the third and were denied entry by the pushing, shoving horde vying for standing room. Then Marcel pointed to a window in the rear of the bus. There sat Claude, smiling broadly and beckoning me to come, *"vitvit, vitvit!"*, (come quickly!) Marcel passed my duffel through the window, then boosted me up. With Claude pulling and Marcel pushing, I made it through the window and Claude made it out the same way. There was barely time to reach out over several heads to shake Marcel's hand and utter a repeated *"Méci, méci, méci".*

"Revené anko," (come back again) they called to me as the bus chortled off.

As the bus sped back down *Route Nationale,* crammed three to a seat with no standing room left, I felt a glow of success. I knew then that I could handle anything that my future years might bring in this still strange but wonderful country.

Pamela Gullard

TOURIST ZONE

Marta and Derrin walked slowly over the blue cobblestones, the *adoquines,* of Fortaleza Street. Marta, an experienced traveler, was empty-handed, carrying not even a purse. Her few pieces of jewelry, bought on other vacations, were locked away at home in San Francisco. She had nothing for anyone to steal. It occurred to her that she didn't even have anything to give away.

She took Derrin's arm, moving with the slightly studied grace of a tall woman. The narrow streets of Old San Juan were a maze. Glowing teenaged girls swung past on stacked heels, their arms entwined with those of their lithe men. Marta thought that the tourists seemed like slow-moving blank sheets absorbing the blue of the streets and the heat and the lingering images of past armies trying to invade this Caribbean island.

Derrin and she passed a lace shop. Heat spilled from the roofs of the shops, and she felt squeezed between ancient buildings. She glanced at Derrin, her vacation buddy. He was balding well; his new sandals creaked. He'd been married twice. She was still married. Or was she?

The divorce papers had come in the mail three weeks earlier. With her mind paralyzed, Marta had signed away her long-dead marriage, walked quickly back to the mailbox, and stuffed in the return envelope. She hadn't lived with her husband in years and wondered why she felt faint. She'd immediately called Derrin and left a message on his machine saying she was ready for another vacation whenever he was.

She and Derrin lived apart and told themselves they couldn't bear being tied down like other people. They'd met as consultants working on a procedures manual for a South San Francisco insurance company that later went broke. They were technical nomads, and they formed the kind of tight, instant friendship that comes during late nights in basement cafeterias. At two o'clock one morning, Marta told Derrin, "You know, what I've always wanted to do is travel."

"Travel?" said Derrin. "Just what I need—someone to go with me." He took her hand. "Meet your travel agent." From then on, they would head for the airport whenever they'd saved enough for another trip. Mostly they went to hot places—Cancún, Rio, even Dallas. Derrin was the most lax of travel agents. He took Marta to their destinations without reservations or plans. He could find a vacant room at the peak of the tourist season, lunch during siesta. Their train abruptly stopped once beside a rocky goat pasture in southern Italy.

"Breakdown?" Marta asked anxiously, thinking of the surly residents in the last bleak town and wondering who would help them.

"Doubt it," Derrin yawned. "Probably a workers' strike," and he predicted, accurately, that it would be over in an hour.

Sometimes after Marta's trips with him, the heat would linger for a while. He would move into her narrow Russian Hill apartment with its attic bedroom. They would set the travel alarm to watch the sunrise and swim in the numbing cold of San Francisco Bay. But gradually the abandon of the last vacation would wear off. One or the other of them would get a new contract and start working killer hours. After a few days Derrin would repack his travel bag and go home to the condo in Pacifica he shared with two other guys.

The street opened to a dusty square of brown cobblestones. The fortress El Morro, which had stood firm for four hundred years, rose in the distance. Sea waves crashed against its twenty-foot-thick walls. Near El Morro's vaulted entrance was a van parked haphazardly in the dust. Black letters spelling *El Tatuaje* waved across its corrugated side. A thrill shivered across the skin of her stomach. Who would get a tattoo in a dirty van with pockmarks like bullet holes around the windows?

Marta thought of the shady street in Milwaukee where she'd grown up. She imagined her mother in the window of their brick house. Her mother would never have gotten a tattoo or even have known someone who had one.

Marta thought of her mother, Rosemary, as a fragile flower. A flower grafted to a woman. She had rarely left the house. She said she had everything she needed right where she was. Her breath was light and quick, as if she was scared to use up too much oxygen. Marta was in algebra class at Estabrook High when her mother stepped off the roof and died. Maybe that was why she always pictured her mother in motion—Rosemary falling, falling.

Marta glanced around the square. She was in San Juan. Derrin beside her. The grimy van ahead.

The idea of a tattoo instantly took hold of Marta. Derrin tugged her hand, but she seemed rooted in the dust. For a minute, she and Derrin stood awkwardly pulling at each other. He could finesse any situation, and she felt him looking at her, trying to find just the right joke to dispel her vacation stupor. He knew that strange cities brought eerie feelings that would disappear as soon as the town map began to make sense.

"Hey gringo," he said, "you lost?"

She nodded, but her mind was filled with thoughts of tattoos.

Derrin dropped the smile. "You OK?"

"Yes," she said promptly, meeting his eyes as proof. He wore a pink polo shirt and chinos with creases. He had a way of rolling his clothes in a backpack so they came out wrinkle-free in the dampest climates. For the first time, she realized how carefully he avoided the bereft look of a tourist.

She hooked a finger in his belt and they started to stroll again, crossing the middle of the square. A tattoo! Ink seeping beneath her skin. Had the tattoo artist drawn those lurching letters on the side of his van? Would he scratch ink over her bumps and imperfections? What would she have for a tattoo? Marta imagined moist green vines spreading riotously across her flesh, their tendrils searching the curves of her hipbones, the roots twisting around her thigh. How would it feel to have a grapevine coiling her waist, or a tree climbing her calf, or a flower, a flower grafted to her ankle?

The side door of the van swung open. A middle-aged, slightly stooped man appeared, the tattoo artist. Marta gave a start. Derrin looked at her, and a faint smile crossed his face.

The artist turned and watched a group of children flying kites on the grounds of the fortress. He leaned against the door with his hand clutching the roof of the van. His arm was a swirl of large-beaked birds and flying banners, but there, at his wrist, twined a single vicious flower.

How about a large heart on her back with *Mother* written inside, a sailor's tattoo? She touched Derrin's arm, but before she could speak he said, "No, you don't want a tattoo." Though his smile was still there, Marta thought she sensed a new gravity.

"How do you know?" Her voice sounded breathless.

"I like you just the way you are, no other decorations."

Was he vehement? Usually Derrin found a joke for everything. In Ixtapa, a two-foot chunk of ceiling fell next to her side of the bed, and Derrin woke, brushed concrete from her pillow, and said, "Now that's a bad dream," and went back to sleep.

"I need to do something," Marta said, "to celebrate my freedom." She waited a moment. "Michel's marrying someone he's known since childhood. I'm finally getting a divorce." Marta wondered if she'd known anyone since childhood. Most of her friends changed with her jobs.

Derrin said, "I didn't think you'd ever do it."

"Actually it was done a long time ago." She could hardly remember Michel's face. She'd torn up his photos years ago. She made herself brighten, but Derrin wasn't fooled and he drew her to him.

"Whenever I get a divorce," he said, "I feel like a failure for about a year."

Marta gave a little snort but felt better. "Thanks," she said. Derrin had a knack for soothing her. The night before, she'd wakened unsure of where she was, then had remembered—the Ramada Inn in the tourist zone. Derrin was beside her, snoring faintly. She counted his breaths to make herself sleep.

Now Marta lifted her chin and kissed his damp neck. "It's not that I feel like a failure exactly," she said. "I'm not anything. I've been careful." She put a hand on his chest. "I've kept working, kept going. But I don't know." She looked down at his huaraches, the leather still pink like young skin. "Ten years. What have I done? Nothing. I don't know, shouldn't I have gone to pieces, been addicted to something, made some kind of big mistake? Isn't that what people do who've had their hearts broken?"

Her heart felt too quiet. She'd married Michel when they were undergraduates at Berkeley. After six months, he said he'd made a mistake. "I just didn't realize marriage would be so"—he searched for the word—"constant. I feel you thinking about me all the time."

Marta squeezed her eyes shut. "Isn't that good?"

He shrugged, "Not for me."

He moved out and joined a fraternity known for serving specialty ales at parties. She called him every morning and left messages with his frat brothers. Then one day, she stopped trying to contact him. She didn't miss him, but now his official absence was like the swooping, weightless feeling of discovering one more step down than you'd anticipated.

Derrin was silent, studying her face. She wished he'd hug her again, but he stood with his hands at his sides. His eyes were clear, alert. He was the kind of traveler who took in details and could recount after a tour just exactly how a culture had changed. He said carefully, "With that damned Michel out of the way, you can marry me."

For a wild second, Marta thought he was serious. This was her friend Derrin, who called himself a reconfirmed bachelor. What did he want?

Triangular shadows crossed his eyes, making him seem hesitant. She couldn't marry him. She couldn't marry a man who spent every spare minute loping around the world, fitting chameleonlike into any society he entered. Oh, there, his face turned into full sun, erasing the questioning. Of course: a joke, part of their old lazy bantering to ease the way into a strange land. Marta smiled, relieved, feeling as if the desire for a tattoo had sharpened her life and summoned jokes that stung with a new kind of excitement. She laughed, "Well, why don't we just scare up a priest after breakfast tomorrow?"

"Good idea," he said, watching her.

The tattoo artist turned away from the kites and, looking straight at Marta, said in rounded English, "In or out?"

Her heart caught. His eyes were so black they seemed blind, yet he plied an art that didn't allow mistakes. Once laid down, the lines of his fantastic images couldn't be changed.

He clenched his fist, making the fierce flower at his wrist seem to bloom.

Derrin pulled at her arm. "You can't be serious. Defacing your body." His eyes were back in shadow, his eyebrows bunched. Had she ever seen him angry? Before, he seemed to accept any new custom.

She was amazed at his disgust. She said, "I need something permanent, something I can't get out of."

He ducked his head. "Think about it. Needles. The ink.
Please—you'll have it all your life."

All her life. Absurdly, Marta imagined her future as a large cartoon balloon. What was she saying in it? What was she thinking? What? She smiled at Derrin, nodded.

He waved a hand at the tattoo artist—a large, American gesture. "Not today," he said. "Just looking."

Marta and Derrin sat by the window of the International Café drinking Puerto Rican coffee and eating French toast heavily dusted with powdered sugar. Marta liked the bitterness of the coffee. She knew Derrin drank it only because he wouldn't be caught dead ordering *café americano.*

Outside, two men in white shorts, no shirts, brought a wheelbarrow to the base of a hotel palm. The shorter man pulled a foot-wide loop of rope from his pocket and slipped it over his bare feet. Almost magically, he climbed the palm, moving first his hands, then his trussed feet up the rough bark. He stopped, tossed a coconut to the man below. The man whacked the coconut open with an enormous machete.

"I've been thinking . . ." Marta said, turning to Derrin.

He looked up quickly. The hair at the sides of his head was still wet from his shower.

"I don't think I want to travel anymore," she said.

He bit a corner of crust. "I could tell."

"I didn't know myself until now."

He tapped his fork against the plate. "Why not travel?"

Marta thought he was going to say "with me," but he didn't. In the past, his restraint had seemed admirable, sophisticated. Now it just seemed tight. Maybe he was the one she needed to get away from.

"I want to stay home for a while, maybe start an herb garden." Go home with a tattoo, something that would make people take notice the way she had noticed the tattoo artist. What was he doing right now? Did he live in his van? A longing pierced her. What on earth was she thinking? That she wanted a man she didn't know?

Derrin had leaned back in the wooden chair. He said softly, "How about just one more trip? I was thinking of Tahiti."

Confusion rose through Marta. She didn't know what to say.

"I like traveling with you," he continued more urgently. "You used to be so enthusiastic about everything, I liked showing you."

"You'd like showing anybody."

"Don't be a fool. I want to marry you. I wasn't kidding yesterday." The embroidered collar of his Mexican shirt lay open at the throat. He touched his fingertips to the bridge of his nose, then picked up his fork again.

Marta felt the heat of the day moving in like fever. Her voice low, she said, "You don't love me."

His chin lowered into his palm, bringing out a small wrinkle at the edge of his lower lip. He'd used tanning lotion already and his face looked baby soft. Silence. Then, carefully, "So what? We like each other. I didn't like my other wives. I've thought a lot about this."

"Not enough!" she cried. The fan above was turning, turning. The couples at the scattered tables seemed to move in slow motion, eating, looking away from each other, drinking bitterness. She said to Derrin, "How could you think that so little would be enough for me? How could you?" But then, who wouldn't, looking at her life?

He formed the crusts into a perfect square and pushed the plate away. His fingers shook. "I miscalculated."

"Badly."

They said nothing. Then he looked up from the table. "You can't deny that we have a good thing going."

She nodded. "I wouldn't want to deny it." She wondered what hours the tattoo artist kept.

Derrin took a slow breath, looked out the window. The two men had their wheelbarrow filled with coconuts. Derrin said, "What if I do love you?" he said. "What if I just don't know it?"

The words felt like part of the heated air. Marta couldn't quite make sense of them. She said, "If we don't hear a tree, it doesn't fall."

A long pause. Derrin put his lips together, cocked his head. "Or something like that."

She matched his half-smile.

Then he sobered. "What would it take to prove I love you?"

Marta had always admired his skill at driving down a price, but now she knew how the poor women at markets felt as their profits dwindled. "You can't prove what isn't," she said. The warm air stirred. She touched Derrin's arm. He hesitated, then put his hand on hers.

Marta stood outside the van pretending to watch the squealing kids. She took a step, then back again, as if resisting a force. She felt a high singing in her head, and her thoughts were jumbled.

Derrin was back at the hotel, lying face down in his red Speedo on the small rectangle of beach behind the hotel bar. She told him she was going shopping. He said not to hurry, he was going to take a tour of the Bacardi factory later in the afternoon.

Abruptly, Marta moved forward and knocked on the van door. The sound was tinny.

The tattoo artist promptly appeared and said, "Come in." Marta followed him, feeling pulled into the darkness by a spicy smell—was it his aftershave, a disinfectant? She couldn't speak and he didn't seem to expect her to. He perched on a high stool next to an empty one, his hands on his knees. She stood with her hand on the green vinyl seat. She was here. She said, "What about AIDS?" Too quick, too nervous.

He smiled. His young-old face was free of tattoos.
Instead, concentric wrinkles eddied away from his eyes and mouth. "My needles are disposable. I'm careful. Either you trust me or you don't."

"I wish you hadn't said the last thing." Her new daring seemed to push her thoughts instantly into words.

The waves on his face deepened.

Her eyes became accustomed to the dimness. She saw a row of clear jars filled with cotton balls on the counter. Some of the balls were soaked in a yellow liquid. What looked like a handheld dentist's drill lay on a stand bolted to the floor, a foot pedal protruding from its side.

"I want one of those." She pointed to the flower on his wrist.

The body is the temple of the soul, Marta thought absurdly. Where did that come from? The Unitarian Church in Milwaukee. She'd gone there for a while after her mother's death. She'd made her father take her. But the services, free-form as they were, couldn't reach her swelling emptiness.

The tattoo artist shook his head. "There's only one of these, and it's on me. Pick again."

"Are you being funny?" she asked. "Why are you smiling?"

"Not funny." He sobered. "It's hard on you. On everyone. I smile to take away my nerves." A small catch of the breath. "How about a butterfly on your shoulder?"

Just like Derrin. Of course half a measure was enough for good old Marta. Was there a sign on her forehead? "No," she said, her voice too loud in the narrow space. "A serious tattoo, like that." She caught his wrist. She knew it would shock him to have her touch him. He was usually the aggressor, the one who left an imprint on the sweet and not-so-sweet.

He looked at her carefully. She saw herself in pink pleated pants. He said slowly, "You have to be a little crazy to want a tattoo."

"Or to give one."

He blinked. "You're the kind who causes trouble later."

"I never cause trouble," she said. She still had his wrist and he didn't pull away. "From the moment you saw me, you weren't going to give me a tattoo. You just like getting a rise out of people."

The man smiled again. He put her hand on her own chair. "I'll give you a miniature rose on the small of your back, like Joan Baez."

She had imagined that receiving the tattoo would be something like sex. It wasn't. She sat on the stool while the artist taped up her T-shirt and iced her back. He worked quickly, wordlessly. Each time the needle entered, a tiny ache bloomed just beneath her skin. The ache grew until she could barely stand it. Then it stopped and another ache began immediately. Despite the pain, she got bored. She'd expected a soaring feeling. Instead, she felt empty, used.

"Done," said the artist, handing her a round mirror with a plastic handle. He held an identical mirror at her back. They worked to get the angle right. Then she caught sight of the angry red and blue spot circling the last bump of her spine. A small hurting flower grafted to her back.

"Oh," she said.

"The swelling should go down in about a week." He spoke matter-of-factly. "You'll like it better when you get used to it. Don't think about it now." He looked tired.

"How do you know I don't like it?"

He shrugged. "It takes people a while to know what I've given them, as opposed to what they pictured."

Suddenly she needed to get out of that narrow, over-spiced room. "Here," she said, handing him a wad of bills in the amount they'd agreed on. She felt awkward. The ache at the small of her back made her uncomfortable.

"Thanks," he said. His eyelids were heavy. Would he go home and watch TV? Probably. Marta saw in the bored circles of his face that her dreams meant nothing to him. He'd used them as a mild diversion for the day.

She opened the door herself and stumbled out. The blinding light almost knocked her down. Shouts. A cry? The crowd of families on the green, the kites tangling, a Frisbee slammed between father and son.

Marta walked the wide dirt path to El Morro. There was no guide, and she wandered by herself from ancient pantry to dungeon to the top of the stairwell leading down, down, down to the sea. She didn't go down. Her spine seemed fragile, and she thought wildly that she wouldn't be able to climb back. She must keep walking.

The adobe wall to her right dropped away abruptly to a tangle of hibiscus, and she found herself outside the fortress, as if expelled. She didn't consider going back but rather walked the high street at the edge of the ocean. Low houses with sloping doors stood shoulder to shoulder. A neighborhood. Singing—or was it laughter?—wafted from a deep window.

The ache sunk into Marta's innards. She sat at the edge of a grass slope and pulled her T-shirt to the side. She twisted to see the rose. No. Not possible. She couldn't see it. Her back went cold around the heat of the tattoo. He should have told her she'd never be able to see it directly. Her very own permanent decoration and she couldn't see it. How symbolic! How fantastically stupid! She pounded the grass until the tears came. You poor motherless child, she thought, you poor little girl with no place to go.

The low sun sent shadows from the houses shooting into the sea, and the sound of waves seemed to surge. Marta stood up. Her knees and ankles were stiff. She walked down the hill toward the hotel. What next? she thought, feeling dark and giddy.

Derrin was waiting for her in their hotel room, lying under the sheet, his bare, sunburned chest bent toward the book he held on his knees. "Just the person I want to see," he said. He smiled but looked wan underneath the new tan.

She sat on the bed. He was her friend. His face seemed full and open after the tattoo artist. "Sick?" she said gently and patted his stomach. She didn't love him, would never marry him, but they had something. More than most.

"Better than ever," he said. He lay down his book. *History of Polynesia.* "I have a surprise for you."

The air conditioner whirred and dripped. Surprise? She didn't want any more surprises. She just wanted Derrin, the man who carried his home on his back wherever he went, like a snail.

He turned, lifted the sheet. On his bare hip, "Marta," laid over an angry red spot just like hers. She gasped. "What did you do?"

"I decided you were right. We're the kind of people who should take a plunge now and again."

"Me," she cried. "I meant me." A strange delight sang in her blood. He did this extravagant thing for her?

He took her hand and laid it on her name, which was warm. "Well, I was listening. I wanted to commemorate a once-in-a-lifetime friendship." The sunburn had caught certain angles of his body, and the soft muscles across his back seemed to ripple.

Friends, she thought.

There was a moment. Derrin took a breath. "So now you have to marry me," he said quickly. "You're free and I'm tattooed."

Oh no. Never. She looked into his face. The little crease below his lip had become permanent. When had that happened? A nerve tugged at his cheek. She had to answer. The sheet smelled faintly of mildew. Beyond the folded black-out curtains, the ocean churned.

She nodded yes. She'd tell him the truth later. He turned back and held her head against his chest. "I've never done anything like this before. I've been afraid. This is my first brave thing. Only brave thing. You've given me back my life."

She remembered Michel's face. The heavy, dark eyebrows, the delicate bones beneath his cheeks. Now, she understood how he felt when he left her. He didn't love her. The pain he caused her was coincidental.

Marta lifted herself away from Derrin. He watched, his pale eyes wide. "I can't do this," she said.

"Don't say it." He spoke carefully. He'd anticipated her change of heart. "Not yet."

Not yet, she thought. She didn't have to make a move yet. Derrin was asking for time, the one thing she had. The sadness in the room grew until Marta could no longer bear it. Then it backed off.

Derrin moved his legs to the side of the bed, found his shorts on the floor and pulled them on. Two stars had appeared past the salt-spattered glass.

"I got a rose at the small of my back," Marta said quietly.

He gave a short laugh. "May I see?"

He lifted her shirt gently. "Hurts like hell, doesn't it?"

She nodded. His hand on her hip was warm.

He said, "You must be tired. I had a nap as soon as I got back from mine."

"No, not tired," she said. "Yes. Exhausted."

"Here." She sat on the bed, her back against the mounded pillow. He took her bare foot in his hands and began to knead the arch as he so often did after their long walks through streets.

Marta pictured going home. Maybe she'd explore San Francisco as a tourist. Learn its history, its special places. "So when are you going to Tahiti?" she asked.

"Soon," he said. "Maybe next month." His warm hands seemed to mold the bones of her foot.

"I'll meet your plane when you get back."

He stopped his movements. "No one ever meets my plane," he said, his eyes shining in the last light of the day.

She handed him a pillow to lean on, thinking that someone outside the window might take them for an old couple, comforting each other. "You can tell me your adventures," she said, "and I'll tell you mine."

ASIA AND AUSTRALIA

Leslie Brody

KYOTO

(The Lover, The Priest, and The Hostess)

The Lover

She never spoke to him, but she'd stare across the room at his table with the confidence of a long-time associate. She was by no means a religious woman, but whenever she looked at him she saw sacred contours. His body was hidden beneath the robes of his profession, but his head above and bare feet below were just enough flesh to titillate. His head was smooth and closely shaven. His robes gave the impression of a body constantly drifting. When she looked at him she craved him and imagined him wanting *her* more ambitiously than Buddha-hood. She imagined him wanting to make love to her more than she wanted him to. And she dwelt upon the act with the ferocity of a woman defending children she already possessed. She dreamed of him. Midnights she stalked the perimeters of the temple grounds mumbling her desires to the goldfish in the cultivated ponds.

The Priest

He was not eager to make love to her. For weeks he had seen her staring at him in an attitude he described in his journal as *mad*. It would be debilitating. It was forbidden. He didn't know her. Thinking about her caused him further obstacles to detachment. He was a talented young man, as determined to achieve enlightenment as she was to achieve union with him. He suspected as much given the unusual circumstances, but could not, for reasons he never understood, stop seeing her. He continued going weekly to the same place at the same time.

The Hostess

I work in this bar. There are thousands of American women like me working in bars like this one all over Japan. I make good money. If you don't have the patience to teach English and you're attractive, it's not hard to find a job. I'd only been here a month before Mama-san pointed out to me how these two would come in every week on the same night, Tuesday, sit at the same table on different sides of the room, and practically drool over each other. I began watching them closely.

The Lover was intent upon seduction. Upon her had fallen a critical legacy she didn't understand. She was connected to all the other inheritors by a thread that had at its point an arrow. To be infected was to suspend all natural life. The heart from the moment of impact becomes inexhaustible. The victim (she in this instance) would either succumb or die. History is weighted down with the stories of sacrificed lovers, and she was bound to them all.

The Priest had a daily routine that included nourishment, hard work, meditation, and a little sleep. He had an enormous appetite for western poetry. While the others slept, he would pull from beneath his futon a volume of Ginsberg, Neruda, or Baudelaire. Each night he would read and reread the poems, then, for an hour or two, write his own in a student's notebook. By day he was a healthy young man working in the temple garden or studying the *Sutras.* At night, cradling his books, he knew himself susceptible to a gigantic passion. He feared nights and meditated more strenuously in an effort to escape. He had a few hours during the week in which to do what he wished. Tuesday night he would go to the bar and she would be there.

I don't know what she did in the day. She was an American, too. I'm sure she had been here for years. She always wore a kimono and would never answer when I spoke in English to her. She talked in Japanese with the other hostesses. They thought she was very peculiar—eccentric they said at first, when they were still being kind. This isn't the sort of bar in which women sit alone, and it was unusual seeing her here. His life was more predictable. He was in some kind of monastery where all they do is work and pray. Priests don't come to our bar, either. Whenever any of the hostesses would go round to sit with him (which is what we're paid to do) he'd very politely ask them to leave him alone. One other thing—they both carried these notebooks, which is something I noticed immediately because I always carry one too.

The Lover sat at the table every week with her notebook and one glass of whiskey, composing fervently incoherent letters for him: "Dear Priest, Remember your concubine." She never considered marriage. Once she'd followed him to find out in which monastery he lived. She'd worn tennis sneakers to mask the echo of her steps on the Kyoto streets, and hidden in doorways pretending to herself he suspected something. But he never turned or stopped the whole length of his walk.

The Priest had imagined her following him once and taken an extraordinarily long way home, savoring her company. He composed himself and refused to turn in order to verify his suspicions. He didn't understand why she had chosen him or why he encouraged her. It had been a soft night, and he led her by his favorite gardens and temples. When he arrived at his monastery, it was nearly time for the other priests to wake and pray.

Now a month had passed since I'd begun watching them. Four Tuesdays passed, and I wanted something to happen. They'd both looked pasty and a little out of control last week. I wanted to be in on it if anything broke. This silent love affair of theirs was driving me crazy. I wanted to introduce them but Mama-san wouldn't let me. She and the other Japanese hostesses (there were two) really loved the intrigue. They thought it was a great joke, the American woman and the priest. They asked me if I thought he was handsome. And when I said, "He's bald, bald men don't turn me on," they said I was young and stupid, and their shoulders shook with laughter. Mama-san told me she was sure something was going on between the two of them outside. I wasn't at all convinced of that—but one night at closing time when I saw her hurrying after him, I decided to follow and see what happened. He was about a hundred yards ahead, and she was trailing him in tennis sneakers, poking in and out of doorways as if she expected him to turn and she didn't want him to see her. I kept myself out of sight as well as I could, but I don't think she ever knew I was behind her. We walked for an hour or so all over the city and neither of them turned once. I turned. If she was following him, and I was following her, it was a good bet that someone was behind me, but there wasn't. After leading us the longest possible route, he eventually wound up back at his monastery and went through the gate. She stuck it out a while, and I waited too, but he didn't come out again. It was almost dawn.

The nights were getting hotter. She began to wear kimonos so thin he could see her body beneath if he would only look. Strange men stopped her on the street and tried to touch her nearly naked breasts. Regardless of how thin her clothes were she was never cool. She believed generations of *succubi* boiled in her—their desires saturating her life. Sleep relieved nothing, her dreams were feverish. Covering her bed with winter quilts, she would slowly bring herself to climax thinking that his body was the burning climate, that nothing could move the heat of his body from her the way the blankets might be shifted aside.

In the beginning he had looked up at her occasionally. Weeks passed, and though he continued to come to the bar, he refused to allow her a full-face view. He kept his face down when he entered, but when he sat, and when he'd rise to leave, he'd steal a glimpse of her. She was always staring and never smiled. She was thinner, more radiant now than she'd ever been. She resembled someone he'd seen in Tokyo when he'd been a student there.

I guess she was attractive when she began coming into the bar, but now she was skinny and pale. She had enormous brown eyes and bushy eyebrows that made the hostesses laugh at her behind the counter. They were all still interested in the romance but accepted its lack of movement far more than I did. She started coming in looking more and more haggard, and dirtier. She neglected washing herself and smelled of heavy perspiration. He was always so immaculate, and I worried that she'd lose some ground if she didn't clean up a little. I considered speaking to her about it, but never did. I told myself that I didn't know enough Japanese to get the point across politely.

It was the middle of summer. Kyoto was pestered by mosquitoes. Each bite she received was a reminder of what she had not done. She was losing herself, and the others were taking over. They wrote in her journal and passed the days waiting for Tuesday. She forgot to eat and watched them ordering and eating her meals for her. They needed the strength to finish their job. She spent more and more time in bed composing postures for the two of them. Perhaps he would rub his shaven head between her legs, and the friction of short hairs would send her legs swinging wildly off the edge of the bed, the world. Perhaps.

The Priest's *roshi* spoke to him, "Something's the matter with you. Can you tell me?" He couldn't explain. He'd sit down in the garden midway through the day. He left a book of poetry out one morning and it disappeared. No one mentioned finding it. The *roshi* suggested he meditate more and do less work if he were ill. He said he couldn't accept privileged treatment. The final Tuesday in August he decided not to go to the bar. He felt tremendous relief having made his decision and stayed in, speaking normally with his friends. He went to bed at the same time as the other priests, but when he saw they were asleep he dressed himself and went to meet her.

It was the last Tuesday in August. I know exactly because it had to be Tuesday if they were there, and it was my final week working in the bar. She came in early that night and sat down as always with her glass and notebook. She looked terrible, like she'd been living in the street or something. She didn't even have the money to pay for her drink. Mama-san was going to kick her out, but I sprang for the whiskey and asked Mama-san to let her stay for this last night. The hostesses were irritated by her presence. She was dirty and smelled, and they said, "This isn't good for business," one after another. The place was empty that night, and they blamed it on her. The priest didn't come in at the time he usually does. After a while we thought he might not come in at all. The hostesses giggled about her abandonment behind the counter. I felt angry with him for standing her up in her condition. He finally arrived near to closing time, and head down as always, he sat down.

She stood up at her table and walked past him in order to allow him to see her body in its almost transparent cover. Although she'd become very thin, her breasts and hips had remained rounded, shaped by the desires of the others. Settling in her limbs the phantoms walked for her and brushed the side of his table with her hand.

The Priest looked at his hands, dark from working in the garden all summer. Hearing her begin to walk towards his table, he was afraid she would grab his throat and cut it. He put a brown hand to his throat.

I saw her stand and stare at all of us. She looked lost for a minute, then, composing her face, walked like a princess to a beheading. Mama-san covered her own mouth—I don't know if she intended to laugh or scream. It was an exciting moment. I was glad they were going to do something before I left this place for good. They looked like two ghouls. I'd become really attracted to them somehow. The woman walked straight ahead not even looking at the priest. It was strange, there were six or seven tables between them in the small room, and she touched each as she passed it, like a blind woman who has memorized the way. When she reached his table she brushed the edge of it with her hand, then continued walking past him out the door. He looked vacant and terrified, watching her in a way I'd never seen him watch her before. His hand jerked up and with an effort fell back on the table again. We all thought he would run out after her, but he didn't.

She was no longer herself. She was a love that had murdered others. She didn't want to kill him. She wanted him to make love to her. She stood in the doorway of the bar breathing deeply. She felt like someone was following her. She didn't know what she was doing outside or what it was she had to do that evening. She remembered there was something important. She felt like she'd been running. There was no one coming after her on either side of the doorway. She thought she could fly, and, spreading her arms, ran away from the bar.

The Priest was not going to follow her. Beads of sweat had broken out above his lip. He sat holding his hands together on top of the table, trying to concentrate, "They're brown, they're brown." One hand would fly up of its own accord if not held down by the other. She had been more beautiful than any other woman he'd ever seen in her thin robe passing his table. Her butterfly eyebrows—he had never seen a woman with eyes as luxurious as hers. He felt spasms in his face and no thought was powerful enough to hold him to that spot. He rose to follow her. There was no reason for them to be apart.

I was wearing a long dress that night. It was some sheer material that our customers like to see their hostesses dressed in. It's not what I normally wear, but nothing about this bar is normal, in the normal sense of the word. It was a long and pleated dress that a previous hostess had left behind with Mama-san when she'd quit the work. Wearing it made me feel like a fairy at a midsummer's pageant. I usually change clothes before leaving work, but seeing the priest run like that, I just followed. I ran outside after them, my flimsy gown wafting up like vestigial wings around me. Mama-san shouted something that I couldn't understand, and I kept going. *He* was already at the end of the street, and I couldn't see *her* at all. I followed him, but a crowd of jubilant drunkards blocked my way. They were emerging from bars all down the street and wanted me to join their closing time party. By the time I'd struggled out, he'd disappeared. I felt guilty. I wanted them back. Weeks ago, Mama-san had asked me, "What's your interest really? Do you want to watch them make love? Do you want to make love with them?" I hadn't bothered to answer her. The other hostesses had giggled behind the counter.

Later, Another Bar in Kyoto

She never spoke to him, but she'd stare across the room at his table with the confidence of a long-time associate.

Leza Lowitz

INNOCENCE

The huge black crow on the balcony of the thirty-sixth floor of the Keio Plaza Hotel was saying something to her in the fading afternoon sunlight through the rain. She had just surfaced from the crowded Shinjuku underpass, which had been as silent as an underwater tunnel, and now this. Ten years earlier, a famous movie star had jumped from the balcony just before evening rush hour on his thirty-second birthday. Now the lone black crow perched on the ledge and cawed into the sky above the din of construction. What was it saying? She was trying to make it out when a man in a dark suit careened into her and mumbled gruffly, deliberately blocking her passage with his briefcase. *Sumimasen,* she said softly, bowing. Walking in Tokyo required concentration; looking for the open spaces in a land where space was scarce and openness was not a quality to be admired. She walked on into the thick air of power of the world she did not belong to, and steeled herself against the crowds. She was realizing more and more that she did not *have* to belong.

The suicide had been a popular TV actor who had played macho roles, and who in real life had kept a male lover many years his junior. His suicide note spoke of his love of Mishima and said, "Father, I will wait for you in Nirvana." She wondered if Inoguchi knew of the actor or the suicide, but he would have been a child at the time, and she doubted he had paid much attention to the incident. As for her, it was her job to be aware of things like that, so she knew. She wanted to know everything, all the time. She knew one thing for sure, that Inoguchi would be waiting for her.

She'd been in Tokyo three years and was still fascinated by how things worked. Effortlessly, yes, but somehow heartlessly. Then, sometimes she'd get the feeling there was a whole world underneath, like when the cherry blossoms were falling from the trees and the drunken revelers sat half-singing, half-crying on their cardboard boxes underneath the fading beauty, or when the crows started to caw their hysterical blind cries as if from a graveyard and no one else seemed to hear them, or when someone bumped into her and she liked the combat. It wasn't life they were celebrating; it was more like people determined to be cheerful at a wake. No, it was the pain of loss. Ever since they'd lost the war. That's what the line was, anyway, but the young people didn't buy it anymore. They no longer needed a reason.

There was a small wooden house wedged between the highrises, maybe a hundred years old. The rain traveled down the small copper chains that hung from the corners of the house to catch the rain and train it down to fall in cups shaped like lotus flowers. Even nature could be tamed. But it could transcend its course and mesmerize.

The wind whipped around between the glimmering chrome and glass towers, sending spirals of paper and cigarette butts spinning in small cyclones at her feet. It had a cold beauty to it, this city, and all the sharp edges made it all the more electric for its having rebuffed the ones who tried to get close to it. In that, it was almost human. And the people still kept trying.

She knew this because there was always some new building going up in Tokyo, even with land prices soaring and the economy in the dumps. This time it was the city hall complex, whose mirrored walls and marble bathtubs would make Gotham City look like some quaint fin-de-siècle charterhouse. They were working all day and all night, these men without shirts, their brown bodies sweating in beads down to their purple and blue jodhpurs with knee-high black *jikatabi,* soft socks with rubber bottoms they wore as shoes. She liked the fact that they would meet the earth's hardness with such softness, while the men who built her country usually wore hard hats, padded coats, and steel-toed boots. The contradiction appealed to her.

When she passed the soft yellow lights strung along the overpass, they seemed to her like lanterns of a boat lost at sea, and she was mesmerized by the men who lived their lives in the darkness, digging at the earth, carving out yet another place for progress, somewhere, somehow. If they could find room for another new building in Tokyo, there was room for anything. Even for her.

She smoothed her pants as the doors to the hotel's lobby opened noiselessly in front of her. To her left, a man in a blue suit entered and exited the revolving door within half an inch of the glass—displaying the precision of a master sushi chef slicing open a fish so that its heart still beat on the plate; alive but no longer living.

She wondered if the actor, Inoguchi, minded her being late as she took the elevator up to the fifth floor, which was really the fourth floor. Here, elevators did not list the fourth floor because *shi,* which meant "four" also meant "death." It was unlucky to have an elevator stop for death, so they just renamed it. It did not, therefore, exist.

She bowed again, this time to the receptionist, who cupped her hand over her mouth as she giggled and waved the *gaijin,* the foreigner, in. The girls at the reception desk always giggled when they saw her, because they didn't know who she was, but they figured she must be *someone* because she got to be in a room twice a week with a famous movie star, who, though happily married, had a thing for her so strong you could sense it—like the first rumbling of an earthquake when you're not quite aware what's happening but you know that something is *off,* something's about to go down. So they sat a little straighter, waited a little more intently, felt a little more alive, valued those minutes all the more. Then, they laughed.

Besides, she didn't seem to care what anyone thought of her. Then there was the fact that her English student followed her around like a schoolboy and even carried her bags when they left together (where did they go?), that was something not many Japanese men did for anyone, especially famous and handsome men like Inoguchi Masao—who didn't have to. But maybe he was just being polite.

When she got to the room, she closed the door behind her, glancing over her shoulder at the girls who quickly turned away, blushing. Inoguchi was studying the script, circling the difficult words with a cartographer's precision, and tapping his foot under the table to the beat of some imaginary linguistic drill pounding the proper accent and syllables into his brain.

"Hi," he said shyly.

"Sorry to be late."

"No problem. I got some time to practice."

She smiled wanly. It was hopeless. It always was. It wasn't that she thought one couldn't learn a foreign language at an advanced age—she thought one could. But that wasn't the reason all the housewives and middle-aged men studied English. They wanted to learn "American." But what was that, anyway? It was hard not to remind them of their failures. Of course, she couldn't help but think of hers.

Learning English, she decided, was a lot like learning to love. One only really felt love's power when it was hopeless.

There were two bottles of Perrier on the *hinoki* table and two cups of coffee in Wedgwood cups getting cold. The tape recorder was red-light ready for action, and a small electric heater radiated warmth from the corner. Inoguchi always brought the water, one for each of them. One must be a magic potion, the other poison, she thought. At any given time she could take the wrong one. . . .

In the conference room next door she could hear the faint applause following the rambling speeches of promoters and businessmen toasting the start of the World Boxing Association Championships, which were to open at the Tokyo Dome, the egg-shaped stadium in the heart of the city, next week.

Everyone, including Inoguchi, had their eyes on Owada, a young welterweight whose time was said to have come but whose irascibility and lack of discipline could get the better of him when it always seemed to matter the most. His father had died a mysterious death about a year ago, and he had been unpredictable ever since. He was scheduled to fight some rich pretty boy with a glass jaw and a body to die for, a fighter whose name no one knew, but it didn't seem to matter at all as far as the purse was concerned. The bets were on. And since they were fighting in Japan, he would undoubtedly win if it were a points decision.

Owada was all over the place—vitamin drink commercials, charity sports meets, government fundraisers. She had seen him fight and had felt that tinge in the bottom of her stomach. He had something. To her, what made Owada exciting in the ring was not the lesser chance that he'd pull through—that was what everyone banked on—but the fact that he might get cocky and really blow it. Being a hundred percent hard-boiled loser was easy, but playing the hard-knocks underdog required a particular kind of tenacity and guesswork, a special kind of psychology that kept your fans wanting you to win even when they knew in their hearts you'd probably let them down again. Owada, like any good underdog, had it both ways. The fans enjoyed it when he did lose, they felt they got their money's worth anyway and were ready to bet on him again just to prove their own capacity of judgment. They'd say, "he had a bad night." Anyway, losing was noble if you'd tried your best. Trying your best was an art form in Japan. They even had a verb for it. *Ganbattte.* Go for it. It was untranslatable, but it was a word heard far more often than *sayonara,* at least in her world.

She saw her reflection in the shiny wood table and ran her hand across the surface to distract herself. Inoguchi's head jerked back slightly. He'd been looking at her.

The Japanese used *hinoki* for the *Noh* stage, but this was no stage, only work, and when she looked at his shoulders, strong from years of professional baseball, swimming, and, now, martial arts, she began to reconsider. She was lonely, in the way that a lifeguard at the beach could feel his isolation. His presence was required, but not needed. So was hers.

Inoguchi wore a black cotton turtleneck and smooth wool Yohji Yamamoto pants in a deep, army green. She threw her bag on the table, pulled out the script, and sat down in the swivel chair without blinking an eye.

His watch was on the table, flat, face up, a gold, Tag Heuer diver's watch with an inscription on the inside thanking him for his fine work in a film about the *yakuza* from a famous American director. He had shown it to her the night they met, when a friend of hers had given her the job, and she had taken it not knowing the first thing about acting or how to be a vocal coach, but only wanting to be in the hub of things, where something might happen. So here she was. But nothing was happening.

"How are you?" he asked in practiced English, looking not at her eyes or her briefcase nor even the script but directly at her lips, if just to see them break out in a smile at him, at something he said.

She smiled slowly and said, "Not too bad."

Her friend Martin was a professional *gaijin,* a foreigner who made a living being a foreigner. Martin had told Inoguchi to watch out for her, how she had some sort of mysterious power over everyone. The truth was, the most dangerous thing about her was that she was purely herself. There wasn't anything mysterious about it, she was just in the right place at the right time. Things happened around her despite how she felt about it. As far as she was concerned, acting natural was still acting. So the Buddhist idea of killing the self, of total selflessness, appealed to her.

Two years after her arrival at Narita, she was asked to teach English composition at Waseda University. If she accepted, she would be the youngest on the faculty, the only foreign woman in the department. Knowing she was out of her league, that her Japanese students probably had a better handle on grammar and sentence structure than she ever would, she had tried to refuse, but that only made them ask her more fervently. No one refused a job there. Finally, so her friend who recommended her wouldn't lose face, she accepted. And her worst fears had come true. She had no business being there at all, walking swiftly down the hallowed halls from which would-be students committed suicide when they failed the entrance exams. She had thought those reports were exaggerated. Now she knew for sure. But still, she taught English like everyone else, attempted to pull the clam-like students out of their shells. She rarely succeeded, but she tried her best.

Martin told Inoguchi he was sure that if she'd had to take the same exams, she, too, would have taken a sword to her belly—if anyone did that anymore (they did not). Still, somehow she had gotten the job, been at the right place at the right time. She could just as easily end up on the street, a place she'd certainly been before.

Inoguchi had said that she must be quite modest.

The truth was, everyone said it was going to be hard as hell to be a foreign woman in Japan, but she hadn't found it that way at all, because she had met that hardness, countered its force with her own. Besides, she knew how to hide her strength and no one knew what to make of her so they gave her anything she wanted, if only to get rid of her.

Many Japanese still thought all the *gaijin* in Japan were just bit actors in an incredibly complicated film. As far as she was concerned, she could play any part they wanted and never lose herself, because her self was not to be found in appearances.

They got down to it.

"You move well," she said, smiling her Mona Lisa smile because this line, like all the others, was dumb and she knew it, and he knew she knew it, and there was nothing either of them could do about it but smile.

"I never danced so close to someone before."

"*Dan-ced,"* she said, slowly and with a hard accent on the *n*.

"Danced," he repeated. "Danced."

"Once more?" she said encouragingly.

"I never danced so close to someone before," he said steadily, deliberately, an edge of annoyance in his voice.

"Excellent. Do you like it?"

"It's perfect. It seems like something I've always done, ever since . . ."

"What?"

"I can't tell you. Yet."

"I'll be waiting," came the coy reply.

They read for awhile, came to the part where they slept together. He still didn't know who the leading lady would be. A *gaijin* for sure, blonde. Willowy. Maybe of a certain age, like him. Michelle Pfeiffer, or Melanie Griffith, or Jessica Lange. What's her name? Meg Ryan would be good.

Had he ever kissed a foreign woman? she wondered. He was studying her lips as she sounded out the words. It was a kind of ritual, him looking at her lips moving slowly, she watching him watching her.

"What's wrong?"

"I feel so awful for what I have done. I should not have taken advantage of you like that. It is completely unforgivable. How can I make it up to you?" He said this last line painstakingly slowly.

She rocked back in her chair, folded her arms across her chest and wondered what he would say after he had made love to a woman—foreign or not.

"No . . . please . . ."

Suddenly, he broke character.

"Maybe in the *Meiji* era men talked like that. Maybe they even thought like that! My grandfather might even have said something like that. He might have even felt that way. But not me. How ridiculous," he scoffed at the script in front of them.

But she read on.

"What century are you from? I don't know how the women are where you come from, but around here it doesn't work like that anymore. I made my choice last night, just like you did. Don't be so chauvinistic."

Whoever was writing these scripts knew nothing about the Japanese, she agreed. It would probably be a big hit . . . Hell, many Japanese didn't even understand the Japanese. But who understood America, either? There were as many different Americas as there were Japans.

"You think this is dumb, don't you?" he asked, putting his hands behind his head and stretching backwards, pushing gravity, feeling her eyes on him and liking the focus it gave him.

"Yeah, it's the worst script I've ever read."

And then, when she laughed he laughed too, because she was honest, and honesty was a valuable commodity in a world of appearances, and he liked it. Besides, they both knew it was themselves they were reading about. They mocked those shadows because they felt superior to the stock lines and awkward apologies. They thought they would both handle it differently.

"Better get them to change the script," he said, his eyes on hers just a bit too long.

"Let's go on," she said, meeting his gaze.

"I can't explain how I feel about you."

She looked down at the page, but the lines were not there. She looked up at him, puzzled. He smiled.

"Explain," she said.

"Explain," he repeated in an exact echo of her accent, tone and pitch, moving his mouth in perfect approximation of hers. She wondered when the film came out if he would sound like some radical Berkeley hippie or techno-punk co-ed, a wry cynicism wreaking havoc with his proper *nihonjin* manners.

"Tell me if I'm doing it right."

"You are," she said.

He took a sip of his Perrier, cleared his throat, and repeated the line that was not the line.

"Say it in a whisper," she said, and he did, brushing her leg lightly under the table with his knee. Then he held his knee against hers.

She opened her water, swigged it out of the bottle. She shifted in her chair, got some height, and moved her legs, turning strict.

"Let's go."

"Is this what foreigners think Japanese people talk like?"

"*Some* foreigners."

"But not you?"

"Don't think so. I don't know yet."

He had a two-year-old son.

She was thinking about that. She wondered if the boy had ever seen a foreigner, if he would cry at the sight of her eyes.

"I'm not telling you everything. I can't tell you what's going on yet. I guess I should just leave now. And we can forget that anything ever happened between us."

Inoguchi put the script down.

"I need a break."

She said nothing, nodded, pushed the script aside, and leaned back in her chair. He leaned forward, and she could smell his clean clothes, neatly laundered and folded with care. That smell comforted her because it was the smell of domesticity and balance, something she'd not had too much experience with in life.

"Come to Okinawa with me," he said suddenly, looking down.

"Okinawa?"

"Yes. Have you ever been?"

"No."

"I'm going next week. With Shizo Yamasuke."

"Yamasuke Shizo? I can't believe it."

"Yes. We are doing a play. Come see it."

Shizo was the famous Kabuki actor, an *onnagata* whose portrayal of women was more feminine and graceful than the real thing. It was said that Shizo captured the essence of femininity better than any other *onnagata* in Kabuki history, and of course, better than a real woman herself.

She was interested, thought she could learn something from his distillations of walk, gait, gesture, expression. The more artificial you looked, the more real you seemed to others, she realized. The artifice was the art, the beauty of it, like a Japanese garden.

She had heard that Shizo made it seem as if he had entered the spirit of femininity and became it, transcended his own gender with that first strike of the bamboo flutes, the curtain rising and the shouts from the third floor flooding the stage, "Shizo! Shizo! Shizo!"

"You can come down and check my English," he offered when she did not respond. She knew that he did not need her to come down to Osaka to check his English.

"How long will you be there?" she asked ambiguously.

"A week."

"I cannot," she said automatically, and then she cursed her impetuousness. Of course she could.

"You will see the show we are doing. We will have dinner. You don't have to stay the week. . . . Just one night."

"One night?"

"You can stay at the Imperial. Unless you have some objection. . . ."

Objection? The truth was, she was totally free to do whatever she wanted with whoever she chose. She had been engaged to be married to a rising young professor, but one day she just woke up and knew she did not want to be an "academic wife." She thought what was the point of all those words and books and plans when what was happening was outside the mind, in the body, and the guts—all those places the modern world had covered up so coldly in circuitry and silicon and high-definition TV screens. She wanted to lose herself, remembering that someone once said, "To be lost in Tokyo is better than to be found anywhere else." She agreed. She wanted to be so totally lost that she didn't even know it. So one day she moved into an abandoned, dilapidated house, a house with two four-and-a-half tatami-mat rooms downtown. The owner had probably died and left it to his children, who didn't tear it down because they couldn't afford the land taxes of building a new structure on it. So it just stood there, and rotted.

She moved in, mended the roof, scrubbed the floors. There was no bathroom, so she went to the public bath. But she liked the public baths. You met people there. Old people. Young people. Anyone.

What mattered was that she was on her own after six years, and it was delicious, that freedom.

This way, she could live within the circle of the Yamanote, the green train that ran around the city like a garter snake. If she lived outside the line, in the landfill, she'd be stuck in packed commuter cars with stale-breathed *sararimen* who felt her up in the morning rush hour and looked innocently into the centimeter of space between their bodies as if that distance alone would absolve them of any responsibility. But it did not.

"The Imperial?" she asked. The rooms were at least four hundred dollars a night.

"You can go back to Tokyo the next morning."

This last, a statement that required only an acknowledgment. She wanted to say yes, but what was holding her back? Some ridiculous moral standard she'd never believed in but upheld because in her world it was morally better to be righteous and then talk about the temptation as something you had conquered, bettered. . . . Yes, it was morally better to be righteous, she thought, but it sure wasn't as interesting.

"But. Your wife . . ."

"My wife?" His eyes widened. "Oh, she will be coming down to join us after a few days. Of course, with my son."

Thus relieved of any lascivious intentions, she agreed.

"Thank you," he said and smiled innocently, but deceptively. It was like a Japanese bath that's been sitting for a while so that when you first get in the surface is hot and you think the rest will be too, but the water all around the center is cold.

"I will send you the ticket."

"Thank you."

"And if you'd like to go to the match, we can go see Owada beat that pretty boy."

"I'd like that," she said.

She looked at his watch on the table. They still had an hour left. She took a breath.

"Okay, back to the script. From the top," she said.

They continued to read and stop, read and stop, for the next hour, not looking up until the receptionist tapped the frosted glass door and brought them hot towels to wipe their hands and faces with before they left.

When they walked out into the street, she asked Inoguchi if he knew of Shimada Yuji, the actor who had jumped off the thirty-second floor.

He said he didn't, so she told him the story.

"Times are different."

They said good-bye at the station, and when she walked home she let the rain fall down upon her and didn't feel a drop of it, not at all. It was then that she heard what the crow was saying: *Now. Now. Now.*

The next day the ticket to Osaka came, and the day after that, she went. Taking a taxi from the airport, the taxi driver guessed that she was

Russian. No one ever knew where she was from, and she liked it. He said he imported vodka, but only drank Japanese *sake.* Didn't want to pollute his tastebuds.

At the hotel's lobby, a woman in gilded kimono played the *koto* on a raised platform, her head bowed in concentration. The music's sharp twangs made her feel something of the primitive, something of what the Japanese islands had once been.

Inoguchi was waiting in the lounge, drinking orange juice from a Brandy snifter. Rehearsal would begin soon.

The play was about a woman who had fallen in love with two men—one a frail intellectual, one a heartless, virile brute. Together they made the perfect man. The story was an old one by now.

When the evening's performance began, the audience rose to its feet and cheered the actors, as if they were at the Kabuki. He threw her a kiss from the stage.

All through the performance, a fly circled the air above the actors, buzzing loudly. The brute murdered the woman in a jealous rage on the eve of her wedding to the intellectual, then, he spit in the face of his rival to soil him. Shizo played both the woman and the intellectual, both in white. Inoguchi played the brute, dressed in black tunic and richly polished leather boots. He had even grown a beard for the part.

After the play ended and the crowd had cleared, she went backstage to congratulate Inoguchi. He kissed her hand. She smelled the leather of his boots. She saw the photograph of his wife and child on his dressing table, and he noticed her looking at them, but nothing was said. They were taken by limousine to dinner, where they had seafood dishes she had never seen before, small fluid sculptures on the black and gold lacquerware plates. She had so much *sake* she could barely stand. Shizo's attendants were in waiting, all young boys with thin muscular arms and high laughter. They laughed, and covered their mouths like women when they did it. They danced and sang together, and she enjoyed it, felt fully alive. After all, she was among actors. They were all actors, herself included, only some got paid better than others for doing it.

After dinner they took the limo back to the hotel. Inoguchi walked her to her room, and they stood outside her door for awhile. Finally, she unlocked the door and went in. He did not follow.

All night long she thought about the evening, decided what he wanted from her had not been English lessons, but had not quite been sex, either. She laughed to think that it was *he* who had been pure and *she* who had been otherwise, at least in mind.

In the morning, she went to his suite for the lesson. When she knocked on his door and he opened it, she could see his script on the desk among a pile of books and newspapers in his room.

He also had various cookware assembled in the bathroom—rice cooker and a *daikon* radish grater, among others, because he refused to pay the high prices the hotel charged when he could cook it just as well, if not better, himself. His parents had run a small country *ryokan,* after all, and he had helped with the preparations. The more she knew about him, the more she had begun to like him in earnest.

He took out his script and put it on the Formica table.

She took out hers, too.

He then took out his watch and placed it face up on the table next to the script.

He opened his mouth to speak, and what came out was not English. It was not Japanese either. They both burst into laughter.

"I'll never really learn English," he said.

"I'll never really learn Japanese," she replied.

"But you know what, it doesn't really matter. Does it? We understand each other just fine. Maybe better, even."

They looked at each other and continued to laugh, because he too, now, was being honest.

"Better get them to change the script," he laughed.

"Impossible. This is the way they like it," she replied.

So he began to read, slowly and perfectly.

She listened to him, glancing at the morning paper, open to the sports page, on his table.

She was surprised to read that Owada had withdrawn from the fight because he had sprained his wrist during training.

"Once more," she said, and he complied.

Still, she wondered: What kind of fighter sprained his wrist before the big fight? A real one, she decided. Someone human, vulnerable, prone to stupid mistakes. At any rate, the bets were off.

He saw her looking at the paper.

"Oh. Owada again."

"Yeah, it's a shame. I wanted to see him fight."

The truth was, she had been attracted to something about Owada from the beginning. She had wanted to meet him. She told Inoguchi this. He smiled knowingly, as if he had seen it coming.

Inoguchi said that he had told Owada about her too, and that he would arrange everything.

And so it was set. Inoguchi would be the matchmaker. They would meet. Another drama would begin.

It had all been staged from the beginning.

This time, she decided, she'd make up her part as she went along.

Michelle Dominique Leigh

AN INN NEAR KYOTO

I'm sitting in a simple room, all pale bamboo, yellow-gold straw, and blonde wood, with green, sandy walls. The windows open onto a stream. I hear the rushing sound of the waters flowing from the deep green mountains, now black with the density of night. The sudden rise of the mountain begins on the opposite bank; I look up the slope to see the silvery blue moon, full, just rounding the high ridge. The black silhouettes of spiky pine trees are backlit by moon-mist. *Semi* (cicadas) rasp their incessant summertime nightsong.

Here at Miyama-so, a mountain *ryokan* forty kilometers north of Kyoto near Hanase village, life is reduced to its essentials. This is a place for eating, for sleeping, for bathing—a place for being. Though one may climb the four-hundred stone steps to the Heian temple, Daihizan Bujo-ji, or perhaps laze along the path that skirts the clean fast stream, there is the pleasant feeling here that there is, after all, really nothing to do, nowhere to go. Miyama-so is the ultimate antidote to Kyoto—that place of too much to do and an infinite number of places to go. Indeed, Miyama-so owners Nakahigashi Yoshitsugi and his wife Kazuko have aimed to create a place for *inochi no sentaku*—a cleansing of the being, a cure for modern life.

"We wish to invoke *kokoro furusato*—a feeling of the beloved past, an earlier, simpler Japan of villages—and so none of our five guest rooms holds a television or a mini-bar, and our guests receive no newspapers," explains Kazuko Nakahigashi. Quietly beautiful, with the soft grace of the traditional woman, she wears pale gray linen mountain pants over a pale pink kimono of delicate loose-woven linen. Within a setting that is as purely natural as possible, she hopes to offer an atmosphere of lyrical happiness—a quality, she expresses in Japanese as *jojoteki* (a singing heart).

After a soak in the elegant beechwood bath, with a floor-to-ceiling window overlooking the stream, I wander the grounds. I am seduced by details: the row of oiled-paper umbrellas against an outer wall, the white-lacquered, red-thonged wooden sandals in men's and women's sizes lined up on the wide stone at the entry, the garden lamps with conical straw wrappings, like winter-wraps for trees. Serving-people and cooks bustle to and from the kitchen in preparation for the evening meal. Nearby in the cook's pond is a crowd of stout, soft black carp, and further up the stream swim small, silver trout and sweetfish.

Mr. Nakahigashi, a chef highly regarded in gourmet circles, offers to *ryokan* and restaurant guests a unique type of haute cuisine known as *tsumikusa ryori* (gathered-herb cooking), which had its origins a thousand years ago during the Heian Period. The food is an inspired amalgam of *shojin ryori* (Zen temple cuisine), *sansai ryori* (mountain plant cuisine), and *chakaiseki ryori* (the tea ceremony cuisine that evolved into *Kyo-ryori*—Kyoto cuisine). All is prepared, arranged, and served with the reverential finesse of *ocha no kokoro* (green tea mind).

The inn's fishermen, gatherers, and gardeners each day assemble the ingredients—the carp, sweetfish, and trout; mountain plants such as fiddlehead fern, trefoil, *myoga*, *yama no udo*, gingko, *kinoko* (mushrooms), wild grasses, and glorious garden-grown vegetables (lustrous eggplants, *kabocha* pumpkin, green beans, sweet potatoes). Each day's menu is newly imagined, built upon what has drifted down from the trees or unfurled from the soil.

My dinner is served in one of four private dining rooms. Course after course of astonishing, delicious food is carried in with noble aplomb by an old man in a gold and black striped, traditional costume of wide, skirt-like pants. The red lacquer tray upon which dishes are placed sits upon no table, but directly on the *tatami*.

There are three silver trout curled at the center of a deep basket full of fresh-picked bamboo leaves, with a small smoking fire at the center, under the fish. There are chopsticks made from just-hewn baby bamboo, bright green. There is carp *sashimi* with raw julienned *kabocha* and mountain *wasabi*, mushroom-stuffed lotus root, a crimson, long-armed, freshwater shrimp upon a sprig of pine, sweetfish *sushi* with fresh and aromatic *sansho* leaves.

A meal at Miyama-so is an experience of refined hedonism, poetic gourmandise; if there is such a thing as sophisticated rusticity, this is it.

The clientele is cosmopolitan, well-traveled, drawn from the somewhat jaded upper echelon of society, here to enjoy a restorative meal or a night at the enchanted Miyama-so. A good bath, a superb meal, the pleasant company of a few friends, a *yukata*-clad stroll through the country quiet of the place, a deep sleep under silk *futon* quilts to the sound of the moving stream—a rediscovery of a lost Japan. But was there ever really such a place? This is like a dream filmed by Kurosawa, a reinvented golden age, a precious Kawabata rhapsody, a theater presenting the Japan of the imagination, deep in the silent green nothingness of the mountains.

Michelle Dominique Leigh

MYSTIC MOUNTAINS: THE SACRED PATH OF THE *YAMABUSHI*

At some time before 4:00 on a July morning in these northern mountains, the sky is light, and I am awake to see it: a fine sunless luminosity in which shivers the ghost of rain. I am on Yudono-san, innermost sacred mountain of the sacred group of three known as Dewa Sanzan. I am here to undergo ascetic training, the hard practices of purification followed by the *yamabushi*, an ancient sect of Japanese mountain-dwelling mystics.

In the room with me, the sleeping forms of fellow female participants. Women I met yesterday, now intimate strangers, we fell asleep exchanging confidences. Of the thirty-two initiates, only five are women. There is a feeling that here females are a species apart, though we all, men and women, white-garbed and shorn of outer-world identities, belong during these three days to ritual space, in which each of us is equally No One.

Our day will begin at 5:30. Today, after sitting chest-deep under an icy waterfall—a practice known as *misogi*—we are to climb the great mountain of Gassan. It is the big pilgrimage, the central test, and I am feeling weak and sick to my stomach—perhaps the result of yesterday's *misogi* under a cold rain.

I don't want to climb Gassan. The day ahead is to be one long ordeal of fatigue, fear, pain, and subjugation.

What am I doing here?

Ten years ago in New York I first learned of the *yamabushi*, shaman-ascetics of the syncretistic Shugendo, a sect of Buddhism that incorporates Shinto beliefs, Taoism, and mystical mountain worship. The *yamabushi* are men of power who practice purification of body and spirit by eating little, training themselves to withstand extreme cold and the heat of fire, testing themselves against the snow-country mountains, meditating, chanting, and worshipping the *kami,* or natural gods.

The highly spiritual lifestyle is built upon the simple, primitive experience of survival, using the natural world as a means of training and hardening the body. There are now only a few full-time, mountain-dwelling *yamabushi,* but those who participate in the ascetic training retreats and rituals, or live in the Dewa Sanzan mountains for some portion of each year, number about one hundred and seventy.

A decade earlier in New York, I had decided that one day I would go to Dewa Sanzan not to visit, but for a personal rite of passage.

Before Yudono-san, I journey first to Haguro-san, "Black-Wing Mountain," the most accessible of the three, and the one where Dewa Sanzan Jinja is located, with the deities of each peak housed in the main temple, Gassai-den. At Haguro-san, I stay alone in shrine lodgings and hike the short, steep pilgrimage path through sacred six-hundred-year-old cryptomeria trees. On the morning the retreat is to begin, I bathe thoroughly, as instructed, performing the first solitary purification. After a night of hard rains, the mountain too seems freshly washed, the early morning sky utterly new.

From Haguro-san to Yudono-san, the road winds through foothill towns and then through Shonai rice-field flatlands. On this day the world is glistening green everywhere, with the thick white of clouds filling low valleys. The road up Yudono-san leads into a primordial landscape—only mountains, mountains, and again, mountains.

Arriving at the *dojo*, or practice site, I am ceremoniously signed in and sent to the women's room to don the white clothing required of initiates. The two women already in the room teach me to put on my ritual garb, which consists of a short kimono, wide-pleated *hakama* pants, waist-sash, leggings, my own white *tabi*-socks, and the head-sash known as *hachimaki*. With all these items tied on, I feel pleasantly contained, bound snugly by bands, knots, and bows.

My fellow initiates give advice: "When you enter the waterfall, go in on the left." "Don't wear the long kimono for *misogi*." "Try to chant constantly while you're in the cold water." They are old hands at this; one of the women has been coming here for fifteen years.

I meet the *yamabushi* Utsumi-san, who took leave of his outer-world job as a truck driver to come here several months ago. He has been performing austerities every day since then. He is not what I imagined an ascetic to be. He seems rugged and vigorous, with the soulful earthiness of those who live close to the land. Utsumi-san has been a *yamabushi* for five years in these mountains. He knows every rock.

The leader is Ueno-*sensei*, *yamabushi* and Shinto priest, a man known in these sacred mountains as "the Bear." A handsome, charismatic man in his forties, the Bear has the voice of a *Noh* actor, a voice that carries power, originating deep in the belly and sing-speaking the long-breathed syllables of chants with otherworldly resonance. He is fierce but good-humored; he laughs when he sees the way my leggings never seem to stay up, but droop around my ankles in stubborn disarray.

The first day's lunch is a tiny bowl of rice gruel and a few pickles. Thinking I should eat slowly in order to feel more full, I proceed bite by bite, taking my time, then look up halfway through my meal—the room is suddenly silent—to find I am the only one still eating. Everyone else is sitting stonily in *seiza*, staring straight ahead and waiting for me to finish. Eating fast, I realize is part of our training. I notice that some people haven't eaten at all.

After lunch we are taught the chants, the meditation techniques, the movements to perform before and after *misogi*. We now have a costume, a new system of behavior, even new words to speak. I am soon to realize that there is no time for anything, even for thoughts; we are made to rush from task to task, from assembly to assembly. Now, the world is this group, and all other realities slip away.

On this first day we walk in the rain to Yudono-san Jinja, a tiny outpost of a shrine with a portly priest in full regalia, a high, rounded rock upon which streams warm red sacred water. Here, pilgrims bathe their feet to heal themselves. It is from this rock that Yudono-san, Bathtub Mountain, derives its name.

We climb through the river to reach the site for *misogi*: a small pool at the base of a cold waterfall, marked as holy by straw ropes and folded white paper. In the water, the first sensation is a painful coldness, gradually giving way to numbness, and then finally to a strange blissful heat that fills the being. Around me, initiates chant vigorously, hands clasped and shaking hard, invoking the *kami*, casting out evil and calling up the good. Afterwards, we run in freezing exhilaration down the mountain for a soak in the hot bath, then meditation, chanting, and dinner, followed by more meditation and chanting until it is time for sleep.

I am interested in the moving meditation, which consists of vigorous full-body movement performed repeatedly; doing this, I feel an irresistible drowsiness. Looking around, I notice that several people are indeed fast asleep in the midst of the chanting, moving group. This technique seems also to alter visual and auditory perceptions, perhaps, I surmise, eventually leading to a trance-state.

Having survived the first day's initiation, I awaken now on the second day feeling ill. I know that I cannot back out of this day's climb to the sacred mountain of Gassan, or Moon Mountain, whose gentle-seeming slope rises high into the heavens with perfect, quiet symmetry. So instead of giving in to my inclination to disappear into my *futon*, I follow the rest of the group on the dawn hike to the waterfall for morning *misogi*, back to the *dojo* again for prayers and chanting, and then a hearty breakfast to strengthen us for the day's difficult ascent. After more prayers and chanting, we are off.

Our first climb is up a streambed that slices steep and narrow through heavy vegetation, then we are moving up paths fortified by rusty chains and thin-runged ladders at an angle nearly vertical. I seek a certain momentum, which I maintain even when tired, knowing that if I stop to give in to fatigue, I will fall behind. I want to get this over with; being not only female, but foreign as well, I feel the task is urgent. It is expected, perhaps, that I will weaken, complain, despair, lose footing, tumble, or otherwise fail. Already a small group is lagging behind, and I am determined not to be among them.

I remember Utsumi-san's advice: "Take steps as far apart as one foot-length, no more. To rest, never sit, but stand. Keep a steady rhythm." Though still feeling ill, I am possessed of an energy that surprises me. I move forward with aching legs, step by step, aware of my body's humble strength. I am grateful to be wearing *waraji*, simple straw sandals that help my toes grip rock surfaces and move lightly through knee-deep, rushing streams.

We reach a rest stop, where an old man serves us licorice-flavored herb tea in his hut. We can't get enough of its warm spicy sweetness.

From here, we can see the big mountains ahead, their great green meadows that disappear into white mist. Moving again, we leave the trees and move into bushes and scrub, then expanses of snow amid green slopes covered with alpine flowers.

As we go higher, the air acquires a chill. Our path moves along the ridges of a series of peaks, a path impossibly infinite, stretching on and on until it disappears into the fold of a far, high hill that I am told is Gassan. I want to rest and take in the beauty of the golden lilies and the tiny pink bell-blossoms that surround me, but I must allow myself only fast glances. The path is often a bed of boulders, and moving this fast, we need to watch our feet.

The *yamabushi* wear bells at their waists, and the ringing accompanies us throughout the day, punctuated by the melodious sounding of the *yamabushi* conch-shell trumpets carried by the Bear and several others to communicate position as we climb. I notice Utsumi-san one moment far beneath me on the mountain, helping someone maneuver a difficult stretch; then the next moment he is far ahead, at the precise instant to catch another climber who stumbles. He bounds lightly up the path with the weightless grace of a deer.

When we reach Gassan's summit, we are moving through milk-white mist. The cold air makes our sweaty skin freeze. We pass a mysterious blacksmith house, a center for esoteric training in austerities; I remember that in Japan metalworking has ancient links with shamanic ritual. But many worlds mingle here: booted skiers clomp past; legions of hikers are dressed as if for the Matterhorn; elderly pilgrims swarm by the hundreds, eating rice-balls on the rocks. We pass a group of *yamabushi* in full regalia, small black hats perched on foreheads, ornate orange silk cording draped over their white costumes. We pay our respects at the tiny windswept shrine; a wizened priest watches as members of our group fling handfuls of coins upon his shrine's three-mirrored rooftop. We are jubilant to be here.

We white-garbed initiates draw curious glances from the ordinary hikers at the summit; when eyes reach me, there is a distinct look of pure astonishment. I have the feeling that we are somewhat frightening to the "regular" people, yet we ourselves are no less regular. The age range of our group is between nineteen and seventy, with the average age perhaps forty. In the group there is a fireman, a retired bus driver, several housewives, an engineer, some office workers. But this diversity is invisible during the retreat, when we have no identities and no status.

I understand the urge among participants to return here year after year, to follow the Bear upon the ritual path of renewal, back to the simple beauty of a more primitive existence.

After a rice-ball lunch at the summit of Gassan, we are eager to descend before the onset of night. The day has grown even colder, and we hurry down, back again through the meadows, the flowers, the snowscapes, through the streams and boulders, the scrubby bush, to the trees again and the old man with his cauldron of sweet tea, back down the steep slopes, and back through the narrow streambed, until we arrive, once again, at our waterfall pool, into which we plunge, of course, for evening *misogi*. This time it is deathly cold. I don't stop shivering for hours. Walking down the mountain to the *dojo* in my soaking kimono, I see the mountains before me with new eyes. They have become real to me, alive; they are no longer just shapes. I am elated, relieved, and empty of thoughts. Yes: I am purified.

On this night, after a hot bath and chanting meditation, we participate in *hi-matsuri*, a fire ceremony conducted by the priests of all these mountains. In the dusky room lit by candles, and thick with incense-smoke and the smoke from the ritual fire, Ueno-*sensei* beats the drum with supernatural passion. He is a man who unites body and spirit—moving through the land with the grace of a tribal hunter, performing the esoteric rituals with fiery intensity. The wisdom of the mountain, the *yamabushi* way, seems to me embodied in this man.

We are feasted, then, at the end of this long and difficult day, with glorious *shojin ryori* dishes: sesame, tofu, mountain greens, tender bamboo shoots, and buckwheat noodles, accompanied by sake and beer. Hilarity takes the place of mental control and discipline. We still have tomorrow's *misogi* and a hike up the rapids to come, but we have achieved our hardest challenge. We have passed the test of Gassan. We are transformed.

The next morning, I am up fast and dressed before anyone. I know the routine now; I am no longer a novice. The final *misogi* is accompanied by a mood of exhilaration mingled with nostalgia. We will soon return to the outer world. What of this experience will remain? I am told by the others that remain it does, that at odd moments—riding the bus, eating breakfast—the memory of a certain chant will sound in the mind, or the desire to do something the hard way will surface. The sight of a mountain, they say, will never be the same. *Yamabushi* mind. As I discard my now-soiled white clothing and begin the return to ordinary life by putting on the clothing I wore when I arrived, I have the impression that I will be back. The mountains will call me.

Michelle Dominique Leigh

ME JANE: NAGANO'S VALLEY OF HELL

"It is the Year of the Monkey," I said to myself. "What better way to celebrate than with a visit to the wild hot-spring-soaking monkeys of Nagano's Jigokudani, also known as the Valley of Hell?" I booked a room at the Korokukan, also known as the Later-Pleasure Inn, packed my snow-boots, my paintbrushes, and my Jane Goodall fantasies, and headed for the Japan Alps.

Driving east of Nagano City in the direction of Shiga Kogen's Joshinetsu Plateau National Park, civilization soon gives way to the quiet grandeur of the mountains. The area is rich in hot springs; one drives through innumerable honky-tonk spa towns until the road dwindles to nothing just past Kanbayashi, and it is there that the real journey begins.

There, at the top of the mountain, at the end of the dwindling road, a sign shows the way to Jigokudani, a snowy path leading into a forest wilderness. Embarking upon the path, lit lavender-blue by winter twilight, one's footsteps made silent by snow, one walks gradually downward and deeper into the forest, hearing no sound but occasional bird-chirps and chatterings—chatterings which, one excitedly realizes, may perhaps belong to monkeys. There is a sweet tingle of adventure on the night-chilled air.

Ah! Finally, a warm yellow light is visible, shining through the trees. The 1.6 kilometer walk is just long enough to bestow a pleasant fatigue upon the walker and short enough so that fatigue does not become despair. From the forest, the inn is a curious jumble of rooftops, passageways, and

Hewlett-Packard, but she was going to do it, anyway.

I told her that I thought Ikeda-san and our other colleagues would understand her position. Maybe, because they liked her so much, they'd even be happy for her.

"You're a pioneer," I added.

Miyuki-san sat up straight, pulled out a handkerchief, and started drying her cheeks. "A pioneer, Rhiannon-san?" she asked, doubtfully. I think she was picturing herself in a calico dress on the bench of a covered wagon.

"You're doing something different. You're setting off into new territory. It's always uncomfortable to be a pioneer, Miyuki-san, but it will be worth it. I think you're very brave."

Miyuki-san needed all her courage in the days to come. Her managers did understand her position. "They are so nice," she wrote in an e-mail message to me, "and want me to come back if I have any problem." But during her final two months at YHP, she wasn't allowed by company policy to tell anyone else why she was going. An American could have joked about it—"Wait and see. You won't believe it!"—but we're raised to believe that we can plug ourselves painlessly into and out of groups. Most Japanese can't. It's not a question of pulling a plug, but of severing cords that grow out of each person in the group and connect her to all the others. The knife, cutting the cords, seems to cut into living flesh.

That's the metaphor I used as I tried to understand Miyuki-san's anguish. I found her one day crying quietly in the ladies' room. In answer to my worried e-mail message, she replied, "Yesterday I felt sad when I talked with a sales manager in Osaka whom I have known since I joined YHP. He does not know that I am leaving. But I am OK now. . . . Rhiannon-san, please enjoy yourself in Japan this month."

I didn't try to persuade Miyuki-san that she'd be better off living in California. She wasn't a portable person, either.

You are plum blossoms on the water,
Petals floating by till they pass out of sight.
I am a willow growing by the stream.
My shadow is sunk in it, and I cannot follow.

—BUSON

Judy Rosen

WEARING THE GOOD RED EARTH, DOWN UNDER

Given a growing global concern for the environment, more and more park rangers have become interested in working internationally. I was one of them. In May of 1990, I gave up my full-time job in one of America's crown jewels for an opportunity to ranger Down Under.

Down Under . . . where constellations appear upside down in the sky, where seasons are reversed, where I had to head *north*—not south—to reach the Australian tropics. And so began my temporary assignment with Queensland National Park and Wildlife Service.

Queensland, a state bigger than Alaska, occupies the whole northeast chunk of Australia. It boasts 332 national parks, offering endless stretches of deserted beaches, pounding surf, and coral-fringed coast. Hundreds of islands shimmer in the Coral Sea along Queensland's 2000-mile coastline. In the Far North, pristine rainforests of the Great Dividing Range spill right down to the sea. Here the two richest ecosystems on earth mingle, the Great Barrier Reef—the world's largest living organism—and the Wet Tropics Rainforest, both designated as World Heritage Areas.

Inland, the "red centre" of Queensland encompasses uninhabitable deserts and endless eucalyptus forests riddled with termite mounds. These, along with the occasional *billabong*, capture the classic Australian Outback. I was ecstatic to land myself amid such biogeographical extremes; Queensland was a microcosm of the entire continent.

My springboard to the largest, most remote national parks was the coastal town of Cairns. Its mile-long esplanade, shouldered on one side by the Coral Sea, and budget-minded accommodations and bustling cafés on the other, belied the wilderness that lay just beyond. Gateway to the Far North Frontier, the sign read, and I sensed my adventure was about to begin.

With only a few dirt tracks penetrating hundreds of miles north, the Cape York Peninsula evokes feelings of the last frontier. This Utah-sized region is accessible only by four-wheel drive and *only* in the dry season! Entire communities gather to meet the weekly mail plane bringing supplies and news from the outside world. Children go to school *on the air*, tuned in by radio to centrally located teachers who serve several remote villages. And *flying* doctors come to the rescue for lack of medical facilities.

I had always felt at home in the wilderness, but with 156 species of reptiles lurking beneath the foliage or hanging from trees, I was constantly on guard. The nearly 400 species of birds and mammals made this a noisy place to camp out. This strange frontier required its own vocabulary to get by.

"Bring your *swag* and *tucker*," Garry advised from beneath the brim of his floppy sweat-stained hat, while preparing for an assignment a few days drive into the heart of the Cape York Peninsula. I was too embarrassed to ask, and even more embarrassed when I showed up without a sleeping bag and food. Along the way we stopped for a *smoko*, where, curiously, no one smoked. Instead Garry stoked a quick fire, whipped out a *billy*, and offered me a *cuppa*. *Spinning a yarn*, I learned that the *salty* and *freshy* exhibits we were employed to develop meant displays on saltwater and freshwater crocodiles.

Living with crocodiles was simply a matter of fact, as we forged through the Cape from our perch high in the cab of a Mack semi-truck. Garry had to remind me only once to roll up the windows at river crossings so the beasts wouldn't swim in. Was he joking?

Nonetheless, we arrived safely at Lakefield National Park, about 150 outback kilometers southwest of Cooktown. The rangers—who protected a vast river system which, during the wet season, burst the banks to form a huge inland sea—were housed in an old cattle station homestead. They greeted us excitedly, not the least because we brought the delicacy of ice cream to their remote duty station. After a hardy welcome, we were put to work, building everything from crocodile exhibits to boundary fences. With only a few rangers to cover hundreds of miles, spouses chipped in full work days too, without getting paid.

We grew close fast, as you can only when drawn together in isolation to perform a common task. Around lantern-dim dinners, we discussed the hot issues of Aborigines (comprising ninety percent of the Cape's population) who were staking claim on national park lands that had been their homeland for 40,000 years. Should Aborigines be allowed to continue to hunt—much less, with high-powered rifles—in the newly designated national parks? What about the use of mechanical equipment to access hunting grounds—another taboo in wilderness areas?

Touchier still was that national parks opened up sacred lands to the general public, something we'd been experiencing with native populations in parks and forests from Arizona to Alaska. In Australia, this was dramatically revealed at Ayers Rock in Uluru National Park. There, in predawn light, strings of tourists traversed the immense bulk of weathered sandstone. This geologic anomaly, known to Aborigines as *katajuta*, is at the crux of their mythological and ritual beliefs.

I found myself siding with the Aborigines. They were here first. Galleries of ancient rock art tucked in caves testified to their endurance in this harsh, open land. This was no longer a monotonous landscape of endless plains and eucalyptus forests, but a network of sacred sites linked by Aboriginal ancestors. Home of the *Tjukapai*, or dreamtime. You could feel their presence everywhere.

This enduring culture lent a vibrant texture to the land and the isolation prepared me for my next Outback assignment,evaluating tours in Chillagoe Caves National Park. Once again, I left the coastal city life behind, where eighty-five percent of Aussies live. I grew increasingly anxious and dusty with each kilometer the little white *coach* carved westward into the interior. One by one, passengers were dropped off in tiny specks of towns until I was the last one aboard.

Hours later, the driver dropped me off with a sack of mail, "I'll be back in a week if you need a ride back to Cairns, he said." I wondered if I'd make it that long, as the last hint of civilization for miles just drove off.

How comical I appeared with textbooks and slide carousels spilling out of my duffle. I desperately tried to hide these props when I met face to face with the Chillagoe rangers. Two were aboriginal, as they should be; after all, it's their land. Two others wore long bushy beards. The ranger in charge, tough and capable, intimidated me from her 4' 11" frame. All wore tan shirts tucked into dark brown shorts with knee-high socks rising from sturdy boots. Their smiles, it seemed, were a matter of courtesy.

"You'll need the Pink Cadillac to get around," Lanna asserted without looking up. She nodded to Jonny who produced a barely serviceable salmon-colored *push bike* with a basket bobbing on front. "Follow the track about 6k to Royal Arch. The next cave tour's at 2:00 P.M." Pedaling the desolate track in the oppressive heat of the day, I wondered what, if anything, we rangers from opposite sides of the globe held in common.

My fears dissipated the moment I set foot in the cool damp reprieve of Royal Arch, a coral reef 400 million years ago. We were given headlamps to explore a labyrinth of tunnels and lofty caverns. Brilliant sparkling crystals hung down from the ceiling, rose from the floor, or grew sideways, draping us like shawls. Mesmerized by these formations, I scarcely noticed the other 50 or so tourists that had gathered spellbound around the ranger. "Where did all these people come from?" I mused. No life stirred for hundreds of miles, it seemed, along the journey to Chillagoe. Yet, sure enough, as I exited the cave into the harsh sunlight, there were heaps of Land Rovers with extra cans of petrol, several spare tires, and gargantuan jugs of water strapped every which way onto fenders and roofs. Tour busses unloaded camera-slung foreigners, all wearing the good red earth from their journey into the interior.

Each day for two weeks I pedaled the Pink Cadillac out to the caves, snatching glimpses of kangaroos bounding in the *bush*. Just when I could recite the tours by heart, Jonny, an Aboriginal ranger, played a joke on me. He had gathered his tour into a large chamber and announced, "Now, our American ranger will guide you out." An hour later, we stumbled into daylight, on the heels of an astute young *bloke* who obviously had been paying better attention to the route than I.

We had a good laugh that night around a campfire as Jonny recounted the day's tale. This led to an all-night session on techniques of nature-guiding and minimizing resource damage caused by thousands of feet trampling through the cave. By the time I had redeemed myself, I was cast off to another assignment. . . .

I landed on the tourist-glittered Gold Coast of southern Queensland, a two-day drive south of Cairns. I felt lost in the frenetic pulse of the Miami-like strip, where high-rise hotels shadowed extraordinary beaches for thirty miles. Luckily, a chunk of forest and mangrove swamp was preserved at Flaeys Fauna Centre. Working in a habitat zoo, I now had close encounters with wildlife I'd only seen at a distance in the *bush*. My heart raced with the sight of a *joey* peering out of its mama's pouch and a *cassowary*—a bird nearly my height—guarding a green apple-sized egg just inches away from me. I marveled at how the biologists handled the marsupials as casually as I glanced at deer and elk in my Rocky Mountain home.

One day, a wildlife biologist brought in a baby koala who'd been hit by a car, and she enlisted me to nurse it back to health. Each day I transported Kia and her personal eucalyptus tree everywhere between the office, home, and the bathtub where she slept each night. I often jumped up and down on a mini trampoline with Kia on my hip to simulate a tree-climbing experience in the wild. "If only I could make babies this cute," I thought, growing heady with Kia's growing attachment to me.

By November, we were all going troppo,that sluggish, dizzy approach to life you get when the temperature and humidity hover around 100. I had moved inland to Forest Hill (population: 200) near a small agricultural college where I spent my final months drafting reports for the national parks. My roommates and I would fight over the typewriter in the early morning hours, trying to finish our work before the stifling heat of the day.

One day, as on many occasions after work, we ducked into the Lockyer Valley Hotel for ice cold beers. It was too hot to eat, but I was lured into the dining room where, to my surprise, a Thanksgiving dinner awaited. "Mellie," I exclaimed to the pub cook, "how on earth did you do this?" She pulled out an American magazine, revealing a gloriously laid Thanksgiving meal. She had reproduced it in perfect detail, down to the neat cranberry and orange slices.

"Before we eat, though, you must tell us what Thanksgiving is about," Mellie insisted. It suddenly dawned on me that not everybody on the planet celebrated the Pilgrims' arrival at Plymouth,a sharp reminder that I was in another culture. On this day, however, the spirit of Thanksgiving transcended the continents.

One of my last experiences Down Under seemed to punctuate the national character. I had ventured by bus to the mountain town of Toowoomba, lured by the "Festival of Flowers," where residents proudly displayed their beautiful gardens. Stepping into a café, I asked the owner about the best neighborhoods to visit before setting out on a walking tour. He drew me a map and tossed me a set of keys. "Take my *Ute*," he said. I soon realized he was offering me,a total stranger,his pickup truck for the day. Though I declined his generous offer, I vowed right then and there to be kinder to visitors pouring into my own hometown each summer.

All too soon, I was homeward bound with a broad perspective to apply to my work in conservation. Through the lens of the national parks, I was struck more by the similarities than the differences between our countries. It was heartening to know that, whether in a bustling American park or a remote wilderness on the Cape, rangers on opposite ends of the earth were working with equal dedication toward a shared vision—protection of the land and its immeasurable gifts.

Touching back down in Denver, the city lights stretched beyond the wing for miles. The Far Northern Frontier was fading to a memory—Nights camped in the Outback, peering up at the Southern Cross through my *mossy* net, unable to sleep for the howl of dingoes and the wingbeats of flying foxes. It was no longer enough to have experienced it. I clutched my backpack, still caked with dust from my adventure Down Under, and knew the challenge ahead: to wear the good red earth of the journey on my sleeve as I reentered mainstream America.

GLOSSARY

billabong: a pond; a bend in a creek or river which has been cut off from the main water course by the build-up of sand and silt during flooding

billy: coffee or tea pot

bloke: man

bush: backcountry

cassowary: large, flightless bird

coach: bus

cuppa: cup of coffee or tea

freshy: freshwater crocodile

joey: baby kangaroo

mossy: mosquito

push bike: bicycle

salty: saltwater crocodile

smoko: reststop

spin a yarn: tell a story

swag: sleeping bag

tucker: food

Ute: pickup truck

Judith Azrael

SKETCH BOOK

My father had many sketchbooks. Some were large and some were small enough to fit into his pocket. I loved to browse through them. I'd find a tree, a sloping shoulder, a woman's sorrowful face. I felt he was enabling me to see through his eyes.

These words are sketches of a journey in Southeast Asia. I dedicate them to my father.

Bali

A gecko pokes out its head from behind my bathroom mirror. Bulging eyes. It emerges slowly. Then it catches each moth and insect from the wall. I watch wings disappear into a wide mouth.

The bar man is speaking about the magic of Lombok. They can put a glass bottle in your stomach, he tells me, or turn your mouth into a weird grimace, steal from you without your knowing or fill you with sensual desire.

He says there is white magic also, magic that can make you fly. Like magic mushrooms, I ask, and he laughs. With mushrooms you only feel like you fly, he says. And no one can see you.

He talks of herbal medicines that can make a woman young again and beautiful, that make a woman's vagina like that of a virgin.

And he speaks of frogs. Only the males sing. If one sings off key, the others complain and nip at him.

Two large carved ducks beside the road and a shop with a sign reading, Various of Duck.

I like watching the women cook in the warungs, small booths set up along the beaches and the roads. They mash peanuts, chili, and garlic. Then they add water to make peanut sauce. They chop tofu. They slice rolled banana leaves which contain a portion of cooked rice. The food is arranged like an offering.

Always somewhere a gamelon is playing, relentless and full of sorrow and of joy, a clear stream of melody moving through the slow afternoons.

The cows here are slender and graceful as deer. They graze beneath the coconut trees. And beyond them is the sea.

There is a small soft lump on my bed. I learn it is a dropping from a gecko. When a gecko calls seven times in its cracked voice, it is said to bring luck.

Warm rain today. A woman is washing her feet in a mud puddle. A child walks beside the road holding a large banana leaf over her head to keep off the rain. A flock of tan ducks is shepherded down the road.

I move to a bungalow on a quiet back road of Ubud. The old man of the family welcomes me with a huge pot of steaming tea. He returns a few moments later to wipe our faint footprints from the shining tiles of my porch.

The villagers are gathered in the road in the twilight to laugh and chat. The men hold their prize rooster, stroking it proudly. Other roosters, each in a curved bamboo cage are set by the roadside. I am told this is to keep them from becoming bored.

A boy named Nyoman has brought me here on his motor bike to see the heron. They come at dusk, hundreds of them, to this small village where they sleep in the trees. They settle on the branches like large white blossoms.

We ride slowly homeward through the dusky night past rice terraces. Beside the road young women are bathing in the stream. Fireflies flicker in the darkening sky.

Each day I stop for a while to watch a huge bull that is being built. It has been carved from wood. Then it is covered with wicker and soft coconut husks. Then a layer of burlap and finally soft black velour. A man glues pieces of red felt around its large eyes and mouth. Its legs are decorated in gold. Its large red penis is erect. The bull will be used for a cremation. The body will be placed inside and then it will be set aflame.

A woman stoops beside a large pile of dirt. She has a basket on her head. She scoops dirt and empties it over her head into the basket until it is overflowing. Now with each scoop, the dirt falls all around her. Finally she rises with the grace of a dancer and disappears down a small lane.

I go to stay by the sea. There is a full moon now and the nights are filled with a gentle mysterious mist. The sea and the sky seem wedded and the air is balmy.

At night the geckos call loudly. And there is a night bird that calls persistently. Music from the distant cafés. Heat. Later a few mosquitoes circle my room. And finally the predawn Muslim chanting. Roosters are celebrating the first light. I don't know how to sleep on this island.

I walk down the road in the warm rain. The mountains are lost in mist. The green ricefields gleam and the thatched roofs look washed clean. I walk past the strange swayback Balinese pigs, their tails flicking as they root in the grasses. Two small girls with wicker brooms sweep bright orange petals from the path.

I buy a carved wooden Buddha. And a small gamelon. I go to a shipping office where two women work for almost an hour preparing a package for me to mail home. They cut down a box until it is the right size and use shredded paper for packing. Then they seal the box and cover it with heavy plastic. With a sharpened stick they punch holes all around the edges of the box and weave blue plastic ribbon to secure it firmly.

Two mahogany butterflies are dancing in the morning light.

In Bali the first child is named Wayan. This is true for a girl or for a boy. The second born is named Made. The third is Nyoman and the fourth is Ketut. If a fifth child is born the name Wayan is given once again. Then Made. And Nyoman and Ketut.

A stream runs just beyond the door of my bungalow. At dawn the women come to wash their clothes there. I wake each day to laughter and chattering voices.

I visit an old Balinese village, a village of the Bali Aga. This is a place where the old ways are still intact. If a Bali Aga marries someone from outside the village, they must leave.

The nights are a cacophony of geckos calling their own names and frogs and crickets and rain.

I scrape my toe open on a rock on the main road of Ubud. There are few sidewalks and walking consists of trying to dodge traffic by walking on a rough stony shoulder. After each rain it is muddy and slippery. Several times a day I wash the cut and apply antiseptic hoping that soon a scab will form. But nothing dries in this humidity. Nothing heals.

I stop and chat with a woman who is sitting beside the road making tiny woven baskets. First she makes careful cuts in a banana leaf. Then it is intricately folded and fastened with a sharpened bamboo needle. I sit beside her and she shows me how to fold and sew.

Black rice pudding is served bubbling hot. It is sprinkled with sugar and coconut milk.

Water buffalo roam the paths of this village. I follow the sounds of gamelons and find a large orchestra rehearsing with their teacher. Someone beckons me in and I listen for hours to metal clappers and gamelons and loud drumming that rises and falls in waves. I wonder if I am being changed by this music, the strange rhythms, the relentlessness.

Offerings are placed at every temple, every crossroad, every doorway. An arrangement of flowers and woven leaves and rice grains. They are sprinkled with holy water.

Clinging to the wide mouth of a cave is a vast colony of bats. Their bodies touch and overlap and cling. Some are sleeping, some moving about, and others are cleaning their young. A priest is chanting and people sit on the earth and pray.

My stomach is ailing and I am given snake fruit or *salak* to eat. First it must be boiled for fifteen minutes. The taste is bland and pleasant. By the next day I am well.

The *echak* dance has a human orchestra. Dozens of barechested men sit in a circle, their voices chanting and croaking and beating. These are sounds I hadn't known a human voice could make.

In the mountains the air is cool and moist. Bright splashes of blue morning glories amidst a jungle of greenery. Monkeys with small tufts on their heads are sitting in the road.

I stand in the crowd and watch giant statues of gods carried aloft on frames. It takes many men to support them. Orchestras pass with gamelons and drums and resounding gongs. The women are dressed in sarongs and temple scarves. They carry tall intricate arrangements of fruit on their heads.

The village boys are filled with longing. Ketut wants a bag to carry his books. Wayan wants a watch he can wear into the sea. They want my scuffed sandals and my sweater and my daughter's photograph. We have nothing, they tell me. I gesture toward the fringe of shining white sand and the sea. We have nothing, they say again.

At dawn I run down to the beach where a boat is waiting. It is long and narrow, carved from a mango tree. We motor far out to sea until we find the dolphins. The sun is rising and dolphins are leaping all around us.

Stacks of firewood are piled between the legs of the huge black bull and set aflame. The crowd laughs and cheers. The bull's bright necklaces and golden halter are the first to turn to ash.

When it grows dark I carry in the mosquito coil that has been lit for me and left on my porch. Then I get a cup of hot lemon juice and honey and sit by the sea. A full moon is sailing through the clouds.

Penang

It is a long train ride from Singapore to Penang. I sit between cars by the open door in the warm wind. I am wondering if I should leave my luggage behind and step off the train to follow one of the paths that wind away through the trees.

It is night and a group of boys is balancing a huge and multi-colored flag on a long pole. They place the end of the pole on their foreheads and their shoulders. They pass it from one to another. There is a full moon and a flag floating against the sky.

Bangkok

A butterfly on whose wings are a delicate watercolor painting. Fine pen lines and then a wash of pale rose and yellow.

At Wat Po I pay thirty baht and set two small bright birds free. A woman has a cage filled with birds. "This will bring you good fortune," she tells me.

The *klongs* are bordered by flimsy wooden houses with decks suspended above the river. Pots filled with bright flowers and laundry hung out to dry. Dogs and cats and birds in cages. Children playing in the muddy green water. My long-tailed boat passes beside a small café where a young girl washes lettuce in the river. Bougainvillea spilling across a wall. A few modern apartment buildings. Gilded shining monasteries. And everywhere there are people cooking, doing their laundry, sewing, eating, sleeping beside these milky waters.

When I want to go somewhere in this vast city, I ask the person at the desk of the guest house to write it down for me. So few people speak English. Even when I learn to say the word in Thai, I am seldom understood. I stand like a child, clutching a note in my hand.

The *tuk-tuk* drivers are often new in town. They don't know their way much better than I do. This one gets more and more disgruntled when he can't find the address of the place I want to go. He is sweating profusely and wiping his face again and again with an old kerchief. Suddenly I remember I have a travel tissue in my bag. He watches in the rear view mirror as I carefully unfold it and then hand it to him. He wipes his face looking amazed by its coolness. Then he grins back at me.

King works at the guest house. She spent her childhood living on the *klongs.* "I longed to be in America," she tells me. "I knew that there I could leave my house and go for a walk." From her house the only way to leave was by boat. And only one boat came by each day.

Wa Pa Nanachat

As a lay woman at this monastery, I am provided with clothes to wear. A white sleeveless underblouse and a white short-sleeved blouse. For a skirt there is a very wide circular black cloth that I step into and then tie at my waist like a sarong.

I have two of everything. Each day I wash the clothes from the day before and hang them out in the sun to dry.

I open the bathroom door gently. On the inside is a hook where a clear shower cap hangs. Inside the cap are two immense spiders.

Squirrels and chipmunks playing on the forest floor. A velvety blackbird with a white circle on its back is singing on a branch.

I rise for meditation just before it grows light. I sweep the forest pathways with a broom of stiff straw.

In the predawn light the villagers come with large baskets of food to offer to the monks. The women cook in the open air kitchen. There is one meal a day at 9:30 A.M. The food is nutritious and plentiful. There is rice, tofu, vegetables, salads, sweets, and fresh tropical fruits. After the meal, when all the dishes have been washed, the women and children lie down on bamboo mats to talk, visit, and sleep.

The meditation huts are built on stilts. Around each stilt is a small cement moat to keep insects away. Today at tea the monks are talking about the ways that ants can cross water. Some find a raft, perhaps a bit of straw to ride on. The smallest ones can walk across the surface. Some wait for the wind and leap.

There is a meditation path beside my hut. At dusk I place a candle at each end and walk slowly back and forth. The candles glow, and somewhere in the trees an owl gives a low hoot. The earth is warm beneath my feet.

There is a small lizard on the tree trunk. It has a brown and white striped back and an orange tail. It curls its tail and then flicks it back and forth like a cat, that same feeling of energy gathering.

It is evening now and there is a sudden unexpected rain. It rustles in the trees. Today I watered the plants around the Ajahn's, for they were withering in the sun. And now the rain becomes a downpour clattering on the metal roof. A bolt of lightning and then thunder.

Mekong River

In Thailand I hear the word *farang* again and again. It means foreigner. Ke owns the little guest house on the river where I am staying. She and I become friends. "The *farang* will go to the monastery tonight," she tells someone. "The *farang* took a shower," her son calls to her as I emerge from the outdoor shower stall.

This morning there is shooting in Laos. Ke grabs her son and runs inside.

I take a bus that follows the river. Now and then there are trees carved into shapes. I see a water buffalo, a large peacock in the branches, a long-tailed boat carrying many people, a deer, an elephant, a dolphin, a giraffe. The Thais watch my delight and make certain I don't miss any.

My bungalow has a mattress on a platform and a warm quilt and pillow. A gauzy mosquito net. The windows are open spaces. There are a few nails to hang things on. From its small porch I can see the river and the hills of Laos beyond it.

Tonight there is a fire in the mountains of Laos. The peaks are outlined with a bright orange glow. Now and then a flame leaps up into the dark sky.

At night the village dogs are released and guard the dusty quiet roads. I walk filled with dread as they snap and growl at my legs.

There is a small monastery down the road from the guesthouse. Only two or three monks are living there on a dusty piece of earth above the river. The buildings are simple wooden structures in need of paint. There is a feeling of peace.

List of gifts I buy at the Laotian refugee shop and mail to America:

1 shirt

1 doll

2 embroidered pillow covers that depict Laotian villagers driven from home by soldiers and crossing the river to Thailand

2 carved turtles

Twilight. The boys of the village and a few men come down to the river to bathe. One boy first hangs his towel carefully on a branch. He takes a few fierce punches into air and then stands on his hands. Now he is ready to bathe.

This is the day of Buddha's enlightenment. In the evening the villagers gather at the small monastery. There are many children and everyone carries flowers and candles and incense. A monk gives a talk in Thai. The only word I can understand is *farang.* He says it several times and everyone turns to look at me. This time the word is welcome.

After the talk everyone pours out into the moonlit night and we slowly circle the temple three times. Then we place our candles on the stone walls. The flowers and incense are also placed there. The ceremony has ended and everyone disappears into the darkened streets. I linger on, watching the candles flicker in the darkness. A monk is standing in the temple doorway and I place my hands to my forehead and bow my head. He bows his head in return.

I sit on the banks and watch the river flowing by. The Mekong moves swiftly and impartially. It sweeps everything along in its current. I watch my thoughts arise and disappear.

Islands: Ko Pee-Pee, Ko Lanta, Lanta Noi, Bamboo

Today the tide recedes so low I can walk to the village across the floor of the sea. I splash through the warm shallows, looking for shells.

There is only one guest house on Lanta Noi. I take a small motored boat to get there. Then Muslim boys with motorbikes offer rides. I climb on the back of a bike and hold on tightly around a stranger's waist. We fling off down sand roads and across meadows. Monkeys laugh in the trees.

There are plants along the pathways that turn limp if I touch them. Their delicate leaves close and droop. When I pass by a little later, their leaves have opened once again.

It takes only an hour or so to walk the white sandy beach that encircles Bamboo Island. How long it takes depends on how many times you bend to gather up a gleaming shell. Or how many times you stop to swim in the shimmering blue sea.

I sit on the rocks watching the sun sink into the sea. Prayer flags wave in the breeze. A solitary fisherman lands in his long-tailed boat and rows with one oar slowly across the bay.

Wendy Erd

THE CYCLO DRIVER'S STORY

"Can I tell you my story?" The cyclo driver leaned over his handlebars behind me and spoke softly. I nodded as I watched the muscular calves of my husband's driver pedal steadily away. They turned a corner and disappeared ahead of us, into the darkening streets of Nhatrang. Along the first block, our carts had ridden abreast until my driver called out to the other in rapid Vietnamese. Then he'd slacked off and fallen behind. I pulled my thin sweater close and slumped down in my seat between the two front tires. In the lingering light, only a few shadows hurried home past the closed shops.

Behind me, I could hear the rhythm of his steady breathing with each push of the pedals. Under the neon lights of the restaurant, this man had looked frail, his tee shirt flattened against his ribs by a warm wind. He'd raced ahead of the pack of cyclo men parked along the curb and bargained me into his rig for a few dollars. Now he worked for the fare. Our destination was six kilometers away, past the cheap hotels, to the Villa on the point, where Peter and I had arranged to meet two other tourists in their room for vodkas after sunset.

He pedaled down the beach strip, past the wooden stalls that sold snacks and shade. Past rental umbrellas uprooted and gathered in the white sand like closed flowers. Past the Green Hat Café, where we'd had a cold beer in the heat of the day. The barefoot vendors had gone home, shouldering their yokes of steamed crab and soy pudding. The town I watched rise before daybreak was folding for sleep.

That morning we'd joined the English women on the Villa's terrace for breakfast, sipping strong French coffee and breaking crusty baguettes.

"You know it's strange," said Joselyn, "but Elizabeth and I really haven't seen many traces of the War."

Above us a lemon parachute, stretched for shade, snapped in the sea wind. I stirred my coffee fingering the "U.S." stamped on the aluminum spoon and gazed across the green water where the jagged rigging of a sunken freighter stretched two fingers above the waves.

Vietnam. The deadweight of the word had hung on my friends' faces before I left home. "You're going *there*?" they frowned. "Is it safe?" We tumbled into a dark morass of memory. I watched war documentaries on TV. A farmer near Hanoi shook his dead daughter's red shirt at the camera, a wailing wife tried to climb into her husband's grave. After a while I snapped them off. I wanted to go as myself, blameless, unencumbered by country.

The wind from the South China Sea picked up my cotton dress. I clamped it between my knees. I felt vulnerable, perched in front of his bicycle taxi in a metal seat and propelled through the town. I leaned back against the worn bamboo matting. Above my shoulder, his voice floated over the soft wash of waves, "After 1975 . . ." he began.

Another story. They all began the same way.

The last three weeks we'd heard so many stories. Our first day in Ho Chi Minh City, we wandered down a faded colonial street to the quay. The muddy Saigon River swept past rusted freighters, sampans and new tour boats that rocked in the gray green water. A street boy spotted us and hung on my arm for blocks, sticky as Velcro, calling me, "Mama," Peter, "Papa." An escapee from Laos shook our hands. Women bicycled by and smiled at us from under the shade of their cone hats, their elbow length gloves white in the brilliant sun.

Small children worked the tourist cafés. At breakfast, Anh, a scrappy ten-year-old with tangled hair, tweaked my chin and leaned against me. She spread postcards, tourist maps, and a handful of tarnished dog tags in front of me. I shuffled through them and gave them back. "Come on Miss, you buy something from me." She took my hand in hers and stroked my fingers, clicking her tongue at my plain short nails. I heard myself arrange for her to enamel them at dinner. She skipped away and I felt as if I'd offered her scraps under the table.

Each day, thin men with hands in their pockets fell in step and asked what country we were from. "After 1975 . . ." they began, and told us of their lives since the fall of South Vietnam. They described what happened when the Americans left, of their attempts to escape by boat, of the family members who made it. Did we live in L.A.? Seattle? We acquired bundles of letters they couldn't afford to send overseas. Two sisters, who had waited years for their orderly departure papers, gave us a picture for their parents in Colorado. In the picture they held hands behind a chocolate cake; the pink icing read, "Two years of separation is two centuries of waiting."

We rested in the shade, under a statue of Ho Chi Minh and waited for a group of giggling students to settle near us like silk butterflies in their white *ao dais.* One girl asked me to pose with her and they snapped our photo, my arm around her tiny waist. Shyly she asked me, "What do you think of us? What do you think of my country?" In 1993, we were symbols of change and possibility, American *tourists* in Vietnam.

After they left, we crossed the street and rode an elevator to the top of the Rex Hotel. We ordered drinks at the rooftop bar and watched swallows stitch together the sooty top of the city. From another table I recognized a boasting southern drawl. "Yeah, me and Ed were past the hooches. I was walking point . . ." I didn't want to be an American here. I would say I was from Alaska.

In the afternoons, I lay on our hard hotel bed, thinking of home, exhausted. Outside our wire-mesh window, a pink sun steamed over the tin roofs of Saigon.

One day, as we rode in cyclos through the clamor of the city, two men burst from a sidewalk throng onto the street in front of us. One chased after the other, his knife stabbing the air. Along the walks, the crowds froze. I jumped down from my seat to run away, but my driver motioned me back, "Get in, get in, not safe." Weaving through mopeds and cyclos, the two men sped in a deadly race down the middle of the street. The traffic pressed inexorably on. I'd seen more than I wanted to. I covered my eyes as we passed them struggling on the pavement.

We'd gone up the coast then, away from the violence, the hustle, the heat, the confusion of a city in change, to the blue waters of Nhatrang.

Now, my husband was nowhere in sight. Except for an occasional motorbike heading back to town, the boulevard was empty along the breaking sea. The faint lights of Nhatrang glimmered behind us. In the quiet darkness the driver's voice formed an envelope around me.

"I was a lieutenant in the South Vietnamese Army," he was saying. "I worked for the Americans."

When the North Vietnamese had captured the city, his troops wanted to commit suicide. He refused. He had a wife and a young son. They sent him to a labor camp in the mountains with his family and his wife's father for "re-education." "I work so hard, so very hard, and for no money. It's been eighteen years."

He looked too young. He would have to be at least my age. In Saigon I'd seen a photo of American GI's under dusty glass in a tourist café. They were boys, laughing, their arms around each other's shoulders.

I thought of the friend I'd talked to the week before I left home. "What would I have said to the guys who never came home, if I'd known then, that twenty years later Americans would be coming back as tourists?" he said. I asked if he wanted me to look any place up for him? He stared over my shoulder and shook his head.

"What year were you born?" I spoke into the darkness in front of me.

"1955." He must have sensed my doubt. He went on, "I was sixteen when I joined the army."

He sighed. The wheeling sound of his narrow tires rose from the pavement. We passed the last hotel on the outskirts of town. A gaudy necklace of Christmas lights hung on branches near the gate. The outside bar was empty, stools upside down on the small tables. The smell of salt and damp sand mingled with the stars.

His voice gathered emotion, "Two weeks ago my wife got a terrible malaria. I begged a friend to loan me money." He left food for his children and bused his wife down from the mountains, to the hospital in Nhatrang. He had enough dong for one night there.

"In Vietnam, if you can't pay you must leave. This morning, I carried her out and lay her on a blanket by the hospital gate."

He brought her a bowl of noodles, but she couldn't eat. A cyclo driver had stopped to talk to him and, taking pity, had loaned him his cyclo for one night saying the poor man could keep the fares he made to take his wife home, to their children.

"I worry about her alone by the gate."

We passed under a streetlight. I turned and looked up at his face. Tears wet his cheeks. He saw mine reflected in the light. "Don't cry," he said, touching my shoulder. "Life is difficult here. You can't worry."

I saw the lights shimmering on the top of the Villa. They shone down on a tiny fishing village tucked at the foot of the knoll. It had been one of Bao Dai's summer homes. Vietnam's last king had slept in these same spacious suites with their Maxfield-Parrish-blue walls and views of the sea. I could see Peter, waiting beside his cyclo. Past him, a private drive wound up to the hotel.

My driver stopped short. "Perhaps you can help me. Do you know where I can get malaria medicine? Anything I could give my wife?" I thought about the Larium we took once a week. Our prescription would last the six weeks we'd be in Vietnam.

"No." I shook my head. "Wait here." I ran to my husband.

He could see I'd been crying. He peered at my driver waiting in the shadows.

"I want to give him more money. It's such a sad story." My throat felt thick.

"Do you believe him?" Peter asked.

"I'm not sure it matters."

"Well, do whatever you need to," he said.

I raced back and pressed twice the amount I'd bargained for in my cyclo driver's hand. Then he was gone, pedaling off quickly through the village.

I walked over to Peter's driver. "Did you know him?" I asked.

He shook his head. "Playboy," he said.

Peter caught my arm. "He doesn't speak much English."

"Good? Bad?" I asked again, determined to find out.

He shrugged and smiled. Then he rode slowly away, back towards Nhatrang.

The English women greeted us at their door. They had the prince's room and, from a tiny refrigerator in their sitting room, pulled out a chilled bottle of Russian vodka. I couldn't drink but sat watching the fishing lights above the white blossoms of frangipani outside their window.

"No one likes to be fooled," Elizabeth said. "Yet isn't it better to let nine guilty men go free than to convict one who is innocent?"

Our last two days in Nhatrang, I scanned the streets for my driver, wondering if I'd recognize him. Knots of cyclos parked outside the cafés. In the sun, the drivers' dark features bled together to form a composite face. I knew the story was true. If it didn't belong to him, it belonged to his country. Still, I was relieved when we left in a hired car for Hoi An that I hadn't seen him.

There was only one hotel in Hoi An for foreigners. The Vietnamese government kept its travelers in tidy groups, like a clutch of golden eggs under a watchful hen. Beneath a broad-leafed tree, the hotel ran a small café. We recognized several people at one table who were traveling the same route north to Hanoi. Michault, a Frenchman waved us over.

"How has your journey been?" he asked.

We pulled up metal chairs and sat down beside him in the dappled shade. I told him I was road weary. I told him the cyclo driver's story.

He laughed. "Once in India, twenty years ago, I had a similar experience." A poor man in Madras had confided his desperate need to go home. Michault gave him a substantial sum for his train ticket and, in gratitude, the Indian gave him his address upcountry.

A blond American couple joined us in the shade and ordered coffees.

Michault leaned over the table, "I found myself near the man's hometown, and rode a miserable bus for three days, across a desert, to visit him." He smiled. "When I arrived, I found it was a colony for lepers."

All of us at the table laughed then, recognizing some familiar irony.

Michault raised a hand, "Wait, there's more." He had returned to Madras ten years later and been amazed when the same man approached him and asked if he would join him for refreshments. Again, he patiently listened to the beggar's identical tale. Then Michault confessed he remembered their meeting ten years before. "I told him, 'My friend, this time you will buy our tea and cakes.'"

The American woman who sat across the table from us gazed over the dry grass toward the hotel. She sighed, "I heard a sad story in Nhatrang."

I stared at her, "Did a cyclo man tell you about his sick wife?"

"Oh no," she said, more to herself than me. Her blue eyes widened and returned my stare. "Yes, he told me that his wife lay on the hospital grounds with malaria, that they were poor, from the mountains." She fidgeted with her napkin. Her face flushed. "Shit," she said shaking her head. "I gave him twenty dollars."

I like to picture him in the mountains. His wife is well. He comes in at night smelling of sweat and the sodden damp of the rice fields. She places a bowl of *pho* before him. He bends his head over the steam and begins to eat.

Danielle D'Ottavio Harned

THE LIGHT IN THE DUST

When the lamp is shattered
The light in the dust lies dead
—PERCY BYSSHE SHELLEY

Alta, an American volunteer, looked out at the coiled wire fence which enclosed Kai Tak Refugee Camp. On the other side of the fence, a Pan Am 747 taxied along the runway. The heaving exhaust made apartment buildings lining the distant hills of Hong Kong shiver like illusory towers in a mirage. Then she heard a child howl, and she looked along the barren strip of land between the administration area and the refugees' living area to find a child sprawled on the ground, holding her bleeding knee. Reaching the child, Alta knelt down just as a blast of Hong Kong's erratic wind strafed the barren field, churning up dust and debris. In the dull morning light, dust sprinkled their hair and arms and stung their eyes like some poisonous shower. The child coughed. Alta pawed the air protectively. She watched fine silt make a paste of the blood that trickled from the child's bleeding knee. Suddenly she rose and urged the child to stand. "Let's go to the clinic," she said.

"Not necessary, clinic." The voice came from behind her, small but determined.

Alta turned on long achy legs to face Sue, her star pupil, a thin, bird-like girl who tilted her head to one side as if listening for a call.

"Her knee's dirty and bleeding," Alta insisted.

The 747 turned on the runway, and a blast from jet engines bombarded the field. Sue's parka surged and swelled, and the billowing parka reminded Alta of a kitten's fur lifting in reaction to a hand poised to pet it. Sue closed one exquisite eye in a wink, as she did when Alta called on her in class. That wink, like fingers snapping, produced a shift of perception in Alta as abrupt and sweeping as Hong Kong's wind. She found herself pondering, as she knew Sue did, how the knee might affect the child's obtaining a seat on that plane across the field. Since the fall of Saigon in 1975, Vietnamese refugees sailed into Hong Kong Bay or walked overland to China, crossing into Hong Kong's New Territories. A fresh decade was upon them, and still their names didn't appear on the Holding Area wall. Alta's body sagged in surrender to the conspiracy, but she insisted, "She should go to the clinic." She was not surprised when the wounded girl veered toward Sue.

"Tee-cha! Tee-cha!" a little band of children called to her from the gate, leaping and flapping their arms.

Alta saluted them with a theatrical wave, then turned back to her girls. They were already trotting away. She watched Sue's parka heave and roll until both girls disappeared into the drifting mob that made up Kai Tak Refugee Camp, then appeared again amidst the jumble of jeans, T-shirts, and sneakers at the gate. They could be American kids, she thought.

Sue's voice ricocheted back to her. In Vietnamese. Then English.

"You will be American," Alta called out.

Her outcry almost eclipsed a more hesitant "Tee-cha." An old man passed very close. His gentle tone captured the spirit of that word for the Vietnamese, a respectfulness he might have used with a maiden aunt. Everyone at Kai Tak Refugee Camp called her *teacher,* the way they must have called all American soldiers *GI* back in Vietnam.

The wind attacked again, sudden and unrestrained. The old man staggered, recovered, and, with a nearly toothless grin in her direction, maneuvered a course toward the airfield and the crowded barracks just inside the fence which was the refugees' home. Alta pushed off in the opposite direction toward the administration buildings and a one-room concrete hut slapped up against a high wooden fence.

On a windy morning two weeks earlier, Alta and Tra, a refugee who was also a friend and teacher, had rushed that fence, winding their way through the gate to reach the outside. A clot of braver Vietnamese had already gathered, their heads bowed toward the ground, their voices a tantalizing undercurrent, like warnings in a dense jungle of a sensed but unseen danger.

At Alta's insistence, Tra translated. "They talk about man on sidewalk," Tra had breathed under the watchful eye of the camp guard. Her dark eyes, usually shiny with expectation, were screened against intrusion. Her customary high-pitched giggle had settled into the hushed whisper of a twenty-two-year-old veteran. "He killed for drugs."

Alta stretched over the crowd to see that, indeed, a man lay motionless on the ground.

"He ARVN, killed by gang from North Vietnam," Tra said this time. In the hearts of the Vietnamese, the war between north and south had not ended.

Shrieking sirens announced a new authority, and Tra offered a final possibility. "Chinese from Hong Kong kill him. Maybe he owe them money."

The Hong Kong Police dispersed from the front and back of black mini-vans, removed little notebooks and pens from their stiffly starched shirt pockets, and prepared to write. Now the refugees reacted like a colony of mute dullards. As if in agreement, the police closed their notebooks, returned to their mini-vans, and drove away, leaving the body for the ambulance.

The office of the children's school consisted of a long metal table with rickety chairs; a desk for Sister Katherine, the Maryknoll nun who ran the school; a metal cabinet; and boxes stacked in rows along the floor—all donated. Alta searched through boxes, always on the lookout for teaching aids. "The meeting over?" she asked. Perfectly timed, her entrance would coincide with the end of the daily meetings.

"Morning, early bird," Molly mocked. She stood on a chair at one end of the room and straightened a placard on the wall: WE INTEGRATE BETTER.

Alta and Molly were stewardesses for an American airline. They'd brought U.S. soldiers into Vietnam; they'd evacuated refugees out of Vietnam; now they were at one of the refugee camps in Hong Kong on their own time, teaching Vietnamese children English.

From her perch on a ladder, Molly nodded to the placard. "In the U.S. last week," she said, "all I heard about the Vietnamese was 'they integrate so well.'" Her long blonde hair had escaped its ponytail and swirled around her face. The light had faded her blue eyes into a sudsy gray. When she spoke Chinese, the refugees saw only those blue eyes and blonde hair, and they could not believe what they heard.

Before Alta could respond, Tra raced through the door. "Hi, everybody!" Tra's ponytail was tied like Molly's, but her thick hair held it strongly in place.

"I read about Charlottesville, Virginia in newspaper today," Tra said. She pronounced the city's name in a way only the initiated would have understood. Gasping for breath, her face rosy, she said, "Very hot in Charlottesville today."

"Congratulations on your transfer," Alta said. She pulled playing cards from one of the boxes.

Tra grinned, "Me and Lonnie go to Charlottesville." She patted Lonnie who sat at the far end of the table cutting colored paper into long segments for her students' art class. "I have uncle in Charlottesville," she said. "Is number one good luck."

Alta turned over a card and smiled at the red queen. Sometimes even the illogical made sense, and this transfer to Argyle Refugee Camp could bring Tra luck. "A crash course in English at Argyle and you'll be on your way," she said.

"Lonnie see her husband in America very soon," Tra agreed.

Lonnie looked shyly at Molly.

Molly's mumble came out more like a growl, "You can learn English right here."

Tra laughed, the refugee's way of covering up an embarrassing situation. "I visit you in America," she said to Molly.

Lonnie turned quietly back to her colored paper.

"It could happen," Alta said. She turned up a knight and realized that a different picture from *Alice in Wonderland* was painted on the face of each card. "At Argyle, I mean."

"Transferring is a one-in-a-million gamble," Molly said. "Your pet, Sue, was at Jubilee for eight months. Jubilee closed. She's been here for seven months. They're moved around and lost, and I'm convinced at this point that the government just reaches down and grabs a handful, any handful."

"Everyone says they're getting out of Argyle by the hundreds," Alta insisted. "Right?" She looked to Tra and Lonnie for confirmation.

Molly looked over to where Lonnie and Tra pretended not to hear her words, and she blushed. She poured tea from a pot into her cup. Then, impatient, she crossed over to the cabinet and picked through the books. "Today it's Argyle, tomorrow it might be Sham Sui Po." She chose a book. "Or right here in Kai Tak for that matter."

"There's a mass exodus out of Argyle. That's a fact, too." Alta realized she was staring at a rabbit with a huge watch.

Molly blew across the worn book and dust flew up, causing her to cough. "You'd think I'd learn to leave this stuff alone," she said. Her words seemed to discourage her, and she dropped the book. "I want to know where Tra and Lonnie are. I want them close by. Does that make me selfish and uncaring?"

Just then, another refugee teacher and two refugee volunteers burst through the door. They shook rainwater all over the office. Someone knocked Alta's arm, and playing cards exploded into the air. She grabbed for them and sent Molly's teacup careening across the table. Oblivious, the newcomers cheered Tra and Lonnie's irregular transfer before sitting down at the table to check the day's class schedule.

"Do my tea leaves let you see the future?" Molly asked, reaching past her to right the cup.

Alta focused on bits of wet leaves that stuck to her cards.

"Letter come from Lim!" Tra's cry interrupted the two women. She waved the envelope with its mysterious foreign stamps.

Molly's laugh was more a sigh of relief, "Maybe the future has arrived first class mail."

Everyone cheered. Lim had been a favorite teacher at the camp's school. The shock had been palpable when he was consigned to Austria instead of America.

Writing in English, Lim described his home town in Austria as a charming place. "I am happy," he wrote. "I am learning German. I not have a job but I will soon have job. Everything is very good."

Alta carefully dried playing cards on her blouse while Molly read the next letter. It was from Lim's teacher. She wrote that Lim was working hard at the Austrian language, but, in this small village, life was not easy for him and jobs were scarce. The people in this town were not sophisticated, not worldly. They did not understand. But she wanted everyone to know she was doing what she could, and she hoped Lim would be accepted at the University of Vienna.

"Sounds terrible," Tra said. "I glad to go to America."

The rain advanced in heavy noisy sheets. Near the gate about forty Vietnamese huddled under the Holding Area's open shelter. Women hunched over suitcases. Men smoked, breathing deeply, holding each cigarette by its pungent end for that last long drag. One man stalked the space in front of a board where sheets of loose paper flapped in the wind, hands in his pockets. Alta imagined him jiggling nickels and dimes—American coins. He checked the paper's list of names in smeared Chinese characters and Vietnamese, the names of people leaving camp for their new homes abroad—his name.

Alta paused for breath under a building's overhang. At the other end, Sue looked disconsolately around at the downpour, her arms filled with bits of muddy paper that blew around the camp. She caught sight of Alta, and a big smile spread across her small face, the one eye closing in her quaint wink. "I clean, like in America," she called.

"Come to class," Alta demanded. She was suddenly and unreasonably impatient with Sue.

When she reached the school, Alta shoved wet hands into dripping pockets, searching unsuccessfully for the playing cards. She kicked a muddy foot at the cement wall, mad at Molly for upsetting her equanimity and making her forget the cards. One of her little girls saw her, and she kicked her foot at the wall. The girls giggled and called out to Sue who'd appeared out of the abating rain. Each girl kicked the wall in feigned anger. As she watched, Alta couldn't help but laugh. They were forever aping her. She'd catch them and laugh, and their laughter would echo hers. She laughed again, glad for the reprieve. But Sue refused this play. Her face was fixed in firm disapproval.

"Inside," Alta shouted.

In the damp classroom, dingy walls consumed a light which squeezed through small dirty windows. Desks dwarfed by a high long blackboard seemed to shrivel into the concrete floor. The wet had seeped through Alta's pores, chilling her from the inside. She shivered, unsure of what she should do with seven wet little girls: free them to change into clothes which the rains would soon soak, if leaking roofs hadn't already managed that; or keep them here and shivering in the cold classroom.

The wriggling girls called back and forth to each other, reverting to their Vietnamese names, oblivious of the rain. Their babble encouraged Alta. She smiled at words she didn't understand, and she felt like a refugee, a stranger campaigning for entry. Her rift with Molly had propelled her headlong into her students' corner.

"Tee-cha! Tee-cha!" Sue called. But for all her desire to speak, her efforts yielded only a choking cough.

A beautiful girl with dark brilliant eyes thumped Sue gently on the back. Her name was Mary. On Alta's first day of teaching, unable to pronounce her Vietnamese name, she's said, jokingly, "I'll call you Mary."

The girls loved the name. When Alta asked the next little girl for her name, she'd crossed her arms in front of her, mouth tight. She pointed to Mary.

"I'll call you Sue," Alta had said. Sue slid one lid down in a luxurious wink, as if embracing a collusion from way back when.

At their insistence, Alta had gone down the line, all seven, giving each girl her American name. That's what they called it, "My American name."

At first she'd been uneasy about what she'd done. In the end, she could hear another awkward ten-year-old telling the third grade teacher in her new school, "You call me Alta." The Mexican family who had lived next door called her *alta*. New to San Antonio from the east coast, she'd found the name exotic; she hadn't known, back then, the family was simply describing her: *alta* meant tall. When she'd found out, she'd insisted as fervidly on keeping the name as if taking up a powerful incantation.

Writing on the blackboard what she knew seven little girls copied meticulously on bits of paper, Alta grinned. She understood the magic in a name.

Alta moved to the guidebook phrases the government thought best prepared future citizens for life in the U.S. Brows wrinkled in concentration, her students buried eager faces in old grammar books they couldn't read. They understood being singled out for this special class as unbelievable good luck. As Alta reviewed the old phrases, Sue, her small face smudged with mud, hinted at answers or encouraged the girls in Vietnamese.

Then Alta moved to a new concept. "Let's pretend you now live in America, okay?"

Everyone nodded vigorously.

"Sue, where do you live?"

"Here," Sue said. She mashed her finger into the desk for emphasis.

"No, you say, 'I live in America,'" Alta said.

"No, I live here," Sue said. Her face wore a determined expression which charmed Alta.

"Where will you live?" Alta asked. "Maybe in one month. You will say, 'I live in America.'"

Sue pulled her jacket close.

No one else spoke, none of the usual encouragement that accompanied a student's bewilderment.

Alerted but unable to disengage herself from the guidebook, Alta turned to Mary. She pictured those high cheekbones and that crooked but sensuous smile on the cover of *Glamour* in years to come. "Mary, where will you live?" she asked.

Mary looked up from her notebook, eyes flashing. "Spanish eyes," Alta called them, and the girls giggled without understanding. "Me, too. I live here," Mary said.

"Tee-cha! Tee-cha!" Sue called. "You forget. My mark."

Alta turned to the blackboard. One of the volunteers had introduced the star system. Now the girls insisted on stars for every correct answer;

they counted the stars repeatedly.

Alta started to place a star by Sue's name, then hesitated. She turned back to the class. Seven little girls sat at their desks, leaning on their elbows, in eager anticipation of the next question, the next picture.

"No star," she said. "You didn't say, 'Soon I will live in America.'"

Silence convinced Alta she had made her point, but then Sue said, "Live here." Her finger mashed the desk with a finality that made Alta surrender. She turned and placed a star by Sue's name.

Behind her, a desk scraped the ground, as if kicked aside. Alta turned back to face seven waving arms. Slowly, she took in the arch in Sue's back. And again. Sue's body convulsed in a rapid succession of shocks that drove her desk forward. Alta told herself Sue was simply anxious to try again. Sue's arms flailed wildly. Racking jolts, like someone being given shock treatments, contorted her body.

"Sue!" Alta ran to the child, wildly tossing surrounding desks out of her way.

The girls crowded close, and Alta pushed them from her brusquely. Kneeling, she reached into her pockets, searching for some assistance: a pencil, Kleenex, a ten-dollar Hong Kong bill. She wrapped the pencil with the Kleenex, using fingers now grimy with dust which lay in her pocket, merciless fingers which pressed against Sue's small jaw until they managed to insert the pencil between clamped teeth.

The girls leaned at her back, calling to Sue in Vietnamese. Again, Alta pushed them aside. "Go get the doctor," she demanded of Mary.

When Mary wavered, she shouted, "Doctor!" Her voice was filled with the fury of helplessness. "Clinic!"

She shoved Mary as if to physically drive her in the direction of the one-room clinic. "Now!"

Mary ran out the door.

Like flies, the girls drew close. They waited that way. Alta restrained the now screaming Sue, trying to keep her from banging her head, worried about the pencil that she'd jammed between the child's teeth and the girls calling to Sue, now softly, now louder.

Time unfolded with an aching deliberateness: the return with the doctor, the shot to calm a now screaming Sue, the assistant carrying Sue to Kai Tak's clinic, the call for a special doctor.

It was not epilepsy.

"Cannot explain," the Chinese doctor said.

Molly and Alta probed the flat gray book of names.

"Her mother has a pass to work outside camp," Molly said. "No father."

"Anyone else?"

"Grandparents somewhere." Then, "Here, I've got them at B-6. No! Wait!" Molly turned pages.

"Come on!" Alta yelled. "We'll begin at B-6."

Rains had washed dust from leafless bushes, exposing quivering naked branches. Air heavy with water dragged Alta down as she pressed across the empty field to the barracks. She heard Molly's breathing behind her, long gulping sighs.

Along the sides of the barracks, women, several with babies strapped to their backs, cooked in makeshift burners, only partially protected from the rain by overhanging roofs. The omnipresent smell of *nuoc mam* pursued Alta and Molly along slippery sideways. Rain dripped from their hair into their eyes.

"This should be it," Molly said. "It's the even-numbered side."

Alta bolted through the entryway. Just inside, she stopped, momentarily blinded by the dark. Unseen life lifted the hairs on her arms. Her eyes adjusted to the dim light from windows up near the ceiling, and she drew back. Her reaction was always the same, the same gasp at the same acrid smell of food and babies and earth. She could taste mold and rot on her tongue, feel infection closing off the back of her throat, a slow steady decay which clung to her as she walked down the long rows of metal beds stacked five high and four deep. A crudely built shelf storing food ran the length of two beds. Alta watched a rat scratch through a bag of rice, and she understood why some volunteers never came into this area. Water dripped from a leak in the high corrugated roof. Her eyes met those of a woman sweeping the space in front of her bed. "Do you know Sue Nguyen?" Alta asked. Her voice sounded harsh and frightened.

The woman shook her head and turned back to her sweeping.

Trying not to drip on those who'd managed to keep dry, Alta asked again, of someone else. And again. The Vietnamese stared blankly. She felt their suspicion creep up her spine.

"They don't know the name Sue," Molly said.

"We'll ask the children," Alta said. Why hadn't she insisted on Vietnamese names?

The children shrugged. Some repeated, "Sue" or "My name is Sue."

Down one narrow side aisle, then another, small children scattering across the beds into the shadows, Alta reached a hammock with an infant. It hung about a foot above one of the beds, and the baby inside was screeching. A small girl sitting on the bed used her foot to nudge the hammock without looking at the infant. Alta recognized her; she was the little girl howling in the dust earlier.

"Sue," she shouted. "Where is Sue?"

The little girl smiled. To each question, her response was the same. "Friend."

"I don't think they're in here," Molly said. Water had caked dust into mud at her ankles.

Something ran across Alta's foot, and she yelped, biting her tongue. She pushed Molly forward. "Let's get out of here."

Outside, they looked at each other, helpless. They ignored the small pre-schoolers who crowded around them, coming from their hiding places in the barracks and calling, "Hiah, tee-cha." They ignored the rain that pursued them.

Then Alta saw one of her girls. "Betty. Betty," she shouted.

"Betty?" Molly said. "Where in the hell did she get a name like Betty?"

Alta shook her head. It was the name she'd given her. Betty looked up but did not move to join them. Then recognition showed on her face, and she ran to them.

"Where does Sue live?" Alta asked.

Betty's voice was hesitant. "She live in America?"

"Here," Alta insisted. She found she wanted to laugh, and she couldn't believe her own idiocy.

Pulling back a strand of very blonde hair, Molly asked the girl in Chinese. Betty looked curiously, unwilling to believe that Chinese could come from that fair face, though she understood her Chinese.

The roar of a Pan Am 747 revving its engines for takeoff made it impossible to hear Betty's answer. Alta pointed at the numbers on the barracks. A blast from the plane's engines tore at their clothes; it scooped mud from the ground, splattering their arms and legs. Along the sides of the barracks, women shielded pots of food with their bodies.

When the noise and wind died down, Betty smiled. "She is nine years," she said.

Alta's finger jabbed the air, taking in several buildings. "What house Sue?"

Betty bit her lip in thought. She looked at the building, then Alta, then back to the building. "She live here," she said and cast a look back over her shoulder.

"You take us," Alta said.

Inside the barracks, Betty leading the way, the two women turned into the cross aisle. Betty pointed to an old woman who was cutting a younger woman's hair. First Alta, then Molly, explained to the old woman that her granddaughter was sick. She needed a relative to be with her. When the grandmother didn't respond, explanation became high-pitched demands, Alta in English, Molly in Chinese.

Grandmother continued cutting hair. She didn't turn her back to them or acknowledge she hadn't understood or even that she had understood. She simply cut hair.

Alta tried sign language. She got Betty to explain in Vietnamese. Unsure of Betty's explanation, she found an adult who knew some English and had her explain. After speaking with grandmother for several minutes, the woman turned to Alta with a half-shrug.

Betty pointed to an old man who sat watching. "Father," Betty said.

"Must be the grandfather," Molly said.

Alta talked with the grandfather. She explained. She had the woman explain again. With a look toward grandmother, who saw only her scissors, grandfather nodded.

Relieved, Molly and Alta ran to the end of the aisle, then looked back to make sure grandfather was still with them. The old man had not moved from his place, except to lean over and pick up one worn sandal from the cement. While they watched, impatient, he reached down and picked up the other sandal. Alta rocked to and fro. Hands behind her back, Molly snapped her fingers. Grandfather put on one sandal.

Alta let out a guffaw. She put her hand over her mouth and looked at Molly. Molly stared around the dark room. Both women looked back for the old man. Grandfather put on the other sandal. Molly laughed, then forced herself to silence. And still grandfather did not come.

The women weighed the old man's painstaking movements, acts of appeasement. They looked at each other again. Then they leaned against the rails of bunk beds, and laughed. Unable to control themselves, they leaned down against the beds and shouted and pounded their chests as if they were choking, and laughed. They laughed until they were weary and out of breath. Then they wiped at the tears on their cheeks. They looked sheepishly around at the grandfather one final time before slipping out the door.

Alta sat beside Sue's cot in the clinic, the soothing effects of her galloping laughter a faraway memory. Since her arrival several hours earlier, Sue had neither opened her eyes nor spoken. A bruise was forming around her mouth.

Thunder roared and lightning sizzled across the sky. Rain exploded against the metal roof. The engine whine of a plane taking off from Kai Tak Airport wrapped around the clinic walls. Alta looked to the door to find Sue's grandmother standing in the doorway, light from the clinic lamps splayed out around her on the muddy ground. Rain drops popped onto her feet.

Alta breathed a sigh of relief. She turned to the doctor. "Please thank her for coming," she said.

The doctor, a volunteer from Hong Kong's hospitals, looked carefully at Alta, then spoke briefly to the old woman.

Without acknowledging him, the old woman looked down at the child who opened her eyes wearily.

Wind slammed the door shut.

Grandmother leaned over the bed, close to the child's face. And screamed. Rage flooded the bed. Spittle blotched Sue's face.

"Stop her! Stop her!"

The doctor's eyes remained focused on his papers. This wasn't his problem.

Alta realized there would be no help from beyond. No magical transfer to another, better, camp. No sudden appearance of a name on the Holding Area wall. She must explain the way immigration to America actually worked. Staring at Sue's small weary face, she willed herself to make everything right, but America was now as incomprehensible to Alta as were grandmother's screams of betrayal.

Each woman held her position on either side of the bed, the one shrieking with rage, the other stunned and silent. Between them, the child sank deeper and deeper into her pillows. She closed her eyes tight, squeezed them tighter, and tighter.

Sondra Zeidenstein

SOFTWARE

I felt tall and white, graceless on the orchid-colored carpet of the elegant reception room of the health salon in Kuala Lumpur, the capitol of Malaysia. My friend, Fatima, a Pakistani, was arguing with the manager. "Look here," she said, "I weigh 119 pounds! But when I started your exercise program I was only 113. I've paid you lots and lots of money. But all that's happening is I'm gaining weight." Fatima's voice was high and loud. There was petulance in her voice and in the lines around her mouth.

"You're eating too much," the manager responded sternly. "It is because of all the travel you do. Here, sign up for more exercises. You'll get a free facial with the first six classes." Her voice was flat, unyielding. She stood behind her desk, a professional smile on her heavily made-up face. "Sign here," she said.

I would hate to be at her mercy, I thought. I was in this tropical country halfway around the globe from my Vermont home to work for two weeks as a consultant to Fatima, my friend and colleague who was with the new United Nations office here. I'd come to the health salon as Fatima's guest after my first day at the office. The manager wrote my name on the guest pass as I spelled it slowly, SALTENBERG. Does anyone know the significance of my name, I wondered, and realized I was still feeling paranoid.

I had never felt that my Jewishness made me stand out in any way from other white people in the years I'd lived in South Asia with my husband and children. Seven years altogether. In Nepal and India in the 1960s, anyone who was white was assumed to be Christian; being Jewish didn't mean anything special to Hindus. In Bangladesh in the early seventies, before the struggle of Palestinians for nationhood gained them power and friends, before the increase in terrorist acts by the PLO and swift massive reprisals by Israel, before the implacable voice of fundamentalism spread into all Muslim countries, I had felt secure and comfortable with my Bangladeshi friends.

I had followed those upsetting events—the hijacking of Achille Lauro and passenger-crammed jumbo jets, the Israeli roundups of Palestinians, the smashing of Palestinian homes on the West Bank to rubble—from the quiet of my home in the woods. I studied the newspapers, watched every moment of television coverage, followed with dismay the monolithic response of American Jews in the name of allegiance to Israel. I knew which side I was on as I buttered toast in my oak-paneled kitchen.

But yesterday, my first day at the office, Fatima had received a phone call. "Do you know that your new consultant is Jewish," the caller inquired. "Don't you know that is a Jewish name? All names ending in 'berg' are Jewish."

"What is this?" Fatima asked impatiently. "She is an American."

"That may be," the man said, "but that is a Jewish name. And we know that all American Jews carry two passports, one American and one Israeli. Our police can put a tracer on her. They can find out everything there is to know in a week. Send me her visa."

I did not hear about this conversation until much later in the day. All I knew was that Fatima had lost her usual smile, her sparkling eyes had gone dull. "Something very irritating happened," was all she would say. "It is spoiling my day. I'll tell you about it later."

Near midnight, Fatima told me what had happened. We were in her apartment where I was staying. We had just said good-bye to dinner guests and were still warmed by the talk and laughter. "I was afraid to tell you," Fatima said. "It's just an annoyance, some busybody who wants to show me his importance. But I didn't know how you'd react, I didn't know how upset you'd be." She sat on the couch, her feet pulled up under her, her bright sari adorning the nubby beige cover.

I felt my body tense inside the flowing silk shirt and pants I'd felt so graceful in all evening. Will they shoot me, I wondered. Will they lock me in jail? I did not want to show the fright which overwhelmed me so unexpectedly.

Fatima went on explaining, "You know it's against the immigration laws here for Israelis to enter the country. Of course my country doesn't allow Israelis in either."

Who are these people, I thought, anger replacing fear, who forbid Israelis to enter their countries? For a moment, I was flooded with self-righteousness. But the question did not remain rhetorical. They are Muslims, I answered myself, like Fatima.

Words and images crowded my mind, called up by the word *Muslim*. This had happened to me before, this rush of past impressions to explicate the present. I assumed it came with age, the long backward stretch of experience, varied, fragmented, yet filed somehow for recall. The word always reminded me of the airport computer where a clerk types in my name and watches information flow in from all over the world, from arrangements made months before, not always accurate, but still miraculous. That must be the way the police work too, I thought now, fright adding a new image.

Arabs . . . PLO . . . Mecca . . . the chain of associations begins. Whole episodes imprint their meaning in an instant. . . . It is two years ago. I am in the living room of a Muslim friend in Bangladesh. The television is on: the image is of a robed Arab, the words are Arabic. The camera moves from his eloquent face and raised hands out over thousands of white-garmented men on their knees listening, praying. My friend is explaining, "It is Mecca. It is the king of Saudi Arabia speaking to the pilgrims who have come from all over the world."

I know that each white-robed pilgrim will soon don the clothes of his own country, board a 747, be met at the airport by cars or rickshaws, travel in bullock carts and country boats and camels, will carry these liquid sounds to remote villages. But the words will already be there waiting. Satellite works faster than cumbersome airplanes.

"What is he saying?" I ask.

"He is saying," my friend tells me frankly, "that Israel is the enemy, that all Arabs must be united against Israel, that that is the wish of Allah."

Another scene flashes, called up by the first. It is the same living room just last week, when I stopped to see that same friend on my way to Fatima's. The room is noisy with children, with television again. This time it is Tony Curtis as "The Saint" blaring over three conversations going at once. I am uncomfortable on the drab hard couch, wood cutting into my thighs; I find the noise dizzying; but I feel at home. At the other end of the couch, a nervous, delicate man leans across his wife to speak to me.

"I just came back from Beirut. I was trapped there for nine months." His English is halting. "I was a student."

"It must have been terrible," I say, trying to block out "The Saint."

"It was terrible," he responds. "We were always in danger. Israeli soldiers know we are Muslims. They don't ask questions; they shoot first."

Seeing sympathy on my face, he goes on. "It wasn't the Israelis' fault," he starts. I'm not sure what the "it" refers to. "There were still PLO left behind after Arafat said they were all gone. And it's true, PLO adults teach the Palestinian children how to shoot, how to throw grenades."

It's the massacre at the Palestinian camp in Lebanon he's referring to, I realize. "No," I say, "it was the Israelis' fault. They should have anticipated what would happen."

He goes on, "We were staying in an apartment building during the troubles. There were some Palestinians taking shelter with us, a businessman and his wife. And they had children." He glances over at his little boy in a blue knit suit, moving little wooden blocks from shelf to shelf, ignoring the grownups. "I couldn't speak to them. I didn't know their language, but they were friendly, and the children always stayed around us. Especially the little girl. She was my special friend. She felt attached to me somehow." I felt a chill.

"Whenever I came into the courtyard of the building, she would stop whatever she was doing and run over to play with me. Then, when the war was over, the Palestinians in our building were told to go back to their homes, that things would be straightened out. They were businessmen. They went back to their home in the camp."

I hear nothing else in the room now. "We didn't know there was a massacre until four days later. We heard about it on shortwave. I had to go there. I saw their house."

The child is jumping at my knees. I turn and see Tony Curtis shouting words I can't make out at a blank-faced blond woman.

"They were caught on the staircase, the mother carrying the two children." I turn back and see him make three dots with his finger, one on each shoulder, one in the center of his chest, for where the bullets hit. "I couldn't sleep for nights."

In Fatima's living room, my anger drained as quickly as it had risen. "He thinks he knows so much," Fatima said, "the way he said it so confidently, that all American Jews have two passports. He's just trying to show off. There's nothing to worry about."

By the morning, I had forgotten all about it. I was busy with my work when there was a discreet knock at the office door. "The car is waiting for the trip to the bank," I was told. "You can go along to get your traveler's checks." I was glad for the interruption. The office was cold and empty, like the building itself, which was hurriedly built on the outskirts of the city, cut off from the natural flow of city life.

At the bank, I sat on a low coral-streaked marble bench across from the tellers and waited for my traveler's checks. I studied the tellers, mostly women, their various backgrounds revealed in clothing that ranged from fashionable to orthodox. One in particular attracted my eyes. She wore what looked like an old-fashioned nun's habit. It was dark brown, of thick cotton, and it cut a straight line across her forehead, down each cheek and across her chin before it fell, in deep folds, over her shoulders and breasts. All I could see of the Muslim woman was a perfect oval face, flattened nose, eyes cast down as if in purdah too, wide curved mouth unsmiling.

I shifted on the bench, the air-conditioning making me chilly. I should have brought a shawl, I thought. I'll get a backache. But it was something else that was making me uncomfortable. They're going to call my name. They have my name from the form I filled out, and they're going to call it when it's my turn. I looked again at the beautiful expressionless face. My mind flashed the image of a beheaded Buddha. I'd seen them all over Asia wherever Islam replaced Buddhism, smashed stone images, noses hacked off, fingers, hands, toes, whatever could be loosened from massive stone, broken. Last night came back to me for the first time.

I had been up in the middle of the night. For how long I wasn't sure. It was a delayed reaction. "Don't worry," I'd said to Fatima before we went to bed. "I'm not upset. As long as I'm not going to be shot or go to jail."

"Nothing like that," Fatima answered cheerfully, relieved that I was being so sensible about the minor incident. "Anyway, if anyone bothers you, just tell them you'll call the American Embassy. Goodnight."

"Goodnight."

It was about three when I woke. There was no sound. The ceiling fan moved moist tropical air silently, caressing my face and bare shoulders above the light sheet. The louvered glass of the windows opened onto a quiet tree-lined suburban street. The doors were securely locked.

I want to go home, I thought, lying there. Two weeks and then I can go, I tried to reassure myself. It feels like forever. Don't think about it, I advised myself, remembering something I read recently by a man who was imprisoned in Argentina, Timerman probably: when you're in prison, the worst thing to do is think about the world outside. I pushed away thoughts of my husband, house, children, dog, my secure life ten thousand miles, twenty hours of flying time away. Once I get past the immigration officer at the airport, I reminded myself.

I rearranged the pillow trying to get comfortable, pulled my knees up to my stomach, realized my breath was very rapid and shallow. I concentrated on drawing air slowly and deeply. It was a struggle, but slowly I forced it to start from my stomach, fill my chest, back, shoulders. If they shoot me, I thought more calmly now, not really believing it would happen, there's nothing much I can do. But that's not what's really bothering me. Its that they picked me out . . . . I caught myself thinking "they," already magnifying one phone call to an organized network. Anyway, someone picked me out as undesirable. Why? Because I am Jewish. Because this is a Muslim country. Because a Holy War is going on.

Behind my closed eyes, my accuser appeared unbidden. He was a stern, bearded, broad-faced man in uniform. His eyes were cold. He spoke little English. "It's not true," I addressed him. "American Jews don't have Israeli passports." He stared without expression.

He's right, I thought. It's as if we did have passports, most of us. Oh why do I have to see from so many points of view, I wondered, annoyed with myself. Why can't I have some simple gut reaction like Fatima. If anyone says a word against her country, against Islam, she takes it as an affront to herself and flares back. Why do *I* have to remember my friend Martha who was pulled from the customs line at the airport in Israel because she is Black and questioned by soldiers for an hour: who are you, why are you here, what do you want, until she was crying.

I know the world is falling apart, I told myself, but I've seen what I've seen. I don't think there is morality in groups, only in individuals. Groups turn into sides, gangs, factions. And look, I'm caught in the middle!

A flash of fear ran through me again. I'll say I'm not Jewish if they confront me, I told myself. They don't really know. That's how I'll get out of this. In an instant the flood of images was so dense as to be overwhelming. I was thirteen when the Jewish camps were liberated. I could not question their compulsion. No, I thought, pulling the sheet up over my shoulder, staring into the cold eyes of the bearded man. Whatever happens, I will never deny that I am a Jew. I will not buy my escape that way. But then, I'll call my Embassy. I stretched out my legs and was soon asleep.

After work, we went to Fatima's health club. It was different from the bare, functional office—subtle lighting, mirrors reflecting gilded white columns, lovely chairs beside glass coffee tables where husbands sat waiting.

In the sauna, I finally began to relax. Sweat poured down my face, behind my knees, into the hollow of my collar bone. It was very dark, the room smelled of wood and heat. The women who sat or reclined on long shelves could not see each other's dark faces and bodies, but still they held their towels modestly over breast and groin. The voices were sweet in my ears, murmuring. It was a friendly atmosphere, but as I felt my muscles soften, I heard Fatima's voice joking in the car as we were driving here, "I talked to him again, told him you had no trouble traveling in Egypt and Jordan. But he said it didn't matter, the police here were much smarter." Tension clogged my pores.

After the sauna, I waited for my name to be called for a facial. Fatima was called first. Then a pink-uniformed masseuse looking at a slip of paper called out, "Sultana." No one came forward in response. She said again, "Sultana . . . facial. . . seven o'clock," and looked toward me. It must be me, I thought and went over to look at the slip of paper. On it was written, *Sultana Ber.* I smiled to myself. They must have heard Saltenberg as Sultana Ber. "That's me," I said and followed the young woman to the softly lit room.

Lying down, a towel across my chest, my face in the practiced hands of the woman who was moving gentle fingers from chin to earbone, pressing there a moment, then down to point of chin, I was infinitely soothed. No one had ever massaged my face before. I heard soft music in the distance and realized it was Christmas music, tinkly sanitized carols. They sounded odd in the tropics, even in December.

I stopped thinking. I heard the woman announce each procedure in her soft voice: "steam . . . blackheads . . . mask . . . hot cloth . . . massage." Only once I opened my eyes and was surprised at the vision above me, the opalescent curves of eyes looking down. Like a cat or a Buddha face, eyes slightly open.

"Your hair is so fine," the woman spoke to me once, "so soft and fine." Otherwise she murmured in another language to the woman working across the room on someone else's face. "Finish," she said finally and I rose reluctantly, wishing it were not over.

Then, just as I was about to leave the room, the masseuse asked me, "Where are you from?"

I felt my nerves tingle with anxiety. "I'm from America."

"Oh," the woman murmured, looking puzzled. "I thought you were *Araby.* Your name, Sultana, the shape of your face . . .I thought you were *Araby,* from Saudi Arabia."

I didn't know what to say. I felt a surge of intimacy. What I wanted to say, maybe because the word Araby reminded me of Romany, was:

"My ancestors are from Romania." But what if she went on questioning me? I was fearful of what the next question might be, or the next. So I just smiled and turned away. Then I heard her say something I didn't understand. I turned back and asked, sharply, "What is it?"

The masseuse repeated her words, "Merry Christmas."

Ann Pancake

KEEPING CLEAN IN KORAT

The Friendship Highway is, in theory, four and, in practice, eight to ten lanes of Thai traffic: three-wheeled taxis, portable kitchens, water buffalo along with their herders, homemade wheelchairs, an occasional elephant, the intermittent Mercedes, and families of four or five wedged onto single motorcycles. Bangkok-bent semis barrel past, their backdraft unbalancing fruit, dumpling, and ice cream vendors toiling on tricycles. Then come the air-conditioned buses where stewardesses serve the new bourgeoisie watered-down Pepsi in communal plastic cups. The "ordinary" buses, the cheap ones, are always overstaffed with renegade teenaged conductors who swing barechested out of the doorless doorways. They grin, baring their teeth against the grit, intoxicated by the danger and howling their monosyllable of English,"You! You! You!" at the anomaly of blonde me waiting on the shoulder to cross.

The "Friend" in Friendship is the U.S., the highway built for the Vietnam War to transport U.S. supplies and personnel deeper into Northeast Thailand to the big bomber bases (Korat, Ubon Ratchathani, Udon, Nakhon Pathom)where our planes took off to carpet bomb Vietnam and Laos. I live and teach in Korat, which, as the "Gateway to the Northeast," was one of the most important military installations. Along with Turkish baths and red-haired Amerasian children, Korat was left a huge airbase that it still uses. Although the Northeast, or "Issan," as it is known in Thai, is the driest and least fertile, thus poorest, region in Thailand, Korat hosts a wealthy military class, and inside the base are the only groomed green areas in the entire city, which is the second largest in the nation. If you can get past the armed guards at the gates, the base offers a lake, a horse racetrack, and a golf course with female caddies in blue smocks and cone hats who will lug your clubs around on their backs, yet another of the apparently infinite variations on Thailand's sex trade.

The base takes on particular interest for me because I arrive in Bangkok en route to this teaching position on May 26, 1992, exactly one week after Thai government troops staged their latest slaughter of unarmed democracy demonstrators. When I reach Korat, I discover that almost no one speaks enough English to talk about the massacre, and those who do speak English evidently consider it an inappropriate subject to discuss with an American woman. The reasons for this silence become clearer as I stay on and realize that most of the Thais in Korat above poverty level, which includes anyone who has had the opportunity for enough education to learn English, have scrambled over the poor through family connections to the military. Consequently, I resort to following the aftermath of what becomes known as "Bloody May" through the *Bangkok Post*. Yet I soon learn that much more instructive, on not only the aftermath, but also the antecedents, of such matters is the day-to-day business of keeping clean along the Friendship Highway.

I approach the Friendship Highway twice daily with two objectives: first, to reach the college on the other side alive (a feat I accomplish only narrowly on several occasions), and, second, to reach the other side without stepping on anything. Buffalo dung dries quickly and brushes off, but roadkill does not, nor do the often unidentifiable "spills"—one unforgettable spill being a hundred-foot-long ribbon of market-ready intestines unfurled along an outside lane. In lieu of guardrails, an unbroken collar of detritus borders the Friendship Highway, about eight feet off the shoulder where some law of physics deposits anything not sticky after the traffic blasts it from the pavement. Because only those "spills" large enough to disrupt traffic-like bloated dogs—are ever moved aside, I follow the intestines through each stage of their decay as I pass back and forth to work: at first, plump, rosy, and blue; by that afternoon, sun-bleached and reeking; finally just shriveled twists adhering to the asphalt. Such is the view from the Friendship Highway, built to facilitate "my" war on Vietnam.

Of course, Vietnam was never "my" war before I arrived in Southeast Asia, much the way America is never "my" country until I leave it for extended periods. While in the U.S., I have the luxury of considering myself an exception to the American rule, a citizen solely by accident of birth. As long as I stay within U.S. borders, I can deceive myself that I share no responsibility with those men making the decisions in Washington, and although I suffer the negative repercussions of their decisions, I accrue none of the benefits. Nor have I come to Thailand with any lofty ideals about helping those less fortunate than I. Three years of teaching English in two other countries have cured me of any such delusions and taught me that the best rule of thumb is to keep a low profile, mind my own business, and check my white (wo)man's burden at an airport locker. I've come to Thailand because I've vacationed here twice before and found its culture interesting and its people amiable, and because the humanities degree that makes me only marginally employable in the U.S. in the best of times is null and void during a recession and because in Korat I've found a reasonably well-paying job. But even while those other two countries reminded me hourly of my nationality, race, and class—attributes of which I'm comfortably oblivious back home—they still permitted me the fiction that my business was mine to mind. No, it has never been "my" war until I move within earshot of the Friendship Highway, and even then, not until I meet the man in the fedora.

A few weeks after I begin my position at a small private college, I'm given a long weekend and take a trip up to Nong Khai, one terminus of the Friendship Highway. I sip Nescafé along a muddy street that dead-ends at the Mekong River, and across that I can see Laos. Although aside from dense, Thai-looking vegetation, all I can discern of Communist Laos are three billboards, each advertising Pepsi. A man in a fedora stops by and while smalltalking about the rain asks my nationality. After I admit I'm American, he takes a seat to confide in me, "I fought in your war in Vietnam."

To me, the "you" reverberates so loudly over the morning torrent that I don't even hear his next two or three sentences. This is the first time, I realize, it has ever occurred to me that it was "my" war. I look down into my coffee cup, then catch from the corner of my eye the gutter that parallels the open front of the restaurant, water-swollen plastic bags pitching through the dirty runoff. But the man in the fedora doesn't notice that I'm distracted. He is a zealot, is more of an American patriot that I will ever be, and, as he tells his story, he spins his hat in his hands with enthusiasm.

"But I never killed anyone, sir," he adds. "I was close, but I thought, what's the use? We all die someday, sir. Everyone dies someday." He end-stops nearly every sentence with an honorific tag the way Thai does, except the gender of the Thai tag depends on the speaker, not the listener, and the man in the fedora has never learned the distinction. Most likely he has never had to learn it because he's spoken English only to males. It turns out that the man in the fedora is a translator, and not just any translator, but a translator for CIA teams making forays into Laos after MIA's.

"Not through Immigration, never through Immigration, sir—we sneak across up the river." He is a true believer, is convinced that all the sightings are for real, sir, and he even gives the "sir" the high tone it would take in Thai. "Always news, news," he says, "but we go and nothing. Nothing." He throws up his hands. I know that every Southeast Asian refugee who enters a camp is questioned about having seen live Americans, and many, believing it will expedite their passage to the U.S., answer yes, but about this I say nothing. Nothing. "I talk to this man, he says see this man at the next village, but nothing, sir. Unofficial, never official," he assures me, and why is he confessing this? Does he expect me to appreciate his efforts? Should I appreciate his efforts?

I was twelve years old when Saigon fell. Our *Weekly Reader* reported only upbeat news, so the extent of its Vietnam War coverage was the return of the POW's whom the little paper portrayed as triumphant heroes. Before that, the war played as lifelong white noise on the TV, a remote backdrop for everything else, birthdays, lost teeth, first days of school, and the arrivals of all five of my brothers and sisters. I couldn't remember a state of unwar. But it was never *my* war.

The man in the fedora continues, tells me he has seen firsthand what communism has done to Laos," Nothing, they have nothing, sir, and they cannot say what they want or move around." He thanks his lucky stars (and stripes) Thailand is not communist."Over here, we can move around. Anywhere we want, we can go, sir. Not like there, sir." At the end of the street and across that slow, milky river lies Laos, per capita the most heavily bombed country in the history of the world. Although the man in the fedora detests communism, he believes that Thailand is being ruined by "the rich people making the farmers go to the factories, sir. There are enough factories in the world to make everything! EVERYTHING!" And he doesn't lay a "sir" on that one.

It's soon after that I begin to notice the trash.

I don't live directly on the Friendship Highway, but within a tangle of rutted tracks that run ankle-deep mud four months of the year and disgorge onto the Highway. Our neighborhood is called the Thai equivalent of "Bamboo Highland," although it stretches from horizon to horizon as flat as this piece of paper and as empty of bamboo. Because we live just beyond Korat's city limits, we have no mail delivery or trash collection. When I first move in and ask my landlord where I was to put my garbage, he picks up a rotting rattan chair that had been left behind by a former tenant and pitches it off the back stoop into the swamp which was, in effect, my yard. "Out there!" he giggles. Appalled to my middle-class American marrow, I pack my garbage out for the first month or two, passing up the half dozen dumps that punctuate our road, including one right across from my front door, to deposit *my* trash in the cans on the far side of the Friendship Highway where a municipal garbage truck occasionally puts in an appearance.

From my favorite noodle shop I have an enlightening view of these garbage trucks. A Thai garbage man has the opportunity to double his wages every day through scavenging, so there is none of the sterile distance of many American garbage trucks where human hands never contact a can or even a lid, a fork-lift picking up a dumpster and tossing it over the truck's head. Korat garbage trucks have a big open "window" in the center of their bodies where a man stands directly in the collected garbage within arms reach of a half-dozen baskets strung along the spine of the open tank. As his colleagues on the ground toss up baskets or cans of fresh garbage, he sifts each into the bed, sorting aluminum, wood, plastic, glass, paper, and any other promising odds and ends into their respective baskets, now and then dancing up and down to tamp down all the useless garbage into the truck guts. What *is* determined useless is hard for me to imagine, since even restaurant and food stall slop, chicken guts, watery rice, and vegetable parings, are carted away in cooking oil tins by elderly men on wobbly tricycles.

After a few weeks, I'm finally struck by the absurdity of dragging all these leaky bags to city limits. Every ounce I produce has to go somewhere, so why not out in front of my house with all the neighbors'? The only real difference in the U.S., or across the Highway, is that there it's carted out of sight to a "sanitary landfill," and although this is supposed to serve as a sort of "germ" quarantine, it still ends up some place on earth. Wouldn't its inescapable presence, I ask myself, mounting higher and higher, make me think twice about the amount of garbage I'm generating? As I watch curious passers-by rummage through the open dumps, I find myself comparing Thai garbage to American garbage, which is always disguised in plastic bags, "lawn-green" plastic, no less, as though if camouflaged it will fade harmlessly into the landscape, all of it tied up with wire twists to protect each garbage maker's privacy.

In Southeast Asia, privacy is a privilege few can afford, including me. When I begin depositing my trash in the ditch across the road, I must be prepared to confront my discarded T-shirt on a kid at the local store, burn any personal mail I don't want gusting around the neighborhood, smell my watermelon and papaya rinds rot, and inhale my own milk cartons smouldering in the night. Sometimes, walking home on sweltering afternoons, I'll let my eyes glaze over and see our neighborhood as simply one enormous dump broken up by a couple of paths, a few houses; then I'll blink to shift perspective and each dump becomes distinct: green gutter dumps, little personal house dumps doubling as urinals, the swamp dump where children paddle around on discarded chunks of Styrofoam, the paddy irrigation dumps, and the pair of acre-sized dumps surrounding the new bourgeois condos for which the developers apparently can't find any bourgeoisie. Then, with the floods in October, we're back to a single, huge, buoyant dump. Dumps feed not only dogs, cats, goats, chickens, ducks, rats, lizards, ants, and certain undiscriminating water buffalo, but also shy and mysterious low-slung, platypus-tailed creatures that vanish under heaps of scorched banana leaves. And lying over it all—lying over the whole province the way scales cover fish—are the plastic bags, as ubiquitous and motile as insects, fluttering across the plateaus before the pre-monsoon winds, snagged by the scores in chainlink fences, dammed up wherever a stream enters a culvert or passes under a bridge, palpitating in the slimy current. If in the States we had to live in our garbage the way we do in the Bamboo Highland, would we become sensitized to our waste, or just inured to it?

When the wind is low and we've had no rain for a day or two, some conscientious soul will splash kerosene around and fire up the dumps. By morning the little ones will be scorched of everything but the recalcitrant sardine can and the maverick plastic bag; but the monster dumps, the ones near the unsellable condos, brighten the sky all night and carry the trash right into my bed. Smoke seeps through the finger-width gaps between the boards of my house even though I've fastened every window shut, and I get up in the morning with trash residue clotted in my throat. The whole neighborhood is phlegm-filled, everyone, even the children, is on their stoops hacking and spitting. In the years before I lived here, through months of traveling in Indonesia, Malaysia, Taiwan, Hong Kong, I was astounded at all the unabashed expectoration for which the Chinese in particular are infamous, and at the time, I chalked it up as a cultural difference. Now, I know it's at least in part an environmental one. It's the same with widespread public nosepicking. "Keep your nose clean" takes on a whole new significance in parts of Thailand where you blow hard at the end of the day and blacken a tissue.

The politics I'm beginning to read in the trash is more explicit on some nights than others. Occasionally I'm awakened by helicopter or jet engines, the Royal Thai Air Force playing with their American-made aircraft, and I lie watching the dump glow flicker on my walls, prevented by this American-made noise from escaping the trash back into sleep. The trash fire soaks into my lungs, and I draw my sheet over my face as a futile attempt at a filter. I imagine what poisons and carcinogens I'm inhaling and calculate the number of days it must be subtracting from my life. Jet Noise, Sound of Freedom: American bumpersticker bravado. I see by my clock that it's three A.M., yet my neighbors are handwashing laundry under my window. American bombers returning here to base twenty-five years ago, I've heard, would first jettison leftover bombs on Laos to avoid reprimands by officers who had ordered them to empty over Vietnam, which was much better defended and more dangerous. Lao, Vietnamese, and Cambodian farmers still strike dormant U.S. ordinance with plows, annihilate their buffalo, lose an arm, a leg.

Three-thirty and the Top Guns have gone home. Often I wonder about the paraplegics on Korat sidewalks with begging cups between their stumps, because the proximity to Laos and Cambodia that made this city ideal for the airbase also makes it a favorite for refugees. When I drop them coins, they return no recognition. They show no hate and no appreciation. I trudge on, keeping to the shade, past the intermittent trash piles and through the odor of rot. Thailand, I think, keeps very few secrets.

More mysterious is the VFW Cafeteria. Adjacent to one of the seediest hotels in Korat, this American war relic might prove a happier hunting ground for the man in the fedora than any place he's visited in Laos. Although it's kept eternally dark—probably to prevent diners from examining what's served—after my eyes adjust I see that I've backpedaled into "my war" from the American point-of-view again. To the left of the door sags a forlorn block of particleboard lockers, each labeled with a scrap of masking tape: "Bob," "Alan," "Skip." The commemorative plaques nearby are now so mildewed I can't even make out what person or event they're intended to memorialize. And behind the bar hang discolored pinups of Asian girls, pink feathers sprinkled strategically over their nipples, reminiscent of the backdrop of every bar scene in every American movie about Vietnam I've ever watched. Sequestered in the booths along the walls are the new Thai middle class dining on poorly prepared and overpriced pork chops and spaghetti, but the tables in the center of the room are permanently occupied by U.S. vets—yes, the ones who just never went home—and the vets are occupied from the eight A.M. opening onwards with Singha beer, Krungthep cigarettes (in defiance of the No-Smoking sign), and a TV that is usually tuned in to dubbed American cartoons, Chip and Dale chortling in Thai tones.

I sit alone over my pinto beans, which are the reason I visit the VFW. They come with a ship's biscuit instead of cornbread, but they still remind me of home. It's like home here in another way, too: in the VFW, the war stops being mine and becomes theirs again. Even though I go for days or even weeks in Korat without seeing another Westerner, I am still invisible to the vets in the VFW. In the VFW, I am comfortably excluded: it is their club and their history.

None of them fits the American stereotype of the Vietnam vet. Twenty years in Korat have eroded any distinguishing characteristics they might once have had until they all look like each other and like any middle-aged retiree on a fixed income back in the States. Paunchy in their polyester clothes, shod in white socks and plastic slippers, many are accompanied by Thai wives with whom they converse only in English. I try, as I finish my biscuit, to rewind time and un-age these women. What were they in 1967? Prostitutes, officers' daughters, sticky rice vendors? The vets swap both American videotapes and VCR's. I imagine them back in their airless houses, the same movies over and over, as they vicariously live in the U.S. for a few hours.

While I pay my bill, I try to get a peak into the kitchen, which is rumored to harbor a spectacular rat population, but it's too dark for me to see, just as it is for me to determine how filthy are the tablecloths and silverware. I exit past the secret contents of the lockers, then stumble squinting into the sun where a legion of loitering bicycle rickshaw drivers catch sight of me and crow in unison that nationwide English vocabulary word: "You! You! You! You!"

As I negotiate the mud and debris of the Bamboo Highland on my way to work, I know that I'll have to suffer the ignominy of rinsing off in the outdoor spigot before I can even climb the stairs to my office, although all the other college employees, from our President down to the battalion of uniformed janitresses, will arrive not only mudless and sweatless, but without so much as a wrinkle in a sleeve, regardless of where they live or how they make their way to work. Fresh from sanitized America, I'm the only person around who hasn't learned how to keep herself clean. In Korat, which has the reputation of being one of the dirtiest cities in Thailand, this is especially difficult; but I've noticed that each Thai, in reaction to the environment, constructs around him or herself, then fiercely defends, a little envelope of absolute sterility. Interiors of homes are spotless, and those wealthy enough to own cars keep them the way the Japanese do, two or three air fresheners, frilly seat covers, and an impeccable wax job. I've watched train passengers board grungy third-class cars, stake out their seat, then draw their indispensable roll of toilet paper—which functions also as napkin, paper towel, Kleenex, and rag—and proceed to wipe down the whole area. Another method of fortifying those hygienic bubbles is through menthol inhalants, the most popular in Korat being "Vapex." Walking through populated areas of Thailand entails passing in and out of nauseating odors, and while naive Americans like myself make the mistake of trying to hold our breaths for the duration of these air pockets of stench, prepared Thais merely whip out their Vapex bottles and snort. Some rub it around their necks for longer-lasting protection, a variation on Vick's Vapo-Rub; and twice, on smelly, long-distance buses, I've watched extended families share one bottle, passing it around and around for the duration of the trip.

In a similar vein is the popularity of body powders, from imported Shower-to-Shower to St. Luke's Anti-Prickly Heat. Few conscientious parents pack their children off to school without a heavy white dose all over their faces. Initially, I thought this whiteface had some religious significance, and I was a bit deflated to learn that it was simply applied to keep them clean and cool. In certain respects, however, the Thai obsession with personal cleanliness *is* Buddhist, a religion that teaches that because we can do little to change our environment, we must attend to our responses to it. Such a philosophy, of course, stands at complete odds with the West's conviction that we modify any object or situation which we find inconvenient, inefficient, or simply incompatible with our point-of-view, then sweep the fallout under the rug for as long as possible. In Thailand, due to the inadequate trash collection and paucity of garbage cans, there is little out-of-sight, out-of-mind. Keeping clean in Korat means shifting the dirt near you to a place a little farther away. It means sweeping the sidewalk immediately in front of your shop into the gutter, pitching the refuse from your kitchen into the creek across the road, throwing the toilet paper with which you just cleaned your train seat out the train window. I once passed up the night market, my usual dining spot, to try a moderately expensive Korat restaurant where the planters doubled as wastebaskets. When the ceiling fan began blowing some loose napkins and plastic wrappers around my table, the waitress pounced on them, wadded them up, and tossed them into the planter where they joined two Coke bottles, more napkins, and sundry chewed-up straws.

The Thais live always in sight of the garbage, and at times climb directly into it, but simultaneously they somehow transcend it. I, on the other hand, am repeatedly embroiled in it, mud-sprayed by a passing bicycle, picking up fungus on my feet, continually carrying in the back of my throat the need to spit, but unable to make anything come up.

It was the height of the hot season, the most difficult season for keeping clean, when democracy demonstrators began protesting the appointment to Prime Minister of a general who had led a military coup the year before. He had insisted he'd overthrown the elected government only to clean up its corruption, and to prove his worthy intentions, he had vowed never to aspire to the Prime Ministry himself. A year later, he changed his mind. The number of demonstrators murdered varies according to the source: Western periodicals say 40, with 300 missing; the Thai English dailies, 54, and 768 missing; and as I talk with different people over the next few months, I hear missing estimates as high as 1500 and the confirmed dead at 300. I flew in somewhat apprehensive, but Bangkok is the quietest I've seen it on any of my three visits because all the tourists have evacuated, as well as a sizable percentage of the Bangkok middle-class who have taken unscheduled vacations to Chiang Mai.

As I dodge from shade spot to shade spot to get a look at the Democracy Monument, the demonstration's focal point, I find myself accosted not by the usual Bangkok gem touts and other con artists, but by young Thais, still in shock, brandishing photographs. Photographs of soldiers beating kneeling protesters about the head with batons. Photographs of headless bodies being rushed away in hotel bedsheets. Photographs of scores of young Thai men crosslegged, heads bowed, on the pavement in front of the Royal Hotel, their hands tied behind their backs in their bloodied, ripped T-shirts. Photographs of similar young men being herded by soldiers onto military trucks and buses. The people with these photographs speak almost no English, so they substitute machine gun noises as they point things out to me. At this point, the Democracy Monument has not yet been "cleaned up," but under the banners, wreaths, flowers, flags, graffiti, and posters, I notice, etched in the stone monument itself, a file of Thai soldiers, lurching, shoulder-to-shoulder, towards what I suppose is "democracy." A barefoot dwarf scurries over to hand me two joss sticks, already smoking, and I join the others making merit at the improvised altar for the dead.

✧ ✧ ✧

No, in the States, I never gave a lot of consideration to keeping clean. My body was something I showered and dressed in crisp clothes from the dryer, something I fed packaged, inspected food. Here it seems I spend all waking "non-working" time either cleaning something or looking for something clean to put in my mouth. While wasting six hours a week handwashing laundry, I become intimate with every stain, discover those surfaces on shirts and skirts most susceptible to soil and am initiated into the virtues of bleach. When the dust ends with the dry season, the insects come with the wet, penetrating places I'd thought impenetrable—sealed plastic bags, my little Japanese refrigerator—eating things that in my American ignorance I'd thought inedible—dry rice, dirty laundry, unused Q-tips. I have no sink, only a spigot in the bathroom wall, and while the tap water back home seemed only distantly related to nature, this water changes color every time it rains, and after a dry week or two, doesn't come at all. What stands leftover in my tub is urine-colored with shoals of sediment wisping across the tiles, but I must bathe in this or not bathe, so I do, watching it coast over my prickly heat, my staph infections, my undiagnosable bumps and rashes. I learn quickly from the vigilance of the middle-class Thais over every object that contacts their mouths. Before eating in roadside restaurants, they tear wads of toilet paper from the ubiquitous dispensers on the tables and wipe down every utensil, bowl, plate, and cup, as much a pre-meal ritual as Americans' saying grace. I buy and trundle home my drinking water in huge, sealed plastic bottles stamped PURIFIED, but the worms I find in one of two of these awake me to the naiveté of my American faith in labels.

And finally, there's the ever-present threat of HIV, epidemic in Thailand because of the sex trade. At times, as I cross the Friendship Highway, I can't stem the negative fantasies of being rammed by a bus, rushed, unconscious, to an emergency room, and waking, hours later, pumped full of tainted blood.

I take a *Bangkok Post* with me that week in May as I board the long-distance bus that will carry me along the Friendship Highway to Korat. A letter to the editor reminds readers that the M-16's used to murder the demonstrators came from the U.S. Still, I learn later that America's responsibility in this massacre pales in comparison to its indirect hand in similar slaughters in '73 and '76. These bloodbaths followed two solid decades of America's arming, advising, training, and subsidizing the Thai military. In the early years, "we" contributed 2.5 U.S. dollars to the Thai defense budget for every one the Thais kicked in. The *Post* lists each missing person by name, age, and sex, all 786, mostly men in their early twenties, but also a fair number of women and some kids as young as fourteen.

The country spends the summer of '92, at least ostensibly, in hot pursuit of these hundreds upon hundreds of missing persons, now assumed to be missing bodies. However, the national game of hide-and-seek soon deteriorates into a snipe hunt. Locals spy a neighborhood military base bulldozing an enormous hole, and the press sprints out to find a new soccer field. A campaigning politician insists he has inside information on the bodies being dumped in the jungle on the Thai-Burmese border, but search teams uncover nothing. Other sources claim they're all being held alive inside a military academy, and the simple discovery by an elderly Bangkok couple of three fresh graves marked "unidentified" makes front page news.

By September, however, when the military parties are narrowly edged out of a majority in Parliament and the heat of summer hysteria has cooled, the missing "Bloody May heroes" are swept away from the headlines into the corners of pages three or four, where they are more often referred to not as "missing," nor as "found," but as "not missing." Were they found dead, I ask myself? Alive? Injured? Were they found at all? For months, the only gesture the government makes towards clarifying "not missing" is to point out the carelessness of the relatives who reported them missing in the first place. Many, chides the Ministry of the Interior, were reported missing twice, and others were actually "staying with friends." When I return to Bangkok in July, I notice that the Democracy Monument has been what the government calls "renovated," every trace of the May events scrubbed clean. The Monument looms in all its magnificent sterility in a cloud of Bangkok exhaust that has already wilted the newly-sown flower beds. The number of those missing shrinks at the same rate as the amount of text giving explanation, and by November I'm nearly overlooking four-line paragraphs at "just over 100," although the *Post* adds that lists compiled by the universities are higher.

On December 4, I come across this article: the Ministry of the Interior's list of the missing is now under 100. The government has decided to count as "not missing" any person who cannot be *proven* to have been at the demonstration. How one presents this proof is not detailed. Furthermore, by the middle of December, the government says, the list will be between 40 and 60, and at that point, the case will be closed, this foul odor obliterated by a nationwide snort of Vapex. I'm impressed by a government that can tell two weeks in advance the final count of bodies that have been missing for seven months. The official 40-to-60 count of those missing is vaguely reminiscent not only of the official 40 slaughtered in May, but also of the official 46 murdered in the October '76 demonstration. Furthermore, this international *faux pas* will be tidied up in a timely fashion, just before the New Year's holidays, enabling everyone to enjoy the festivities then begin 1993 with a clean conscience.

The plot is so transparent to me as I follow it through the narrow window of the Thai English language daily that I'm astounded it seems to disturb no one else. What's being propagated in the Thai language papers? Are people protesting, but the *Post* isn't covering them? Is the deceit obvious to me only because I'm an outsider? Does it outrage me only because of my aseptic American origins? Does the populace regard the affair with the same attitude that makes popular St. Luke's Anti-Prickly Heat powder and the never-leave-home-without-it roll of toilet paper? I haven't the language, the information, or the understanding of the culture even to know *what* is going on, much less draw conclusions about why. By December, I have to revise my generalizations about Thailand's lack of secrets, at least when those secrets pertain to its own machinations, and not America's.

I realize, after months of trying to keep clean that "my" implication in the whole mess was smeared in my face within four days of my arrival, although in my initial disorientation, jet lag, and unfamiliarity with trash, I didn't process it until much later. It is May 30, 1992, Memorial Day weekend, no less, when I first pull into Korat via the Friendship Highway, ten days after the massacre. *My* government, or so I heard on CNN before I left home, has reacted to "Bloody May" by announcing its suspension of all joint military exercises in Thailand. Imagine my surprise when I disembark the bus into a twenty-five-year flashback to Isaan's heyday as America's "unsinkable aircraft carrier," the whole city infested with American military personnel and that hackneyed carnival atmosphere that accompanies them wherever they go in Asia. American boys in their civvies swarm Korat's single pseudo-mall, drawn to this one icon of the West like flies to rotten fruit. Blonde butch cuts fondling Thai "escorts" careen around corners in *tuk-tuks*. Every hotel, bar, and restaurant with the means for an English marquee trumpets, "Welcome Operation Cobra Gold 5000!" And the bicycle rickshaw drivers are in their glory, stationed at every watering hole, whooping "You! You! You!"

In the midst of the uproar, my employers give me a welcome dinner at the Sri Pattana Hotel, and as we eat our dessert, a group of sweat-drenched, camouflaged Americans tramp in to suck down bottles of purified water and gape at a listless Chinese girl singing sentimental songs. While blundering out, they knock a rod of beaded curtains off the dining room door, then hurry away as if no one will notice. At the time, I didn't even consider what they'd been doing all day in the heat and whether it was a "joint operation" or not. I'd been moved into a temporary apartment without running water and was totally engrossed with just keeping myself clean.

Operation Cobra Gold 5000. It sounds like a cigarette brand or a motorcycle, a malt liquor or an amusement park ride. The Operation of May 17-20 was code-named "Operation Destroy the Enemy." No "Desert Storm," "Just Causes," or "Restore Hopes" here; a military dictatorship has few reasons to cultivate the consent of those ruled. Because my employers foul up all my immigration papers, I must make regular visits to City Hall, where I get to know a self-important functionary whom the other office minions refer to as "the General." Strutting around on a pole-stiff leg on which he pivots to great martial effect, the General has established his office status by cloistering his desk in semi-privacy behind two gargantuan file cabinets in the corner while the underlings, as in every Thai bureaucracy, are jammed in rows upon rows of desks laid end-to-end like dominoes, all tottering with stacks of ledger books and documents. The General speaks excellent English. He is of that age. After only a few months, I realize that the only Thais in Issan with fluent English are men the General's age who worked very closely with the U.S. during "the American War." One afternoon the General leans forward from behind his desk, so near me I can smell the grease in his metallic hair, and purrs, in a confidential tone, apropos of nothing, "*Your* country and *my* country have been *good* friends for a *long* time."

An American can get into Vietnam these days almost as easily as she can get into Thailand, and the tourist promos claim we're just as welcome. I begin to plan to finish the academic year in March, then fly to Hanoi, to see for myself. But despite my efforts at keeping clean, I pick up amoebic dysentery, and after four months of clinics and pills and no evidence of its surrendering, I finally have to return to the States. Where it's easier to think myself clean.

Marilyn Krysl

DEEPER DARKNESS

Human rights are universal and indivisible. Human freedom is not separate from these: if it's denied to anyone anywhere, it is therefore denied, indirectly, to all.
—Vaclav Havel

Photograph: moonlight on the Indian Ocean. I look at this photograph now, a layer of light across surf, and try to imagine Richard de Zoysa's body washed up on the beach south of Mt. Lavinia. *What goes around comes around,* and, among things that come around, I think of the L.A. riots. As it happens those riots transpired on the same day the Liberation Tigers for Tamil Eelam in Sri Lanka massacred some seventy Muslims as they slept.

The notion of a simple vacation seems laughable.

I no longer imagine I can "get away."

In 1992 I worked in Colombo for Peace Brigade International. April is the hottest month, and it was hot the day I set out with Sam and Francis on a packed bus to visit the Sri Lankan Bar Association. Crossing the city was like traversing a giant botanical garden: humidity and chlorophyll, laced with the hot cries of parrots. There's a patina of the quotidian—school children in white uniforms, women in saris doing their marketing, the tri-shaw driver in a sarong pulling up to the curb, summoned by two businessmen in western dress. But beneath this sense of the ordinary, workaday world, darker water runs. How much Sri Lanka's dubious human rights' record results from colonialism and how much from the vagaries of caste and ethnic oppositions is an academic question. Both factor in. Inescapably I see through a Western lens. The image of the sari, for instance, suggests—to me—layered secrets, the hidden beneath the visible. The colonial legacy, on the other hand, seems all too blatant.

I was more aware than I wanted to be of my whiteness as I strolled a street or entered a shop. At the same time, though, it's precisely because of my white skin that I was in Sri Lanka working for Peace Brigade International. P.B.I. began its escort work in El Salvador and Guatemala in the early Eighties, and volunteers came to Sri Lanka at the Bar's invitation in 1989. Government death squads had disappeared thousands, and six lawyers representing families of detained persons had been murdered. P.B.I. operates on the assumption that governments don't want to lose their foreign aid, and thus can be expected to avoid incidents which might be witnessed by foreign visitors. Simply being in the company of a foreigner is pretty good insurance against vigilante attack, and P.B.I. can activate its Emergency Response Network if one of our clients should be arrested. The organization is nonpartisan and nonviolent, as its clients must be. We don't intervene in partisan politics or escort government soldiers or guerrillas who espouse the use of force, but we can protect law abiding citizens caught in between.

The edifice that houses the Bar Association dates from the Nineteenth Century, its architecture suggesting the British gentlemen under whose tutelage and to whose specification it was built. Ms. Udugama introduced us to Mohammed, a Tamil-speaking Muslim in his thirties. Mohammed projected a fiery energy. Fearless and angry, I thought. You have to be both to bring a case to court here, and it also helps to have protection, which is why Ms. Udugama suggested this meeting. Mohammed practiced Aryuvedic medicine, one of south Asia's traditional methods of healing, but harassment by the police forced him to close his practice and go into hiding. Now he wanted to bring charges against the men who murdered his sister: a son and his father, the father a prominent government official.

Mohammed's sister, a widow with four children, and like Mohammed, a Tamil-speaking Muslim, lived in southern Sri Lanka where Sinhalese predominate. The son of the official owned the plot next to her house and wanted to buy hers as well. She refused and was murdered in a dispute over the property line, and Mohammed and his brother witnessed the murder.

One might wonder why murder in a property dispute wouldn't be treated as a criminal act, subject to the usual prosecution. But fourteen years of one-party rule has failed to the extent that both vigilante groups and public officials flout it with impunity. And indeed, soon after the murder, Mohammed's brother was arrested. Police had attempted to arrest Mohammed as well.

Sinhalese comprise 76% of the population, Tamils 18%, and Tamil-speaking Muslims 5%. There are also a few of the original natives, the Veddahs, and a few descendants of Dutch immigrants called burghers. Since the Sinhalese majority came to power after independence, Sri Lanka's become a country where you may come under suspicion simply by being Tamil. Though Tamil-speaking Muslims consider themselves a group apart, anyone not Muslim may not see it that way. You may come under suspicion because you speak Tamil; if you join a political party other than the UNP, or if you join a labor union; if you publish a newspaper which runs articles critical of the president or of government policy; if you write such articles; if you represent any of the persons described above in court, and sometimes even if you're a judge hearing such cases.

Mohammed's brother had been in Colombo's Wellikanda prison for thirteen months without being charged. Police appeared at his mother's house unexpectedly, hoping to find Mohammed or to frighten the family into revealing his whereabouts. Occasionally Mohammed stayed at the home of one of his friends, but most of the time he slept "in the jungle." Though he'd sneaked home a few times for just a few hours, he hadn't slept in his own bed for more than a year. We couldn't do anything about Mohammed's brother, but Mohammed was someone we could help: a law-abiding citizen who wanted to bring charges against his sister's murderers and his brother's abductors. In all likelihood we'd be able to protect him by accompanying him armed with cameras, and, as our flyers read, "visibly embodying international concern."

There's a world of difference between shaking hands and taking the hand of someone with whom you spontaneously feel intimately linked. Mohammed took my hand in his two. He did the same with Francis, and with Sam. He was grateful. Francis and I decided to forego returning to the house for clothes and toothbrushes. Sam took the news home, and Francis, Mohammed and I headed for the bus station, bound by the intimacy of our mission. We were in this together, and as we rolled south past crashing breakers, Mohammed again expressed his gratefulness.

I reminded him that our presence in Sri Lanka wasn't without self-interest. In a decade when ethnic rivalry and the state violence that seems inevitably to surround such conflict is becoming the order of the day in industrialized as well as developing nations, my fate is inextricably linked with Mohammed's and others like him. For we live in a time when the state, as Murray Bookchin has written, "is not merely a constellation of bureaucratic and coercive institutions. It is also a state of mind, an instilled mentality for ordering reality."

The state of mind in Sri Lanka, Mohammed explained, is vastly determined by revisionist history, especially as chronicled in *The Mahavamsa*. Begun by Buddhist monks in the Sixth Century, this text lauds Sinhalese kings who united the country in the name of Buddha, protected the monks and preserved the teachings. The colonial powers viewed *The Mahavamsa* as an accurate record of history, an endorsement which influenced subsequent Sinhalese scholars to do the same. By the 1930s politicians were invoking the work of these scholars in order to associate themselves with the notion of a great Sinhalese past. Thus, once the British granted Sri Lanka independence, the dominance of the Sinhalese came as no surprise.

The Mahavamsa was brought "up to date" in the late Seventies by a committee commissioned by then-President J.R. Jayewardene. The work, originally written in verse dialect, now includes a Sinhala prose text which elaborates the original stanzas, and new chapters in Sinhala (plus a few in English) which chronicle events from 1935 through 1977 and celebrate Buddhism as a force central to the nation. *The Mahavamsa,* Mohammed suggested, had become a text which encourages the Sinhalese majority to think of itself as an "ancient race" descended from Indo-Aryans in north India and thus distinctly prior and superior to the Dravidian Tamil minority. The process seems akin to the religious right in America glossing the Bible and bringing it "up to date" in such a way as to "prove" God's on their side.

By the time the bus turned inland, it was getting dark. Wet paddy fields shimmered in the moonlight. It was almost ten when Mohammed said, "Here's the police station. My mother's house is close by." We got down and turned off onto gravel, then a dirt path. At the third house Mohammed called out. A child appeared in the lighted doorway, then more children, a man—Mohammed's brother-in-law—and several women, one Mohammed's mother. Mohammed explained why Francis and I were there. Immediately we were welcomed into the family's affiliation. Except for Nauma, twenty, who spoke English, the women went off to prepare food.

English was Sri Lanka's official language under the British and after independence, but in 1956 Parliament declared Sinhala the official language. Subsequent legislation privileged Sinhalese students for University entrance by requiring Tamils to score higher on qualifying exams. The conflict, which had been brewing since independence, then came to a head, and Tamil youths responded by forming the Liberation Tigers for Tamil Eelam. When the Tigers attacked Sinhalese policemen in the northern Tamil province, ethnic war became fact.

Though the war continues, the Sri Lankan Parliament has reinstated English as an official language and declared Tamil an official language as well.

Nauma offered us towels and soap. After we washed, the children crowded around, and Nauma introduced Ithiyas, a shy eight-year-old adopted by this family after his young mother was drowned. She was a victim of the JVP, a Marxist Sinhalese youth group powerful in the Eighties and given to dispatching those they considered politically incorrect. But Ithiyas was still too young to understand political maneuvering. He looked at me eagerly, his eyes liquid amber. I was immediately in love.

Francis and I needed to contact Colombo, and Ithiyas, Mohammed, and Nauma came with us to a neighbor's house to use their phone. On the way I asked what Ithiyas' mother had done to rouse the ire of the JVP.

"She didn't want to join," Nauma said. "Like many people, she wanted to stay out of fighting."

"Ithiyas was four," Mohammed said. "They took her from her house, and Ithiyas ran to us for help. Later the headman found her body washed up on the bank."

Though Nauma later insisted Ithiyas understood only a tiny bit of English, he seemed to sense what we were talking about. He touched my arm, pointing toward a line of trees visible in the moonlight. Then he uttered the one, and only one, glittering English sentence I was to hear him speak: "There is the river."

Late in the Eighties when the anti-Indian JVP threatened MPs with murder should they vote for the Indo-Ceylon Accord, President Jayewardene decreed that each MP might marshal a hundred and fifty "bodyguards" for personal protection. This mandate for private armies legitimized a state of mind which "legalized" government death squads and political thuggery. Combined with the 1978 Prevention of Terrorism Act, this state of mind has had disastrous repercussions for Sri Lankans. The Act makes punishable "terrorist" or "subversive" acts, including non-violent advocacy of secession; permits detention of suspects without charges for up to eighteen months, arrest without warrant, and search and seizure "on suspicion;" prevents magistrates reviewing arrests or ordering release of detainees; denies detainees access to legal advice and visitation; and allows confessions under duress as evidence in court.

The P.T.A. also gives the president authority to declare a state of emergency. With the exception of one six-month period, emergency regulations declared in the 1983 anti-Tamil riots have been continuously renewed. In this country where the sons and daughters of the Sri Lankan elite studied at Oxford and Cambridge, where the literacy rate is still 88%, emergency regulations have been used to prohibit public meetings, affixing posters, distributing leaflets, and to ban newspapers, censor broadcasts and proscribe political parties. When an opposition group, Voice of the Clergy, brought charges against a police inspector who confiscated their leaflets, the Supreme Court found in the group's favor, but the government paid the inspector's fine and promoted him.

I'd heard plenty of stories about death squad goons. The stories resemble the testimony by a village woman interviewed in 1990 in the *Bulletin* published by Article 19, the London—based International Center Against Censorship.

> They surround the young men and take them away. Then they bring a person covered fully except for his eyes. There are two holes for his eyes. This is the bogeyman. He is one of the boys they have taken and beaten up and tortured. He is asked to point out suspects, and when he nods his head at anyone they are taken into the forest. There they pound them and maul them till the blood flows down. In the end their bodies are burned.

The songs of birds near Mohammed's house had that resounding clarity that comes only in the silence of early morning. I lay and drank in those sounds, then the footsteps of someone on the path in front of the house. I remembered then what I'd read in the 1992 *Canadian Human Rights Mission to Sri Lanka Report*. Sri Lanka is part of

> the global economy in which net transfers of financial resources since 1983 have been flowing from the southern hemisphere to the north in increasing proportions. The Third

> World is part of an economic transformation from colonization to 'neo-colonization' in which the international financial institutions play an increasingly influential role.

The report concluded that "economic policies that foster the absence of economic vitality, equity and opportunity can be viewed themselves as violations of human rights."

Then I remembered my dream. In Mohammed's mother's house, wearing a clean, white negligee Nauma had fetched from a trunk, I'd dreamed I walked the unobstructed strip of Colombo beach where you can stroll barefoot all the way south to the Mt. Lavinia hotel. In my dream an American friend and his wife had built a house there. Dark and shaped like a wedge, it resembled a bunker. To my dismay this bunker extended all the way to the water. Now no one could walk this length of sand. Anyone who came within sight of this obstruction would find their attention torn from the solace of the natural surroundings—white capped breakers, expanse of strand, gulls, light and the cleansing, satisfying crash of surf. They would be forced to contemplate the ugliness of the bunker and of its meaning.

Francis and I breakfasted with the family on bread, tea and bananas. Afterward we walked with Mohammed to the police station, wearing our I.D. cards, carrying cameras. Mohammed explained that Francis and I were international observers and asked to see his file. The sergeant refused his request, but all of us were treated courteously.

Walking back, Mohammed was jubilant. Our accompaniment had allayed his anxiety. He felt he could stay at his mother's now in relative safety. Though his village was too far from the city for our team of five to accompany him on a twenty-four hour basis, we agreed that one of us would pay a visit once a week and also appear with him in court.

We got ready to leave. Nauma wanted to send along food and small gifts. Always in this work so much affection was given us that I sometimes forgot the potential for danger. The P.B.I. training had included being wakened in the middle of the night, roughed up a bit and taken away at "gunpoint," then interrogated blindfolded. In fact the P.B.I. house in El Salvador was bombed once, but no one was hurt, and another time two volunteers were attacked on the street and suffered minor knife wounds. In both cases the team alerted our emergency response network, refused to be intimidated and got back to work. Nothing particularly intimidating has happened to the P.B.I. team in Sri Lanka, possibly because the regime doesn't enjoy the indulgence shown El Salvador during the Reagan administration.

We don't risk much here, but our clients risk danger continuously. I admired Mohammed's courage, the courage of his family. Ithiyas' eyes seemed to have become deeper and more beautiful overnight. His sentence, *there is the river,* leapt in my mind like a solitary fish surfacing in moonlight. His mother must have been beautiful. But I didn't try to imagine what she might have looked like. I didn't want to visualize her face pushed down into the water by force.

Richard de Zoysa had been a journalist, actor, and television personality whose writing documented human rights' violations. On the night of February 17, 1990, he was abducted from his mother's house by six armed men. Though the Superintendent of Police had been informed that an armed party had obtained Richard's address and was going after him, and though the de Zoysa home is within sight of the police station, police took no precautions. Richard's mutilated body washed up several days later on a beach south of the Mt. Lavinia Hotel.

Rolinde and I arrived early to accompany his mother, Dr. Saravanamuttu, a handsome woman in her fifties, to court. She offered us tea, then lit a cigarette. "I smoke too much," she said. "It's part of this mess." She was due in court because a defamation case was brought against her by a police officer she'd identified and charged in the death of her son. While watching television on May 15, 1990, she'd recognized Superintendent of Police Ronnie Gunasinghe as one of her son's abductors. Since she had no other children and therefore felt she had little to lose, she brought charges against him and another officer.

During the proceedings, P.B.I. volunteers had accompanied her and her lawyer twenty-four hours a day. When her charges were dismissed on grounds of lack of evidence, the Bar Association and the Opposition party called on Parliament to set up a Commission of Inquiry into these charges, but before Parliament could act, Mr. Gunasinghe filed defamation charges, thus precluding parliamentary debate. Dr. Saravanamuttu then organized The Mother's Front, an organization which, like its counterparts in the Americas, works to gain release of the detained and to determine which of the missing have been disappeared. Though she believes the publicity her son's case received here and abroad offers her a measure of protection, she was neither relaxed nor resigned. "Sometimes

I still wake up in a sweat," she said. "I still practice obstetrics, but I don't do deliveries now because I'd have to go out at night."

At the courthouse, she put out her cigarette. Large numbers of police stood outside and in the hallways. Delay of the judge's arrival seemed a tactic calculated to increase tension. When she first filed charges, her lawyer received threats, and she herself received a letter which read in part, "Mourn the death of your son, as a mother must do. Any other steps will result in your death at the most unexpected time."

Secretaries in saris fanned themselves with pages from briefs. Dr. Saravanamuttu read through the statement she would make when called to the stand. Suddenly the judge appeared, and we rose. His announcement that the hearing would be delayed until July came as no surprise. Postponement is another obstructionist tactic.

Peter, a P.B.I. volunteer from England, liked to go to one of the tourist hotels Sunday afternoons for high tea. Colonialism's lingering presence in such rituals is ineluctably part of modern Sri Lanka. Consciousness of authority was ever in the air—to be invoked, obeyed, disobeyed—as was the knowledge that where there might be disobedience, force would be in order. Part of this matrix was an elaborate awareness of racial difference, partly the residue of caste, also surely the product of three hundred years of European supremacy. Whiteness was associated with wealth, authority, and that fantasy, absolute freedom. Thus wealth, authority, and freedom were things to be valued, or defiled. You saw it in peoples' bodies, eyes: the things powerful white people have done have been noted with rapt attention, gazed at, admired, desired, coveted, reproduced without judgment.

Yet it's precisely pale skin and its privilege which give P.B.I. volunteers from Europe, Canada, the U.S., Australia, New Zealand, and Japan visibility and thus the power to protect those we escort. We use the system against itself. Together with those we accompany, we invoke an international realm where this racist remnant of colonialism is means to a greater good.

How deliciously *criminal* I feel, transgressing.

Peter, Francis and I went to Anaradapura, several hours northeast of Colombo, to attend a pretrial hearing. One of our clients had brought charges against two policemen for the rape and death of his sister. Police had suspected her of involvement with the JVP, but she was never arrested and charged. Instead a group of men, including local police, arrived at the family's home, restrained her father and brothers, raped her, then took her away. Her body had not been found.

Anaradapura isn't a place where international observers put in regular appearances, and our arrival at court at 9:30, a half hour before the hearing, caused consternation. The bailiff immediately inquired why we were there. When we told him, he went off, then returned and announced proceedings had been set back to 1:00 P.M. At 1:00 I sat beside another plaintiff whose hearing had gotten set back. "Something drastic must have happened," he said. "This judge hasn't ever set back the time of a hearing."

Two policemen, defendants in the case we were observing, were marched into the dock. At a previous hearing, the prosecution had made arguments in favor of trying them. This occasion was for hearing defense's evidence why the case should not go to trial. Testimony was in Sinhala, but two reporters present passed notes to us to keep us informed.

Our presence would exert pressure on the judge to rule in favor of a trial. If he did, there was the very real possibility that these two men, whether or not they were guilty, would be found guilty, simply because the government is trying to polish its human rights' image. If the trial received heavy publicity, the men would probably be given harsh sentences in order to demonstrate that Sri Lanka was indeed prosecuting perpetrators of violations. I understood our presence in that courtroom would be a factor in any loading of the dice. I also understood that given the crudeness of the state's state of mind, there wasn't much we could do about this. And in fact, though P.B.I. tries to keep a low profile, our photographs appeared the next day on the front page of *The Island,* one of the country's three mass circulation papers.

One of the arguments against a trial was that, since the body had not been found, there was no proof that murder had taken place. Still, I thought of the woman in question as "the dead girl," someone I wouldn't meet. When the judge announced his decision to hold a trial, the faces of her father and brothers shone. For them a great victory had gone forward. They'd taken a frightening chance, and their first display of resolve had succeeded. I watched them, aware that they'd shown a courage that I with all my western "advantages" might not have been able, in similar circumstances, to muster. I wanted to say, "Thank you. Thank you for your example."

For I felt, as I almost always did with our clients, that I'd been magically infused with their courage. I'm often fearful, and a coward, and I long to be otherwise. I can scarcely get enough of the daring examples of others.

I set off for Mohammed's, my last visit before I would leave Sri Lanka. His first appearance in court, accompanied by Sam, had gone forward without incident, but though Mohammed badly needed money to support his family and his deceased sister's children, he was afraid to reopen his practice. The bus wound through jungle and paddy fields, countryside as much like paradise as anything I've seen. Still I was aware that, beneath the banana leaves' fans, runs a darker current. Rocked by the bus, in sweltering heat, I dozed, dreamed. In my nightmare my daughter and I walked a city street in the States. Suddenly a group of men surrounded and separated us. My daughter's face registered terror. I was forced to watch them force her down onto pavement.

I woke with a start and discovered I'd slept past my stop. I called out: the other passengers were amused, and I had to get down and take another bus back. I managed to shake off the nightmare only when I reached Mohammed's mother's. There Humaizera, her thirteen-year-old granddaughter, was in the midst of the coming-of-age ritual that marked her first menstrual period. It's the custom to seclude the girl in one room for the seven days of celebration, during which friends and relatives pay their respects. For the first time the girl is allowed to wear saris, and if the family can afford it, she's given a new one each day for seven days.

We were on the front porch taking photographs when a police car came by, slowed. I pointed my camera toward the car. Instantly the driver sped away.

Toward evening Nauma invited me to bathe in the river. Though I didn't want to pollute the river with soap, I'd didn't want to refuse. I put on one of Nauma's house dresses, we walked down to the bank with the children. Bits of sunlight through leaves were white flecks on the water. A bird called. Ithiyas skipped stones. The dress spread around me in billowing swaths. I felt like a throwback to some earlier species, a sea cow with filmy fins, mythic, ancient. In this state of mind, I remembered the woman from another part of the island who'd told me about the army passing through her village. The soldiers hadn't been able to engage the guerrillas, though they were around, taking the occasional sniper's shot at their government counterparts. On the pretext that some villagers were guerrillas disguised as farmers, the soldiers arrested all the men they could find and held them captive. Then they herded the young women to the riverbank and raped them. Some they shot, others they beat senseless. They shoved broken arrack bottles up the dead girls' vaginas, then dumped the bodies into the water. I still remember her words. "We watched those dead girls float down."

"Returning violence with violence multiplies violence," Martin Luther King Jr. wrote, "adding deeper darkness to a night already devoid of stars." As I write this, a year later, there seems less and less point in trying to distinguish between institutionalized and random ruthlessness. Every day the evidence accumulates. The Liberation Tigers for Tamil Eelam massacre seventy Muslims on the same day riots break out in L.A.; rioting citizens murder Turks in Germany seeking asylum; Leonard Peltier continues to serve a life sentence in the U.S., convicted on dubious evidence of shooting a state trooper at Wounded Knee; someone in Oregon dumps the mutilated body of a four-year-old girl into a rest stop toilet; Guatemalan soldiers torture and execute Rigoberta Menchu's mother; James "Tiger" Knowles of the KKK lynches a black man named Mike Donald; vigilantes harass Vietnamese-Americans as they try to make a living fishing off the Texas coast; Arabs sell kidnapped black Sudanese children for less than the price of an international postage stamp. And then, out beyond these individual atrocities, lie the mass graves of Kurds and of Sri Lankan school boys.

Once back I'd had to get through a time of transition in which I'd felt awkwardly out of place in my own country. Stepping off the plane had seemed a descent, and for weeks, which gathered into months, I'd wandered in a peculiar kind of hell. I had the sense in the supermarket, at the bank, in traffic, that the people around me had been desensitized. They seemed to float in a haze of Novocain, while I stood exposed, without buffers. I wept copiously and often because I didn't know any other way through my distress, my loneliness, this alienation from my culture. I noted with bitterness that I was back where what constituted the good life for quite a few of my compatriots was making the fast buck, then going blank in front of the tube, or going shopping with an eye for the latest in leather, or starting the new romance novel picked up idly on the way through the checkout. I thought the ignorance and self-satisfied greed of some of my fellow citizens was what dismayed me, but the truth was that I was my problem. I was homesick, heartsick, and filled with longing for the affinities I'd left behind when I left Sri Lanka.

In this distemper of mine, I'd remembered the last time I accompanied Dr. Saravanamuttu to court. Leaving for her house, I'd found myself reviewing our Colombo neighborhood where two decades of Sri Lankan history had left their mark. During the government's vendetta against the JVP, all the houses on the street had been searched for suspects. A member of the ruling UNP party who'd lived in the house we later rented had been murdered on the doorstep. And across the street was an empty lot where, in the 1983 anti-Tamil riots, a Tamil family's home had been burned to the ground.

Dr. Saravanamuttu's niece drove us to the courthouse. The streets were tiled with blossoms brought down the night before by a hard rain, and I was filled with hopeful expectancy. This time when the judge entered and we rose, his Honor announced he was stepping down. Another judge would hear the case at a later date. We adjourned with Dr. Saravanamuttu's lawyer to an anteroom to confer. He'd learned off the record that the judge had lost his nerve. A car which didn't belong to anyone in his neighborhood had begun to appear regularly near his house.

Dr. Saravanamuttu rolled down the car window and smoked. There was no satisfaction for her in those moments. Impatient drivers blew horns, people queued for buses, street vendors hawked their wares, and I reflected on my relationship with this woman. Given that we live in a world where violence was increasingly someone's solution, she and I shared a frightening fate.

She'd told me that morning that she planned to go abroad for a while, and I'd asked if she'd thought of leaving permanently.

"It's what the authorities would like me to do," she'd said. "So I won't. Besides, what's left of my family, they're here. In spite of Richard's death, I still love Sri Lanka. For me, it's still the sweetest land there is."

Now, all of a sudden, she turned to face me. Her eyes were watery, as though she might be on the edge of tears, and at the same time there was in them a sort of fierce light.

"If I could have done something to save my son," she said, "I would have. But they don't come to bargain. They come in the night when you're alone, and for one purpose only. They come to murder, they like murder, they are murderers, men without mercy.

"If there is justice at all today," she says, "it's a faint glimmer at the end of a dark, long tunnel. But I swear I will not give in to them. I will fight, I will crawl along that tunnel."

Edith Pearlman

THE MESSAGE

On a small stone balcony in Jerusalem, across a round glass table, Carolyn was guardedly looking at Terence. Terence was looking at his bowl of yogurt and apricots; he was not complaining; he was practicing his customary comfortable silence while his mind whirred.

She leaned forward. "I should have bought cereal."

"That's all right." His eyeglasses glinted at her. "The coffee is delicious."

It was Terence's first visit to the city that Carolyn knew well. There was a further imbalance: she spoke serviceable Hebrew, whereas he spoke only English, French, and German, though he read both Latin and Greek. And the weather had made itself his enemy the moment he stepped off the plane. Carolyn knew the weather. She spent every October in Jerusalem, renting the same apartment—it was the pied-à-terre of a Tel Aviv family, complete with two sets of dishes and even two sets of ashtrays—and she always packed for a burst of autumn warmth. This hot Saturday morning her skin caught whatever breeze there was; her arms and throat were bare in a gauzy halter that was almost the same golden brown as her recently dyed hair. But Terence had flown in unexpectedly from a conference on epistemology in Zurich, bringing only his professor's wardrobe. He'd inherited a taste for drab clothing from his Methodist forbears—their daughter teased that he'd inherited the clothing itself. Last night he'd worn a dark suit and tie to a restaurant where every other male patron had on a short-sleeved shirt buttoned imperfectly over a paunch. He had gone to bed in his underwear—he would have melted in his flannel pajamas—and this morning his face seemed almost as white as his round-necked undershirt. A man with a malady, she'd suddenly thought, her composure sagging. But no: Terence was always pale, just as he was always thin. When they'd met, thirty years ago, he was already slightly stooped.

"I'm used to your hair being gray," he said mildly. "Is this what they call henna?"

She caressed her nape. "Cognac is the official name. In Jerusalem all women of a certain age dye their hair."

"Cognac. . . . I didn't know anthropologists could go native."

"Well, no. But I'm not a professional anthropologist." She smiled, trying to lighten the exchange. "I'm not a professional anything; remember?" She had a couple of Master's Degrees: certificates but no status. She currently held a grant to study the residents of East Talpiot, one of the oldest Jerusalem suburbs. Once a year she squeezed airfare out of the little grant, and paid a month's rent on this apartment in the leafy Emek Refaim neighborhood. During the other eleven months she lived in Boston with Terence, and taught sociology in an adult center, and wrote a paper or two, and attended a few seminars. "I'm a bronze-crested dilettante," she said now. "Maybe somebody should get a grant to study me."

He looked at her with a brief intensity, as if studying her might be a good idea. She knew that look. It meant that he was thinking about Wittgenstein, or maybe Kant.

He had arrived yesterday, Friday. He would leave tomorrow. "The conference is wretched," he'd said over the telephone on Thursday morning. "I'll skip the banquet, come spend the weekend with you. If my arrival won't be an inconvenience," he'd added, not ironically, merely considerately.

It would be a great inconvenience. "Wonderful!" Carolyn had said to Terence, south warming north, wife deceiving husband, Mediterranean splashing onto Swiss shrubbery. "I'll meet you at the airport."

"Not necessary."

"The cabbies would skin you. I'll be there!"

Then she'd had to climb the stone stairs, to knock on Natan's door, to explain the situation, to endure his immediate fury.

"Twenty-eight days a year we have together, and now you rob me of three of them!" He'd held her by the forearms and shook her slightly. "And Saturday night, we have tickets for the quartet!" he remembered.

"I'm sorry," she said. What a bellow! "*You* go to the concert."

"Alone? Bite your tongue! You are *sans merci,* like all lovely women. Without compassion. *L'lo rachmim!"* he wound up, though he usually spoke Hebrew to her only when within earshot of American tourists. "Carolyn?" he then inquired, signaling the end of his outburst.

She was silent.

"Oh, your Christian tolerance," he sighed. "A Jewish woman would have already told me to shut up. I'll visit my daughter this weekend. I haven't been to Haifa for three months. I'll play with my granddaughter. Little Miriam is a beauty, too. Okay?"

He scowled at her and then grinned. Gold flashed from the brownish mouth that always smelled of tobacco, though he smoked only five cigarettes a day in her presence, numbering each one aloud. She figured that he consumed fifteen or twenty when she was out conducting interviews. Their aroma had seeped into her apartment. Luckily she found it aphrodisiac.

He was tall, wide, big-bellied, large-freckled; a teacher of high school biology, retired. His apartment, up one flight and across the hall, was a mirror image of hers. Since his wife's death six years ago he had turned the place into a kind of terrarium. Mushrooms flourished underneath panes of dark glass. Thistles dried on a loveseat. Vines, climbing up strings, completely enclosed the balcony. Sometimes Natan and Carolyn made love within this green tabernacle, lying on an old mattress pad. The morning sun, penetrating here and there, further mottled his piebald back.

Her balcony—the balcony of the Zebelons of Tel Aviv—betrayed its owners' indifference to horticulture. A single orange tree grew crookedly out of a tub. In the center of the table Carolyn kept daisies in a jar. Across the homely bouquet she and Terence now made their plans. They would return to the Old City, would continue through its labyrinth. Yesterday at one of the stalls she'd bought Terence a loose, woven, collarless shirt striped in purple and orange; he'd smiled and named it "the Garment." He had walked contentedly beside her; in his usual attentive silence he had observed alleys, excavations, beggars, and corners golden with ancient dust.

Now he studied the city map. "This afternoon let's visit the University. We can take bus number Four."

"If we don't mind waiting for it all day. The busses don't run on Shabbat, not while the sun is up. But about an hour into the darkness they move again, glowing, all of them at once, like night-blooming plants. . . ."

The telephone rang. It rang again. Terence raised his eyebrows.

"I've got a machine," she told him.

The instrument was nearby. Her own voice floated onto the balcony, first reciting practiced Hebrew, then English ". . . return your call as soon as possible."

The caller was a breathless American hanger-on; everybody knew her, and everybody avoided her. "I haven't even laid eyes on you this visit," she wailed into the void. "*Please* get in touch."

Carolyn, smiling at Terence, turned her thumb down like an Emperor.

"Do taxis run on the Sabbath?" he asked.

"They do; and. . . ."

The telephone again. This time the caller was one of her Yemenites from East Talpiot. The woman's Hebrew was accented but clear, "Madame, I cannot meet with you on Wednesday; my son returns from Army. Maybe Thursday? At ten in the morning?"

Carolyn nodded, as if the women could see her.

"Your appointment with the hairdresser is changed," said Terence. "From one day—I heard *yom*; that's day, isn't it?—to another *yom*."

"Almost! It was an interviewee; but you're right about the switch in day. What an ear you've got. A month here and you'd be bargaining with the *moniot*—the taxis. . . ."

A third ring. "I've received more calls this morning than all last week," Carolyn said. "My friends are putting on a show for you," she added, her real voice intertwining with her recorded one, though they were both real, weren't they; the difference was temporal, not essential.

Natan. The caller was Natan. Natan the mischievous, Natan the yea-sayer. He spoke in the Hebrew tongue, in case Terence was listening. He spoke in the vocabulary of an acquaintance, in case someone else was listening. His tone was perhaps too rich. But the message was unimpeachable.

"Carolyn, this is your pal Natan. I have come to Haifa to visit my granddaughter. We have bathed three times already. The buoyancy of the sea has made me young again. In the blue depths I thought of my green balcony, and I call to ask you to water the vines on my behalf. I will return on Monday."

She had inclined her head slightly at the first sound of his voice. She was afraid to straighten it, as if the gesture might give her away.

"Another *yom*," said Terence.

"*Yom sheni*. Monday," said Carolyn; and now she dared resettle her head on her neck. "My upstairs neighbor is in Haifa visiting his family; he asks me to water his plants."

"You are not telling the truth."

". . . Pardon?"

"Forgive me; you are not rendering the message faithfully."

Carolyn closed her eyes. "He mentioned swimming with his granddaughter. It was rejuvenating. I believe that was all he said, except for naming his day of return. The sea is blue, he said."

"He said your eyes are blue," said Terence.

She opened them now; but his gaze was elsewhere, resting on the little telephone table just inside the archway. His lips pursed with distaste.

"I will tell you what he said, your friend, Mr. Etan. . . ."

"Natan," she helplessly corrected.

". . . Mr. Natan, he said that your eyes, though not as blue as the sea, though green, really, have spokes of a darker color." His voice labored, as if he really were translating. "Your eyes remind him of a tropical leaf."

"He didn't say that, any of that, Terence, honestly, what are you imagining?"

He continued to stare at the telephone and its attachment. "He said that when his arms are encircling your naked back, he thinks he is touching silk." He paused to hunch and then widen his shoulders as if trying to wriggle out of a jacket; Carolyn longed to help him, but there was no jacket. "The small rough mole on your collar bone makes his blood pound. He yearns to fall into your lap, to lick your salty belly."

In all their years together Terence had never spoken to her in such a manner. Once or twice he had admired a piece of jewelry, and he had often thanked her for her graciousness to the junior faculty. Otherwise they spoke of his work, her work, their children; friends; books. Their lovemaking was conducted in peaceable silence. Silence made guilt endurable.

"He yearns to hear you laugh," said Terence to the answering machine. "He finds it thrilling. He thinks he cannot live without your voice. He thinks he cannot live without your presence . . . without you."

Again, the familiar silence. Carolyn considered rising from her chair, kneeling before her husband, acknowledging the declaration that she recognized as his own, the avowal that had been wrung from him as if by thumbscrews. But no; melodrama would shame him; and besides, if she got up she might fall. Her trembling hands rummaged through her new hair; her wrists crossed in front of her breasts; finally her splayed fingers came to rest on the table. Still seated, she watched his profile. Two drops of sweat slowly made their way down the side of his neck. When the second had spent itself on his undershirt she said in a low tone, "My final round of interviews is nearly over. The research is finished. I'll be coming home in November for good."

He flushed purple, as if enduring a merciless spasm. Then his normal pallor returned. He wiped his mouth with his napkin and looked at his watch. "Shall we be on our way?" he said, and left the balcony.

"Put on 'the Garment,'" she called after him.

But when he came out of the bedroom he was wearing one of his usual white shirts.

EUROPE

Kelly Cherry

AN UNDERGROUND HOTEL IN LENINGRAD

I was standing at the window of my room in the Sovietskaya, gazing into the courtyard below. All at once a *window* whizzed past my line of sight—a pane of glass exactly like the one I was looking through. It touched down with a tremendous ringing noise and splintered into silence. In the afterhush, I glanced up and saw in their various rooms four or five hotel guests, all with baffled and blank expressions. Then the man whose window had fallen out smiled guiltily and shrugged and the man with him slapped him on the back. The first man began explaining loudly that he hadn't done anything; he hadn't even been near the window. Across the courtyard, another man leaned out of his open window, calling condolences. A fourth man laughed and turned back into his room. Nobody ever came to sweep up the glass. That might have been laziness, or it might have been prudence: you wouldn't want to be under it when the next window came crashing down.

Imant was waiting for me. He had met me at the airport, with Emil, Ilze, and Rudolf, and then followed the bus to the hotel. Imant didn't know Leningrad well. We were all tired, and Imant's face was drawn. He had a friend in Leningrad and he'd been hoping we could stay there, but it developed that the friend was out of town. Naively, I suggested to Imant that we could go to another hotel, surrendering the Sovietskaya to my tour group. That was when he explained the regulations to me: no visitors in your room after nine P.M. I still didn't understand why we couldn't register as Mr. and Mrs. Ivan Ivanovich Ivanov. Imant's eyes lightened as he saw what the problem was. "Oh," he said, "you thought we could simply sign our names! Is not the way here. One must present one's passport." He meant the internal passport Soviet citizens are required to carry. Once Imant had asked me if it was true that in America anyone was free to travel anywhere.

"Of course," I said.

He didn't say anything for a long time. Then he said, so softly I could barely hear him: "*Free*. . . . Sweet, sweet word."

After further discussion we realized we had no choice: it was too cold to sleep in the car. (We left summer in Riga, and went to Leningrad to catch winter whipping around the corner.) We had to find a hotel; we'd fret about the rules and regulations later.

It was still light when we started searching, but the light drained away quickly, as if somebody had pulled out a plug. (Or, seeing that this was a Russian sky, threw the plug away, since all Russians *know* plugs are unhygienic.) Reflected in the black canals, neon signs seemed to swim like brightly colored fish. The streets of Leningrad are broad and beautiful; I opened my window a crack, and air poured in like water. Ilze and I didn't care what it did to our hair.

Imant and I waited while the others went in to see about a room, but there was no room in this inn. We set off to try another hotel, but I felt subdued. And the next hotel had no vacancy either. Nor did the one after that. We had been driving around Leningrad for two or three hours, and in the end Imant took us back to the Sovietskaya. The trio went in to ask again for rooms. It was our last chance, and this time they struck gold, Russian gold. There were still no vacancies—but the clerk at the desk gave them the phone number of an *underground hotel*.

Now that we had a place to go to, the others stayed in the car while Imant and I went into the Sovietskaya, so I could collect, from the room I was supposed to share with Vera, the overnight things I would want.

"Did Indra bring you something to the bus?" he asked, looking around the room. The package was on a shelf. "But you have not opened!" he said, taking it down.

"I waited for you."

"Open now," he said. "I want you to see—"

They were cups. Not the hefty red coffee mugs I expected; these were delicate teacups with matching saucers, two of each, handpainted against a light brown background.

"Teodor made," he said. "They are very fine, no?"

"They are beautiful." And they were. "I don't want to take them with me. They belong in the farmhouse."

For our farmhouse we now had a painting, a photograph, and two teacups. On winter afternoons, when the sun was sparkling on the snow, we would sit in our kitchen and sip tea from works of art.

Imant had said everything in our house would have to be "very fine." He was going to try to get a Dutch sideboard from someone he knew who had one for sale; the furniture in Soviet stores is all knockabout stuff, jerry-built, but you can get good things privately. Still, neither of us had owned fine furniture before, and I asked Imant why he was concerned about it now. He was laughing, though, as always, more with his eyes than out loud. "Someday this house will be famous," he said. "People will come from all over the world to see it and so it must be very fine house." That wasn't all. It also had to have alligators in the pond. "You're putting me on," I complained, but he said, "Yes, yes! Russian alligators," indicating a body length of about ten inches. He had already decided we'd have several cats, and a Borzoi puppy for me. And, of course, our allotted cow.

I tied the teacups up again in their newsprint and tucked them back on the shelf.

It was time to ask him about something that had been bothering me.

"You must have been in love when you got married before," I said. "How do I know there isn't going to be a Wife Number Five? I'm willing to live in the Soviet Union as your wife, but actually, I can't think of any place in the world I'd less like to be a divorcee in."

"You only wife I want."

"Yes, but," I said, unable to stop, "is the way you feel about me"—I didn't know how to put this—"is it any different from the way you felt *before*?"

"You are asking me," he said, "what I cannot answer. I do not know how—" My face felt numb, as if the world had just blown up in it. He said again: "You ask me what I do not know how to answer."

I put together my gear for the night and gave it to Imant to carry. Walking back down the long hallway, weighed down by my flight kit and string bag, he said in a low but distinct voice: "I would give my life for you." I looked up, jolted. "I cannot live without you," he said, "I cannot." I smiled at the key lady at the end of the hall as if Imant weren't saying these things to me under his breath, but words which might be only romantic in other circumstances take on a startling significance when you know they could be overheard by the KGB.

"That's what I needed to know," I said.

We needed a gas station, and it had to be the kind of gas station for which Imant had coupons.

The beauty of Leningrad, simply speaking, stuns. The whole city is a measured spread of pastel set against a pewter sky carefully engraved with clouds; it's like a formal garden in which the ornately trimmed shrubs are made of stone. At night, the city's breath seemed cool and moistened, and the dark streets glistened. We spent another hour looking for the gas station, which we eventually came upon behind another building. I can't exaggerate the difficulty of these ordinary tasks.

And after we found the filling station, we still had to find the hotel. Now, like all underground activities, this "hotel" was certainly known to the authorities. The room shortage being what it is, private citizens, or comrades, rent out spare rooms for a few untaxed rubles. Some of these rentals are quite well organized: word is passed from guest to guest, or through official hotel employees who presumably receive a kickback, and if a hotel is booked up, it refers its overflow to another hotel. Upstairs, it may be, or next door. Again, the room shortage being what it is, the authorities look the other way.

It took us another couple of hours to find our hotel; it was in a monolithic apartment complex in the suburbs. I thought we'd never find it. I asked Imant if the KGB were following us; he said it was possible. I had an idea. "Why don't we let them go in front," I said, "and then *we* could follow *them* to the hotel?" It was getting late and every back alley and dead end we went down made it later. When we found the right complex, we couldn't figure out how to get into it. At last in utter disgust Imant jumped the curb, drove across three backyards and brought us to a halt in front of a building in a row of buildings. The only thing distinguishing it from the others was its number. We gave three cheers, discreetly.

Emil, Ilze, and Rudolf went on up. Imant clasped my wrist. "Kelly," he said, "do not speak to these people, okay? You will be my Latvian wife, okay? They may be frightened if they know you are American."

I nodded and followed Imant upstairs. Our friends were on the landing, talking (Russian) with the two old women who had answered their knock. They seemed agitated, and I immediately imagined some misunderstanding and dire consequence, but the only problem was that the room had only one bed. Neighbors upstairs had another room, one with two cots. At the time I didn't know what they were discussing; Imant introduced me to the ladies, I smiled, our friends raced upstairs, and I tried to cover up the name tag on my flight bag with my right hand while keeping my ringless left in my pocket and then remembered that in this country it should be the other way around. I kept saying "*Paldies*," the Latvian word for "thank you," whenever anyone spoke to me. Our room was just inside the door to the flat, and as soon as we succeeded in getting inside and shutting our door, I sank onto the bed in relief. The room was small—and wonderful. A window looked out into the lives of other people in lighted rooms across the way. The wide bed had been pushed against a tapestried wall. The mirror was on top of a piece of furniture of indeterminable function. I got out my contact lens equipment—aseptor, cleaning solution, and so forth—set it on the table and took out my lenses.

There was a knock on our door. Before we could stop her, the larger of the two ladies was in our room, urging cups of tea on us and talking a mile a minute. She was thrilled to be entertaining foreigners—Latvians—and she headed straight for the things I'd put on the table, picking them up and looking them over and seeing, of course, the American labels. Imant launched into an explanation; I could make out that he was telling her that he had to import these things for his wife. I couldn't say anything; I couldn't, for that matter, even see anything. When the woman left, I sighed my second sigh of relief. Then she came in again, with great hunks of bread in her hands. *"Paldies,"* I said. She made motions that plainly meant, even to my myopic eyes, that Imant ought to fatten me up. "*Da*," Imant said. She seemed satisfied at this and left, and this time she didn't return. It saddened me to think she might not be so friendly if she knew I was American.

After she left, the apartment grew quiet; you could almost see the silence settling, like a cloth over a table. I stood at the window. In the building across the way, lights were going off. Soviet citizens go to sleep at night just as American citizens do: so much the better if they can sleep together, making love instead of war. I put on my long lavender gown with the low neckline. Wind was clawing at the trees, but in our small room we were safe. I could have holed up there a year, at least. Imant felt at home too; while I was looking out the window and musing, he drank both cups of tea and ate all the bread, and I gave him an apple from my string bag and he ate that too, and then he leaned against the tapestry on the wall and began to be happier.

Was everyone else asleep? I opened the door, stealthily. The rest of the apartment was dark, but to get to the bathroom, which was only a few feet from our room, I had to pass an open area from which a prodigious snoring issued. I crossed and recrossed on tiptoe, and then, having accomplished that much without waking anyone, Imant and I discovered that our bed creaked. Someone has told me that at one time the peasants used to overlay their hearths with broad platforms that became their beds at night, so that, in effect, they slept on their stoves. At least stoves don't creak.

We were making so much noise anyway that I asked Imant to teach me some Latvian. After all, I was passing as Latvian. And though the Latvian language, unlike Russian and English, isn't rich in vulgarities, it does have some words that were pertinent to the occasion. But Imant refused to teach them to me. When I asked why, he stammered and said that his *mamina* had brought him up to be "modest." On the other hand, she had not brought him up to be modest in a foreign language, and he wasn't at all averse to learning a little basic *English.*

Later, with the light out, as I was drifting into sleep, Imant began to speak Latvian. He was speaking his mother tongue, but as far as I was concerned it might as well have been tongues. My face was buried against his chest, and the mysterious words fell softly on my head, as if I were being anointed. I stirred, but he continued; it was almost a chant, alien and ritualistic, and I became alarmed. I thought he might be talking in a kind of half-sleep, that he might have forgotten I was only pretending to be Latvian, even that he had confused me with Frederika. I tried to interrupt, but he covered my face with his hands. His words were swift and sometimes so muted I could hardly catch the hard and palatalized *k's* that lend the Latvian language its characteristic sound. In Imant's gentle and hypnotic voice, the words seemed almost less sound than shadow, and gradually I grew used to them, like beginning to see in a dim room after coming in from a brightly lit hallway. Secure in his arms, I gave myself over to this grave music and closed my eyes. As naturally as day becomes night, the words became silence. The transformation was scarcely noticeable until it was complete, and silence filled the room. Then Imant spoke in a normal tone in English: "All these things I have had in my heart to say you, but my English is too poor. So I have told them to you in Latvian."

Sunday morning, Emil rapped lightly on our door, took the car keys from Imant, left two boiled eggs on our table, and ducked out again. We were late getting down, and just as we thought we were ready to leave, I realized I'd better pack all my stuff and lug it along with me. I didn't think our landladies were light-fingered but they'd be bound to come in and take a look, and any of a dozen articles could have made them suspicious of my nationality. "Yes, yes," Imant said, smiling, "they are very curious. They are very typical, these old women, for they are simple but they are good." They brought us more tea, more bread, but I was kept busy biting my tongue. Imagine how hard it is not to let slip an "okay" or an "all right" or a "hi" or "thank you"! I was restricted to my *paldies*, which I used indiscriminately, looking helplessly at Imant whenever any longer speech was called for. I'm sure they thought he had married an idiot.

Emil, Ilze, and Rudolf were waiting in the back seat of the car. It was a brilliant day, not too cold. The first leaves of autumn lay on the ground but the trees were mostly still dark green, and the wide streets brought a bright blue sky clear down to eye level. Leningrad's palette is more variegated than Moscow's or Riga's but its hues remain subtle; only the sky, the trees, the myriad canals will sometimes leap to the front of the stage like a *corps de ballet*, and dazzle. There's also, as elsewhere, the red of the banners overhanging the streets or draped across the cornices of factory plants and warehouses.

I've heard that many of these oratorical oriflammes were hung up to commemorate a given Party congress, and then after the congress no one had the nerve to take them down; and so they accumulate, congress to congress. They all say things like: COMMUNISM IS THE PARTY OF PEACE, or WE ARE MAKING THE WORLD SAFE FOR ALL PEOPLES. My favorite slogan was, TO LIVE, TO WORK, TO STUDY—LIKE LENIN! It struck my funny bone.

We parked, and walked to a café—to several cafés, in fact, before we found one that was open. Along the way, Imant practiced *basic* English, at the top of his lungs. I tried to hush him up but he argued, "Is okay! No one will understand," and the more I blushed, the louder his voice grew. He was testing his new vocabulary in sentences. "Is right way to use, yes?" he would ask, and Rudolf, coming up behind us, would say, "What does it mean?" Finally I capitulated: "Imant is learning the English that textbooks leave out," I said. Rudolf begged, politely but urgently, "Please, will you be so kind as to teach me too?"

So I rummaged around in the back of my brain for some expression or idiom that was slangy without being obscene, and so help me, what

I came up with was this: "Wow, look at that pair of knockers!"

"Woo, look at that pair of knoak-erz," Rudolf repeated, his face contorted excruciatingly.

"Knockers," I said.

"Please, what are knoak-erz?" he asked.

I tried to explain. "Well, you know," I said, "a woman's chest. That is her bust." There was complete incomprehension on both their faces, and in desperation I shouted, "Breasts!" I didn't know I was going to announce it so forcefully, and put my hand over my mouth, too late. Imant laughed. "I think you knew all along," I said, accusingly.

He wanted to know "if all American breasts are knockers."

"Only big ones," I said. "You're supposed to stand on a street corner, see, and then when a big-breasted woman walks by, you nudge your sidekick with your elbow, like this"—I nudged Rudolf with my elbow—"and you say, *Wow, look at that pair of knockers*. I promise you, this will make you extremely American."

"Knoak-erz," Rudolf said, with enormous seriousness.

"Knockers," Imant corrected him. "The *s* is between an *s* and a *z*. Woo, look at that—"

"Not woo," I said, correcting Imant. "Wow."

"Is impossible. How can there be such a sound as this: *ow*?" He made a face. "Americans," he declared, "are a peculiar people."

By this time we had reached the café; Emil and Ilze had caught up with us, and we were all standing around waiting for a free table. One of the patrons in the process of leaving was about five feet tall and five feet wide, with a grand smile displaying her gold tooth; as she walked toward us, she rolled from side to side like a sailor. A Russian grandmother, surely. She was reclaiming her coat from the attendant when I happened to catch Imant and Rudolf staring down at her ample bosom. Imant nudged Rudolf with his elbow. "Woo," Rudolf said, "look at that pair of knoak-erz!"

"Oh no," I said.

"Knockers," Imant said. "Yes?"

"Yes. . . . I mean, no!"

"But what is wrong?"

"Those are not knockers," I said (in a low voice, out of the side of my mouth, to Imant).

Imant looked perplexed. "But they are breasts?" And when I assured him they were indeed breasts, he was visibly relieved. "Big breasts," he said. "And so, knockers."

"Right," I agreed, once and for all. Besides, I didn't really want him to become overly American on this score.

The café didn't have the fish we ordered, so we opted for eggs, although we'd already had eggs once that morning. But the waitress tipped us off to the eggs not being fresh. We wound up with the third—and last—item on the breakfast menu, beefsteak. I asked Imant if orange juice was ever available, and he set off in search of some. I don't remember what he came back with but it wasn't orange and he'd had to go to two other stores to find it. He didn't mind. Rudolf said to me, while Imant was away from the table, "Imant is cheerful today." Rudolf looked as earnest as ever. "Yes," I said, "thanks!"

We wanted to visit Petrodvorets, eighteen miles outside of Leningrad, an incredibly profligate spill of pleasure palaces and parks centered around the Grand Palace for which Peter himself is said to have done the first sketches, but we didn't know the way. I wasn't even sure it was within the permissible limits except by Intourist bus, but of course it is. I was jumpier than I needed to be. And yet, how do you know what's *appropriately* jumpy? We were heading out of the city, in clear weather, light breaking on the Neva in waves like water. A cop flagged Imant down, and he pulled over to the curb, got out his papers, and walked around to the back of the car to meet the cop. I had no way of knowing what this was all about. I tried to quiz Rudolf but he turned my questions aside. Emil shook his head, but whether he was shaking his head at me or over me, I couldn't tell. I did my best to look natural—also as if I weren't an American staying in an underground hotel—but I couldn't help casting furtive glances over my shoulder. When Imant returned to the car, he didn't say anything. After several minutes of studied nonchalance, I blurted out, "Why did he stop us?"

Imant seemed surprised by my question. "Why?"

"Did we do anything wrong? Did you break a Russian traffic law?"

"No," he said, as if that fact had been obvious to everybody, including the cop.

"Was he looking for someone?"

"For whom would he be looking?"

"I don't know," I said. "Smugglers, maybe. Counterrevolutionaries. Enemies of the State."

"He was not looking for anyone."

"Do you mean," I said, slowly, "that he stopped you for no reason at all? Just to check your papers?"

"Yes, of course."

"Of course?"

We spotted a palatial-looking residence and hiked down one hill and up another to get to it. Stone lions guarded the gates. The palace was decayed and deserted, a windswept outpost, as if the czars had dug in at the last affluent fort. There weren't any czars here, however; only two or three contemplative picnickers eating their lunches singly in the "backyard," which looked more like the north forty. We paced the patio, looking down on the solitary lunching people. The formal layout of the former lawn was traceable under the overgrown grasses, and wind rippled the long grasses like green water.

I wanted to take pictures but my companions wouldn't let me; this wasn't our destination, and they wanted me to wait for the real thing. This was just your average spare palace, left lying around like a calling card from an earlier age. *Sorry, sir,* says the card, *but you were out when I happened.*

The real thing was a good deal farther up the road, and a herd of Intourist buses penned in the parking lot made it unmissable. The whole affair is nearly as elaborate and decadent as the Tivoli Gardens, though higher-minded. From Peter's summer palace, steps pitch steeply down an escarpment to a string of parks on either side of a shimmering ribbon of tame water that unfurls into the Gulf of Finland. Viewed from the palace, the figured symmetry of hedgerows and footpaths is breathtaking, but at the bottom of the steps you join the throng of tourists meandering through planned walks past ingeniously contrived fountains and mechanical amusements. You blink before so much gilt—the very air seems like beaten gold. It's all enough to give a good Bolshevik nightmares, or at least dreams of capital gain. Children hop back and forth between a cupola and the sidewalk, giggling and shrieking as they aim to anticipate the next "waterfall" from the rim of the cupola. Toy ducks quack in a pool; you'd have to feed them toy crumbs. The event that took my fancy was a mechanical garden: there were big, painted, metal flowers that spouted like whales, and a tree with spraying branches. Coney Island, Disneyland . . . what won't people do, to entertain themselves and stave off death? We bought ice cream.

As we rounded a bend in the path, the Gulf of Finland came into view. Just before you reach the water's edge, there's a cottage now used as a museum; many of the visitors were headed there. Our friends joined the queue for the current exhibit, while Imant and I went shoreside to talk.

A mere eighteen miles away is Finland. It seemed I could reach out and touch it with my fingertips. We leaned against the railing. There was a bench but it was totally occupied by two old Russian women, reading. "You could ask them to move over," I said, but Imant whispered back, "I do not dare." The pair held their books up to their noses. Imant ambled casually around to the back of the bench and peeked spylike over their broad shoulders. "They are *very* serious," he said, reporting back to me. "I think they must be retired Communists." We tried hard not to let them see us laughing.

"Did you ever think," I said, catching my breath, "of leaving?" Imant followed my gaze to the horizon.

Almost automatically, our voices dropped. "Everyone thinks I want, but this is where I belong. If I had been some years older when the war came, then, to be sure, I would have sailed to Sweden on one of the boats. There were such boats." Imant was five-weeks old when the Nazis occupied Riga. Why had his father stayed? I asked him. Imant said, "Of course. He did not think that it would be like this. Now, is my home, my people, and I belong here. A man must live in his country."

There was never any question of persuading Imant to leave; aside from considerations of law, morality (he thought defecting was wrong), and homesickness, for Imant to leave the Soviet Union would be even riskier for his work than moving to the Soviet Union was for mine; I knew this even better than he did. A young composer who writes on a large scale—symphonies and oratorios—can, in the Soviet Union, be performed and recorded; money is rarely available for that kind of large-scale thing in the United States, and although Imant would be able to write his *Magdalen* in the United States, he'd probably have to scrap most of his other compositions. Finding me a typewriter in Latvia, however tricky, still wouldn't be as difficult as finding him an orchestra in America.

"Sooner or later," I said, "after I'm living here, in your country, I'll have to write about it. If only incidentally."

"Yes, yes, is true, I understand."

"Will they make trouble?"

"There will be interference—of this I am sure. They do not know how *not* to interfere. But I think it may not be so bad. They will let you publish in America, I think. They will see that it is good for everyone that you live here and write."

"Will they let me send my manuscripts to America?" Again, it was a question that, according to the Helsinki Accords, shouldn't even have to be asked. My manuscripts would be my personal property, the property of a U.S. citizen, and I should be able to mail them to my agent, who would sell the first rights in North America.

"But why not? I think so," he said.

We looked out over the water—the jumble of rocks first, then the sun-spangled waves, then the jeweled horizon—toward Finland. Our hands, on the stone railing, touched. "Almost it seems," he said, "as if you can reach out and touch—"

I thought he was going to say Finland.

"—freedom."

The day's light had begun to go underground, like all radical activity. Our friends came out of the cottage, and we walked—a little faster, now—through the park, over one of the bridges to the other side of the blue ribbon, and back to the steps. I must say they seemed steep to me. I stopped to rest two-thirds of the way up. "I hope I get to marry you before we get old," I said. "You'll probably be bald by the time they let us get married."

"The men in my family do not go bald," he said, reassuring me. "Only a little."

"That means time is on our side," I said. But I was lying, and we both knew it. The crowd of tourists had thinned, and the weather was growing chill. Imant turned his collar up. We had a long ride back, and it was dusk by the time we got there.

It began to rain, a clear, steady, autumnal rain, the kind of rain that puts things in perspective. We were in the café at the Sovietskya. One wall of the café was glass, so from where we sat we could watch the rain spattering against it, and across the driveway, the grassy circle changing colors from green to black. I had brought the teacups, Imant's present to me, down from my (official) room—Imant would take them to the farmhouse—and he unwrapped them for everyone to see. Even the waitress oohed and aahed. Just one table was oblivious. While Imant was putting the cups away, Rudolf leaned over to me and said, "KGB." I thought he was pulling my leg, as Imant did fairly often. The only people at that table were kids. "You're teasing me," I said.

"No," Rudolf said.

I looked at Imant. He was tying the string around the teacups. "Rudolf's joking, isn't he?" I asked.

"No," he said.

I looked again at the table of kids. "How can you tell?"

Rudolf answered, "One knows, that is all."

"They do not talk with one another," Imant said. "They try to hear what others are saying."

"But they're only kids—"

"Very often, a young person does something wrong—he takes something from a store, perhaps, or he tries to buy and sell on the black market. Then when he is caught, he is given a choice: to go to prison or work for the KGB."

We finished eating as fast as possible, got our gear together, and vamoosed. I don't know whether we were followed or whether, if we were, it was by the kids from the café.

It was early evening by the time we found a wine shop where we picked up the night's supply, and dark by the time we found a candy store. Emil and Ilze disappeared into the candy store for twenty minutes. The shop window glowed brightly through the rain, and my red umbrella finally got some use when Rudolf borrowed it to dash in after Emil and Ilze.

I had taught Imant another word: *privacy*. To Emil and Ilze and Rudolf, he had said, "I wish to have some privacy with Kelly tonight." (That was only for show, because he had to say it in Latvian before they could understand.) But Rudolf, in his halting English, said they hoped we would come to their room for a little while first. We would have a kind of party—a very quiet kind of party—in our underground hotel.

At our underground hotel, Emil, Ilze, and Rudolf decided to buy cigarettes across the way, so Imant and I went inside and waited for them by the window on the first landing. Light from the streetlamp, made misty by the evening rain—now slowed to a thick drizzle—shed a nebulous glow on the wet pavement. Three forward-pitching backs made a lunge for the store door, like football linemen. Emil and Rudolf were on the two ends; Ilze was in the center. Ilze had sharp features, eyebrows carefully etched on a small face, and she spoke only Russian and Polish.

I thought of the other two, Rudolf and Emil: the one, Rudolf, with a young man's acute sensibility lending him outward elegance and a piercing inward sense of betrayal; the other, Emil, so much the man Rudolf would become, the inevitable older version, edges worn, the style grown scruffy with time and circumstance, the passion more accommodating, less ambitious, more forgiving, enthusiasm reserved for the attainable and not dissipated in dreams.

Dreams. Suddenly I wanted something to signify that my life here was real. I asked Imant if he knew what an engagement ring was. "Yes!" he said excitedly, "I like this custom very much!" He said he would have a ring made for me. "I know a place," he said, "where they are making very fine jewelry." But he didn't think he would be permitted to send the ring out of Russia. "I will send letters," he said. "Each night I write to you and tell you what has happened in the day, and in morning I send."

We had somehow managed to shrug off the consciousness of time: it seemed as though we could wait forever by that window, speaking softly in a bare, echoing hallway, and never run out of time. I asked Imant if there was any chance we could be married in a church. He was greatly excited by this notion also, and exclaimed, "Yes, yes! I have not been married in a church before." Considering the number of his civil marriages, I had to laugh. But Imant was serious.

He is Lutheran, though about Catholicism, he had said, "I like this confession very much." (He'd have had trouble with the Catholic ruling on divorce!) Before the war, the majority of Latvians were Lutherans, about one quarter were Roman Catholic, and nine percent were Greek Orthodox. There were smaller but significant numbers of Russian Old Believers and Jews. In answer to Imant's question, I had explained that I was brought up more or less as a Presbyterian. He looked perplexed. "We have no Presbyterians here," he said. However, when I mentioned Calvin, he'd immediately produced a book on Luther and Calvin. The pictures of the two dour theologians were unmistakable in any language.

Now Imant said, "Sometimes it is allowed to marry in a church if it is discreet." (Sometimes the churches are so discreet you can't even find them. We knew there was one church in Leningrad where concerts are held on Sunday morning, but we couldn't discover which one.)

And then I recalled a scene from ten years ago. Night, in the old town of Riga: Imant opens an inconspicuous door, and I find myself in a cathedral. There is incense. People are kneeling, praying, rising. There aren't many of them, and some are so old that it seems a miracle that they can get up from their knees. There is one young girl, with a kerchief pulled so far in front of her face that I can see her face only when she turns and looks straight at me. Imant guides me out, his hand on my elbow, and neither of us ever refers to any of this.

I had wondered at the time why Imant was showing me this. To show, without stating it, that the Soviets discouraged religion; to show that people worshiped despite that. But did he also mean to convey a sense of his own spiritual longings, to suggest that here, in a church, was where I might find a side of him that not many people knew?

I began to think how much time had passed since we'd come in from the car. "Where could they be?" I asked. And for the first time we looked around us and realized that we were in the wrong building. Imant slapped his forehead and laughed. "Well," he said, "they are all the same, these hallways, no?"

We sat on the cots in a room smaller than many closets. There were no chairs, for the simple reason that there was no space for any. Overhead, an unshaded bulb dangled at the end of a string, glaring like an open eye. We had to keep our voices to a whisper. It wasn't the merriest of atmospheres, but we were merry. You're pretty much forced to be, on red wine and *marzipan.*

Imant asked everyone to estimate my ring size, and, by comparing the circumference of my ring finger with Ilze's, decided what size he'd order. If he couldn't send it to me, it would be waiting for me.

Meanwhile, Rudolf also arrived at a decision: he would learn to speak English well enough to conduct a real conversation in it when I returned. I grew sentimental about the English language, as a language that makes its own music, and then about Russian, which is also beautiful and rich in insight as well. Latvian isn't so beautiful, but it has other virtues, and the most beautiful of all is Estonian. By way of experiment I asked Rudolf to say something—the same something—in Russian, Polish, Latvian, and French. Emil threw in German, and Imant contributed Estonian. Then it was back to Rudolf for the English translation, but he was suddenly overcome by embarrassment. I had to look to Imant to persuade Rudolf to let me in on the little set speech. Rudolf had to struggle through the sentence, putting a period after each word. "We wish to thank you, dear lady, for your company and kindness in being with us." I knew if I started crying I wouldn't stop all night, so I smiled just as if none of us understood that we might never see one another again.

You could of course forge for yourself an iron heart to set in the place of this old mortal heart. This old mortal heart ticks like a time bomb, but the new heart lies in your chest like a dead weight. You try to walk and it drags you to the ground, you try to swim and are drowned. That heaviness keeps you in your place—your only place. This is a type of imprisonment. You would rather explode.

We set my travel alarm for six and woke to its clatter. Oddly, we weren't depressed; the thin light outside our window, the sense of secrecy and importance that attends any leave-taking done while most people are still sound asleep, buoyed our spirits. We packed efficiently—we were getting to be old hands at that—and when we were ready, Imant went to pay the landladies. The larger one came to see us out. She was in her robe, her hair looked as if she'd been fighting it during the night, and sleep still creased her cheeks, but she would have liked a chat. She stood with her hand on the doorknob, and she didn't want to let us go. I was afraid I'd muff the whole affair at the last minute, and as soon as we could slip out the door, I began to back down the stairs, saying, *"Paldies, paldies,"* but she wanted a final word with Imant. On the way to the car I asked him what it was. "She told me," he said, "my wife is pretty, I must take care of her." He grinned. I made a mental note that when I wrote my Michelin guide to underground hotels, this one rated four stars.

We waited in the car for Emil, Ilze, and Rudolf. The weather on this last day made it clear that we really were in a new season now: a brisk and freshening wind, sky so blue it seemed as if the last traces of summer had been swept from it only that morning, and a fallen leaf stuck against our windshield like a deciduous parking ticket. The canals glint, glitter, wink, shine, blind, flash, and glow—how can anyone be sad in Leningrad? But anxiety nips at the heart like a dog at a rear wheel, and by the time we reached the Sovietskaya, I felt emotionally out of breath.

Imant didn't see me onto the bus, because his scheme was to follow the bus to the airport. I couldn't see out back from my seat; I could only hope he was there. Then when we were out on the road that led to the airport, a little yellow Fiat overtook us, horn blaring, and all its passengers waved like crazy at ours.

But at the airport, I couldn't find them. We were driven one way; they had to come another. We learned that we had a half hour yet, the news I was praying for—but what good was a half hour without Imant? Finally, we collided on the main floor.

"I am as excited as on the first day," he said, "but I know it will be okay. You will be back soon, I am sure of it."

"Before Christmas?"

"It is possible. . . . Yes, yes, I think so! I must make the house warm for winter."

We had gone off by ourselves and were sitting in the waiting room.

"You should keep your name when we marry," he said. "Here, is done very often when the wife has work of her own."

"Don't forget to take the things to the farmhouse—"

"They are calling your plane," Imant said, and suddenly everything became terribly bright and hectic and unreal. I said good-bye to Emil, Ilze, and Rudolf. The room all around us seemed to be in flux, but for that moment we were as isolated as an island. Ilze and I shook hands; Emil kissed my hand, and Rudolf was about to, but he looked so wildly forlorn that I pecked his cheek instead. Then there was nothing more we could say to each other, and we raced to the boarding station, the three of them following Imant and me. Imant, handing me over to the check-out officials, kissed me loudly and proclaimed for all to hear, "I love you." A short while later I was miles *above* ground.

Lee Sharkey

WALKING WITH LENA

I'd been in Russia about a week, long enough to eat a loaf of rye bread, to hear the *babushkas* grumble *"oy"* in the market, to be impressed by the generosity of the people and depressed by the overweening bureaucracy, when two women I did not recognize, one in a long blue dress coat, the other in a black leather miniskirt, appeared at the door of my dormitory room at the Pedagogical Institute, where I would spend the semester as an exchange professor of American literature. Word of the Jewish-American had traveled fast in Syktyvkar, the capital city of the northern Komi Republic, which borders Siberia on the east and reaches north into the Arctic Circle. My visitors had come to invite me to a Rosh Hashanah celebration. They were expecting fifty or sixty people, said the more matronly of the pair, who spoke for the two of them, her words deliberate, alert gray eyes smiling a welcome. I thanked her and quickly accepted. She would come for me Sunday at five.

To meet my Russian counterparts. . . . My heart thumped loudly in the cave of my chest. Would we look alike? Would we have songs, prayers in common, common language across the continents and generations?

Months before, I had learned from a woman from Syktyvkar whom I met at a gathering of my Jewish group in Maine that Jews in this city had begun to reconstruct their heritage. Her father had told her on his deathbed that he was Jewish, that he had relatives in America. She was trying to track down her family. I was on a complementary quest. Dressing for that evening, I put on the gold and coral pin that had been fashioned from a necklace my grandmother carried as a girl of twelve from her birthplace in the Ukraine to America. To wear it in Eastern Europe made me tingle with pleasure, as if I were completing the wiring of an inner circuit.

✧ ✧ ✧

Displaced from Moscow, Lithuania, and the Ukraine, the Jews of Syktyvkar remember little of Jewish religious tradition. In our gathering place in the community center for a local industry, the candles were lit before the meal, but there was no *b'racha.* A young woman gave a brief speech from a prepared text explaining *akedah*, stressing the sparing of Isaac and God's providing the ram as surrogate offering. As always, I thought of Isaac lying terrified under the knife, but she told the story as if she were imparting information. We drank cognac instead of Manischewitz, and wished each other *le shanah tovah.* I proposed a toast, in which I said, "I'm grateful to be here; many, many American Jews, I among them, are also studying and recreating our traditions." A boy just back from Israel stood up and told the gathering, "You are my family, but Israel's my home now. It's warm there."

Late in the evening, as an old record spun out Yiddish tunes, a half dozen celebrants rose to sing and dance, casting auras—past their loosened skin and stiffened limbs—of the young men and women they had been when they first acted out these lyrics of flirtation and complaint. Among them was the mother of Lena, my guide and interpreter; a handsome woman, she took obvious pleasure in the performance. As for the younger members of the group, who watched with mild interest, Lena observed that their Jewishness had been defined from without, by the declaration of nationality each citizen makes at sixteen on their passport. Its infamous fifth line declares them Jewish *or* Russian, Russian *or* Komi, Russian and hiding a heritage so as not to be discriminated against. Lena learned just two words of Yiddish from her communist mother—*meshugene* and *mishegas.* I was interested to note the overlap with the six-word Yiddish vocabulary I inherited from my capitalist mother.

Lena told me she might soon need to decide, again, if she was Russian or a Jew. When I questioned the need to choose one over the other, she reminded me of Pamyat'. Although she had no desire to emigrate to Israel, the renewal of anti-Semitism might make that option more compelling. In the meantime, Russian Jews are stepping forward as Jews by gathering in public places to educate themselves about their history, to celebrate new-found traditions.

Already, though, Syktyvkar has lost much of its Jewish population. Dora, Lena's friend in the miniskirt, her co-worker at a local public school, has a sibling and both parents in Israel; she plans to go there to live with her husband and nine year old, a bright-eyed boy who gathered up his courage to speak to me in English ("Hello. I am pleased to meet you. How do you like our city?"). Most of the young will leave. Descendants of German Jews who fled to Russia are also—oh, irony—"returning" to Germany. But this evening in this room everyone looked and sounded Russian. When a song I've danced the *horah* to a hundred times, if once, announced itself through the speakers, I joined the circle of dancers. But the steps were not the ones I knew. I worked to follow.

Throughout the evening, Lena interpreted for me and a sequence of partners in conversation—a young journalist married to a poet, a recent *émigré* to Israel returned for a visit, a thin, sad violinist for the musical theater. Lena's unobtrusive attentiveness revealed intelligence, a balanced temperament, and stamina. Later, lying in bed, I turned over what she had told me about herself. She was someone I might have been had my family moved east, as hers had, instead of west from the Ukraine. A native of Syktyvkar, she had studied English at the Pedagogical Institute, where I was teaching, and become an English teacher and assistant principal at a local school. Except once briefly to India, however, she had never traveled to an English-speaking country. She lived with her mother and seven-year-old son in a three-room apartment. The first time I'd talked with her, so briefly, at the door of the dorm room, I'd recognized someone familiar. Being with her at the Rosh Hashanah celebration had deepened that sense.

What did I pick up on that night, when we were not yet friends, that intimated all we had in common? Only later, when she appeared at one after another of my lectures, did I begin to learn the depth of Lena's attachment to literature. Only later, when I visited her classroom, did I see how much she, too, lives in her teaching. In a letter she writes:

> An idea has come into my head—to organize a party devoted to Robert Burns. This is not because of the date . . . simply my wish . . . and of course my love of this poet. The first I heard of him was when I was a teenager. . . . I even learned some poems by heart. Now I decided to help my pupils to love him too. Every lesson we speak a little about his life, translate and explain his poems, a poem a lesson. What's more, I gave many of my pupils something to learn and the whole class will learn his poem "My Heart's in the Highlands" and a song, "Auld Lang Syne". . . . The pupils are happy. So when all the teachers are coming to an end and thinking about the rest, only I am all busy with my party. That is in a few words all my life.

The intimacy I came to feel with her, which made our linguistic and cultural differences seem mere stuff, could I have felt it with a non-Jewish Russian woman? A Jewish Russian man? Was knowing she was Jewish my *sine qua non* for seeing her as family? But there was so much more than that.

My colleagues at the Pedagogical Institute were bright and literate, dedicated and dogged within a wearing, Kafkaesque existence. But only Lena had *read* Kafka. As an adolescent she had come across Ilya Ehrenburg's memoirs, and subsequently sought out all the Modernists he writes about. While her classmates were being charmed by the Impressionists, she was steeping herself in Modigliani. In the basement stacks of the public library, Lena's mother had found the one copy of Kafka's works in the city and brought it home for her daughter.

"We're in *The Castle*," I observed to Lena one day when she kept me company as I waited an hour and a half for my salary, while five bookkeepers scrambled back and forth on unfathomable errands, and dozens of faculty members stood in line behind me. She chuckled, then regaled me with stories of the petty tyranny of the bookkeeper at her school, who refuses to explain the calculations she uses to arrive at the teachers' salaries. Walking me home, she described the transformation of the rector of the Institute from innovative teacher to complacently obstructionist administrator: "The leather armchair and the trips to the Education Ministry removed him from his senses."

We were to have gone that day to visit Lena's mother, Celia, at the library. A former engineer, she had worked on diesel locomotives in Soviet Asia until she married. Her husband, a bright and shining graduate of Moscow University, could not get a position teaching history in the capital because he was a Jew. He was appointed instead to the Komi State Pedagogical Institute. In Syktyvkar, there was no work on the locomotives for Celia, but her science and engineering background won her the post of patents librarian at the public library, a job she still holds forty-five years later. She was to have given me a tour. But if the wait at the cashier's window hadn't intervened, I still would not have got to see the library that afternoon. The electric power had failed there, as it did in my dorm unpredictably for indeterminate periods.

"Sometimes, walking with a friend," Grace Paley writes in her "Midrash on Happiness," "I forget the world." I was gratified to hear Lena's response to Paley's stories, which I regularly read aloud to anyone who will listen: "It's as if I've known her all my life." We too walked and talked like Faith and Ruth in the story, as if the talk itself were our destination. I tucked my arm into her arm so we wouldn't slip on the ice, in the snow, so we made a Russian pair, for the pleasure of it. Sasha, her son, who was most often with us, taught me the word for *mitten* on the day he lost one, and Lena crooned a lament for lost mittens as we walked through the sub-zero afternoon. Sasha would run ahead, then return to us as we talked about our lives, about what Gertrude Stein calls the "bottom nature" of men and women, about our cultures from the vantage point of critical insiders. We were headed for Lena's apartment. At the end of such visits we would run the process in reverse: scarves and hats and coats would come off the hooks and out of the wardrobe; Lena would pull on her boots, slip into her long coat and button it to the fur collar, fit her fur hat snugly to her head. She and Celia would decry my lack of serious winter clothing, then she and I would set out into the dark toward my place. After the first visit, I didn't need her guidance home, but I never refused her offer to walk me half way. The cold was often bitter; talking with her, I forgot to feel it.

Between our walks, the hours of our visits spread out in that small but comfortable apartment, which didn't look quite like the other apartments I knew in Syktyvkar. Though the furniture was identical, Communist standard, the artifacts that filled it weren't—the portrait of Akhmatova on the cabinet; the dolls from India; the hand-carved and painted Komi animals; the pieces of wood with swirling grains, found objects, pinned to the wall; the bookshelves filled with classic and contemporary Russian poetry, with Russian, American, and British literature, including Celia's prized collection of Jane Austen. The piano. On one of the shelves sat a photograph of the fine-drawn face of an intellectual, Lena's father, dead these fifteen years.

On my first visit, Lena pulled out book after book of Tsvetayeva's poetry, showed me photographs, and read from her work. I listened to the cascade of nursery rhyming through which the tragedy of that poet's life and suicide sang out, and thought of Sylvia Plath. On another visit, she played a record of Langston Hughes's poems performed in translation; I was able to make out the key words of "The Negro Speaks of Rivers" within impassioned cadences of her native tongue. She told me stories of Jewish actors and writers whose careers had been cut short by Stalin. Through my ignorance, I glimpsed traces of a human story larger than either of our cultures.

One afternoon Lena invited me to her apartment to introduce me to Vladimir Vysotsky. So much was she taken up with revealing everything to me in just a few hours that she didn't glance once at the platters of tiny open-faced sandwiches she had prepared and laid before us. Vysotsky, poet, actor, songwriter, was known in the '60s and '70s by everyone in the Soviet Union, though as an artist he did not officially exist. Tapes of his impromptu concerts spread across the country, copies of copies of copies, blurring with their increasing distance from the source. The voice, however, was unmistakable—hoarse, raw, passionate, and the lyrics like nothing people ever heard. He spoke in the vernacular, he told the truth. He savaged the absurdities of Soviet life.

Lena first heard him when she was twelve, on a vacation with her parents in the South. A boyfriend had a tape he played for her. She had never heard such singing, such a use of language—Konsomol songs had not prepared her to think such a thing could exist. She did not know what to make of it, but a window opened and her spirit flew out into a wider world.

Her father, driven in his work and a devoted communist despite state-sanctioned anti-Semitism, demanding and authoritative at home, forbad her to listen to Vysotsky. But Lena did what she needed to do. Her ideal of a man formed around the figure of Vysotsky: passionate, visionary, utterly honest. She tried every time she went to Moscow to see him perform in the tiny experimental theater he acted in—in avant garde performances of Brecht's good person of Setzuan (ungendered in Russian), and as Hamlet, where he sat onstage in blue jeans strumming his guitar while the audience filed in.

Vysotsky died of heart failure at forty-two. Thousands thronged his funeral. Unlike Stalin's funeral, where people were crushed to death, the service for Vysotsky was peaceful, a final tribute to his spirit.

I nibbled and listened. Lena pulled articles and photographs from a two-foot-high stack of folders, and laid all of Vysotsky's records on the sofa around us. She read and translated poems. Finally she played his songs—she knew the precise place on the disc where each one began—and I too heard the power and beauty in his voice. She translated, told me what was untranslatable.

No one good or brave or strong enough to stand up to the system appeared in Lena's life, and her relationships with men never lasted. When she decided to have a baby, she got pregnant by a transient worker; she did not tell him her intention, or about the pregnancy. Sasha is a delicate, fair-skinned, straight-haired redhead. He does not learn quickly, and Lena works with him every evening on his schoolwork. Sometimes she forgets he even had a father, a state of mind I was often in myself when I was raising my child alone. But Sasha looks nothing like Lena; his genetic father is written all over him. In a few years, someone will ask him a question he won't be able to answer, and then the wondering will begin. Will he resent Lena for what she's done? She has an address for the father's family. Her son may want to track his father down. "Won't he be surprised," is her only comment.

There is what I need and what she needs. I do something for her, so she tells me. She is tired, watches the nighttime soaps instead of reading. I remind her, perhaps, of something she has put aside. "You're not good enough to be an actress," pronounced her father. "Go study to be an English teacher."

"She used to write poems," her mother told me.

"Now Sasha is my poem," she replies.

She writes, "Did we really make friends? How did it happen? We didn't have a lot of time to recognize each other." She is afraid I won't understand why she aches with tiredness and turns off the light on the book she is reading. She thinks I may judge her. I need to tell her about my years of tiredness, when I fell asleep every night with a stack of papers beside me, when I couldn't be sick because there'd be no one to take my child to school. My mother's step as she pulled herself up the stairs after work to work again is imprinted in me. I need to say, "this too will pass."

The solstice was upon us, Chanukah was coming, and there were four dim hours of daylight in each twenty-four. I hungered for a festival of light. A voice gathered deep inside me until I heard, *Before I leave, I want to worship in Russia.* What did I mean by that? To bow my head? To raise my voice in praise? To cup my hands around a candle flame and bring light to my eyes? To sit with Lena and her mother at the table, to join the branch that forked three generations past, to sit with my sister here, as anywhere, at home.

Lena and I sat on the sofa bed in the room she shares with Sasha and turned the pages of her photo album. Her father, young, thin, with a full head of curly hair, tucks his five-year-old daughter to his side, the bond between them unassailable. She has his eyes and his focus. (In a similar picture, my father stands beside me at summer camp, his hands draped over my shoulders, assuming possession. I peer into the sun and smile.) In school photos, the girl gives way to the gangly adolescent, the hair lengthens. The coed at the institute might just as well have been a classmate of mine at Brandeis. The young teacher puts on glasses and trims her hair. Then comes Sasha, dozens of photos of him. He's two or three, they're in Odessa in an antique car, he's got the steering wheel, she wears a flower-print dress and jaunty bowler hat. Her white arm folds across her waist and tucks into his arm. This is the photograph she wants me to have. The page turns, she puts on weight, her hair whitens and she cuts it short.

The table set with bowls of garnet broth. It was the sixth night of Chanukah, I'd brought some candles, an assorted handful, and asked if I might light them, say the blessing. A five-pronged candelabra placed before me, single candlesticks beside it made a sixth and seventh. I lit the wicks and sang the prayer I hadn't sung since my son's childhood; I forgot a verse, my voice weakened as I reached for the high notes. But Celia smiled, perhaps remembering.

We talked, we ate, we talked. Most people over thirty I met in Russia could not summon the heart for politics. But this is a political family. Lena's mother is keenly interested in her country's struggle toward democracy; Lena's brother was allied with a colleague of Sakharov's, and exiled to Komi for promoting a memorial to the thousands who died in prison camps throughout the republic.

"Why this difference in attitude?" I asked.

"The family history," the brother answered without hesitation, and traced a line back through scholars and rabbis, five generations of book people, a hundred fifty generations of people of the book. A heritage. A set of values, of responses.

And Celia danced, her center of gravity low in her body, weighted and sensuous, lifting her arms to clap above her head, a smile spreading over her face until it flooded her full cheeks, her high cheekbones, her dark eyes that filled with generous light. Her woman's pleasures, her childhood pleasures, her mother's mother's knowledge moved in her steps. I stood and swayed to Celia's rhythms, Lena threw a window open. Then we three danced while cold air pulled the flames.

Nadja Tesich

LOVE

(From the novel *Far From Vietnam*)

She fell in love the way they had predicted and said it would happen some day. It was love at first sight—the moment she saw him—long dark hair, deep brown eyes with the most beautiful lashes. Better looking than any man ever, it had to be him, nobody could compare with this one. And there was something totally lonely in his eyes, the feeling of sadness, of imminent disaster—she recognized him by this—her old self—and what she had told Pascale once about her early death. This didn't make her unhappy, on the contrary.

Right after Spain, she saw many posters of the same face from different angles in black and white—in some he wore a beret, in others not, in some he was in full combat gear, in others he smiled. But each picture had that special longing around the eyes. She read everything she could find about him, but there wasn't much, mostly political pamphlets, thin, badly printed; she wanted real details about his life. He had asthma, she found out, and she wondered how he managed in the jungle with all those flowers blooming day after day, all the time. Her admiration grew; he was stubborn, didn't give up. But the really decisive moment, when the feeling of love crystallized (she would think later), happened when she read in *The Permanent Revolution* how after the takeover, right after the victory in Cuba, he had turned down this big position as minister of something or other and had despite general protest declared, "I am leaving, my mission is elsewhere." And then he took off for Bolivia. She couldn't think of any other gesture that would reassure her more; he'll always be different, she thought. He didn't put it quite like that, out of politeness and respect for those who stayed; he spoke about the revolution spreading like fire and so on. In the pictures of him and Cuba, it looks like a celebration—young bearded men, all handsome, wave their guns—it's the end of Batista. Yet she remembers the film she had seen with Pascale, a Hungarian or Yugoslav war film in the Latin Quarter, and in it a young man says to his friend, "Tomorrow a new government starts, a real one, we fought for it, didn't we? Tomorrow we'll have everything in order, the laws, the housekeeping, the rules for execution. These last twenty-four hours are the last ones of the revolution."

That's why, she thinks of Che; "I'll never get married," she tells Pascale.

Of course loving him had its disadvantages—she couldn't walk hand in hand, kiss on St. Michel near the river on the bridges, not like other people on Sunday or any day when the weather was good. She would have liked to do it briefly, for a week maybe, to satisfy the yearning that had to do with the landscape, the beauty of Paris, maybe just once she thought, but didn't linger on it. The others would have laughed had she said something, probably considered her nuts, crazy, cracked. It was best kept secret, her lonely passion, but maybe it was better this way—all the usual public signs of affection only diminish it. This life, ordinary life, was denied to them from the start. It left the other one.

Even though she couldn't walk with him arm in arm, she took him along everywhere, on the street, on hundreds of marches, Rome, Berlin, as the Vietnam War suddenly transformed the Latin Quarter and he unified them under the same flag of permanent rebellion, everyone young running, chanting "Che, Che, Che," she louder than the others. That they loved him too produced no jealousy or exclusiveness, if anything it proved her own love, vindicated it, a way of sharing. But the time came when marches and chanting weren't enough, that's where she differed from the others on the street, in the nature of her obsession. He was real, alive, not made out of paper. Somewhere in Bolivia.

She knew he had left Cuba but the Cuban government though friendly didn't help. She even detected some suspicion in the embarrassed official she saw at the Rue Sainte Anne, a wiry fellow with a cigar. When he asked why she needed this information, she couldn't easily explain. And of course she couldn't approach the Bolivians—he was an outlaw there. The information had to be gathered slowly; the months passed. It helped that Latin Americans loved talking, sharing secrets, a dangerous activity since everyone knew about the latest uprisings before they happened. Some information was wrong, wasted time, like the Argentine boy with whom she went out just for this reason—he claimed he knew a lot. It turned out he knew little, loved tangoes and dancing in general, was very good at it. Finally, holding her tight one night, he said, "Why are you interested in him, what difference does it make, where I come from we are all as good as Ernesto." He wanted to explain how different they were from the others, Brazilians, Peruvians, and the rest, more civilized, virtually Spanish. That lead came to a stop.

She couldn't ask openly and directly for reasons having to do with suspicion, the fear of laughter. And being American didn't help, she saw that—every Yankee was a potential CIA agent and of course some were. Around this time she started telling lies, and some she believed herself—how her father was murdered, how her grandmother was an anarchist (that was true in a way), but from this one grain of truth her tales changed to include all the rest—how it was an accident she was born in the U.S.; at home nobody spoke English at all. Maybe these stories helped, maybe it was her natural ease in inventing herself, but it was really through Pedro, the *concièrge* at the Argentine dorm that she got the lucky break one night. He was feeling nostalgic, lonely, and tired, and he put up a sign on the window that said Gone for Repairs, then invited her to have a drink at the café by the park. After the third beer he said, matter-of-factly, without any questions, that he knew Che's cousin, a girl who lived near Notre-Dame-des-Champs.

Clara looked ordinary; glasses, hair pulled tight, and like most women, her ambitions were of this world. She said Ernesto is crazy to abandon his wife and children (new information), who does he think he is, Jesus Christ? The entire family disapproved. She was studying medicine in Paris, he was a doctor already. "If he wants to help the poor, why doesn't he open a hospital at home? They need them. Why Bolivia?—what a waste for an educated man to go traipsing around the mountains," she said. "Men have bizarre notions about what it is to be a hero," she added, somewhat bitter, then asked, "Are you writing something about him or us?" Yes, she was writing about both, she told her, but there wasn't enough information. "It's because they don't care about us," Clara said. "We are all lumped together under Latin America; before you do it, you should know more, nobody would ever confuse a Frenchman with a Swede, would they?" She was the one who confirmed the asthma story but was harsh, "Imagine a man with a severe case trying to be a hero in the mountains. He is mad, and no medicine anywhere. I wonder what he does when he has an attack." They chatted, Clara grew relaxed and revealed everything—that in fact she didn't know him at all, had seen him only once but they had a cousin who did, a man who married a Peruvian and stayed in Lima.

"I should go there," she muttered.

"I wouldn't," said Clara. "Buenos Aires is more interesting. Why not write to Lima instead? Do you want his address?" She gave everything, including the addresses of other relatives, phone numbers, but extracted a promise to tell her if she went to Argentina soon. She had a package for her mother.

It took months to get an answer from Peru and, then, having received it, to write to another person, a friend in La Paz. This second man was vague, couldn't promise anything in a letter, he said. If she comes to La Paz he'll be able to show her the scenery and introduce her to his family. She wrote in French, he answered in Spanish which Pedro translated. No names were mentioned, but she was sure scenery meant something else. It took additional months to get a passport, the quality of the forged ones had declined since the bookstore where they could be bought had closed and the best technician had left for the States. For obvious reasons she couldn't use hers, any other nationality was less dangerous in Latin America.

Just as she started to despair, Pascale offered her hers. She didn't need it just now. They examined it together. Pascale's nose, strange in life, was just about invisible in the passport thanks to a bad photo. "We both have blue eyes, just dye your hair black," she said, "and if you stick to the same shirt and my gold chain, you might pass."

She didn't ask why Anne needed it, assuming a love interest, as always her main preoccupation.

This settled, she had to translate, be a tourist guide, do any extra job to save for the passage. It looked like it would take a long time when suddenly it turned out she was able to go for nothing thanks to an agent at Air France who only asked her to take a suitcase for him to La Paz. And put her dirty underwear on top, this way they didn't look any further. He was apparently a nice man, she never met him, he was doing this for Pascale. Several times before she had done him a favor, would let him use her old shed in Montparnasse during lunch hour, the only time he could meet his lover who didn't want to go to a hotel. She was a married woman but very romantic. Because of this, he did small favors for her once in a while, Pascale said. In fact now she revealed that he didn't even know that she, Pascale, wasn't going to La Paz, "but since you have my passport, you are Pascale," she said and laughed as always.

She swore never again, what if the man appears right at the last moment and discovers she was not Pascale, what if everything turns bad? At Orly, nervous, heart pounding, she was to go through the usual police check when the stewardess grabbed her and led her with a smile through another door with the rest of the crew. They were casual, it looked like they did this all the time. She sat in front, in first class, empty except for a silent German couple and an American nun. In first class, everyone was in disguise.

She slept most of the trip, drunk on champagne and the fear of the night before.

The passport check in La Paz was effortless, the official seemed drowsy, barely looked at her passport or her. She had nothing to be afraid of after that. Outside, a man in a navy jacket, vaguely European, waited for the suitcase. She recognized him by the description; he immediately recognized the tan leather suitcase she had carried on board. He pretended to be a relative, he kissed and hugged her but grabbed the suitcase firmly and without talking dropped her in a hotel that seemed to be in the center of La Paz. From this trip she learned something important—not to be nervous about passports, the officials only looked for the most obvious things. And women they ignored. Of course her hair was different; together with Pascale she had picked a very dark shade, packed more bottles for the future.

Nothing had prepared her for La Paz that first day, the shortness of breath, the dizziness that came with high altitude. It was one thing to read that it was the highest city in the world and another to breathe it in. And the colors, the yellows and reds of wool hats, the shiny blackness of braids. She knew that first day she had left Europe behind; this was another world, the landscape resembling her image of the moon. She'd better learn fast.

She could vouch for the CIA—they were everywhere in La Paz and easy to spot because of the shoes and clothes that looked like a costume of what the CIA should wear. Crew cuts too, and rosy freckled skin that never tanned. She herself would have done a better job of it, at least found a better type of face—why did they always have to be so blond and bland here where color dominated? And they didn't try any real sort of camouflage, not finding it necessary. Relaxed, matter of fact, they hung around the same bar in La Paz, called El Topo, drinking whiskey and gin. It was fun pretending not to know while they gabbed stupidly in half-loud whispers with total disregard for the locals, in the conviction that Indians are too dumb to speak English. They simply couldn't imagine them comprehending. Code words were used at El Topo like "Operation Monkey" or "Operation Cynthia"—how transparent. They liked this part she observed and remembered her own childhood, the games of hide and seek in Racine. One of them, the young one from Illinois, was cute. She wanted to ask him "what the hell are you doing with an outfit like this?" but didn't dare. Instead she drank with him and he tried to find out what she did. Even when drunk she revealed nothing because the more she drank the better she lied, her real life escaping out the window; on such occasions, she could invent so well and be so convincing about imaginary sadness, she herself cried. She enjoyed it, a temporary rest from urgent matters, from the real sadness, the core of her mind. She told him her brother had disappeared, a student, and she was to look for him and then leave when it got hopeless. "You see," she said, "my parents are convinced it's a woman."

"Let's hope you don't disappear," he said. "Where did you learn to speak English so well?"

"In Paris and London," she lied, "and I had an American boyfriend."

Obliquely she hoped to learn about Che's whereabouts but didn't get too far—he was getting too interested in her, too inquisitive, so she stopped going to El Topo for good.

Her main contact from Peru had disappeared—she found out almost right away. When she went to see Clara's cousin's friend, he wasn't there. The family that lived at his address high up on the edges of La Paz knew nothing about him, they had just moved from Le Sucre. She waited outside still hoping for someone to tell her more. A neighbor, a woman, said "gone away"; a man shrugged his shoulders; another implied that his throat was cut. Between them they spoke a language she couldn't comprehend, and she couldn't describe him well. She had never seen him, it was as if he never existed. Yet she came again to the same house on the outskirts hoping for something. Without him she had a problem—he was going to show her the scenery which she was sure was a code word.

Going back the last time she saw an Indian man near the house; chewing coca leaves, he stared openly; his teeth were black. He followed her at a distance all the way to the hotel but didn't enter.

She had been in La Paz for two months, walking, looking, and everything was fine except her money started to run out. She felt trapped—to try to work in a city where the natives were out of a job was hopeless and the two embassies were out of the question—to the Americans she couldn't prove her existence without a passport, and she didn't go to the French, afraid of being discovered. The way out, the last resource, to be shipped home, which embassies did occasionally, was denied her. And she had nothing of value except the asthma medicine and her gold chain. Trying to sell Pascale's gift at the market she stumbled on a young priest who said she could eat with them, a group called the Brothers of Mercy.

He was a handsome man, originally from Nimes; in its contours his face reminded her at first of her friend George and of Saint Paul. But his eyes had the look of something that knows itself watched, and while they talked she had a peculiar feeling—everything they said stood for other things. He knew of a cheaper hotel, accompanied her there. They seemed to know him well. She would never know if it was because of him that the first man appeared, disappeared, but others came after him, never staying more than a day. They said nothing. Nothing happened. Yet their appearance had a pattern, the eyes carried messages she wasn't supposed to decipher. They didn't trust her, she thought, and why should they? Normally you have to prove yourself first. She decided to do something, this could go on forever, a letter would be the best.

She wrote, "You can trust me, I can help," and gave it to the same Indian man she had seen at the market and in front of the hotel. He was the only one who stayed constant, the others came and went. The letter wasn't addressed to Che, there were no names used, just his symbol on the envelope, a star done with a magic marker. This was a risk, she knew—he might give it to the police or CIA, a possibility. Briefly she wished she could confide in someone, but the young priest had disappeared, they told her.

A week later, as they passed each other at the market, a man slipped a note in her pocket. After that he moved away and watched her. Written on notebook paper, Che's letter was hardly longer than hers. "Go away, please," he wrote in French, "I don't need anyone. You can't help, would only make matters worse." She answered immediately, giving it to the man she thought of as the Indian with gray hair. "You are wrong," she wrote, outraged, "nobody would suspect me, I could get you medicines, anything, think about it, try me for Christ's sake!" She was making a pest of herself, begging him, something she had never done before for a man.

On the third day of her third month in La Paz a man appeared in the early morning hours inside her room and said "*Vamos*." He terrified her, after all the door had been locked. She had been waiting for something of this sort but at that moment she is uncertain, she has no proof of anything. What if he is with the police. He is impatient, edgy. Once again he says, "Let's go."

She packed in two minutes, in fact she had been packed all along. It's early now, cold, the street is silent, bluish from the invisible sun. She thinks she hears birds' wings, a train whistle far away; a feeling of destiny is in her lungs—when you can't retreat, when everything has been chosen and is somehow out of control. He puts a thick wool poncho on her and a wool hat; suntanned with black hair she likes to think she looks *mestizo*. Dark glasses cover her eyes. He has them on too. Together they get on the train which is surprisingly full.

He said nothing all along, was either asleep or bored. In the middle of nowhere, he motioned her to jump. The train had almost stopped. He stayed on. Another man waited outside with a truck. He said nothing either, looked like a farmer of sorts. They went on like this forever, not talking, which she found hardest of all. When the truck stopped at some point, another man with two small horses motioned her to get on one, a sickly looking animal resembling a donkey. This part took forever as the landscape changed, over broken hills, rivers in deep ravines. There were no people anywhere but she saw villages in the distance, a sign post said Iripiti, five kilometers. They stopped, to rest again, she thought, but they had arrived. Dismounting, a sudden sensation of danger, of someone aiming at her back. She ducked and turned around.

She saw a man partially hidden by the trees in front of an earth-colored hut. He was chewing on a pipe but was otherwise recognizable.

"I thought you'd be puffing on a cigar," she said for some reason. His hair is chestnut, not black.

"I have none left," he said. "I wouldn't mind."

She pulled out the inhalers and the pills for asthma, but first gave him a pack of *Gauloises* Pascale had forgotten at Orly. His eyes are blue gray, slant a bit when he laughs. "You are fast," he says. "Come."

Inside, on one wall a map of Bolivia and a detailed one of Santa Cruz. A violent smell of earth, grass, and sweat. The three of them and a Peruvian drink something yellow and sharp, then two men get up and leave. She hears distant voices, the neighing of a horse far away. Through the door red mauve on the treetops, a flutter of invisible birds very near; soon the trees are all black—the sun has set. In the hut his pipe glows like a firefly.

"What should we call you?" he says.

"You pick a name," she says.

"I've always picked mine. Here's to your new name," he says, touching her glass.

At this moment, it is certain she is in love with the picture and the man, had been in love all along, maybe she had him in mind when she spoke about love before, maybe she had always been in love with one and the same face.

She came in March; by June they were separated. She was to go elsewhere, following this advice, and would soon come back. She never made it. Later, they spoke about a woman Che knew; sometimes she was referred to as Russian, other times German or Polish, and her names changed in the papers but nobody was sure she ever existed. Her hair was long and black then, she was safe—nobody would recognize her and all those who could were dead.

This portion of her life she never told because it was too private to tell—the core of what's important had to be protected. But she knew even then something wonderful and sad, that with him she had attained the best and it couldn't be repeated. Protected with this, she would laugh much later when they spoke about Ernesto Che. They knew nothing at all. He loved good cigars and wine, and even had a weakness for certain chocolates. And there was a large mole in back of his neck and one big toe was much larger than the other. No, he was not a saint. Sure he spoke about his love for the masses, the need to feed the poor and give them bread but there was more. Even though she was young, much younger than he, she saw that his life, or what others call "living," was not enough him, never would be. He had to move forward, invent the new—their ideas on love and revolution were similar, that's why they got along so well. But it was too brief, and the memory of him would always be linked to something unfinished, and all her thoughts of love to unbearable sadness.

Vicki Goldsmith

RUNNING AROUND THE BLOC

Packing for a year in Poland, I made sure I had plenty of running socks, my Thinsulate mittens, and a new pair of Nike Airs. I figured correctly; it turned out that I wouldn't be able to buy those things in Warsaw. In the States I'd been spoiled, blessed with the beauty of Michigan's Upper Peninsula and a group of hard-core runners as friends. Now, unless I was very lucky, I'd be running in a city alone, and I didn't want any excuses to stop.

We spent our first ten days with the dozen other Fulbright teachers at an orientation in Cracow, one of Europe's oldest and most beautiful cities. The first day Cracow seemed romantic: we were surrounded by a soft, lovely mist, like a light fog that hasn't quite risen in the morning. The second day we realized why. Our guide explained, "We can see the air here because of the heavy pollution from our Russian-built steelworks." Since it was 65 degrees and sunny, I decided to run anyway and took off for an hour. I returned coughing, choking, and grateful Gary was not assigned to Cracow. During the hour I saw one other runner. He was wearing gloves, a wool hat, two pairs of sweats, and a mask.

When the orientation ended, we took the northbound train to Warsaw. The morning after our arrival, I decided to check out the neighborhood running conditions. Fortunately the University of Warsaw had assigned us to an apartment in a suburb called Zoliborz, away from the congestion and the maze of high-rise apartments downtown. Looking through the grapevines that covered our patio, I could see the obvious route to take, a wide, tree-lined boulevard with charming sidestreets.

The reason the street was wide, I discovered during the next hour, was that it was a major bus route. At three-minute intervals a bus would crawl past me like a sick dragon and cough diesel fumes in all directions.

The second deterrent was the dog population. Almost every pedestrian had at least one dog. Apparently it was popular to raise two puppies from one litter because several people had leashed twins. Since the average Polish apartment has only two rooms and a kitchenette, I was surprised to find such large breeds: Labs, German shepherds, Great Danes, Afghans, Doberman pinschers, and sheepdogs. Warsaw has a leash and muzzle law. Some owners obey it, but even a muzzle didn't have much effect as I passed. Neither the dogs nor their owners were accustomed to seeing runners, especially women runners. Each dog went into action, leaping, barking, sending the next dog into a similar frenzy. The owners stared, open-mouthed, some with shock or disgust, others with amusement. A few shouted questions at me in Polish. One small old man smiled, raised his fist, and yelled, "Bravo!" I returned with my seven miles in, but I knew this couldn't be my regular route.

The second time out I tried the sidestreets. For an hour I went up and down the short blocks looking at flowers and rowhouses. I met fewer dogs and stares, but the curving streets would often dead-end and break my rhythm. The bricks and cobblestones were charming, but they jarred my skeleton and were difficult to run on. After two weeks of being continuously lost in what felt like one of those mazes I did on paper as a kid, I longed for a woods.

Paper is scarce in the East Bloc. Typing paper is a luxury. Sometimes whole towns are out of toilet paper for days. If you have access to a Warsaw phone book, you have clout. I went after, and found, another rare paper product—a map of the city including suburbs. In addition to bus and tram routes, it had the answer to my problem. Green sections. Parks and woods of Zoliborz. I taped the map to the bedroom wall and memorized my way to a small woods about three kilometers away. The route took me past scenes unfamiliar at first, but soon to become routine: women lined up at the fruit stands waiting patiently for cabbages and apples; people in front of the meat stores at 10:00 A.M. to be first in line for the 11:00 A.M. opening; black market money changers (referred to as "bankers" in the neighborhood) asking me, "Change money? Change money?"; school children laughing as I passed, slapping their fists and yelling, *"Tempo, tempo"* until I was out of view.

I found the green section of my map, but my first attempt to enter the woods was the usual Polish lesson in patience: no prize is attained without a line to wait in or an obstacle to overcome. The trees were surrounded by a high wire fence that continued for more than a mile, a mile of narrow sidewalk sandwiched between the tramtracks and the bus stands. Finally I came to an entrance, but the *milicja* were there in their blue uniforms pacing. I thought perhaps they were guarding the entrance. I stepped up my pace and ran past them. Nobody stopped me.

On the outskirts of the woods were small groups of men taking their morning *piwo* break. Each man carried a couple of beers, which he downed in the five or ten minutes he had before returning to work. Farther into the woods were more groups: grandmas watching toddlers play in the sand; farmers with horse-drawn wagons gathering wood; priests walking in pairs; more dogs walking their owners. For the next two weeks I explored trails, listened to ravens and jackdaws quacking around me, discovered the little fences Poles make by braiding forked branches. Twice, three deer pranced out in front of me. For the first time since my arrival in the city, I looked forward to my hour alone. I decided I was the only runner in Warsaw, but at least I was safe in the woods.

I was wrong on both counts. One morning as I neared the exit of my woods path, a man walked toward me. As I always did to accommodate walkers, I stepped off the trail and ran beside it to pass him. As I moved back onto the path, I felt his hand on my leg and heard his deep voice, like an animal laughing. Later I thought what a shame it was those two miles home weren't part of a sanctioned race. I screamed, kicked him, and escaped unharmed, but I was afraid to venture into the woods alone again and furious that he had cost me my perfect running spot.

For awhile I stayed on the road beside the woods, where the priests walked. Then one morning I saw an animal rarer than a deer—another runner. Equally shocked to see me, he smiled and said, *"Dzien dobry."* I returned his "Good morning." He stared at my shoes and asked me something in Polish.

"Nie rozuniem po Polsku," I replied. I didn't understand Polish.

"Francuski? Angielski?"

"Tak," I answered. I could speak French or English. He seemed disappointed. He looked at my shoes again and said something. I recognized the words for *American* and *shoes.* He motioned for me to show him the bottoms of the soles, then rolled his eyes heavenward and smiled. Lifting his foot, he showed me a sole nearly gone, glued and reglued. In his next question I heard the word *"maraton."*

"Tak," I answered. *"Dwa . . ."* I had run two marathons.

Accenting the first syllable, he said, *"Berlin,"* then picked up a stick and wrote in the dirt, 2:56. Despite the language barrier, we were having the universal runners' conversation. When I left him, I knew his 10K times, that he had cartilage trouble in his right knee, and that we were to run together the following Saturday at 9:00 A.M.

When I arrived at the small plaza beside his apartment, my new friend shook my hand and taught me the word *Czesc,* the Polish equivalent of *Hi,* less formal than *Good day.* By moving his finger around his watch and shrugging, he asked how long I wanted to run. I moved my finger once around my own watch face, a miniature Monopoly board with a tiny man in a top hat pointing to the hour with his umbrella. My friend laughed and said, *"Amerikanski."*

We started running through a small neighborhood which was wealthy by Polish standards. It had individual houses instead of rowhouses; yards, which by spring would be filled with roses, hollyhocks, poppies, and irises; cars in private driveways; even an elaborate doghouse. We passed through a small woods, then a larger one. As we ran, we exchanged names. Mine was close to Victoria, the name of the big tourist hotel in Warsaw. His was Miatek. We began constructing what would for nine months be our own language, a combination of some German verbs, French for family relatives, our native tongues for long stories, and a lot of drawings in the dirt or snow. When something was pretty, he said, "beautiful," I said *"piekna;"* then we both added *"jolie"* for good measure.

The green on my map went only as far as a little cluster of streets I'd never seen, but whose names I'd translated: Alphabet, Writer, Rhythm, Papyrus, Illustration, Encyclopedia, and Poetry. By 9:45 that Saturday morning we were moving through those streets, across the city's one four-lane expressway, past tethered cows and horses, up a steep hill. Suddenly we came to a huge forest. To my surprise Miatek led me through a few trees to a three-and-a-half kilometer circular path wide enough for a car to drive on. Halfway around the circle we met five of his friends running the opposite direction. Like him, they were mostly in their fifties and were part of Warsaw's small core of serious runners. Miatek introduced me to Marek, Gutek, Bogusch, Wojciech, and Kuba. The men shook hands with me, smiled, and stared at my shoes. The only young member of the group, Wojciech, spoke English and offered to translate for me. The group's two-hour daily runs were perfect for him, he said, because he was training for the Boston marathon. I asked what his job was. "My card says *athlete;* I train every day," he answered. His reply was modest. I learned from Miatek that Wojciech was the fastest runner in Poland. He was hoping to get passports and visas for him and his girlfriend Eva so he could win some money in the marathon and look for a scholarship at an American university. About three hundred Poles a day lined up at the American Embassy to apply for visas. The forty percent who got them usually succeeded because they had a savings account and a family, reasons to return. Wojciech had both and thought his chances were good.

In the middle of each circle we ran, the group stopped for *gymnastiques*, stretches and calisthenics that lasted five or ten minutes. No one stretched before or after the run, and no one got chilled or stiffened up as a result of stopping in the middle. No one except me, that is. I wasn't used to the distance and wanted to keep moving. Each time we completed the circular track, someone suggested we do one more *ronda*. The talk was familiar: how far we were going, how long it was taking, who had knee trouble, where the nearest water pump was. It was remarkable that any of them escaped knee problems; they were running in old, ragged shoes. The best running shoes available in the country were what Americans would call "bottom of the line." They cost about twenty-five dollars, or the Polish equivalent of a month's salary. Miatek's shoes were three years old. In addition to his regular runs and races, he ran three or four marathons a year in them.

After three rounds on the path Miatek and I left the *grupa* and retraced our route home. It was the first time I'd run fourteen miles since my days of marathon training.

Through the winter months I met Miatek four days a week for a ten-mile run. I told him about Gary's new job as coach of the Warsaw baseball team. He told me about his daughter's open-heart surgery and his wife's work in Canada. We complained about the meat lines and taught each other the names of flowers and animals. He pointed out leaves full of holes and said, "Chernobyl." He brought us homemade meat dumplings. I took him aspirins, unavailable in Polish pharmacies. We joked about bugs we swallowed as we ran, the "only meat in Poland without a line and a ration card."

In mid-January Miatek told me about a local race scheduled for the following Sunday. Was I interested? If so, he said, I shouldn't worry about the doctor's permission slip required of all runners; he would take care of everything. *"Nic probleme."* All I had to do was be ready to go at 9:00 A.M. Since the race was at noon, I wondered why we were leaving so early, but I had already learned that the simplest task can take half a day in Poland, so I was ready to leave right after breakfast.

It was snowing the day of the race. Wojciech, Kuba, and Miatek picked me up, and we walked to the bus stop, discussing what we had just eaten to get ourselves ready to race. When I mentioned my banana, they started razzing me about being a rich American, able to afford oranges and good running shoes.

I soon saw why we wanted a three-hour headstart. First, the bus ride took an hour, since the race was in the south end of Warsaw. Second, we had the ubiquitous line to stand in. Sometimes it took three lines to accomplish a task: for example, one to get a shopping basket, another to wait for a product, and a third to pay the cashier. Today there were two queues, one to handle medical permission slips and another to take application forms.

In this city of one and a half million people, only about 125 turned out to race. Since there were three events—a 2K, a 4K, and a 6K—about half of those were children running the 2K for fun. I saw about a half dozen women, all in their twenties; one was Wojciech's girlfriend Eva. She introduced herself and took me to the women's dressing room, the lounge in a small health club. I asked if she was excited about the prospect of visiting America. "Yes," she replied, "very excited. Wojciech is hoping to run his fastest time. And I think we will be married soon."

All 125 entrants had to line up behind one man at the table. As promised, Miatek produced a paper resembling a doctor's prescription stating I had been examined and was in good health. It was signed by a doctor I had never met. In the second line Miatek picked up two entry blanks for the 6K and began asking me questions in Polish. When I recognized the word for *year,* I assumed he was asking "How many years?" for the age division. I gave him the Polish for forty-six. The question, as it turned, out, was for my year of birth, but it didn't matter that I'd knocked a few years off my age because the only times reported after the competition were those of the winners of each race, in this case Wojciech for the 2K, Wojciech for the 4K, and Wojciech for the 6K. He had decided to run all of them as a little training exercise for Boston. The route was a 2K circle around the bottom of a small man-made ski hill. Runners in the 4K and 6K repeated the circle. Otherwise the race was the same as always—I double-knotted my shoelaces, swore near the end I'd never enter another competition, and got passed by a nine year old on the finish line.

When all the runners were in, the mob started walking down the street en masse. Miatek explained, *"Restauracja. Herbata."* Were we all going to a restaurant for tea? Wojciech caught up with us and explained that the awards would be given out at a nearby restaurant because it was too cold to stand outside.

In a large room resembling a warehouse converted into a roadside dance hall, twenty families sat devouring their Sunday dinners—chicken, potatoes, green beans, and apple pastries. We—all 125 of us—found seats and ordered tea. The president of the running club, who was wearing a New York Marathon T-shirt (acquired honestly, Wojciech told me), was the master of ceremonies. He opened a case of Russian sardines, began pulling names out of a box, and awarded can after can to the seated runners. "This is what you call in America 'door prize,'" said Wojciech. "We in Poland are very poor, but we think it is better to award something than nothing." I agreed. "He's calling your name," he added, nudging me toward the front of the room. As I walked forward to get my prize, people smiled, applauded, and stared at my shoes. When the box was empty, the M.C. gave awards for the three races. "Trophies" were beautiful cut-glass vases, a specialty in Poland. The third time Wojiech returned from picking up his prize, he whispered to me, "I don't know where to put these. My apartment looks like a crystal shop."

"And you'll be needing all the space you can get when you and Eva get married," I said.

He looked surprised. "No, we will not get married for a long time. We are still very young."

I heard my name called again, and everyone applauded. Wojiech explained, "He made a special category for you because you traveled so far to be in this race." I walked forward and received my second can of sardines. Evidently Miatek had told everyone I was coming because this time, as I returned to my seat, a reporter joined us to interview me for the paper. Our M.C. brought me another prize, a little lamb made of sugar and decorated for Easter. Unlike Wojiech, I had no trouble figuring out where to put my award. It became the centerpiece on our coffee table, and we looked at it every day as we waited for Easter.

A few days after the race Wojiech phoned to say that he and Eva had their visas to America. "Was it difficult?" I asked.

"No, very easy," he said. "We got in line at dawn. We were given numbers 284 and 285. We waited all day for our turns. At 2:30 they called us in for the interview. Ten minutes later we had our visas. No trouble." I gave him the phone number of my daughter in Boston and wished him good luck.

Spring brought new life to our route. The women in line now waited for strawberries, cherries, gooseberries, and currants. The "bankers'" rate of exchange had tripled since September. Miatek showed me new trails surrounded by violets and forget-me-nots (called "do not forget" in Polish). Cuckoos called back and forth to each other until the woods sounded like a clock factory. Alphabet Street was ablaze with color; here hollyhocks, those horsey flowers I pictured thriving only behind gas stations and garages, were cultivated into gardens of tissue paper pastels.

Near our circular trail was a clearing where I had seen stork nests the size of our dining room table. One day, as we ran past, a stork stood in the field. It resembled a mechanical toy as it moved its head out in front first, then comically pulled the rest of its body along. As we watched,

Miatek looked a little embarrassed, then said he wanted to tell me a custom that Poles have that I would find hard to believe. Since storks are considered lucky in Poland, he explained, parents tell their children these birds bring babies. His expression said, "Can you imagine anything so silly?" His jaw dropped when I told him that in America, with no storks, we tell the same myth.

Our strange salad of a language was becoming very workable, though we had little time left to use it. In April Gary gave a series of poetry readings all over the country. Among the many surprises the tour provided was new running turf. On the Czeckoslovakian border I ran up mountains and through a village where Heidi's grandfather could have lived. On the Baltic I found a spot where I was literally running with one foot in the woods and the another on a beach where swans fed. Running in a new town meant a chance to check out the local movie theater, bakery, and cathedral. My shoes were no longer new, and I had learned to look past the stares into the shop windows.

When we returned to Warsaw, Miatek had good news. Wojiech had won $1,000 in Boston. I asked when he and Eva would return. "Not soon," said Miatek. In Polish he explained that the young couple was washing dishes in a restaurant. Then he held up his hand and slid his wedding ring off and on a couple of times.

"Did they get married?"

"*Tak*. In New York."

Neither of us was surprised. Laughing about Eva's triumph, we ran past three men in business suits, huddled together like schoolboys telling secrets. I had noticed other men looking conspicuously out of place in the woods. Miatek pointed at them, scowled, and said in English, "Drugs." In Polish he explained that these businessmen in their three-piece suits often sold drugs on our running path. Miatek complained regularly about Polish life, especially the women, who spent too much time on "dance, cigarettes, *piwo*." He was disappointed that they didn't exercise.

Our time was running short. I wondered how I would say good-bye, even if I'd had the language. The week before Gary and I were to leave Warsaw, Miatek and his family had me over to dinner. We couldn't converse easily, so we spent the evening eating soup, ham, salad, and bread, drinking wine, and looking at family photographs—high school graduations, the wedding, the infant Anna in her christening gown, her brother Andrew with his swimming team. I asked for a piece of paper, drew around Miatek's foot, and put the drawing in my purse.

The last time we ran together, we were quiet. About a mile before our usual stopping place Miatek paused and stared at me a long moment.

He gave me a quick hug, smiled, and ran back into the woods without looking back.

Our last weeks in Poland were spent in the center of the country in Chelmza, a tiny town, poor even by Polish standards. Gary's baseball team had decided to hold a training camp, and Chelmza's soccer field was one of the best. While the Sparks did their morning workouts on the groomed grass, I explored. Running into town, I passed a cemetery as large as the town itself. Outside its gates sat women selling dahlias and roses tied with ribbons and asparagus fern. The road led past the graves of infants, little unmarked mounds of dirt like covered papooses, then a section of toddlers, the family plots, and the nuns' corner. Women carried water to wash the gravestones and water the flowers that adorned almost every grave. Later I would return to read the stories locked in the dates on those stones. A block away was a thirteenth-century cathedral. Three times in those two weeks I ran past a double-file procession of people in black carrying a coffin from the cathedral to the cemetery.

The cathedral spire, visible for miles, became my compass point when I ventured into the countryside. Away from the coal dust of the town, the scenery looked like a French film. Boys carrying loaves of bread rode their bicycles through the mile-long stretch of linden trees that lined the road and relieved us from the strong sun. A horse-drawn milk wagon raced me every morning. Lured by wagon wheels the farmers put out for them to nest on, two storks flew above my head almost close enough to touch. Farmers on three-legged stools looked at me in awe as they milked their cows. If a woman runner was a strange sight in Warsaw, it was an even more bizarre one here.

By the end of the second week the farmers, whose mouths had dropped the first day as I ran by chewing on a stalk of wheat, were waving as I zigzagged between their chickens and geese. The last day I ran in Poland, a farmer who spoke broken English walked down the road and asked where I was from, what I was doing in Chelmza, why I ran down the road every day, and what kind of farms we have in America.

After I left him, a woman on a bicycle stopped me to say that the farmers on the road were curious about why I ran. Her English was good, so we talked for fifteen minutes or so. She was fascinated by the idea of running, but said, "The women here do not exercise this way. I ride a bicycle every day." We lamented the fact that I was leaving; we both wanted to have coffee and talk about women's lives in our countries.

I was having a hard time leaving this country, its people and its images, particularly Chelmza. I had gotten to know the sweet young men on the baseball team, Pete and Marek, Jacek and Pizza Hut, nicknamed for the American T-shirt he wore most of the time. I had watched them break their first windows and give up their summer family vacations to train for this strange sport, new to most of them. They brought me flowers to say good-bye, pink carnations, which my tears watered all the way to the airport. Reaching for a Kleenex, I pulled out the paper I would need at the sporting goods store on my first morning in the States—Miatek's shoe size.

Simone Poirier-Bures

CRETE, 1966

In the photo I remember, Maria looks straight at the camera. A smile flutters at the corners of her mouth, as if she is hesitant to show her ferocious pride, as if she dares not enjoy this moment, surrounded by her children, lest some jealous god yank it away. She rests her hands on the shoulders of Ireni, who barely comes up to her waist. Somber Ireni, whose eyes are large and unsmiling. Smaragdi and Katina stand at their mother's right, their heads reaching just to and just below her shoulders; Katina, distracted by something, looks off to the side. Yannis, at the left, is barely as tall as Smaragdi, though he is older than his sisters. He stands a little apart from the others, as if, as the only male, he feels a need to disassociate himself from the women.

There is something hopeful in their expressions, in the way they are poised there, their faces curious, expectant, as if they are used to standing on the sidelines watching, waiting for things to happen.

Behind them, the stuccoed wall is yellowish-brown and peeling. It's the wall of my house, the one I occupied for four months, twenty-five years ago. Theirs, very much like mine, stands directly across the street. I remember also in this picture the hindquarters of a donkey, a brown shaggy one who carried things for the old man who delivered goods to the small store a few doors down, but perhaps I am confusing this photo with another.

Maria's husband Giorgos is missing from this family portrait, but that is usual. Every morning he would leave his house at dawn, return for the noon meal and a few hours' rest, then leave again. He would spend his evenings in one of several *tavernas* along the waterfront. I seldom saw him at home, though I waved to him whenever I saw him along the old harbor, bringing in his catch. And he would wave back, in front of the other fishermen, giving a surprised but pleased smile to this young foreign woman. A friend of his wife's.

The *Yaya*, too, is absent. Maria's mother, all in black, would sit at her chair by the front window watching the goings-on. Like all *Yaya*'s, she knew how to stay in the background, to help when there was work to be done, but otherwise, to remain invisible. I feel her hovering behind the photo, silently moving her toothless mouth.

They are all frozen in that moment—yet as I think of the picture, time softens, moves. Maria stands below my window, yelling, "See-moan-ay! See-moan-y!" It is 10:15 A.M., far too late for decent people still to be sleeping, and anyway, she has something to tell me, or she is lonesome and wants some company, or it is the day for making some Greek delicacy and I must come and watch so I can learn how.

It is 1966 and I am twenty-one. I am in Chania, on the island of Crete, searching for something. Some truth that keeps eluding me. Some peace I long for. I am fleeing old griefs, trying to lose myself, find myself.

I am not completely alone; I am part of a small group of temporary expatriates—Canadians, Americans, Brits. We all live in the old quarter, in ancient three-story houses built by the Venetians in the fourteenth and fifteenth centuries. We live there, instead of in the newer parts of the city where there are flush toilets and running water, because the streets in the old quarter are narrow and picturesque, because the rent is cheap, and because none of us cares about flush toilets and running water. We are all there for our own reasons—we do not ask each other such questions—and together we form a community of sorts. We go to the *tavernas* at night, dance with the sailors, drink too much, help each other find the way home.

Much of my day life, however, is with Maria. She has "claimed" me. When we walk through the neighborhood she holds my arm and tells the people we meet: "*Apo tin Ameriki*." I correct her gently: from Canada. She shrugs and laughs. Wherever I am from, it does not matter. She was the first to have me in her house, so now I am known as "Maria's friend."

"Come to my house for some *raki*," a woman down the street calls out to me. "No, Maria says to her fiercely, she cannot. She is with me." Later, Maria tells me: That woman is not a good woman. But Athena, as she is called, will not give up so easily. When she sees me coming down the street without Maria, she rushes out to speak. She is thirtyish, a few years younger than Maria, but unmarried. She lives with her sister (also unmarried), and with her mother; occasionally she goes out with men from the nearby NATO base, and this makes her vaguely disreputable. I am curious about Athena, this loud, persistent woman who dyes her hair red, who hovers on the edge of respectability, but I do not wish to offend Maria, so I decline her invitations.

In the evenings, when I slip out to dance with the sailors on the waterfront, to drink, to behave in a way that is totally unacceptable for Greek women, I wonder what Maria thinks, at home, alone with her children. The rules are different for me; this is part of my appeal. "Come with us," I say to her one Saturday evening when the winds are warm and we can smell spring coming. "Giorgos never stays home—why should you?" She clicks her tongue and throws her head back. I have proposed something preposterous, impossible. I might as well have proposed that we fly to the moon. She laughs, chides me for being so silly, but she puts on lipstick, and I know she is tempted.

At first I thought I was merely her trophy—something to show off in this city of few westerners. But Maria remained my friend long after it was expedient or prudent.

✧ ✧ ✧

"See-moan-ay! See-moan-ay!" she yells through the front window. It is unshuttered and open because it is a lovely warm day, even in mid-January. Behind her stands Yannis, ready to supply the appropriate English if I do not understand what his mother tells me. He is eleven, small and sturdy, with a curious, intelligent face. He is learning English in school, and eager to try out his new words. When his friends invite him to play kickball down the street, he demurs, telling them he can't right now, that his mother needs his help. I understand enough Greek to catch this and to know that we could manage without him. He looks at me shyly; I am not like Greek young women; I tease him, and he hides his smiles.

Maria's friend Varvara has invited us for coffee. I must come now. Varvara is one of the band of gypsies who winter over every year in Chania. I know this because I have seen her pull her small cart laden with colorful woven blankets and rugs through the narrow streets of the old quarter. She is short and compact like Maria, with dark fierce eyes like hers. But Varvara has a shrewdness about her. I do not trust her. A few weeks ago, I bought a blanket from her; later I discovered I had paid far too much.

I am surprised to learn that Varvara is Maria's friend, as the gypsies are not well-liked here. Faces tighten, mouths curl as the gypsies pass. But I do not question this odd alliance. I, too, am an outsider, and I, too, am Maria's friend.

The gypsies are encamped behind the old city wall, a few minutes walk from our street. Yannis may not come, it is only for the women, Maria tells him. Yannis turns away in disappointment. The *Yaya*'s face appears in Maria's front window. She will watch the children. It is a beautiful afternoon, and as we walk I tell Maria about the blanket. She throws her head back and laughs. In Greece, anything is fair in business.

The path to the encampment takes us along the top of the old wall, now crowded with tiny, whitewashed shacks. In the five hundred years since the wall was built, the inner face has totally disappeared; the town has sloped up to meet it. Only when you stand at the edge and look down do you realize that you are on a wall and how high you are. Maria and I stand there for a moment, looking down. In the clearing below, about two dozen tents form a tiny village, complete with rickety-looking wooden wagons, a motley group of horses and donkeys, a few old cars. A trash fire burns on one side, upwind from the tents. A dog barks. It is eerie to see this scene, like something out of time, something from the Middle Ages. I want to express this observation to Maria, but it is too complicated for my simple Greek vocabulary, so I smile and squeeze her arm, and we follow the path down.

As we approach the camp, we become the focus of attention. I am suddenly aware of my long yellow hair hanging loosely to my waist, my blue eyes. The dark eyes of the men follow me, openly, aggressively. They resemble Greek men in their darkness, in their luxurious mustaches, but their faces are narrower, their cheekbones more pronounced. I hold Maria's arm more tightly. One of them asks us what we want there. Maria tells him in a loud voice that we are looking for Varvara's tent. He points the way. I realize, then, with a sudden twinge of fear, that Maria has never been here before. Is this all some elaborate trap? Has Varvara tricked Maria into bringing me here so that I can be stolen, then sold as a white slave? The youth hostels in Europe were full of such stories.

A man approaches us with a proprietary air. He jerks his head to the right, indicating that we follow him. He spreads his arms out and around us, as if to shield us from the curious eyes of the others. I feel Maria relax a little. "Varvara's husband," she tells me.

Their canvas tent, like all the others, is a grayish, stained tan. Through the partly open front flap we see Varvara, who rises to greet us. We take off our shoes before we enter, leaving them with the others in a neat row outside. The inside is both roomy and cozy. Layers of blankets and rugs in patterns of bright blue, green, and red pad the floor. Varvara and her husband exchange a few words in their own language; the husband darts a last look at me, then leaves, pulling the door flap down behind him.

Varvara invites us to sit down on the carpets and we do, forming a circle around a square slab that holds a small stove and a few cooking utensils. I am not sure what to expect from all this, but I suddenly realize that being invited here is a great honor. Maria seems to understand this too, and nods at me solemnly. Varvara lights the stove, a tiny one-burner, fueled by gas. She takes a handful of coffee beans from a burlap bag, puts them in a flat, long-handled copper pan, and shakes them over the fire for a few minutes. The tent fills with a wonderful burnt-brown smell. While the beans cool, she opens a long brass cylinder and begins to assemble what I see now is a coffee grinder. It's a beautiful thing, obviously very old, the elaborate engraving well worn. I wonder for a moment, how many generations of gypsy women have owned this grinder, how many continents it has traveled.

As Varvara grinds the beans, the tent smells more and more aromatic. I wave my hand in front of my nose and say *"orea,"* beautiful, beautiful. Varvara nods at me gravely, but says nothing. She places a few spoonfuls of the powdered coffee with water into a small brass pot, then adds a few large spoonfuls of sugar. When the coffee froths up, she fills three small white cups, paper thin, and hands one each to Maria and me.

Now Varvara smiles. "Welcome, my friends," she says. We sip our coffee slowly. Varvara inquires about Maria's family; Maria inquires back. She asks me about my health; I ask back. We are formal, ceremonial. Here, in her own element, Varvara is beautiful. She has loosened her hair and it hangs over her back in a thick mantle of glossy black. She looks softer than before, yet at the same time more powerful. I let the strong, sweet liquid linger on my tongue. Though I have had Greek coffee before, this is the best I have ever tasted. I am in a gypsy camp, I say to myself. A gypsy has called me "friend." I forgive Varvara for the blanket.

You come down through one of the narrow, twisting streets, barely wide enough for a small car, and you come upon it: the old harbor, opening before you like a flower.

A wide paved area separates the buildings from the water, very much like an Italian piazza, which is appropriate, given that this part of Chania was built by the Venetians. At the edge of the piazza, the water is deep, and small fishing boats pull right up to the edge to unload their catches. Mid-morning they bring in the octopuses. Glossy and silvery gray, raw octopus looks like the internal organs of extraterrestials. There is something vaguely obscene about those thick, slimy appendages; cooked up, however, they are an amazing delicacy. The fishermen throw the octopuses by the handfuls on to the pavement, then pick them up and throw them down again, beating them like this to release the dark blue inky substance and to tenderize them. The octopuses are then hung on makeshift racks and lines to dry, and the fishermen wash down the pavement with buckets of sea water.

Sometimes it's sea urchins they bring in, one or two buckets of them, their greenish-gray shells bristling with needle-sharp spines. Inside, flesh the color of smoked salmon. I have never tried them—they are food for the wealthy—though I am told they are wonderful. Mostly though, the boats are full of fish and octopuses, and all morning the air is briny and aromatic. By noon, all trace of the fishermen is gone.

Everything around the old harbor is a bit shabby. The facades of some of the buildings have begun to crumble. Old paint peels from walls and woodwork like outgrown skin. Some of the buildings are whitewashed, but most are not, unlike the picture postcards one sees of sparkling white Greek villages. Here the buildings are mostly a drab gold—the color of limestone—or light ocher, or the grayish tan of unpainted cement.

Still, there is something enormously pleasing about it all. The crowded buildings face the water like flowers facing the sun. Roofs of red tile and wide doors painted a glossy blue flash patches of color. Old oil cans grow huge red geraniums. The rounded domes of an ancient mosque, a legacy of the Turkish occupation, shimmer in the sun like white hills. A bright-green fishing boat is moored on the water. Everything seems harmonious, comforting. On fine days, the restaurants spill out into the piazza. Tables and chairs appear on the pavement, inviting. On weekends, the aroma of roasting meat fills the air.

On my way home from the *Instituto*, I stop at one of the sweet shops for a *galato-buriko*, or a bowl of rice custard, or a piece of *baklava*, and look out at the harbor water. Sometimes blue, sometimes black, the water riffles lightly or bristles with foam, depending on its mood. Though the ancient sea wall contains it—a small opening permits the comings and goings of small boats—the harbor water is never totally placid, more like some wild thing, barely domesticated. And it seems emblematic somehow, of all of Crete: Hungers surge up, then subside, waiting for their own good time. A thin layer of order overlays roiling chaos. Apollo and Dionysious held in delicate balance.

✧ ✧ ✧

At the Instituto Amerikaniko-Helleniki I teach three classes: a group of twelve- and thirteen-year-old boys, a co-ed class of about a dozen high school seniors preparing to take the Cambridge proficiency exams, and a group of seven or eight local merchants.

While the other shopkeepers take their meals at home, sleep with their wives, or do whatever they all do between one and four in the afternoon when the shops are closed, these men spend an hour, three afternoons a week, practicing their English with me. They range in age from their late twenties to late forties, and their manner toward me is formal. They call me *Miss,* and hold doors open for me, bowing slightly, as if I were a visiting dignitary. I acknowledge their deference with a smile, wondering what their wives would think—their husbands treating a woman this way, while *they* are expected to obey and please.

We spend about half of our time in general conversation; I gently correct their grammar and pronunciation and supply words when I can guess the intent. We converse mostly about *"Amerika";* they are passionately interested in "*Amerika.*" They have heard there is a sexual revolution going on there, and they are eager to learn how it works. "In America, is it true that a girl can go alone at night with a boy who is not her brother, and her parents do not know his parents?" I am careful with my reply, aware of my position, a single woman about whom there is already too much speculation. And in Chania, the old codes still prevail: a boy who dishonors someone's sister is likely to feel a knife in his back.

"It's very different there," I tell them. "Being alone together does not necessarily mean that something shameful will happen." They wrinkle their faces in puzzlement. They would never believe that a man sleeping alone on the third floor of a house would not sometimes wander at night to the bed of a woman, sleeping alone on the second. They would never believe that a woman who dances the *hassapico* with sailors and sometimes sits on their laps, and drinks with them, and sometimes walks home alone with one and lets him kiss her, does not allow him other things as well. But all that is part of my other life, my life in the old quarter. These men never go to the old quarter.

These men live in the better part of the city, in houses with water heaters, small refrigerators, stoves. Their wives do not carry the Sunday roast to the bakery down the street to be cooked in the public oven for a few *drachma* like Maria does. Their wives wear wool and rayon instead of cotton, their coats have fur collars. And at night, when the tavernas crackle with music and the scent of grilled *brisoles* wafts through the air—when *retsina, metaxa,* and *ouzo* flow, when feet fly in dance, plates crash on the floor amid cries of *"oopa!"*—these men are at home with their wives and children.

I know this because I regularly visit such a home. On Saturday mornings I privately tutor the younger sister of one of my thirteen-year-old boys. There are no English classes for ten-year-old girls, and to send her with the boys would not be proper. The father is not among my businesssmen, but he could be; he and they are the same. My pupil's house is relatively new. The surfaces are smooth, the corners of the rooms sharp and well-defined, unlike the rooms of the houses in the old quarter. There are plenty of windows, covered with lace curtains and hung with heavy drapes of velvet and brocade. The chairs and sofas are heavy and ornate, solid looking. In this part of town, you never see bedding flung out over the balcony to air like you do in the old quarter.

The mother is attractive in a plump, soft sort of way. She smiles sweetly and greets me graciously in spite of the cheap cotton skirts and shabby tops I wear. She, too, calls me *Miss.* I call her *Kyria—Mrs.* Like Maria, she speaks no English and relies on her son to translate. Unlike Maria, she shows no curiosity toward me. Each time I come, she offers me tea in a flowered china cup, then leaves the money for each lesson discreetly on the sideboard, near my coat.

One Friday, the boy says to me after class, "My mother, she say no come tomorrow. Come Sunday, for to go on picnic. Three o'clock. We go to country. You come?"

When I arrive, slightly before three, they are all waiting. The children are happy to see me, and the mother looks both pleased and relieved, as if she had feared that I wouldn't show. The *Kyrios*, her husband, acknowledges me with a slight nod. This is only the second time I have seen him. On the day of my first lesson with his daughter, he nodded at me on his way out. I suspect he had stayed behind to catch a glimpse of me, to make sure I was "safe," and to give his approval. A *Yaya* appears from one of the back rooms. I have not seen her before and wonder whose widowed mother she is—his or hers. It's impossible to tell. She is dressed all in black with a black wool kerchief pulled over her head like the *Yayas* in the old quarter. She is the one link between these two worlds. She is not introduced.

A big, black Mercedes waits out front. The *Yaya* sits in the front with the man and woman, near the door. I sit in the back between the two children. The girl, who is still very much a beginner in English, holds my hand and looks at me adoringly. The boy keeps smiling, as if he can't believe I am really there, his English teacher, on an outing with his family. The adults sit stiffly, silently, in the front. I wonder briefly whose idea it was to invite me. The children's? The mother's?

Kyria says something in Greek to the boy, gesticulating with her head that he should tell me. "My mother she say to tell you that the orchards will be beautiful today." I smile at her: "I'm looking forward to seeing them. I am very happy that you invited me to come." She nods as I speak. She understands more English than she lets on. She translates my words to her husband and returns her eyes to the road. He glances at me through the rear-view mirror. He seems aware of me, but not aware; I am part of the women's world with which he need not concern himself.

His wife, however, pulses with awareness. Throughout the ride I feel her controlled attention. Though she speaks mostly to her husband or looks out at the countryside, she is acutely aware of what is going on in the back seat. If we all do not have a wonderful time, she will blame herself. This is my first encounter with upper middle-class Greek life, and I am carefully taking it all in, noting how different this woman is from Maria, how different they all are from the villagers I have met, and from the people in the old quarter. Maria and I would be singing by now. Laughing out loud. Exclaiming over the beauty of the hills. She would be teaching me the Greek names of things.

The girl beside me squeezes my hand. "Is good day, yes?"

There is a tacit understanding that I speak only English, so that makes it difficult to communicate with the adults. The school is total immersion, and we teachers are discouraged from admitting to any knowledge of Greek. I suspect I have been invited along to give the children a chance to practice their English. Why else? *Kyrios* and *Kyria* do not ask me about life in *Amerika,* or my life here, or what I think about things. And yet I feel they are studying me, discreetly.

The country house is utterly charming—whitewashed stucco and surrounded by a low stone wall. It is grander than any of the houses I saw in my wanderings around the island, though it is still relatively simple. *Kyria* points to the small outhouse, apologizing profusely for the lack of an indoor toilet. This strikes me as very funny, given my own living conditions, but I suppress my smile. Wide windows look out over row upon row of orange trees.

Huge baskets are unloaded from the trunk of the Mercedes, and there is a flutter of activity. The women will not let me help and shoo me out of the kitchen. The children hover around me like bees.

"My father say to come and see the orchard," the boy says.

Kyrios stands at the door fingering his worry beads. The children and I follow him out. The day is glorious, the air dazzling in its sweetness, and I want to jump into the air and shout with joy. But I control myself, as seems to be required, and smile demurely. Two donkeys tied to a stake by a shed stare at us with comic faces. I have a particular fondness for donkeys, and rush over to stroke their necks and ears. *Kyrios* gestures for me to get on one of them. It's the first time he has addressed me directly. The children shriek with glee when I swing my leg up over the donkey's back. They quickly climb onto the other one.

Their father takes the reins of my donkey and leads us down the rows of the orange grove. The trees are much smaller than I ever imagined they could be, with enormous bright fruit hanging heavily from the branches. *Kyrios* pulls down an orange the size of a cannonball and slices it open with a knife he pulls from his waist. Then he presents it to me with a little bow. I am reminded again how everything in Greece seems fuller, riper, bursting with life. Even the oranges are unrestrained, glorious in their hugeness, their sweetness, their intense color. By now I have lost all reserve and exclaim aloud at the beauty of everything. "It's all so lovely! Lovely!" I tell them. "I feel like a queen!" The children find everything I say and do amusing, and laugh and laugh.

When we get back to the house we find a beautiful meal laid out on a long rectangular table in a shaded area outside—feta cheese, black olives, bread, *dolmathes, taramasalata,* two kinds of beans, several plates of things I don't recognize, and a huge bottle of *retsina*. We are all more relaxed now, more comfortable with each other. Even the *Yaya* nods and smiles. The sun beats down, waves of fragrance waft in from the orange grove. After a few glasses of *retsina*, *Kyrios* raises his glass and sings a few lines of a song: "*Ego tha kopso to krassi, ya sena agapi mou chrisi. . . .*" His wife throws him a disapproving glance and mutters something, but too late. I clap my hands, delighted. A drinking song! This is the first sign of passion I've seen in these upper middle-class Greeks.

I insist on learning the song, and sing it over and over, a bit tipsy myself by this time. My pupils and their father sing it with me. *Kyria* sings a few lines herself, though she looks uncomfortable, as if she is doing something vaguely improper.

After the meal, the children and I take a last stroll through the orchard. It's a wonderful afternoon, and I am sorry when it ends.

On the way home we are again subdued, polite. My hosts ask where I live so that they can deliver me to my house. I protest that the streets are too narrow for their car, and ask to be let out by the old harbor, saying that I will walk the rest of the way. I do not want them to see where I live. I do not want them anywhere near my life there.

✧ ✧ ✧

My class of twelve and thirteen year olds was my favorite. A teasing, affectionate relationship existed between us. They found me endlessly amusing, and I was charmed by their small compact bodies, their dark curious eyes. Once when I came into the classroom and turned on the light switch, nothing happened. I flipped it off and on several times while the boys watched me. Nothing. Things often didn't work in Greece, so I shrugged and said, "I guess we'll just have to have class in the dark today." They all burst out laughing. One of the boys climbed up on his desk and turned the light bulb; another flicked on the switch and the room filled with light. We all laughed together. I had enjoyed this trick as much as they had, so when I walked into the classroom the day after my visit to the orange groves and felt an expectant tension in the air, I figured something was up.

One of the boys had just finished writing something in Greek on the blackboard and was hurrying back to his seat. All sixteen of them were watching me, suppressing grins.

"Aha," I say, going along with it. "Someone left me a message. Help me translate it." Titters all over the room. "It's nothing," the boy whose sister I tutor says. "I'll erase it for you." He gets up and approaches the board. But something in his face makes me want to know what the words say.

"No, let's figure it out. It'll be good practice. Let's see, the first word is . . ." I squint at the Greek letters and sound out "*Ego* . . ." Someone from the back row calls out boldly, "*Ego tha kopso to krassi*." General laughter. I glance quickly at my friend in the front row who hangs his head sheepishly. Obviously, he has told his friends about our excursion, and they have seized on the part they found most interesting.

"Oh yes, the song I learned yesterday," I say, feeling a little chilled, the private made a bit too public. "I like Greek songs. I'd like to learn a lot of them." The boys are restless, whispering things to each other, their eyes flashing a kind of wildness. One of them calls out something in Greek that I don't understand, and they all laugh again. The laughter has a new, aggressive edge.

"What did you say?" I ask him. He is silent. "Someone tell me what he said." No one answers, and a thick tension hangs in the air. Finally, I look at my friend in the front row. He, after all, started this whole thing. I ask him evenly, "Please tell me what he said."

He swallows hard and says, "He said that perhaps you would like to learn, um . . . *Krevata murmura*."

"And what, exactly, is that?"

He looks exceedingly uncomfortable, as does the rest of the class. But I persist.

"I don't know how to say in English, but it means the things a man and woman say to each other when they are in bed."

The boys are absolutely still, studying my reaction. The air crackles with danger.

"I see," I say. "Thank you for your translation." Then I turn to the rest of the class. "Take out your homework now, and let's see how well you've done on the exercises for today." I go on with the class as usual, though I smile less and make no joking asides as I usually do. Something between us has changed.

On my way home, I try to figure it out. A single woman drinking wine and singing—did this somehow mean sexual availability in the minds of these twelve- and thirteen-year-old boys? The harbor water is greenish black today; two small boats, moored in the protected area, rock gently in the lapping tongues of water. Beyond the seawall, the water is deep blue; whitecaps surge and break. It's the same water; only the seawall separates it, only the seawall tames it. How easily things can turn, I think, how easily things can careen out of control.

Sharon Chmielarz

TRACKING DOWN NANNERL MOZART

The journey to the Mozarteum in Salzburg began forty years ago, in the brick A.H. Brown Library on North Main in Mobridge, South Dakota, a musky smelling refuge on the prairie. Three blocks from my childhood house to Highway 12, one block north, then east over a broken sidewalk, past St. Joseph's, the park, the lawyer's pretty back yard, across the dirt alley, a half block more and through the North Main door. Marble floor inside, cool on a summer day. Exchange the dust of the streets for dust of old books. Browse in the three stacks. Hide in a book, slip down its stairs into a world of green lawns and wrought iron fences and fathers who not only read but build houses with libraries, like the Mozarteum, before which I now stand, thirsty, slugging down the last of bottled *Mineralwasser* bought in the Makartplatz. My pudgy matron's hands about to track down (between the lines) the character of Maria Anna "Nannerl" Mozart.

Inside the Mozarteum's marble hallway I try the library's cupboard-like double doors, turning the handle down. The door remains firmly shut. *"Neun Uhr dreissig!"* a muffled voice insists from inside. 9:30. I look at my watch; it's 9:27. I sit down to wait on the hallbench.

The library, on the second floor, stands off from the main activity in the Mozarteum—its concert hall and music rooms. Clusters of future singers and instrumental soloists gather inside and outside the building's nooks and practice rooms. Threatening youth: all talent and enlightened arrogance.

Had I even heard of Mozart when I was their age, in the fifties? I remember struggling with the second clarinet's part to the overture of Die Fledermaus, *a piece our band director Mr. Green has selected. Mr. Green comes from "Out*

East." He is highly respected in town though everyone suspects he eases his nervousness by keeping a bottle of whisky in the band room desk drawer.

Some morning band period, when he sits before us on his high director's stool and taps his baton on his music stand for our attention, doesn't he say, lips tense, brown tweed jacket reeking of cigarettes, "Our next piece, written by Strauss"? After beating that to an inch of its life, surely we move on to some watered-down arrangement of "Eine Kleine Nachtmusik," and he points out to us the name on the music sheets before us on our music stands: W.A. Mozart. But what is a name compared to the rat's nest of staffs and notes and illusions we have to blow our way through!

The Mozarteum library is a suite of five rooms: two reception areas, the stacks, the director's office, and a back room. The set of doors I've attacked open to the director's office, which I enter at 9:35. I hang my bedraggled coat on a hook and set my dripping umbrella to dry in the corner. The secretary directs me to my left, to the stacks. This is the largest room, the heart of the suite, where book spines wait for the grasp of a human hand. Book cases line the walls. Castors direct ladders from the *A*'s to *Z*'s, neighborhoods of light and space. A heavy table invites reading and note taking. Daydreaming. Wonderful double-paned windows ajar in the corners complete this set for a Masterpiece Theater library, scene one, take one.

I introduce myself to Frau Geffray, the librarian. No check-out, no; I'm to help myself to the stacks and card-catalogue; if I have trouble finding anything, she's here to assist. She returns to her blinking cursor; I begin to work the saurian way, with pen and notebook, red-eyeing the selection of books, articles, and manuscripts about or by the Mozarts. The room is immensely small; an old, thick book, housed in crumbling leather, furnished in fine print on ivory-colored pages.

Silence reigns. The only interruption comes from the upper echelon. Frau Geffray is third in hierarchical rank; above her is Johanna Siegel (who's away on vacation). On the peak is *der Herr Direktor.* Outbursts from his office set off a nervous chain reaction through secretary and assistant in his office down to the librarians in "my" room, a wifely, after-he-has-stomped-through-the-house fluttering. Just like my childhood; I catch my heart quaking and feel right at home.

Der Herr Direktor, I gather, is delivering a speech somewhere in France the following week. It is Frau Geffray's job to read and revise it. It is the first of her many talents as a "librarian" that I come to admire. (She is French—I believe. Does she have to be extra sharp because she's not native Austrian??)

The *Herr Director* is a man without a *"von"* (foundation of sand in a

Germanic hierarchy). Worse, his last name, translated, means "peasant." This makes me feel at home. But what must it be like for him? Imagine "Sir Peasant" as the director of the Metropolitan Opera. The starch in the European class system is indeed crumbling. Bauer's family has had a long and slow evolution toward the Herr Direktor's current status. Good old democracy. Good old public education.

How did my peasant ancestors practice their creativity? We couldn't afford a fortepiano; we had to rely on crude instruments, on our voices and the urge in our big, shuffling feet to dance. Polka. Our vocal music was unorganized, happenstance. Anyone free to join in and harmonize. The necessary bass might be missing or present. We did with or without. Professionals like the Mozarts did not leave things to chance; it was their job to provide and create.

I spend two weeks in the library. Many days I am the only reader. One day, however, an older, distinguished looking man (i.e., he's retired but wears a suit) appears at the door humming a melody. He can't remember, he explains to Frau Geffray, which piece of Mozart's music the tune comes from. (I'd never heard it before.) She immediately tugs a ladder to a section, climbs all the way up, opens a cupboard door that I haven't noticed because it blends so perfectly into the wall's scrollwork above the book shelves. She pulls out a manuscript, totes it down to the table, unrolls it, and points out the section in the score of the melody he's been humming.

My grasp of who-wrote-what had not improved much after high school graduation. I remember taking History of Drama at the University of Minnesota in the seventies, in one of those huge lecture halls the University is (sometimes unfairly, I think) known for. One night the instructor, Arthur Ballett, is late. To soothe the waiting, 6:20 P.M. unfed beasts, an assistant pipes Mozart in over the loudspeaker system. When Ballett walks on stage to lecture, he peers into the cave of dark rows before him and asks who in the class knows the name of the composer. Well, of course, it's Bach, Beethoven, or one of them; not one person in that five-hundred-seat hall raises his/her hand. Perhaps the aficionados are put down by the question—too easy, but it and Ballett's incredulous reaction to our silence inspire me. Instead of taking History of Drama II, I start listening closely to music. That leads me to Mozart. And twenty years later, in a North Shore cabin, to reading a condensed version of his family's letters, and to the discovery of his virtuoso sister.

During my second week of research Johanna Siegel comes back from vacation. I've seen only her name: signed on the response to my initial inquiry letter and, on a rainy Saturday afternoon in a museum in St. Gilgen, listed in the credits to a documentary on Mozart. (Nannerl Mozart lived in the village of St. Gilgen during her marriage.) Johanna is slim and brunette and tall and ambitious and sets for herself the task of moving to new locations all the books whose places I've become possessive of during my first week.

I work in the library daily, arriving exactly at 9:30—one day I'm late and apologize—leaving for the one-and-a-half-hour lunch break, and continuing till late afternoon closing. The long lunch break often irritates me. I usually spend it walking. Caught up in the compulsion of research I feel walking should be strictly an after-business-hours activity; at noon it's a waste of my time. This makes for an ill humor when I hit the street for lunch.

God! To stand on a hill in a good old Midwestern gale! I'm so tired of the smell of roses and sweat, Der Drang, *the claustrophobia, the pressing in of a crowd, the staircase closeness, body to body pushing forward; nameless, faceless, formless function: appendage to throng pulsing through city vein; host, rabble, pedestrian, tourist, prey for hotels and service; rabbit dependent on the fox for little rooms and little tables of* Lebensraum.

The overflow spills into the parks. Behind the fence and hedges, the street din fades but not the hot group-life: a milling stopping only to pose: here, by a mermaid with leaf epaulets which spout water. Click, click. There, by the horse fountain, its view completely covered by the group having its picture taken in front of it. A fleur-de-lis of water jets above the heads in the fourth row. It will make an unusual glint in sun light when the photo arrives months later in a manila envelope stamped "Do not Bend."

Repeat all noise, all tourist scenes five hundred times five thousand.

I am so much the solitary one here, such a lonely member of the Drang, *I would stammer if asked to speak, it's been too long since I've talked to a human about anything besides directions or food:* Wo ist . . . Kennen Sie die . . . Eine Nudelsuppe, bitte. *I'm not lonely for people but for a friend. Someone to talk to normally. Someone whom I don't feel self-conscious walking in front of. Though when I get tired enough, this self-consciousness passes, too. I could care less. Or when I have a glass of wine, when I relax. . .*

I carry das Glas Rotwein *out of the café to the sidewalk tables, closing the door—I think—cleverly by butting it shut with my backpack. But I get stuck, hung up in the door, nailed; I can't move. My glass of wine in one hand, my cane in the other. Christ! I'm swinging by my pack on the door. "Can you help me?"* "Können Sie mir bitte helfen?" *I ask —far too softly—of the guy who's sitting closest to the door, but he moves to the end of a table bubbling with the beer-bellies of soccer fans. A round of jokes has them all roaring. The petitioned doesn't want to miss a line. Jerks! Somehow, I pull out of the harness, still holding the wine, and remove my jacket, pinned by its hood to the door.*

Toward the end of the second week I'm thinking I've accomplished little compared to the information still lodged on the shelves around me. Although I'm now using the library's copier, i.e. feeling free to ask Frau Geffray to copy pages for me, there are many articles—at my slow, translating and note-taking pace—I'll not get to.

So, bold-American me, already having edged over the 12:00 closing boundary, I gather my nerve one noon to ask if I may stay in over lunch. Break the rule. The sound of the librarian's quiet chatter flows from a room I've not been in, the back room, past the reception room (the left wing to the Herr Direktor's right wing). I knock on the open door. Peek around the jamb. The librarians are at table, eating. *How* they are eating!

At work I bring a brown paper bag, one side I use as a rag to wipe off the crumbs of the teacher who sat at the table before me, the other becomes my place mat. I pack any kind of food which can be prepared fast and eaten faster. With fingers. Carrot—not sticks, but the carrot chopped in two to fit a plastic bag. Possibly a sandwich—a slice of bread wrapped around a piece of cheese. An apple.

Frau Geffray and Fräulein Siegel have spread white cloth placemats over the worktable and set them with a plate and small fork, knife, stemmed water glass, and a green bottle of sparkling mineral water. As I stare, Frau Geffray's spoon is dancing mid-air above the slice of cataloupe on her plate. Johanna Siegel nips at cracker with cheese. Their "no" to my question is quick and gracious, and I quickly and graciously leave the library to its superiors.

Back in the street I search for a navigable route through the crowd and find help in the guise of perambulators, a couple of them. The mothers aim their missiles, a.k.a. baby buggies, right toward the crowd's ass and legs, and split the hips to make a path through human wall. I, on cane, limp right along in their wake. At the rear bumper of a van parked half in street, half on sidewalk, I take a quick left and escape the bottlenecked Getreidegasse. Why would anybody walk in the Altstadt unless absolutely necessary?—Because, Dodo, it contains a vestige of the world in which the Mozarts were born. Why you are here!

It may be that Charon was a former librarian. Later that afternoon, "my" librarians provide the boat, a book, which takes me through time far more easily than walking through streets. Open the cover, and I'm in the Mozarts' apartments, in the Getreidegasse and the Hannibal (today Makart) platz. Turn a page and I'm smuggled into an armoire. Hidden behind the Mozarts' clothing (smelling of powder), I can't see the lines in their faces, but I can hear them prattle and swagger and whisper and curse and pray and eat and do their lessons and fart and ply their skill on the clavier and iron their lace. Mother, father, son, daughter, dog—Bimperl—, maid, Tresel.

Stopping at the Star Brewery, #23, I gawk: here Tresel, the Mozart's jill of all trades, bought the bucket of beer for the family. On hot August days like today Wolferl and Nannerl dropped in to drink at this oasis. And the neighborhood's folks still come. To eat and drink and sit and talk and smoke. And now, the pilgrim: me. Amen.

Under my saurian eye the Mozarts live like Mary Norton's *The Borrowers,* tiny people alive in the folds of a letter, under a baroque gem in a palace, a walled city set in a valley in green mountains. The Salzach winds through it, the *raison d'etre* for a bridge, boats. The river breathes the cooler night air during the summer *Hitze*; its bank wonderful to stand on during fireworks, a grassy stage for outdoor concerts. An echo resounds from city walls—the notes in "Eine Kleine Nachtmusik." The shadowy cloak of the imperious archbishop falls over the rooftops.

Mozartiana makes good soap, good grist for gossip. The neighborhood girls chatter *schadenfroh* as they fill buckets at the fountain in the Löchelplatz in 1778. Musicians whisper and hoot from music stand to music stand. Tragedy and comedy in a little mountain town setting. The rambunctious youth gets kicked in the ass by his boss's stooge, leaves for the big city, falls in love with a beautiful soprano, Aloysia Weber, an unrequited love, so he marries Konstanze, her youngest sister, the Cinderella in the family. (*"Martyrn aller Arten,"* "Martyrs of all Kinds," an aria Wolfgang composes; including his sister, he has plenty of female models.) In his father's eyes any woman marrying Wolfgang, and certainly penniless Konstanze, embodies the paternal prophesy of doom—a brood of babies and the sire's/composer's ruin. The son's impracticality drives the controlling father to near distraction. Meanwhile his daughter, fated to be the brilliant has-been musician/spinster, falls in love with a captain of insecure finances, gives him up for her father, i.e., his peace of mind and her financial security. Finally, at thirty-three, she signs a contract for a marriage of convenience. As I spy from the keyhole, Nannerl's image becomes clearer. She is rummaging for balance: stewarding her talent, adjusting to her retirement at seventeen as Wunderkind and relieving her father of one financial worry by marrying.

Denser crowd at the museum door—das Mozart Geburtshaus in der Getreidegasse. *We enter the stairwell like cattle being loaded into a train car (This simile pops first into mind in a German-speaking country. They'll never live it down.) Once through the door we slouch shoulder to shoulder up a chute, two flights of century-old stone steps, accompanied by various smells and languages, including Italian. It'll be a long time before I again imagine Italy as* la bella paea.

If you dawdle one second in line, if you fumble getting out your wallet, say, someone steps ahead of you. Der Drang *is completely autocratic: it doesn't matter* why *you need more than lock-step time, i.e., if you have a gimpy leg, or if you are struggling with a crying baby—you must hustle.*

At the top of the stairs the cashier sits in her booth. I slide fifty shillings under the wrought-iron bars—and she gives me fifteen back! The old people and children's rate! God, that's scary. I must have "jowls." "When you're tired," my husband has always told me, "your face goes from round to square and your jaw bones sink into jowls."

They have sunk all the way today!

Nannerl is the most beautiful young woman in Salzburg; daughter of Leopold and Anna Maria, sweethearts—married for love. In 1747 the Salzburgers dub them the town's most beautiful newly-married couple. After their brilliant son quits home, takes the distance he needs in order to achieve his full genius, Nannerl remains like a possession of her father. She's bored. Restless. Unproductive. Prone to illness. A clavier teacher. Amanuensis to her brother. Small-town, beribboned, dirt-poor socialite. Besides her musical life—playing for herself, friends, and neighbors—the one *divertissement* in Salzburg is the court theater, right across the square from their flat; Nannerl and Papa attend as often as they can.

Nannerl's decent dress, the one she wears in her 1784 portrait (a sign of middle class families or aspirants, to be immortal like the royals via portrait/photo), is brown with a pink *tuch.* Pink plumes accent her foot-tall pompadour. She wears this costume all season long, to all twenty-four plays. From her seat in the close, candlelit theater, the stage offers Nannerl some needed distance from life; she laughs at the actors on the boards: the bad woman, Hedda Grandmouth, and the virtuous woman, O. Bea Dient. Nannerl laughs so hard she cries; she cries so hard she leaves the theater with a splitting headache.

Papa Mozart, Leopold, loves drama's thunder and lightning; (after Nannerl's marriage in 1784, he finds refuge in the theater for his own loneliness). His habitual attendance is enabled by the theater's director. Schikaneder (later librettist for *The Magic Flute*) gives free tickets to the Mozarts, not only in exchange for work Wolfgang has done for him, but also, I think, as a token of Schikaneder's camaraderie with professionals who understand, gut-to-heart-to-mind, their craft and art. He, Nannerl, Leopold all pine after the love of performance, excellence, better positions, fewer pupils, and more money.

Trapped in the letters they write, the Mozarts live. Between the lines I intuit conversion disorders. Is Nannerl sick about giving up an acknowledged career?—She smiles graciously before she turns to throw up. She wants to die? —She sleeps and sleeps. She's forgotten the past?

Whatever memory of stardom is left, seeps under the attic door, travels down the nerves regulating the stomach and twists itself around, squeezing. She suffers from headache. Murderers appear in dreams. Doors to rooms stand shut. The mind's eye pans servant's quarters, sees a roster of her duties. In the teacher's music room the bewildered lover jumps into Figaro's wardrobe. He wonders at the connection between his sweetheart's indecisiveness at his proposal (registered as constriction in her stomach) and the explosion under her ribs which his embrace trips.

Nannerl's aloneness might be expressed by a painting of a gown hanging in a tree, blowing crookedly in the wind. Nannerl would recognize the color. The same brown as her wedding dress.

The Mozarts love to walk, e.g., to the pilgrimage church outside of Salzburg, Maria Plain, but a beautiful sunset or lofty mountain peak doesn't appeal to their nature. Much more interesting is discussion of music, money, jobs, gossip, mathematics, clothing, Fenélon (regarding the education of girls during the Period of Enlightenment), coach styles, politics (i.e., stupidities), philosophy, instruments. They appraise and assess a new fortepiano in a count's Italian villa or in a countess's Viennese salon with the same love Americans show when kicking tires in a showroom. "If I could only afford a Scottis!" the Mozarts moan.

Reading/listening in on the Mozarts' monologues in untranslated letters is like trading in the stereo for CDs. The characters jump into the closet with me. These good honest Germans—their phrase, used to delineate themselves from their Italian colleagues and other nationalities netted within the Hapsburg Empire—are heroic and stupid and un/lucky and hungry and greedy—just plain working stiffs/artists struggling to make ends meet and, betting on the power of brilliance and genius, trying to connect with fame/riches. Their phrases are butterflies, they hover with courtly, intricate gestures—"I kiss your hands a thousand times"—they light with grace on the horse apples in Salzburg's streets. Leopold, the great paternal controller, advises Nannerl on menstruation as expertly as he suggests librettists to Wolfgang. Instead of our bedtime *adé,* "Don't let the bedbugs bite," Mamma tells her children to shit in their beds and make a mess of it. (Use of reverse psychology? An expression based on some ancient Indo-European phrase from which the English phrase "loose as a goose" is derived?) Wolferl writes his cousin, *das Bäsle* Thekla, lascivious letters from the room adjacent the one in his brain in which he hears the sublime sound he translates via notes onto paper. (10 May 1709: "Blow into my behind. It's splendid food, May it do you good," and ". . . my arse indeed is no Viennese. Please turn over, *volti subito.*")

This morning I don't feel alone sitting on the edge of my bed in the hotel room. My arms and legs and hair still feel shower-clean, free of grime and the million daily baptisms of dirt, the million goose jobs in the streets, à la bus exhaust. I've begun to take great care now to keep odorless. My armpits and all openings. I've begun to look for signs of internal disorder by inspecting the morning stool before flushing—certainly the habit of a lonely person. The small b.m.'s are proof of different eating habits: insufficient amounts of fruit and water. It takes great amounts of slick toilet paper to clean properly—which I do because I want above all for my underpants to be clean when I'm the only one in the cobble-crowd crossing the street who gets hit by a taxi. This is the miser's and hypochondriac's and recluse's and worrier's anal preoccupation.

Recently a picture book has been translated from German into American; its subject is excrement: *The Story of the Little Mole Who Went in Search of Whodunit.* Perhaps the Mozarts' was the only culture and language in which Freud's work could have originated? In a language where the gender of the sun is feminine and the moon, masculine. Rivers and mountains and valleys masculine. Kitchen and toilet feminine. Chair and table, wardrobe/armoire and wine and coat and *Dreck* masculine. Chalk and *Scheisse* and responsibility and power, feminine.

By daylight and with otherwise sound mind, sitting at a table in the Mozarteum, reading their exchange of letters, I follow the Mozarts on their rounds. I can see Papa's irony and compulsive managing and ambition for his son. I can feel Mamma's desire to please, to do all things right, i.e., according to Leopold's/Papa's plans. She doesn't like being away from home; she misses her dog Bimperl, she asks Nannerl to give the dog a kiss on the nose, worries that Bimperl will not recognize her when she returns. (She won't; she will die chaperoning Wolfgang in Paris and be buried there.) While Wolfgang's out looking for work, she stays alone in one cold Parisian hotel room after another, a downward spiral towards ever cheaper rooms. She dreams of home cooking, home, meaning German. Oh! for a bowl of liver dumpling soup! The Parisians could take all that tough gristle they call meat—at an outrageous price—and shove it.

But where now under my intrusive magnifying glass is Nannerl? Ah! There she is. She has torn to bits every letter she's ever written to her father and run off, down a narrow lane, a *Gasse*, into one of Salzburg's churches, Trinity Church, or the Cathedral, or St. Peters, or Child of Loretto, or Maria Plain, to pray at least once a day.

The new Ursulin convent is in Glasenbach. I do not visit it. I want to see the "original" church, the one Maria Anna Mozart prayed in. I want to climb the same hilly street she climbed, say, on a late September day in 1778 when the buzz of approaching tumult and catastrophe warned Europe of war, when already ten years ago Nannerl has reached the summit of her career and still has over forty years left of her life to kill. The Ursulinenkirche, the church up this mountain, home to Saint Cecilia, patron saint of music, would have been one of her haunts.

"You go to church too often," her father and brother scorn. Attendance at mass seems the only thing Nannerl doesn't follow her father's advice in. Is cultivating Catholicism her act of rebellion? In the kingdom of saints and martyrs, whose godhead is the Divine Martyr/Sacrifice and whose saints enter heaven through the door of martyrdom, is Nannerl happy, spending her life usefully—so others may live more selfishly?

Every century six or seven people lose their lives on this hill in rock slides. The predecessor to this Ursulinen church slid down the mountain in a rocky avalanche. Then Count Thun (of the shadowy, ubiquitous Thun & Taxis family), stepped in, and, as Archbishop, had the building I stand before, begun in 1669 as replacement.

Classic Mozartian scholars like Walter Hummel paint Nannerl in a very sweet light, obedient and gracious. Possibly. But I no longer trust a scholar from the '50s writing about women.

On the way up hill to the church, I pass a tributary of a street, a passageway less than three feet wide, a channel envisioned by an architect during a bad dream: he is trapped in a closet that extends left, left, left under a series of arcades. He designs a cataract of a path used by day and night.

In the mid-sixteenth century the architect's dream becomes reality. On early winter nights without a fingertip of lantern light to follow, peasants and Bürger walking in this Gasse share the architect's nightsweat: the pitch before each footstep, the whorl of confusion—which way?—, the noose of danger—the next turn may put us in harm's way, the corner niche where thieves and the bad lurk to do us in.

"Nannerl"—Maria Anna Walpurgia Ignatia Mozart! Woman twice hexed—to be born in a century with its Rapunzel tower for women, i.e., the home,—and to be born to a family with a brilliant brother and a designing father with only enough money to launch the career of one child; his better bet, the son. *Wenn das Wörtchen wär nicht wär, wär mein Vater Millionär.* If! If it weren't for a little word like "if" things would be different. Obedient, gracious Nannerl would tour like Josepha von Auernhammer, Maria Paradis, Madame Bitzenberg and Therese Friberth, women listed as professional musicians in 1796. With no more talent than Nannerl's, *they* made it. Nannerl's name is sadly absent from the professionals' short list.

Two hundred years after Nannerl I reach the sanctuary of the Ursulin Church. O ye latecomers and sceptics, enter and be blessed by a rose glow from three marble altars, an architectural forest of shadow and light! Over my head, God and His furnishings: dome of heaven supported by pillars in red and pink marble, the blue globe, palm leaves, golden sunlight, candelabra. Angels and a dove and a Joan of Arc-type figure appear alive and well, passing through a battlefield of dead and half-dead figures, banner aloft and flying (with angels) over wounded bodies. Jesus appears, still holding his cross, looking fully recovered from nail wounds. A host of holy ones circle the dome looking more like women than men, like Joanna and Susanna in flowing robes, strong as the Karyatides, the priestesses whose bodies are the columns which support the weight of a temple.

Someone's nightmare's become another's daydream? Here is something for Nannerl to believe in. How lovingly the pink cherubim—alive in the flicker of candlelight—press against the Sower's frame. How happy their dimpled bellies. How simply and sweetly they accept the red light from the candle hanging on a carved silver arm on the wall.

Hope lies overhead in the vanguard, along the horizon of the dome, where the instruments of God—horns, organ, bass violin, lyre—wait the song of victory. Deo placet musica. *As it pleased the music maker who prayed alone under this dome of silence.*

Helen Barolini

GOING TO SICILY

The trip was going to be a *stronzo*. It was reminding her of a Rome traffic jam once near Ponte Vittorio when a man in sunglasses and an open shirt had gotten out of his blocked Fiat 500 and, from all the hundreds of jammed cars to choose from, had directed his clenched fist at her, screaming, *"Stronzo!"*

Connie had told Giorgio about it that night.

"Do you know why he chose me in all that mess to call a shit?" she asked.

"No, why?" Giorgio had asked, idly attentive, getting out of bed to find an ashtray.

"Because he was an elephant!" said Connie.

"Now what do you mean?" Giorgio's forehead had creased with impatience.

"That guy was like the elephant they use in logjams in India or somewhere to pick the one log out of thousands that has to be removed to unblock the jam. But I didn't realize it until after. If I had caught on in time, I would have taken the whole thing differently."

"What would you have done differently?" he had asked, back in bed with her, smoking, more interested now.

"Instead of just sitting there, or giving him horns, I'd have waved and said, *'grazie.'*" It was a kind of *satori* between us. You see what I mean?"

"It sounds like the same kind of rationalization that analysis leads to," Giorgio had said. For he was a physicist, full of a logic that she never knew what to do with—that meant he didn't take her seriously.

And now this trip: a *stronzo,* and she needed no divining elephant to tell her so. She stood at the rail of the boat watching the lights of Naples recede. Tomorrow morning they'd be in Palermo where they'd rent a car to drive to the Sicilian poet's villa for the interview. By Monday back in Rome for the evening classes at Centro where she taught English to Italian businessmen and students like Giorgio.

The trip had been worked out through Giorgio's connections. Someone had been able to secure them an appointment with the poet in Sicily who was a recluse as well as a celebrity. The idea was that Connie would do an article that, together with Giorgio's photos of the illustrious freak in his lonely villa, they'd sell to some big-paying American magazine.

The trip had a meaning in the beginning: they'd use the money they got to find a flat in which to be together. As Giorgio put it, they couldn't marry yet, he was still studying; but they were serious fiancés. They met now in her big, heatless, bathless slum apartment off Campo de' Fiori whose rooms she sublet to three, or four, or half-a-dozen others, depending on her finances at the moment. Giorgio lived at home, the twenty-six-year-old child of doting Italian parents *per bene*. And Connie?—past thirty, American, a hanger-around Rome for years teaching, dubbing, translating, writing, subletting, living, waiting.

Giorgio leaned over the ship rail and a line of the Sicilian poet's came to her mind: "but if the fleeting is dismay/eternity is terror. . . ."

There it was: their relationship—another one in her curriculum vitae—was destined to be fleeting. She woke at night, sometimes, sad at Giorgio's not being there. He had never spent a whole night with her, for his mother would have gotten anxious and begun to worry the father who had a bad heart. Giorgio said it was natural that his mother worried and waited up for him. Connie said nothing.

They met after class in her place, and after making love against the background commotion of her tenants, they went out to eat in one of the nearby *trattorie*. She missed the idea of waking with Giorgio next to her and seeing him shave in the morning while she took a bath—finally, in their own home, with hot water and no boarders.

She scorned this square part of herself that was no part of the scene anymore. But what could she do? She loved him. Enough for a lifetime?—for that eternity the poet called terror? For having children and growing old and bored together? With Giorgio who was still his mother's child?

Giorgio, with irony, called her Signora de Staël, referring to the casual hospitality she offered the artistic and intellectual transients who either rented or visited her place. Electronic composers, sculptors, starlets, poets, pushers, fags, Fulbrighters, and method actors made Connie's rooms the freak-out of a French salon.

Connie was an innocent, a flower-child before they had sprouted, the pourer at a perpetual Mad Hatter's tea party in a falling apart *palazzo*. She was attractive in a floozy, tartish way, and she liked to recall that in her first Rome years she had had as student (and lover) a now rather well-known actor who would have been the father of her child if she hadn't gotten an abortion. She still read of his life and loves in the magazines at the hairdresser's. His first literary woman, he had told her in those days before he made it and she was still under the illusion that teaching was only temporary, that she was going to be a writer as soon as she got down to it—which meant getting enough sleep at night, having her old Olivetti portable repaired, and eating a non-Italian breakfast in the morning so that she'd have the strength to think. Somewhere, in one of the fourteen rooms of her place there was a copy of the American magazine that had printed her poem to Giordano Bruno. His statue stood in the middle of the market square, and it was his backside she saluted each morning when she went to the latrine on the balcony.

When it became clear she wouldn't be a writer, she settled for interesting vacations. One year, dressed in cowboy boots and a Scotch plaid cape and wearing the *cache-sexe* given her by a former student, she went to Tunisia with a Japanese painter named Yuki. They took a guitar along hoping to fill it with hash. But somewhere near salted-over Carthage, they quarreled. She returned alone to Rome and threw his stored canvases into Campo de' Fiori where the market people found them the next morning and sold them from their stands along with eels and *broccoletti*.

Connie (short for Concetta, for she was Italian-American) painted in her spare time while listening to French conversation records. Each winter she came down with a succession of colds that cost her thousands of lire in Kleenex and made her painfully aware of her American-reared frame which, after years in Rome, still asserted its imperative: a longing for central heating and hot water.

Connie's famous gaucheries were never malicious, but sprang from unquenchable ingenuousness. In her innocence she had had two very similar experiences regarding hands that convinced her that the lottery numbers corresponding to hands would someday have to come up for her. The numbers were two and eleven, but since the incident had happened twice, she added two two's to the one's of the eleven and got what she felt must be her true number, thirty-three. Her age. Dante's.

The incidents were these: once in her class, in the usual bantering way that she found put her Italian pupils at their ease and helped them speak more freely, she had singled out a young man with a "And who are you?—Napoleon, with your hand in your jacket that way?" only to have him withdraw a stunted arm and withered claw from concealment.

The other time, at home, she had called out from the far end of the corridor to a friend at the door whom she hadn't seen for a long while, "Aha, so you've come back to me—empty-handed!" And he, one chance in a million, held up a bandaged stump and said, "Yes, the four fingers are lost but maybe the thumb can be saved."

So when is there an end to innocence—after how much clumsiness, after how many abortions, how many trips to Tunisia and back?

Connie looked out at the dark sea and considered. Her life was like her home: a patchwork, a flimsy arrangement, a passing parade of beats and bohemians to whom she could not anchor. But could she commit herself (like being frozen forever in a photo) to marriage or work, or whatever, before she first knew how to define herself, who she was? She couldn't. And that was why, she concluded, no one—certainly not Giorgio—took her seriously.

He came over and stood next to her at the railing. "What are you thinking about?" Even in lovemaking that's how it would be: What are you thinking of, he'd say . . . that you're as beautiful as the sun . . . besides that? . . . that I'm afraid to lose you . . . *Stupida!* In two, three, five years we'll remember what you said and laugh about it.

Really? Where would they be in five years? He in Parioli with an Italian wife and an important job. But Connie?

Still they were persisting in the illusion of a future together. With this trip they could make thousands of dollars if they were lucky. Why not? A few such pieces and they'd be set up forever. Forever? *L'eterno è terrore.*

Cosa nostra they called themselves going to Sicily and doing their thing together. Giorgio was always saying, "We go well together." He liked being with her because she was amusing and pretty and a good sport, not as demanding as Italian women. He liked the way she, American, spoke Italian. It made him tender toward her, he told her. And she liked being American in Italy. It made her in turn tender toward her lousy childhood in Chicago where she had only been a wop.

January. It was a strange time of year to be going to Sicily. There were, in fact, no tourists on the boat for the overnight trip to Palermo. Just Neopolitans or Sicilians chatting and eating. At dinner she and Giorgio sat at a table with a complaining woman who force-fed her two apathetic, sallow-faced children with little squeals of *Mangiate! Mangiate!* It made Connie a little sick. Straight Italy—not the way the movie stuff, or Arcadian whitewash—always did.

Palermo pained her. Her grandparents had sailed from there. Why should she be afraid of Sicily, she wondered as she looked with growing panic into the staring eyes of the dirty children who followed her and Giorgio in the streets.

They were soon out in a rented car, and they headed down the Palermitan coast toward the point where, on a promontory jutting over the violet sea, the poet resided in a place called Villa Luce.

"You know why I hate him, this prince or duke poet, whatever he is!" Connie said suddenly.

"Only a baron," Giorgio said affably. "And what does it matter? Everyone is a baron down here."

"It does matter! Those barons are the ones who drove my grandparents out. Did you see those poor kids in Palermo? What have the barons ever done for their poor except load them on boats and ship them to America like garbage?"

"Well, he personally didn't have anything to do with your grandparents."

"Oh yes, he did—and does. It's a question of mentality that's never changed."

She looked gloomily out at the passing landscape lit by the tepid winter sun. Would I have liked this better than Chicago, she wondered.

"The thought of him disgusts me."

"You've said that," said Giorgio.

"Holed up all his life in the family villa doing nothing but writing poetry. I've written poetry, too, and my grandfathers were fishermen and goatherds!"

"You've told me."

"I'll tell him, too—in French."

"He'll be interested."

"Don't be mean."

"How could I be mean to you?" he said with sudden affection. Then, after a long while, "What are you thinking of?"

"Oh, all sorts of things . . . like who am I, where did I get on, where do I get off? Where, in fact, am I going? And what about you—will you be here next year, next week, tomorrow?"

"Tomorrow for sure. You Americans! Can't you be content with the moment?"

"I'm going to be thirty-four."

They were coming to the end, she and Giorgio, she thought as they drove on with the sea there lapping on the shore like a pumped-up heartbeat.

They stopped for espresso in the village, a wretched cluster of hovels, which was the poet's postal address. The dingy bar was oppressive with silent, watching men. Connie went to wait in the car while Giorgio asked directions to the villa.

"What took you so long?" she asked when he joined her.

He laughed. "When they heard where we were going they filled me in on the local gossip: they say the poet had only one amorous experience in all his life. Someone got him a peasant girl one night, and from that single encounter a son was born. But the Baron refuses any contact with mother or child, and they'd be living in misery if the local doctor hadn't known the facts and convinced the Baron to make some anonymous provision for them. The boy must be about fifteen or sixteen now but his father has never wanted to see him."

"How gross!"

"Still you like his poetry—or don't you anymore?"

"I *do* like his poetry. He's a real poet. But how can it be?"

"It can be, if you don't think about it, you thinking American."

The villa gates were opened by a caretaker (the procurer of that peasant girl? Connie wondered), and they drove up a long avenue bounded by olive and citrus groves. Laid out in front of the villa was an exotic, repellent garden of cacti. Beyond that was a cemetery plot of little white crosses aligned symmetrically.

The poet stood at the portico of Villa Luce restraining a snarling wolf-dog on a leash. "Thank you for letting us come," said Giorgio as Connie put her hand into the soft white pulp of the poet's. Giorgio had made a deferential bow with his handshake.

"Are they family graves?" asked Connie, looking toward the plot of white crosses.

"Oh, yes," the poet lisped. "They're Thales's family," and he bent to stroke the still lunging dog, "and his family is mine. By metempsychosis."

The poet was dressed for a summer day. He wore a beige linen suit with a silk foulard knotted at his neckline. Giving Thales over to a servant he led them through several antechambers to a large salon. The cold was more penetrating than it had been outside. Connie thought of her own unheated flat in Rome where she at least had a portable kerosene stove to take from room to room.

The cold of Villa Luce was total and ineluctable. It intensified the dark shabbiness of the rooms, rooms filled with family pictures of sour-looking Sicilian aristocrats, dusty suits of armor, torn banners, glass-enclosed cases filled with the what-nots of past bored barons and baronesses, the fraying upholstery of the gloomy maroon furniture on which they sat.

The poet, a man of sixty, was old beyond reckoning. His face had the sallow tones of a broth made by slowly extracting the juices from flesh.

Flaccid skin puckered into heavy creases and sagging jowls from which a wispy moustache gave a touching air of whimsy. His hair was parted down the middle into limp, grayish sweep bangs. He looked at his guests with eyes that alternated pride with sudden abstracted looks of anguish.

They conversed politely. Connie thought of mushrooms: decadence being cultivated as one cultivates mushrooms, in the dark. The poet was saying he had produced, in his lifetime, three dozen poems. Perfect examples of Sicilian baroque the critics called them; polished fragments of a world caught on the brink of extinction.

The cold bit into her bones. She and Giorgio huddled in their coats watching their breath form as they talked. The poet, aware of their discomfort, finally took notice of it conversationally: "It's never really cold here as it is with you in the north. What cold we do have lasts no time at all—it doesn't seem worthwhile to put in heating and change our habits for so little."

Connie began to feel she was immured there, sure that she would never again be able to rise and would, finally, be laid to rest among the dogs under another white cross. She cast desperate looks at Giorgio who, with the excuse of photographing, was now moving around and warming himself. When she heard the rattle of china and footsteps of a servant in an adjoining room her spirits rose: tea was coming . . . or, better, perhaps the hot tangerine liqueur punch that is a Sicilian specialty.

"I hope you like Sicilian ices," said the poet, as the servant handed around dishes of an elaborate frozen dessert. "It is our *chef d'oeuvre.* I have always been a glutton for ices and this, I assure you, is the queen of all. I had it made for the occasion."

"That was kind," said Connie, aware of the mockery of his tone.

Poking at her ice, she watched as the poet lapped at his, giving it complete attention and sensual abandon.

Then, just as unaccountably as the fact that her ice was melting in the cold of that room, her revulsion turned to compassion. She felt compassion for her brother poet's hidden life; compassion for her grandparents who had been torn like weeds from their land; compassion for Giorgio who was now and always would be his mother's boy; compassion for herself and her fears.

Why should she be afraid of Sicily and think she had to placate this wild place, make overtures of peace and friendship to it, wish it well? It was she, now, who would send Sicily out of her life, not Sicily and the barons who would expel her.

She put down the dish of untouched ice, refusing it, and putting an end to the interview before it began. There was to be no story, there was to be no further pretense of an arrangement with Giorgio. What there was, instead, she realized was a *satori*—with the poet as the unblocking elephant. She was getting unblocked of Giorgio and Sicily all at once. The trip was no *stronzo* after all but a moment of unique grace.

"I also write poetry," she said to the poet, looking into his bleary eyes.

"Complimenti," he murmured politely.

"Perhaps you'd allow me to translate any new unpublished work you might have."

"I have nothing more. I have written thirty-six poems and that is all. Thirty-six . . . a perfect number. One mustn't push fate, you know."

"Yes, I know. My number is thirty-three—also perfect. But if you don't write poetry, what will you do?"

"I will wait to die," he said pleasantly, smiling.

She understood. One can't push fate, he had said; if one is born as he was, part of a complex eternity, one must refrain, accept, wait. Her good luck, instead, was that she had been given the fleeting.

On the boat back to Naples, Connie told Giorgio what he already knew—that there would not be a story, that the trip hadn't worked along the lines they had planned.

"I know," he said easily, and she sensed his relief that they were finally accepting their relationship on its own impermanent terms.

"But it was a good trip, just the same. At least for me," she said.

"Oh? Why is that?"

"I found out something about myself. Who I am."

"And who are you?" he laughed.

"A Sicilian who is getting away," she said, returning his smile.

Joan Silber

THE DOLLAR IN ITALY

Jill isn't sure why her ex-husband is coming to visit. It's fine with her, as long as he doesn't stay too long. Tiziana, the neighbor upstairs, has suggested that a father who visits should pay child support, why doesn't Jill ask Bob for money? Jill has told her this would be like squeezing blood from a turnip, a phrase that was tough to translate into Italian. Bob is okay, Jill says; Tiziana doesn't believe her.

A lot of people are traveling these days. They stopped when the Gulf War was on, but they started up again when the dollar rose for a brief while, and they're still at it. In Rome, where Jill lives, the airport is busy now. It looks like a shopping mall on a heavy Saturday, except that uniformed guys with machine guns are standing around the entrance. Jill has not brought Lisa, her daughter, because she still thinks the airport is one of the unsafe spots. Lisa, who is seven, is waiting with Tiziana and is probably driving her crazy.

A throng of people is walking into the roped-off Arrivals area, and Bob is there with them. He has a big canvas duffel slung over his shoulder. Jill waves. He looks dazed and rumpled, the same way he always looks. When he sees Jill, he seems mildly startled, not as happy as she expected.

What did she expect? When they reach each other, they hug and do a fast friendly kiss. He is getting a little bonier around the nose and looser around the chin—older. Her too. So what? "Hey," he says. Jill asks how was his flight? How bad was it going through customs? Did he bring Lisa her Ninja Turtle watch? Jill is going to have to do all the work of talking until he decides to wake up more. Everybody else on his goddamned flight looks combed and eager and fresh.

Jill can never decide whether it's better to like him or to set herself against him. Her ex-beloved. What about the eight years she lived with him—are they a mistake and a stupid waste, a dead loss? And what does that mean? What's gone, what did she miss by being with him? And here she is now. So what?

He likes Rome. The last time he visited he talked about getting an apartment here, to be near Lisa. It was just talk, the kind of thing people say when they've eaten well and they're walking up a hilly street with the umbrella pines in silhouette. Jill can't believe he'd leave New York for long, and she hopes he hasn't mentioned any of this to Lisa.

Jill has a tiny rattletrap car, a rusted-out thing that her friends call one of the ruins of Rome. Last time Bob spent half his time here taking it apart and putting it back together again; he made it worse. "Hello, Baby," he says now to the car.

When they pull up outside Jill's apartment building Lisa is looking out the window and shouting down at them in her little, yelpy, shrill voice. An old woman on the street scolds Jill for letting her daughter lean out like that and then she shouts up at Lisa. Lisa looks subdued. But when Jill and Bob go up the stairs inside, Lisa is running down to meet them. She shrieks at the sight of her father. She is all over Bob, a little whirlwind of daughterly ferocity, an imp of desperate love. Bob is in heaven, as happy, Jill thinks, as he will ever be. Jill can hardly watch.

"Hey, Lisa," Bob says. "Your hair is different. Let me think. Was it blonde before? You dyed it, right?"

"It's *longer,* " Lisa says. "I have long hair."

"You sure it's always been brown?" Bob says. "Maybe it was red. I think, yes, red."

"It was *purple!*" Lisa decides. "Purple and green. You don't *remember!*"

They go on like this for a while. Jill gets coffee ready. Lisa has gotten to the Ninja watch and is eating a roll and talking at the same time. In her school there's a boy named Beppe and he's a *stupido.* (Lisa has a crush on him, which means she likes to hide and shout gross insults at him during playtime, usually words having to do with vomit.)

Lisa goes to an American school, but a lot of the kids are Italian. English will be an asset for them later, their parents think. In the schoolyard they all revert to Italian; Lisa has picked up some amazing slang, metaphors Jill can't decipher, and it's just as well. During the Gulf War there was a bomb threat at the school and a guard stationed outside. A lot of the Italian kids left the school. Beppe left, but he came back.

Jill might have taken Lisa out of there too, but it so happens that Jill teaches there herself. She did what she could to be safe. She didn't bring Lisa to the American Express office, to McDonald's, to the English-language movie house. On the street she had Lisa speak to her in Italian.

Bob didn't know about any of this. It was during one of his silent periods. The war in the Gulf was fought and settled without any word from Bob. Lisa tried to phone him—she was old enough to try to do this—but he was never home. Even later he wouldn't say where he was. Out of town, with a girfriend, just busy, who knows? Jill doesn't want to know any more. She doesn't want to bring this up again—what's the point?—but if he stays too long she will.

Lisa is showing him what she got for her birthday. It's a doll that looks just like a little hooker; that's what she wanted. Jill doesn't believe in imposing good taste on a seven year old. The doll has on a gold lamé dress and what used to be called go-go boots. "Guess how much it cost?" Lisa said. *"Cinquanta mila lire."*

Bob clutches his heart and pretends to fall to the floor in a dead faint. *"Cinquantamila . . . madonna."*

"You spent that much?" he says to Jill when he sits up. It was her money. What is it with all these Americans who think she's living in some backwater where everything is dirt cheap? How come they're so surprised all the time? At school one of the teachers said she walks around feeling like money is bleeding out of her veins; she said this in class and it frightened Lisa.

At the moment Lisa has Bob wedged against the wall and is clambering over him like a Lilliputian. Bob says he didn't sleep at all on the plane. He's been up for over thirty hours. Maybe he'll take a nap soon. "You can't," Jill says. "Sleep now and you'll have jet lag for a week." She makes him get up and walk around. She gets him to drink more coffee.

Lisa instructs her doll to keep Bob awake. The doll walks around on Bob's head, the doll bips him on the nose. The doll dances up and down on a fairly touchy part of his lap. "Don't go to *sleep,* " the doll says. Lisa is drinking coffee too, a little bit of it in a mug of hot milk.

✧ ✧ ✧

Bob is out cold on the sofa by noon. He lies with his face down, his ponytail tucked down like a little feather. Lisa is disappointed and has gone back upstairs to Tiziana's to sulk. Jill reads a magazine in the kitchen, as if she could forget he's sprawled out and breathing in the next room. It's ridiculous that he's here except that hotels are expensive (everything is expensive here now), and Lisa needs to see him. But Jill's afraid of what she'll say to him by the end of the week, either in anger or in that terrible, fake, eager agreement.

They're a bad combination. She is worried about what will happen if they stick around each other too much. They once set a building on fire together. By mistake; hardly anything they were doing then was on purpose. They were using a woodstove in their loft, and the stove was hooked up to a chimney that hadn't been cleaned in probably fifty years. It was a drafty loft with one puny radiator and the stove made it cozy and homey. They knew enough to always put out the fire before they went to bed, except that night they were fighting and they didn't. They were fighting about who was a selfish, unbearable person. Lisa was a tiny baby then. They woke up when the dog started barking. (Bob still has the dog, a big Lab named Krypton.) Jill remembers a feeling a like a razor in her heart once she knew what the smoke was; Bob was pouring water at the wall and shouting to her. She got Lisa in a big blanket and ran out with it held over both of them like a tent. The smoke wasn't so bad but Lisa was making those little, hollow, baby coughs under that wool tent.

On the street, the weather was cold enough so that when the fire trucks doused the building the water froze on the brick in icicles. Everyone from the building hovered around her and Lisa; they kept asking about Lisa. Jill was trying to find Bob. When she saw him by a lamppost, with the dog running around at his feet, they looked across at each other—stricken, crazy, ruined. It did not help that they were in the same boat; it was a horrible boat.

They got Lisa to a hospital and she was all right. As it turned out, the building was all right too. The worst damage was in their loft and the neighbor's, both without smoke detectors. At the time, Jill remembers, she was so glad that no one was hurt; she thought she had never known before what being grateful was. Later the neighbor wanted to sue them, and the landlord made threats. She and Bob were living in Brooklyn then, the worst time in Jill's life, while the legal snarls went on between insurance companies; these may still be going on, for all Jill or Bob knows. Neither of them has held an apartment in their name since then.

For a while, when Jill first came to Italy, she really did sort of forget about that time. She was with Giancarlo then, and, while his English was good, their conversation had certain limits of vocabulary, of convenience; they stuck pretty much to the here and now. His friends lengthened and re-pronounced her first name, which does not sound like a name to Italians; forget *Jill.* But now it's the same as if she were anywhere; she walks around with her underlayers of old feeling, her sudden jolts of memory.

She's lived in Rome for four years now. Things have happened to her here; she has spots all over town where she was blissful or miserable with Giancarlo. Giancarlo always said he didn't like Rome. He used to complain that Rome was too un-modern, too crowded with other centuries.

When he was a teenager he rode his *motorino* through the Forum for spite, he wrote graffiti on the walls of churches. He regrets that now, but kids still do it. Maybe Lisa will be one of those teenage vandals, if they stay here that long.

Jill was a teenage runaway herself. At sixteen she was in New York working as an exotic dancer. She still has a tattoo from that time, a blue rose above her left breast. Bob loved it; Giancarlo was not too happy when people saw it at the beach. Only recently has it fully occurred to Jill how surprising it will look when she's an old woman—a blurred inky flower on her skin. If she takes a new lover at seventy, she'll have to explain it all over.

✧ ✧ ✧

When Bob wakes up from his nap, he can't figure out where he is at first. He's on his stomach on a sofa in a room with a terra cotta floor. A rush of brilliant daylight is streaming through the window.

He thinks it's good he slept. At home he's used to being awake and alert in the middle of the night, stuck in bed waiting for daybreak; in those hours he feels as if he's lying in a ditch. He hasn't slept right ever since the art gallery he runs started heading toward bankruptcy; this is not new for art galleries but he can't believe how much money he's lost. The sheer amounts, thousands and thousands, make him want to howl in agony. How did this happen?

He's had to do some things, like cash in his life insurance policy, which he promised Jill he'd never do. He might not tell her while he's here. He's never been good about giving her money for Lisa, and now he doesn't see how he can. Jill won't yell at him, but she'll be stony and disgusted. When they were getting divorced he used to think, no more fights, at least, after this. He didn't know beans about it.

Bob can't get over how much money he's lost; what if he never gets over it? At times he hears himself praying. He is not a believer, and the prayers have no content; they're just names, a repeated invoking; it soothes him to speak on a plane that has nothing to do with money. But now he sees himself slipping into pleas and hope, attempts at private bargaining. Bribes are next, he knows. On Jill's block there is a little cement shrine built into the corner of a building, a dusty ceramic Virgin in a curved niche. People put flowers there, bouquets still wrapped in cellophane. These are requests. Bids for special favor.

And what if this sort of thing worked? What would that mean? It frightens Bob to think of; so petty, so tricky, so cheap. Bob wants to rise above things: isn't that what he's supposed to learn? He is here for the company of Lisa, which, like prayer, gets your attention elsewhere. (Although it's her money that's lost, if you want to see it that way; he doesn't.) With her hair long, she looks like a little Afghan hound now.

How did her hair grow so fast? He is angry, when he thinks about it, that Jill keeps Lisa here in Rome. Why is Jill still here? She could move back now, without Giancarlo. He knows she isn't idling here to spite him, but she might as well be. Even on this crappy couch, he slept so well now, with Lisa in the next room.

All week Bob takes Lisa to the park as soon as she gets out of school. It's a beautiful park, full of palms and cypresses and fountains and topiary. It has swings for Lisa, a slide.

Jill pictures Bob on a bench, watching Lisa as if he's waiting for her to do him good. Lisa knows this or knows something. She's too lively around him; she gets really monkeyish and loud if he laughs. Jill would rather not see this. When she lived with Giancarlo, she used to take Lisa back to New York herself. She would stash Lisa with Bob and stay alone with a friend, be single and light.

At night Bob sleeps on her sofa now. The first night Jill brought in the blankets and the towels, just in case there was any question in his mind. But in the morning when she saw him asleep in his underwear she felt badly, as if she'd been mean and heartless. As if she'd made him go to waste. Someone should admire him, half-naked like that. Not her though. Let him cover himself up.

Lisa has been going through a phase of being very curious about bodies; she spies on Bob at night, Jill knows. A few months ago they were in a church with a dead saint's body miraculously preserved—beyond putrefaction, although it looked pretty black and mummified to Jill—under its satin dressing. Lisa, who has seen this sort of thing before, got very interested all of a sudden in the mystery of the flesh: Has anyone ever been born without skin? Are men's bones made of the same thing as ladies'? What happened to the saint's penis?

These are questions Lisa would ask anywhere, but Jill, being a mother, is sorry now that Lisa got such a long look at that leathery skeleton in its reliquary, the bitter remains.

Bob has made a few vows to himself. He doesn't want to become cheap, a worrier over spent nickels and wasted food, a high complainer and low tipper. If he gets like that, there won't be much left of him. Already he is getting a little like that, he can see. In restaurants he suffers great torments—he talks Lisa out of getting the *prosciutto* and melon and then he makes her eat an expensive dessert. He embarrasses Jill in her neighborhood *trattoria* by almost sending back liqueurs that are in fact free.

He and Jill are trying so hard not to fight with each other. Lisa starts singing to herself when there are big silences at the table. She does "The Itsy Bitsy Spider" in a small, mumbling voice. She tells long boring stories about Beppe and Jennifer and Luca and Miss Bridgewater at school.

She also has some brat moments, which do in fact distract them. She does *not* want her mother to get the black squid-ink *risotto;* she makes vile retching noises the whole time Jill eats it. She does *not* want her father to tease her one more time about her hair, and she says, *"Stupido!"* very loudly at him with a little smile on her face. "Chill out," Jill says. "Right now." Bob suggests they leave her in the restaurant, a threat Jill never uses.

Lisa acts hurt; she comes over and settles down in Jill's lap, a tired baby once more. Jill doesn't remember too much about being this age herself. Later she fought with her mother, tooth and nail, and she believes that if she hadn't fought she would've had no life except as a crushed daughter, a furious humiliated creature. But sometimes, when she's playing with Lisa, she remembers bursts of affection from her mother, things she had forgotten. *Kitten face.* Her mother used to call her that. How can that be?

Lisa is nuzzling in the crook of Jill's arm. Bob is busy adding up the check. Jill remembers when he was much more dashing and spendthrift—was that better? When Lisa was born and Jill's mother came to visit for the first and last time, Bob took Jill's mother out to Lutèce for lunch. A restaurant like that must have terrified her, but how could he have known that? He thought everyone liked glamor; he was a little too caught up in that sort of thing, Jill thinks, but he was always gallant and free, an easier man.

Bob is thinking how he misses the time when Lisa was smaller, when you could make up anything and she believed you until the very end. A squirrel the size of a refrigerator; you couldn't get her to buy that now. She talks a lot now, she talks Italian to him for spite.

"Hey, spaghetti-head," Bob says to Lisa. "Hey, mop-hair girl of mine."

"He called me that before," Lisa says. "He *repeats* himself."

The waiter is hovering around them. For a moment Jill is afraid Lisa is going to call the waiter stupid or something much worse, but she really never talks that way to strangers. Only to Jill and Bob and now the alluring Beppe.

"Moppo," Bob says, "if I didn't repeat myself, how would you remember all the interesting things I say?"

"Giancarlo never repeated himself," Lisa says.

There's a bad silence. Even the waiter looks worried about them. "I don't think I know this child," Bob says. "Does she look familiar to you?"

Lisa wails in protest but she's still smiling her thin brat-smile. Bob is tired, it feels very late at night to him. What about Lisa in the next decade, is he up to it? Every day she gets older and stronger and better at stirring up trouble.

Jill really would like to leave her right here in the restaurant. Tiziana says Lisa is too young to eat out at night anyway. But here they are.

On the weekend Jill goes to the park with Bob and Lisa. The weather is sunny and beautiful, and the park is crowded; little Italian kids are running around in their cute fussy outfits. The youngest ones hold balloons and look dazed. Infant boys are being coached by their fathers to run after soccer balls.

Bob is in a good mood. He has bought a copy of the *Herald Tribune* and is catching up on the day-old sports news. It makes Jill a little lonesome for Giancarlo, who used to try to explain soccer to her. When Bob groans over a score, she says, "I'm not asking." They lean back in the sun with their eyes closed, as if they were at the beach. Bob wants to know if she gets homesick, and she says not any more usually. Also, Jill tells him, she likes teaching art to the high-schoolers, who are chattery but not hard to handle. Bob says, "Not hard for you," which is nice of him.

Lisa is running to the swings and she wants to be pushed. Bob gets up and pushes in a good sweeping rhythm; he gets her soaring. Lisa swings for a long time, with her legs stretched out, and then she runs over the grass, through a brick arch that is part of the ruins of a villa. Bob thought it was fake at first, but they don't have fake ruins here. Jill hopes the sight of all these broken remains is consoling to him (if that's why he's here), signs of somebody else's rises and falls. His business must be in horrendous shape, from the hints he's been dropping. She should be sympathetic but she isn't. Jill's glad he has life insurance at least to take care of Lisa, since she doesn't. Otherwise she doesn't expect much from him.

Lisa is by the fountain. She wants to do one round on the kiddy car ride, and when she gets on it, she doesn't wave but stares ahead, with her hair blowing behind her like Snoopy's aviator scarf.

"There she goes," Bob says. "Our own hot rod mama."

A woman watching her son gives them a sweet smile. They must look like a regular family, how could the woman guess different? Jill doesn't think she and Bob should ever get back together, but at times like this that fact hurts her feelings. Look at them, all rosy and fond; look at Lisa zipping around the track, poor Lisa. And yet they could be worse off. They could be enemies; they could still be at each other's throats, she and Bob. Instead they have behaved as well as they could; they've tried to be decent in these later stages. So they have not, altogether, wasted each other.

The last time Bob was here, when Jill got sick with a bad flu, he brought her magazines, he drove Lisa to school, he tried to fix the car. She thinks of him peering under the open hood, tinkering blindly with the car's wiring; it's not a bad picture. She is thinking so happily of the back of his head, with its wispy ponytail, that she has to stop this sort of thinking, and she's glad when Lisa comes down from the kiddy car ride.

"Speed demonette. We're training you next year for the Indy 500," Bob says.

Lisa of course doesn't know what that is. When Bob explains, he says, "Just don't learn to drive from your mother."

"Excuse me," Jill says.

Bob says the car was fine when he left here last time. It's the way she rides the clutch that ruins it.

"I drive in Rome," Jill says. "That's enough without treating the clutch well at the same time."

Bob says he'll have to give her a lesson.

"It's my car," Jill says. "I don't tell you how to run your business."

"Thank you so much," Bob says.

Bob is here for three more days, she better be careful. But he started it, as Lisa would say.

Lisa decides Bob has to buy her an ice cream bar and they go off together to the refreshment stand. Lisa comes back with chocolate smears all over herself.

"Bath time when we get back," Bob says. "I left the water heater on because I *knew*."

"Nobody keeps the water heater on all the time here," Jill says. "I told you before. You did the same thing last time." And Lisa's too old for mid-day baths anyway. He probably still thinks she takes a nap. "You leave it on all day while I'm in school," Jill says. "You leave it on all night."

"So what?" Bob says.

"And then when you finally go home I'll have to pay the fucking bill."

"Send me the bill," Bob says. "If it's so important."

"Maybe I will this time. I should."

"You're ridiculous," Bob says. "You are."

Are they going to start? Once they start going, they won't stop. They'll forget that Lisa can hear; they won't care. Lisa is right there, with a pinched, wincing look. "We have to go home," she says. "I have to have a bath."

They walk, without speaking, on the leafy paths, under the arcades of trees. The sun is pouring down on them, in vain.

"You're not walking fast enough," Lisa says.

"Know what we have for lunch?" Jill says. "We have that peanut butter your father brought us."

Bob says, "Did you ever get peanut butter stuck to the roof of your mouth?" He does the usual clogged diction, he goes into the whole routine. Lisa laughs; what a nice child. Actually, Bob is funny at this. Lisa is making a big production out of her hilarity. She is working herself into a little choking fit of giggles.

They leave the park by the gate that leads right out into a busy street—cars are streaming by them from out of an underpass. "This is so unsafe," Jill says. "I hate it."

Bob says, "It's not so bad if you know how to cross." How does he know?

Meanwhile Lisa is shouting at someone across the street. It's Beppe, she sees Beppe. He's with his mother, a pretty woman in a tiny stylish skirt. "Beppe!" Lisa shouts. *"Stai zitto!"* Beppe looks around amazed, as well he might, since he hasn't been saying anything and he's just been told to shut up.

"Beppe!" she shouts. "Your head looks like puke with ca-ca on it!"

Beppe stops at the edge of the road, listening.

"I see your pukey head, Beppe. Do you see me?"

Beppe yells something back at Lisa—something in Italian that Jill can't follow—and then it's too much for him, he lunges out. Beppe runs into the street right when a car is coming out of the underpass, and Jill hears herself and Lisa screaming. They can't see—cars on both sides are in their way—but there's a squeal of brakes.

When the road clears, Beppe is being hauled off by his mother, who has him by the elbow. He is still standing, which Jill takes to be a good sign. She waits with Lisa until they can run across the road—it is a very long moment—and then Beppe waves to greet them. He thumps Lisa on the arm; he seems to be fine. The car is still stopped, and Jill sees through the underpass that another car has driven into it and crumpled its back bumper.

"Oh, God," Bob says. The two drivers are getting out, about to yell at each other.

Jill is thinking how much worse it could be; they are all thinking that. Lisa is crying. Beppe's mother is kissing his head. Jill and Bob are looking at each other. Bob's face is wild and scared; Jill is bleary and worn-out. The two of them are remembering the night of the fire, what it was like outside their building. They remember how much they wanted to get away from each other, how different they believed their trouble was to each of them, and how they couldn't wait to have it to themselves. Now they stand at the side of the road and nod at one another; they speak to Lisa until she calms down; they know each other so much better now.

Michelle Blair

ETERNAL CITY

And there I was, southbound in third class, passing yet another long night standing in a corridor, my elbows at the window, my face in the cool humidity, my hair unbrushed and fluttering out behind me. I'd been traveling for weeks now, the backpack-gamut of so many countries in so many days, though I prided myself on a difference: *my* lone journey was with no backpack, rather a fat, shoulder-debilitating red bag, and I stayed in cities or towns for more than an instant, and I did not speak English, and I pretended I wasn't American, and I kissed as many boys as I could. I never slept with them, though—I'd never slept with anyone!—though I was not averse to it, should the right Mr. Accented Right turn up.

That particular night, the endless train I was taking from Holland chugged diagonally through France and Switzerland and, by daybreak—my nineteenth birthday—into Italy. In Torino, the sun rising slow and pink through a fog of humidity, I took a stretch on the platform, squatting down and rising back up. I lit a cigarette and felt instantly nauseous and faint—it was barely six, too early, with no breakfast or previous night's dinner, just an insomniac's headache and hazy stare. I wished I could feel something, some sense of the now, but everything seemed so nonexistent. Nineteen was nonexistent, this trip, my entire life, nonexistent. Not speaking the language, whichever language, was the least of my alienation. It was that every country, every moment, seemed such a different reality from the previous, that it was hard to keep track of who I was, the many *me's* that had developed, then flitted away. I'd been giddy, carefree, clever, sexy, in turn—all of the things I wasn't at home, back at the hip college where I felt forever unhip, where all I could do was pine to be someone else. Who exactly that was, I didn't know, but I hoped to find her here and to hold on to her, to bring her back with me for good.

In the evening, at Stazione Termini in Rome, I was met by the gentlemanly Mario Benuti, a friend of a friend of my dad's, and by Mario's friend, Giulio Mercurino, with whose parents I would be staying. I would not be able to stay with Mario as originally planned in New York, as his father was visiting from out of town. In a blue Renault, I was whisked to Via Dalmazia, where, once inside the large apartment that housed the many members of the Mercurino household, there was immediately placed before me heaping plates of pasta and bread and sausage.

The family was kind and lively and we had fun, attempting to communicate: they would point to an object, write the word in Italian—*pane*, for example—after which I would write its English correspondent, *bread*. Mamma would pronounce it like so, comically, *brie-eda*, making even the consonants have vowels. She did the same with *forchetta*, (fork), which she pronounced *fork-a*. There was a sloppy but good-looking man at the table staring at me, who was the cousin of a sister-in-law. He drew a detailed map from Via Dalmazia far into the city's center, and told me, in pidgin English and Italian, that first thing tomorrow, I *had* to go to Piazza di Spagna. It was the best place in all of Rome.

Soon, I was ushered into a room the size of an opium den, barren but for an antique chiffarobe and a single bed, where I slept comfortably and safely for the first time since the whole trip; and, the next morning, I found myself at the famed Spanish Steps amid the tourists and cameras and souvenir peddlers and grungy youth, of which, I supposed, I was one. Even at 10:00 A.M., it was sweltering in late July, quite opposite to Scandinavia or the lowlands where nights were cool enough that I'd worn a jacket and days always provided some sort of breeze. Here, I was dripping hot, day and night. Yet, in attempts to camouflage what I considered a despicable body, those sticking-together thighs, I had condemned myself to wearing a long dress. It was made of black velour and had faded till the once-rich color looked a filthy gray. It attracted the heat like a sponge and stuck to every part of me.

I watched a mime perform and smiled at him until he took notice; then, aimlessly, I sat by a flower bed, about three-quarters of the way down the zillion steps, where a little fountain's spray reached my sticky skin. I was all sluggish sensation, so tired from the already five weeks and still two more to follow, depressed to imagine how I was going to occupy my time. Of course, I was having the time of my life, but . . . I didn't know. There was something, I felt, missing. I prayed it would be just around the corner.

At the bottom of the steps, I saw a guy dressed all in white—white V-neck shirt, white Bermuda shorts, even white shoes, clogs. He was walking around, calling *"ciao,"* to his right, to his left. Having not yet met any stray Italians, just the plump, sixtyish Mario, and the plain Mercurino family, I wanted to meet this guy. I could just picture him, lounging by a kidney-shaped pool, wearing a skimpy bathing suit, jumping in to pull a long-legged girl off a raft, holding her close, ravaging her.

"Ciao, bella." He surprised me, on my step. I was nowhere near as attractive or thin or worldly as the girl in my fantasy. But here he was. This close, I could tell he wasn't a boy. His black hair was streaked with a few strands of gray. He had a little birth mark just under his right eye. When he smiled, his tight tanned skin became grooved, the lines at the corners of his eyes reaching down like sunbursts.

"Why you not smile?" he asked.

"Look," I said, flashing a smile, "I'm smiling."

"Non, non, I don't see thees."

"How did you know I spoke English?"

"Yes, it's true, you look Italian, but if you was, you not be sitting here pretty girl alone like this, not talking to no one, not smiling, looking so sad on thees beautiful day."

"Well, I *don't* know anyone."

"Ah, *mi dispiace,*" he answered. "I am so sorry. Why it's?"

"I only got here yesterday—it was my birthday, even—and I'm staying with this family who are friends of a friend of a friend. So . . ."

"*Povera ragazza, povera Americana.* And sure you've not had the birthday celebration, no?"

"No." I was skeptical. I couldn't imagine why he was talking to me. But what could I have said: Go away, I don't talk to male strangers? All I'd seemed to do on that trip was talk to strangers, *especially* if they were male.

"And you not had the real Italian champagne, or the homemade pasta like only Italian can makes them?"

I shook my head. "I just got here."

"Allora," he said, lighting two cigarettes, giving one to me, "I am Alberto, I make invitation for you. Tomorrow, you come to my studio—I am fashion deesigner—and I make for you the special birthday meal." He stared into my eyes, as if he were trying to hypnotize me.

I was a little nervous about the whole thing. He was very macho, I supposed. But I couldn't imagine anything going wrong. I told him okay.

"*Molto buono.* Tomorrow at one, then? Right here by this fountain is okay?"

"Okay," I said.

He put his hand on my upper arm as he rose, kissed me on each cheek, and walked away, his clogs clonking on the stone. *"Ciao bella,"* he said, turning his head back to me and winking, *"á domani."*

Until tomorrow . . . would he accost me in his nearby, so-called studio? Maybe, I thought, that was just what I needed. A real Italian man to teach me something about *amore.* I thought of "The Ballad of Lucy Jordan," a song I'd heard for the first time just last week, in which Marianne Faithful sings, *"At the age of thirty-seven, she realized she'd never ride through Paris in a sports car, with the warm wind in her hair."* I so wanted to learn about men; I so wanted to be held in someone's arms while drinking Italian champagne; I so wanted to drive through Paris in a sportscar with the warm wind in my hair. If I never did, I, like Lucy Jordan, would jump from a window to my death.

Meanwhile, there was still a lot of today to get through, and so I began walking, walking, walking in the debilitating heat. Standing at counters, I stopped just about every hour to recharge myself with an espresso. I bought a *panino* or two, nothing much for lunch. Eventually, I found another plaza, this one called—if I was deciphering the map correctly—Piazza Navona. In its center bubbled two fountains; at its periphery were numerous cafés and restaurants and side streets whose names I would whisper to myself, not understanding the words, but loving to mimic the accent. No matter how ridiculously I overdid the cadences, it did not sound like exaggeration. Still, I was tired, and the day was so long and hot and empty. I sat on a ledge, shading myself from the high sun. I sipped a cold orange soda.

A man came walking toward me, sitting just a few feet away. Something about him—the faded aqua pants and aqua sweatshirt over which fuzzy dirty-blond hair curled; his eyes, which were aqua, too, and beautiful—intrigued me. He looked like a poet.

"Una sigaretta?" I asked, pantomiming a cigarette at my lips, not knowing the verb for *to have.* He leaned over to give me a Marlboro, just as another man sat down in the space separating us. This intruder ended up lighting the cigarette for me.

"Di dové sei?" he asked.

"Non parlo. Scusi."

"Parle français? Habla español? Sprechen zie Deutsch?"

One by one, I shook my head. "English," I told him flatly, wishing he would go away and I could talk, or at least attempt to talk, with the other man, the aqua one.

"Ah, *si,* I should have to known. You have an English face."

It was a stupid thing to say. Out of the corner of my eye, I saw the other man looking at me. "Actually, I'm not English, I'm American."

Just then, the other man rose. Damn, there went my chance . . . but he walked in front of the intruder and stood before me. His eyes, I now saw, were lighter even than his clothing, see-through green as Caribbean seas. *"Nous marchons?"* he asked, in a French that I miraculously understood, and I promptly responded, *"Oui,"* and rose from the ledge to join him, throwing a neutral *"ciao"* over my shoulder at the intruder, whom we left looking foolishly alone.

So there we were, the beautiful aqua man and me, and my prior wandering and loneliness evaporated instantly.

"Je m'appelle Luca," he told me.

Luca . . . what a beautiful name. I didn't know why he spoke French to me, but that was fine, I couldn't speak Italian. And French was so romantic, the language of love. He told me he'd just come back from Marseilles and had no place to live; he was staying, temporarily, in the woods. His parents had died. He had a sister in Rome, but she wouldn't allow him to stay at her place. I couldn't imagine such coldness from a sibling. But he said that she didn't like him. I couldn't imagine that, either. He seemed so likable, so sad and frail. And when, in a cool vestibule beside a *pasticceria,* he kissed me, closing his eyes and gasping *"Wow-a"* in my face, I hoped that we could, maybe, find a place together.

At four, he had an errand to do; I didn't know what, and I didn't care, just as long as we would reunite. And we would, he assured me, in just one hour, at a certain tree he pointed out on an island at a busy intersection.

Spending that hour dilly-dallying nearby, so as not to lose my way, I imagined, for a terrified instant, that he'd ditch me, wouldn't show up again. That was what guys did, at least often enough back home. That was why I'd never *really* fallen in love yet, and never actually made love. I was grateful to spot Luca at five on the dot beneath that tree, visible even from way across several streets, his hair blond and fly-away, his clothes shimmering in the still-searing sun.

We ran across the heavily-trafficked street and up behind Piazza Venezia. This piazza too had many steps, but also had a garden to the right and woods to the left, down a lonesome road bearing the marker *"Senso Unico"*—which I was certain was some kind of existential slogan meaning "unique sense," but which I found out later means only "One Way." Luca led us to an isolated spot beside a mammoth rock formation, thirty feet high and wider still, in front of which a bench faced outward, presenting the entirety of Rome spread below us. It was picture-perfect. We sat down on the bench. We kissed some more. I felt his chest tremble, his hand clench at my shoulder. Then, before I knew it, I felt my head being pushed toward the open fly of his aqua trousers.

"Dai," he whispered, *"dai, dai."*

I didn't know what he was saying, although I did, of course, understand what he meant. So that was when I moved up in the ranks, however belatedly, that was when I gave my first blow job. It was awful, but it wasn't. It was easy enough not to pay attention to the crick in my neck or the pressure deep at the back of my throat, because he was loving it, I could tell. Those sounds, those movements, the way his hands wove through my hair and around my neck told me so, and since he was having such a great time, I was sure I was, too. I was sure I was in love with him by then, and I wanted to give him *everything*, sex, of course, but even more, whatever I had to give. But I wanted to wait, at least a little bit, until the time was right. I didn't want it to be all wanton and hurried and crazy, out there in the open. I wanted it to be a slow lead-up. I told him I hoped tomorrow would be the day. He didn't seem to mind at all.

It was nearly dark when we left those woods, Luca guiding me to the bus that would take me back to the Mercurinos. I'd completely forgotten about them, hadn't called once during the day just to touch base, and now I couldn't find their phone number. Luca pressed close to me, his lips on my neck but his eyes on the street, while I called Mario Benuti, who reprimanded me for my inconsideration. It was too late for me to call my hosts, he shouted; was this the way young people behaved in America? I apologized profusely. I'd lost track of time, I told him. What had I been doing all day? he asked. Walking around, I answered. He said he would come pick me up and, although it would be crowded, I would have to stay with him for the night. He would call and wake the Mercurinos to let them know that I was okay, as they had been so worried.

As we walked, I felt strangely outside of myself. I had been outside of myself plenty on this trip, but now was different. Now, I wanted to be outside of myself in order to know who I was. "This is me," I was telling myself, emphatically. "This is me, with this beautiful, beautiful man I love and who loves me." I didn't know how to relish it enough.

Soon, we arrived at the head of Piazza di Spagna, where I'd started that morning, so many piazzas and so many hours ago, where I'd met Alberto, and where Mario would pick me up. I didn't know if it was better or worse to let him see me waiting with Luca, so, when I saw the blue Renault approaching, I let go of Luca's hand.

"*Demain*," he said, which meant we'd meet again tomorrow, beneath our tree.

Idling his car, Mario got out to open the passenger door. He gave me two kisses hello. It seemed he wasn't angry anymore.

"Well, I'm glad you're all right," he said. Arms akimbo, he looked me up and down. My hair was messed, my dress rumpled. I smelled terrible, grit and sweat all over my skin.

"You are such a little girl," Mario said, and laughed. I didn't know why he said that, but I knew he was wrong. I was not a little girl. I was nineteen! I was old! More experienced, wiser, happier, than I'd ever been. With exaggerated gentlemanliness, Mario led me into the passenger seat, closing the door for me and everything.

In his three-room apartment, he handed me a towel and a pair of stiff, brown pajamas, before opening the king-sized convertible couch where I would be sleeping. A freestanding shower stood in the corner, which Mario told me to use. I felt extremely exposed, washing myself completely for the first time in who knew how long, behind the green curtain. I wanted to enjoy, but I sensed Mario hovering just outside.

"Mario?" I called, once I'd turned the shower off.

"Si?" he replied.

"I'm going to get out now."

"Oh, oh, okay, so I guess I'll leave the room . . ." he said, then asked, still in the room, "Did you eat dinner?"

"Yes," I lied.

I heard him leave the room, and I stepped out quickly, hurriedly pulling on the uncomfortable pajamas before I'd even fully dried myself.

"Well, then," he returned quickly, "if you're not interested in dinner, we can go to sleep."

I looked at him, waiting.

"I told you that my father was staying with me," he said. He sounded mad again. "He's here from Trieste. So, we've got to sleep together in this bed." He pointed to the opened couch. "Is that a problem?"

No, of course it wasn't. I was exhausted after the long day. Anyway, why should I feel weird about sharing a bed with him? I'd trusted people even stranger than he. He had been helpful to me. *I'd* been the one who'd been bad, irresponsible. I got into the bed and wrapped a small portion of the covers tightly around me.

Ten minutes later, Mario's hand reached toward the front of my shoulder, pressing it so that I rested on my back. I could feel his breath near my neck. Then his body slid over, his leg landing on mine.

"You are such a little girl," he said. His hands reached over.

I froze. The worst thing was, I felt I owed him, somehow.

"I'm not going to do anything. I just want to hold you. You are such a little girl."

I turned onto my side again, away from him, and passed the entire night with his arm around me and my eyes wide open, my entire body rigid and sensitive to any stray movement on his part. Thankfully, he really didn't do anything more than hold me, like he'd said. But I imagined he would have, had I been more game, had I been more like the girl I'd been with Luca that afternoon. But that was different, I loved Luca.

The next morning, Mario drove me to the Mercurinos', who were only glad to have me back, and Mamma served me pastry after pastry and cup after cup of *caffé latte*, and in the afternoon, I went to meet Luca beneath the tree. I never did go back to Piazza di Spagna again, so I didn't know if Alberto waited long, or if he even showed.

Luca must have gotten there early, as I arrived exactly at one. He must have been as eager as I was. He wore the same clothes as yesterday. Again, we climbed to the back of Piazza Venezia, and this time, on the way to the woods, he reached behind a rock into some bushes, to bring out his sleeping bag.

"C'est ici que je dorme," he held apart branches and twigs, *"exactemente ici."* We walked to a clearing and he spread the sack over the dirt and rocks on the woods' floor.

From my shoulder bag, I extracted the pristine beige case that held the diaphragm I'd bought just before I'd left New York. I took the little travel tube and huddled behind a nearby bush. I felt so mature as I inserted it for the first time of actual use. "I am a woman about to make love to the man she loves," I thought to myself. "This is what I came to Europe for." When I lay down on my back and Luca touched me, it felt as though we were butter, some kind of dissolvable substance, melting into each other; I couldn't tell what limbs were his or mine, whose sweat was whose, there was so much of it. I couldn't have said it was perfect, that there was no pain, because there was—flashing-lights kind of pain. Every part of me burned in waves, starting from where he'd crashed through. But I didn't care. All I could see was his face, the long pale lashes over his aqua eyes. We were so close just then. The way he looked made me know that this was just the way it was supposed to be. I was so happy to have found him, to have been given this greatness.

"*Tu á New York mucho* boys?" he asked later, as we zipped and folded and rolled the sleeping bag back up. I knew he was feeling the same closeness to me—it was so sweet that he was jealous of my boyfriends in New York.

"Non," I told him truthfully, *"rien de* boys *á New York."*

Not long after, as we walked to Piazza Navona, where we'd met yesterday, I could feel the stickiness between my legs, and a soreness in muscles way unreachable somewhere; I was conscious of my lower body with every step, as though I'd been riding a horse or hiking. It was notable, aching, and yet marked something so wonderful. I'd finally been let in on the secret. I'd finally arrived. Luca led me diagonally across the square, until we rested on the curved edge of a fountain. He dunked his head in the water and came up, thrashing like a wet dog. I took my hairbrush from my shoulder bag and leaned toward him, smoothing back his hair so that, despite blemishes and tooth-discolorations, with his straight nose and clear eyes and fair complexion, I thought he looked like a movie star.

Since it was still so hot, we moved to the shade, sentimentally sitting down upon yesterday's ledge. It felt as though we'd known each other much longer, communicating in some pre-verbal sort of way. Language was not important, I realized; when you don't have it, you must communicate by other means, by touch or gaze, by *soul*. That was how we communicated. I felt it every time I looked at him, just by being there.

At four, church bells rang nearby, and I was reminded of Mamma Mercurino, whom I'd promised to call. I didn't want to disappoint her and the family again. I rose, leaving my bag by Luca's feet, and strolled across the square into a side street's espresso bar. I reached her, said I'd be home for dinner. I was excited to pretend to be an Italian daughter—free summer days, mother to fix me meals and tell me I was too skinny, lover waiting for me on a ledge or beneath a tree—rather than to be the lame American daughter that I was back home, trying again and again for things I would never get and didn't even understand.

The brightness of the huge piazza was blinding, like an overexposure, when I came out of the darkened passage. In the haze, people appeared as haloed stick figures, as did Luca, faraway, with my red canvas bag on his lap. His hands were in the front pocket, searching for cigarettes, I figured. Of course, he wouldn't find them there, as I kept them in the back flap. He unbuckled the two clasps of the middle, and, like a surgeon, reached his hands way into the belly of the bag. Well, he wasn't going to find them there, either; why would I have stashed them so inaccessibly away? All I kept in the buckled main part were personal things: hairbrush, cosmetic bag, diary, address book, and the large passport-holding travel wallet that my mother had given me for the trip.

"What are you doing?" I asked, cheerfully, when I got back to him.

He looked up quickly, shaking his head. *"Je ne sais pas,"* he said. I didn't know if he was saying that he didn't know what he was doing, or that he didn't understand the question, since I'd forgotten and asked it in English.

"Ici les cigarettes," I said, taking the bag off of his lap, reaching into the back flap and handing him the pack and lighter.

"Je suis mal," he told me then. *"Trés, trés mal."*

We smoked in silence for a while. I felt a little sick myself. What was he talking about? What exactly did he mean? Suddenly, there seemed to be some kind of conspiracy going on.

"C'est le drug," he told me, *"c'est l'heroin."*

The word sounded lovely. "Heroin?" I repeated, but my accent made it ugly.

"Si." He lit a new cigarette with the last one.

"*Tu sais un* addict?"

"Non, je ne suis pas une addicte."

I was more curious than shocked. Or maybe I was so shocked I didn't even realize I was. How long had it been since his last fix? I wondered. Now that I looked at him up close, he did appear kind of peaked, his skin paler and clammier as we stayed on in the heat. Actually, he looked terrible, not at all the handsome man he'd been just minutes before, with hair now matted as a Rastafarian's, and yesterday's clothes wrinkled and spotted from being in the woods. Actually, he looked about ready to puke.

"So . . ." I trailed off, realizing just how tired I was, having not slept last night, having not slept much, period, for weeks. I didn't know what to say anymore. I wanted to get away from him, and yet, of course, I didn't. I wanted to stay with him forever, move here, and never go back. Wouldn't that be wonderful? I couldn't just chuck out everything we'd shared in the past twenty-four hours simply because he used heroin. It wasn't like he was a junkie, he'd just told me he wasn't. I shouldn't be so quick to judge.

"*J'ai rien de* money." He faced me, clutched my shoulders. *"Je suis trés mal."*

I rubbed my fingertips together. "What do you need? How much. How much *de* money?"

"Dix mille."

I went into the middle part of my bag to get my wallet. But it wasn't there. I checked in the other pockets, before finding it in the front, where I never kept it, where Luca had been looking before. Had he taken it out and stuffed it back quickly when he'd seen me approach? Had he really tried to steal from me? But nothing was gone when I opened the wallet, all of my money, traveler's cheques, passport, mother's credit card—"just in case"—were intact. I guessed I must have put it there after all, accidentally, what with everything going on. I gave him twenty-mille lire, worth approximately twenty dollars, and he placed his lips against mine for a full minute.

Since yesterday, he'd carried over his shoulder a coarse, brown leather handbag, flowers engraved on its front flap. It was hippie-ish and didn't suit him, obviously a woman's bag. He pulled it over his neck and presented it to me. *"Pour toi,"* he said, and then, "I love you." He sounded silly speaking English. I thanked him and took the bag, slung it over my own shoulder.

I followed him to another plaza, this one tiny, fifteen minutes away. There, with the money I'd given him, he bought us icy beers and crusts from the pizzeria shop, the dough fresh from the oven, drizzled with olive oil and sprinkled with salt and pepper and oregano, although he barely ate his.

Campo dei Fiori was different from the other squares I'd been to over the last couple days. The sun barely made it through the buildings. There were no peddlers or performers, no landmarks but for an imposing obelisk in the center, the base of which people sat upon. They were not "the beautiful people," nor were they tourists. Their hair was stringy, their teeth imperfect, their faces drawn and blotchy. It was clear that they too were *mal*. Luca seemed to know everybody. I stood at his side as he exchanged greetings, every single one of them furiously smoking, speaking Italian rapidly. I didn't understand a word, felt very lost, despite Luca's hand in mine. I noticed a tattoo that most of them had, a delicate blue cross: some had it on their forehead, conspicuously between their eyebrows; others, like Luca, had it on the back of their hand, on the middle knuckle. That was when I realized he'd lie to me, that he *was* a junkie, and so was every person there, even the girl, younger even than me, pushing her baby in a carriage.

Mostly, I felt bad for Luca. It wasn't his fault that he'd lied. He probably didn't even know what he was saying, given the state he was in. And the waiting wasn't helping. We'd been there for at least two hours, but their connection hadn't come, and I had to leave, if I was going to get back to the Merucrino's, like I'd told Mamma Mercurino I would do. I wished I could take care of him, wished I could spend the night with him, wished I could at least call him on the phone, but I couldn't.

At my bus stop, he grabbed me tight, smushing my face against his chest. He thanked me a million times, then reminded me about the tree, about meeting at one tomorrow, as if I could have forgotten. Even after this whole strange day, I still couldn't wait until then, to be with him again, in the woods, in the piazzas, even doing nothing. Tomorrow, I was sure, he would feel better. After I boarded the bus, I could see him squinting through the window. When he found me, he gave me the hugest, happiest wave. Everyone knew that nothing was ever perfect in love. Everything was going to be okay.

How long do you wait, I wondered, as the minutes move away; how long is long enough, before you just get up and go? Thirty minutes is probably the limit, I decided, before you become a pure fool. Nonetheless, the following day, I waited for Luca beneath the tree for over an hour, in fact, for one hour and ten minutes, including my excited early arrival. And even when I finally rose to walk away, I continued to turn my head round, walking virtually backward, so as to check just one more time, to make absolutely certain that at any minute he would not be flying, filled with apologies, across the intersection to the tree. Even as it receded, I strained to focus on that tiny spot, but all I saw was an empty patch, people rushing before and around me, locked in their own days. I got as far as five blocks before I thought to go back for a fresh look . . . because maybe I'd left too soon? Still, he wasn't there. Then I was sure I'd missed him, idiot that I was, in the time since I'd walked away. Damn, it was all my fault. I should have stayed. Now he was gone, and I might never find him again.

Methodically, I went to each of our spots. This took hours, of walking, of buses and subways. I don't know how I managed to find each, I'd been in such a daze previously, but I did. I was on a mission. I went to Piazza Navona, where I walked a tight-rope line twice around the entire huge, rectangular square. I went to Campo dei Fiori, but it was deserted of yesterday's group, now just pigeons and the smells from the pizzeria filling the air around the statue. I went last to the back of Piazza Venezia, where I discovered his sleeping bag rolled tight, wedged into the bushes. Had he even slept there last night? I ripped out a back page from my journal and wrote him a note, bidding him *adieu*—I really wrote that, and added, ". . . parting is such sweet sorrow"—and invited him to visit in New York. I signed it with my address and phone number.

It was so hot, my feet moving like tombstones one ahead of the next. Nauseated, I returned and sat down beneath the tree, where, two days in a row, he *had* met me. Why not today? What had I done wrong? Had I not given him enough money? Had I given him *too* much? Had he had an overdose? Or had he—I could barely even think it—just been using me?

I would never know.

I sat there until it was time to catch the bus that would bring me back to the Mercurinos and the dinner table, where I sat rigidly, smiling like a horror-flick dollie, while the entire family gabbed joyously in a language I could not understand. Though a huge meal had been prepared, I couldn't eat; I could only drink wine from a two-liter-sized unmarked bottle, red so dry my tongue and mouth puckered. I didn't even like wine. At ten, when everyone went to bed, I remained at the table finishing off the bottle, my heart poking in me like a swallowed chicken bone. I wrote in my journal, plotting my future. I would leave tomorrow, I had to, the same urgent way I'd had to leave New York for this summer vacation to begin with. A severe headache started growing, less from the wine than from the revelation of how very lonely I'd been on this trip.

It was a relief to say it. I'd been lonely! I'd been sad, confused! I'd been so tired, running from one episode to the next, as if it might obliterate . . . what? I didn't know exactly, but I was suddenly very glad to be going home, to take that pressure off of myself. I knew I'd learned something. I might still be alone, but, now that I'd traveled by myself in Europe, now that I'd had conversations with strangers and had conducted an entire love affair in French, now that I'd had the dramatic and heartbreaking experience of waiting beneath a tree in sheer stupidity for a junkie who would never show, things would never be the same. They had to get better.

And the rest of the trip?

I wasn't worried about it, how to spend the time. I'd go somewhere, sure, it didn't even matter where, it could be any number of cities where I'd had a time: London, Brugges, Paris, Amsterdam, Copenhagen, Stockholm; or it could be someplace new, Venice, perhaps, where I might hook up with a band of international youth who would play guitar and sing and dance, who would picnic on the Lido at midnight, and share sleeping bags on the train station's mildewed cobblestone; where I'd meet more people, drink more *aranciatas*, and laugh and flirt and kiss a few good men; where maybe I'd even find the *true* one this time. I still had twelve days left.

Lisa Solod

A MONTH IN THE COUNTRY

We lay in the Auberge La Treille, three hours outside of Paris, sweating in a bed barely off the floor, the window above us too high to afford any breeze—if there was any to be afforded—and listened to the trucks, the motorcycles, and the little, rattly, noisy cars stop at the corner, gun their engines, and take off.

Outside the window, people talked as loudly as if they were sitting on the foot of our bed, throaty sounds and unfamiliar words that were like the constant irritating drip of a faucet. My son Andrew tossed and turned in his portacrib; in the still bright evening light, although it was nearly ten o'clock, I could see a large wet sweat stain beneath his head.

In our hot and swollen bellies lay the remnants of a terrible and too expensive dinner; the wine had been cold and good so Robert and I had drunk too much of it. Andrew had eaten nothing; he had pushed at his cold hamburger (made especially by the kitchen at what exorbitant cost we would know when we paid the bill in the morning) and told us quite specifically that he wanted to go home. We tried valiantly to explain just how very far away home was.

A day earlier, we had arrived at Charles DeGaulle Airport, and, to save a day's fee on the rent-a-car, we had taken the bus into the city, then caught a metro, dragging too much luggage—crib, stroller, suitcases, diaper bag—down the thousand steps underground. It had been a long trip. None of us had slept much, and, overcome by travel, I had had a moment's hallucinatory terror when, in the desecrated bowels of the subway, I saw large groups of people huddled around the television sets that were everywhere attached to squat concrete pylons. The viewers seemed preternaturally intent on what was on screen and all I could think was: What horrific disaster had happened now? Plane crash, assassination, invasion? But the monitors had been turned instead to good news, nearly forgotten. The long-ago triumph of the moonshot and landing flashed over and over and over as the television sets followed Armstrong's historic steps. An anniversary celebration of some sort. And so the hordes of travelers, native and tourist, who gathered around the small tubes, viewed—with what seemed like genuine pleasure and interest—my country's last moment of unadulterated greatness.

I watched the rest of the crowd, my son Andrew sunk into my hip, and leaned against my husband Robert in exhaustion, confusion, relief. After a moment of dead and total silence, Robert turned to me and said, "Do you know where I was when this happened?"

I shook my head, too exhausted to think, watching nervously for the train and trying at the same time to shift Andrew's weight. Then I said, "It was 1969, right?"

"Right," Robert said. "Right. I was in Kyoto. I had gone up the mountain with my Zen friend, you remember. I told you about him."

"No," I said.

"Well, I did," Robert said. "You just don't remember. . . . Anyway, we came down the mountain and no one else was on the streets. It was eerie. And I thought: What the fuck is happening? What's going on? Well, it turned out the streets were empty because everyone was inside watching TV." Robert paused and fixed his gaze on the fuzzy black and white astronauts. He pulled his tobacco out of his back pocket and rolled a cigarette. "We watched, too." He shrugged.

"When was that again?" I asked. Confusion suddenly took over completely. I couldn't get the memory straight at all. "When?" I said. "*How* long ago?" Andrew wiggled in my nervous arms.

"Hey, what's the matter?" Robert gave a short laugh. "Are you feeling old, or something?" He laughed again, more ruefully, then leaned to kiss me. I pulled away. I wanted the answer to my question first. "*When*, when was it?" I asked him.

"It was a little more than twenty years ago," he said. "Honey, you know. Sixty-nine."

"Oh, God," I said. "I thought it was thirty. For a moment I thought it was thirty years." The panic that had washed over me subsided a little, but only a little. For a moment I didn't believe him—it certainly seemed like much longer than twenty years. I leaned into Robert and he held me.

"It's okay," I said. "Jet lag, maybe."

"Maybe," Robert said, as the subway pulled loudly to a stop. "Maybe." He looked at me funny, hoisted Andrew up onto the train, sat him down, and loaded the luggage. I had to be dragged from the screen. I had suddenly become interested.

Now, lying on top of the covers, I thought about how Robert had first proposed this trip as a way of showing me the real him, a way of letting me in, of making our marriage work—a marriage already too many years old for any traditional form of resuscitation. Robert proposed a trip to his homeland, his country of birth, to which he had not returned since before we met nine years ago. He had dragged me here in some final attempt to try to make me understand him, and the first thing I had seen was disaster.

But if I knew why he was here and why he wanted me here, I was going along with him for reasons far less known. I felt as though I had already lost hope, even with this new drastic attempt. All I could really think about was what I might do so that he would understand me. What *could* I do? I had nowhere special to take him.

"Is it possible to die of heat and noise?" I asked as I took the worn sheet and tried to wipe some of the wetness from my body. *I have got to sleep*, I thought. *I have got to or I will die*. In response, Robert lay his hand on my belly. It felt like some strange and crawly animal. I pulled away. "No," I said. "I can't, it's too hot. I'm too exhausted."

"So, it's bad," he said with the accent that still haunted his English, especially in moments of exhaustion. "It's bad, I know. I'm sorry. It'll be over tomorrow. We'll get on the road; it'll cool off."

"If I make it."

"You've survived this far," he laughed. "I feel sure I'll see you in the morning."

I looked at his tired face in the light from the window and he looked all of his forty-five years, even more. He was, after all, ten years older than I, and I suddenly had a premonition he would die here, in France. He would leave me in a foreign country with a baby, his body to get home, and no way to communicate with anyone. I imagined him dying quietly in his sleep beside me, or stepping out onto the street too fast and being run down by a little Mini racing to Blois. I had had the same vision, I realized, as he leaned over the metro tracks to look for the train: I saw him falling, falling, and then the subway, bells ringing, sliding over his body.

Over the past few months I had imagined Robert knocked on the head by an I-beam in a freak street construction accident; victim of a hit-and-run while out walking the dog; slumped over at his desk at the university, unconscious from a heart attack and no office hours that day. Every time I looked at him I saw death. Part of that omen was rooted in reality. For at least three years I had been urging him to get a physical. He smoked too much, ate as he liked, got little exercise. Like all the French born in the forties and fifties, his teeth were rotting in his mouth. He was soft and often tired. (Although I realized, gratefully, he had carried our mounds of luggage with ease down and up stairs that would have killed me.) But when I brought up his health, Robert told me that the French had no fear of death. Because they embraced life with huge passion, fervor, gusto, drank it up, and enjoyed all its bits and pieces, death was just the expected end: nothing to fear, merely the price to pay for a life lived well. He reminded me that *his* countrymen were not obsessed, as were we Americans, with cheating death; his country's magazines and newspapers were not full of life-prolonging recipes, tips on how to stay forever young. He reminded me, too, that he liked women with a few miles on them, and that I should give him the same due. Aging in his country was expected, not dreaded nor feared. He so completely ignored my pleas, my fears, that they had taken on a life of their own. My fears threatened me, now. It was likely that Robert's resistance to death meant that I, as preoccupied with it as I was, would be the one to die first. There I would be, struggling against my fate, whispering to Robert on my death bed, with my last futile breath, "Raise Andrew right."

Yet part of these death visions I kept seeing were, I knew, a comment on the state of our relationship—a kind of wish-fulfillment, a need for some larger force to take the decision out of my hands. I lay my hand gently on my husband's still warm, still alive, leg and said good night. He turned and slept an old man's sleep while I lay awake, watching the baby's troubled breathing, the sweat shiny on his round white forehead, visions of mortality crowding the room.

In the morning we packed the car and got on the road to Blois. I strapped Andrew into the back seat, set his toys out beside him, and climbed in, too, while Robert acted as chauffeur. The day was warm, the windows were down, and occasionally I would hear my husband take a breath, deep into himself, as if he were breathing in something absolutely life-sustaining. We were on our way to the coast, to Brittany, to meet some friends of Robert's who had rented a summer house near the water. Robert had lived with the husband, Lawrence, years ago when they were young and in school. He was the oldest friend my husband had, and despite their irregular correspondence and the long time between visits, his best. Lawrence had married Fiona, a British woman, a few years after I had married Robert, and they had a young daughter named Elizabeth, nearly the same age as Andrew. Fiona was pregnant again. I had never met them. We were to spend a month in the country with Fiona, Lawrence, and Elizabeth.

I liked the sound of that. A month in the country. Perhaps I could be like Oblomov and take days to get out of bed; perhaps I could languish, as I hadn't done since Andrew was born two years ago; perhaps I could rest and think and get restored. Perhaps I would even be able to decide how my life would be for the next thirty years. Could I lie on the beach and listen to the pounding surf? Watch Robert and Andrew walk and walk and walk until they were mere specks on the horizon, then anticipate their return—Andrew's hands full of shells and sand, Robert tan and happy and calm? Perhaps the four of us would cook large communal dinners—paella, ratatouille, roasted chickens—the children bouncing around our feet, fighting and playing and yelling. Perhaps after the children went to bed we would sit around a table and talk about politics and art and raising babies and I would learn new things and become once again inspired. Maybe I could even see what Robert had brought me these thousands of miles to see. Maybe he could figure out what it was he was looking for and could point it out to me.

What was wrong with Robert and me was nothing evil or unthinkable. There was nothing terribly wrong at all. That was part of the problem. The rest was that lately what was *right* seemed purely accidental. When things were going well, we would often look at each other as if to say: isn't this fun, why do you think that is? But we could never plan for one of those golden moments. We could never be sure one would happen again. Neither of us wanted the weight of this trip to be as large as it was—even when Robert had proposed it, he had been almost casual—but somehow it had taken on a life of its own. Maybe our only final and real hope was not that we could fix what was wrong but that we could learn to accept what was right.

"It's beautiful," I said, looking out the window at the nearly deserted ribbon of road, the too lush greenery, the impossibly tended gardens. Robert had conjured up these images for me for years, convincing me that the reality could in no way meet his description. But it did and I told him so. "You were right."

Robert smiled, tenderly, I thought, as I caught that smile in the rear-view mirror. Then, slightly overwhelmed and trying not to spoil it, I leaned my head back to sleep. For a while I was lulled by the wildly curving road, but sleep wouldn't ultimately come, and so I watched the road from my half-lidded eyes. Andrew was sleeping beside me, breathing quietly, contentedly, his head lolling against the seat belt. I disentangled him from the belt and lay his hot head on my lap. I stroked his sweaty hair and watched the tiny farms slipping by, and another hour passed.

Suddenly, in less than a moment, out from a forest in the distance I saw twin concrete towers mar the pastoral landscape like some deadly mirage. Although I was sure of what I was seeing, still I had to ask, "What is that?"

Robert only shrugged. "It's a nuclear power plant. We have a lot of them. Didn't you know that?" He stared at the concrete towers for a moment himself. Then he admitted, "It does look shocking. It does, when you come up on it like that, so suddenly. But I guess we have learned to live with them. They're there; there is nothing else we can do."

I watched the towers get bigger and bigger, saw them dwarf a small and beautiful stone house and the large vegetable and flower garden that seemed to sit almost literally at their base. "It must be awful to have to live that way, right beside death, so large and looming. I always thought people lived farther away from those things. How do you think they do it? How can those people tend their vegetables, their flowers, and see those horrible towers hovering over them every day?"

"I will never understand why you have such a problem with death," Robert sighed. "It's all around us, after all. You know that. How can you be so naive as to think it isn't always around us?"

What could I say to him that wouldn't reveal too much? I couldn't tell him that I dreamed of his own death almost daily. But I could tell him that I had known full well and first hand about death since Andrew was born, that once a woman pushed new life from her womb, she could no longer be naive about life or death. Because death *is* always around is precisely why I fear it.

During the last few months of my pregnancy, I had huge horrible nightmares, full of monsters and ogres and ghouls. I would wake shaking, nearly wetting the bed, the child who would be Andrew pressing on my bladder, yet what I really felt was some evil force sitting on my chest, sucking away my breath. The monsters had been so relentless that I finally had to take sleeping pills in order to get through the night. The nightmares left with Andrew's birth. Now I only dreamt about death during the day. Now I only thought about one particular death—Robert's.

But Robert found reassurance in death. Where had he learned that: up on that mountain with his Zen master? Is that where he had found what made him so calm, so controlled, so aloof? Well, what he had learned drove me mad with its peace. His acceptance of death was infuriating. All the more because he could seemingly accept the finality of the end of life, but he could not let go of our marriage. Each time our relationship seemed in its final death throes, he was the one who would go to it and, mouth-to-mouth, breathe life back into it. Then our marriage would stand up, shake off its black death shroud, throw down the scythe, and go on for a few more weeks, a few more months. Robert, who thought death was natural, was the one who kept wanting to save us.

"You're a day late," Lawrence said by way of a greeting, scolding. But then he threw himself at Robert and they embraced and kissed. It was wonderful. I had never seen Robert kiss another man before. I liked it. I liked the passion I saw on his face.

Watching, I stumbled with Andrew in my arms and Fiona reached to help me; already she was large and showing, and when she put her arms around me I could feel the child inside her. "Robert wanted to show me some castles," I said. "We took the long way."

"Ah, the castles," Lawrence said with a huge grin, "the symbol of France's ruined aristocratic past. Now we pay large numbers of francs to see places where once we would have been the servants, admitted for free, and kept until we dropped. Those wonderful cold and damp dark places where Kings walked." He turned to me. "How were they?"

"Beautiful," I said. "Beautiful and sad."

"Exactly!"

Lawrence took me from Fiona's arms and embraced me, kissed me, too, quickly on both cheeks, but I felt his heat. The passion around me was contagious. As he held me in his arms, it seemed that a month here would not be long enough. Here, it was clear, were people actively cheating death. Robert was an amateur compared to them. Could I learn their secret? In just a month?

"Allison," Lawrence said, "it is wonderful to finally see you."

I looked around for Robert, anxious to see if he noticed, as I did, what Lawrence and Fiona really offered, if the transfusion of their happiness was what we had come for. But Robert had disappeared onto the terrace; he stood under a small tree, cupped his hand, and lit one of his hand-rolled cigarettes.

He seemed for a moment like someone I had known long ago, an old friend I was coming upon again after a long absence. He seemed purely and utterly at home. I knew I was the visitor on his turf. As I watched him, Robert noticed, suddenly and delightedly, the lunch laid out on the terrace table—cold vegetable pie, a dish of fresh cherries, a bottle of chilled Saumer-Champigny. He whooped with joy. And then he laughed, made a show of pointing to the wine, said "You remembered!" and immediately opened it. He poured four glasses, called us outside and handed them to us. He laughed again, waved a cigarette and glass, and drank a large gulp before he toasted. "To us," he said. "To friendship and a month in the country."

We spent sunny mornings on the beach, driving the half hour from Malansac to Damagan with the car loaded—towels, coolers of juice and water and fruit and cold pasta, pails and shovels and sand sifters, blankets and chairs, books, and a radio. We set up camp near the water, and Robert took Andrew into the cold wet ocean until they both emerged, lips blue and trembling. In the afternoons we drove more slowly back home, put the children to bed and often took naps ourselves, or shopped for dinner, or walked around the tiny village. Then supper preparations would take the rest of the afternoon, the dinners just as I had imagined, huge and filling and satisfying, sauces whipped up with baguettes, bottles and bottles of wine uncorked and emptied. The children would drop, exhausted after their baths, and we would put them to bed again, fighting sleep ourselves.

For all the time it seemed we had, Robert and I had too little of it to talk at any length and so the fighting stopped; and, odd or not, the lack of privacy in the tiny stone house protected rather than oppressed us. At night, after the day was done and the next one mapped out, we would slip between the soft cool sheets in our tiny bedroom and he would reach for me and I would respond and we made love more than we had for years. I had nothing to think about while we made love; no life existed outside the tiny, full house. Robert's hand fell on me in what seemed like new places. I grew used to the long days and making love at night in the pale lightness of our sloped-ceiling room seemed natural. Night fell only after we were asleep. The heat now embraced me.

One night after we had made love, I watched him roll a cigarette in the light of a still bright sky.

"Me, too," I said, and we smoked companionably, intent on the simplest of acts, as we had been when we first met. I wanted to ask what had gone so wrong to bring us to this place. But what I talked about instead was Lawrence.

"He's interesting, your friend," I said. "He's quite mad, really, it seems. And then again, scarily sane." What I meant to say was what I had noticed the moment I walked into the house: Lawrence makes you happy like I have never seen. What is it? What can I do to imitate that?

Robert said, "He is the most interesting man I have ever met." Then he laughed. "He's very special. He wants to know everything and remembers it all. But more than that he wants to know everything about *you*. He can draw from you things you don't want to tell." He paused for a second and thought. "He's done that with me, a lot. He's gotten me to reveal myself completely. He's told me what I needed to know to make a hard decision." He drew in smoke from the disappearing cigarette, and added quietly, "You might have noticed that he does this while revealing almost nothing of himself."

I had, but it had not disconcerted me. I felt like I knew as much about Lawrence as I needed to, for now. I was happy enough just to sit and listen to him talk about things other than himself. I had no desire to ask him questions that would force him to reveal what I was not interested in. And although Lawrence, more than once, overstepped the boundaries of my most private self, I did not hold it against him. I could see what he was doing and steered our conversation other ways. I had had enough of introspection, of self-searching, of recrimination, of examination, in the last few years. I was on holiday.

I also knew that, were I the person I had been even ten years ago, I would have mistaken my affection and Lawrence's interest for a mutual sexual passion, or perhaps even true love. We might well have fallen into bed together. But the relationship—such as it could ever have been—would have lasted exactly fifteen minutes in real time and about fifteen years in memory. It would have changed my life, although I wouldn't have known it at the time. It would have been another of those relationships that, in retrospect, always looked like salvation, and were hauled out and set up as examples when the current one wasn't working.

"That's okay," I said to Robert. "I don't mind Lawrence's not revealing himself."

"Okay for him, but not for me?" he asked.

"What do you mean?"

"You allow him his privacy, you encourage it."

"And?"

"What about mine?"

"You're my husband," I said. "I'm supposed to know things about you. I'm supposed to ask. I *should* know things others don't. But I don't.

After all these years you still hide from me. You may not think I allow you your privacy but you take it anyway. You only tell me what it doesn't hurt you to reveal." I took a deep breath. Here I go, I thought. "Why are you so intent on saving us?" I asked, before I could decide not to. "I don't even know, sometimes, if you love me."

Quietly, with a hand on my leg to soften his cruelty, Robert said, "I don't know that sometimes, either."

After eight years I had no tears left, but still I felt the blow. And yet if I couldn't cry I couldn't get angry either, for didn't I feel the same way? Didn't I wonder, too, what it was I felt? And how long any of it would last?

"You brought me here to show me something," I said, trying to fight the despair that was creeping in. "What was it?"

"I'm not sure," he said. "I thought it was Lawrence, someone who knew me before you did. Someone who has loved me a very long time."

"But it's not?"

"I don't know. It just seemed important for us to make this trip. I thought we could find some small thing we had missed, something that might help. I don't understand why you're so ready to let it go."

"I'm not so ready," I said. "I've done my share of fighting, too, fighting for it, against what made it bad—when I could figure out what that was. Now there's Andrew to think about. . . ."

"I know," Robert interrupted quietly. He smoked for a few moments and then smiled at me. "It's been good here, hasn't it?"

"Yes, it has," I agreed. But I could not let it go. "Yes, it's been good, but is it sustainable?"

"Is it ever?"

Silent for a long while, we sat up in bed. Then Robert turned to sleep. And as the night finally darkened, and I was still awake, I thought: all right, I'll try. It had to be possible, here at least, to try.

Two weeks passed. In the mornings we were on the beach; in the afternoons, Fiona and I would walk to the markets with baskets and bags and spend time searching for fruits, breads, vegetables, spices. I'd wash the clothes in the tiny washer and she would gather them in her strong arms and hang them in the sun. Robert and Lawrence watched the children for hours; sitting on the rattan porch furniture, the men rolled cigarettes, had loud discussions in French, read the day's papers, mended toys, talked to Elizabeth and Andrew seriously about how to play well together, about how to share, about not hitting and banging and screaming. Andrew and Elizabeth basked in their daddies' attentions and were calm for minutes at a time; they would splash in the outdoor fountain, naked, delighted with their freedom. They were always filthy and muddy and happy.

We settled into a rhythm. Sometimes during an afternoon Robert would even come up to me and put his arms around me or place a hand on my breast. For no reason. Once, while we were making love, he told me he loved me. I couldn't answer. But it was nice, I thought later, as I lay on his chest, nice that he said it at all.

One night, late after dinner, as we sipped Calvados and I watched Robert and Lawrence debate the merits of France's social welfare system, I realized once again that in all the time I had known my husband, I had never seen him talk to anyone but me like that. In all our years in Boston he had never made a good male friend; the people with whom we spent our time were friends I had made, or acquaintances from his university. Dinner party discussions were interesting but somehow unlively, and he had no one with whom to spend a quiet, private moment away from me. Once a week I would see a friend, alone, for dinner or a movie, but Robert never went out without me. Letters from Lawrence would arrive sporadically, and once in awhile the two men would call. That always made Robert happy for a few days, but then he would sink into himself again, and I would plan the social calendar, checking with him only out of sense of wifely loyalty: he had little on his slate that I didn't know about.

There had been so many times I couldn't imagine why I had married Robert, except that I had loved him once, I remembered that, and I liked him still, enormously, most of the time, even if I had no idea how to please him, and less idea how to tell him what pleased me. But suddenly here in the country there were moments when I could imagine myself with no one else. Only moments, slight and fleeting, but I wanted to hold on to them, impossible as it seemed. And our time in the country was running out.

Close to the end of the month, as Robert was helping Fiona clean up in the kitchen, I leaned over to Lawrence and said to him, "You're very lucky, you know."

"You mean Fiona," he said. Lawrence was just mad enough to know what you meant without your having to tell him. His voice was always loud and energetic; he moved with an intensity that could have been frightening had it not been softened by his too-thin body, an ethereal white skin, short dark spiky hair, and pale green eyes that made him look somehow as if he were from another planet. He wasn't beautiful but you always thought he was. I nodded. Yes. Fiona.

Lawrence leaned back in his chair, tipping it to the wall, and blew smoke into the night air. "Did Robert ever tell you about Francoise?"

"Only that he was in love with her," I said, trying to be flip; it came out mean-spirited instead. Lawrence laughed.

"Don't worry about her," he said. "We all loved her. She was the most beautiful woman any of us had ever seen. I expect she still is." His words came across soft and easy, tinted with the British accent he had picked up from Fiona. "After she and Robert broke up she came to me to see if I could give her what he had been unable to. I lived with her for a while, too. But she left me, like she had Robert, still looking for something else. Who knows what? A stronger man, perhaps, someone more stable, someone who could provide her with a life other than the one she had."

I was bewildered. "But look at you," I said. "And Robert. Both married, with families. Stable as can be. I don't understand."

"Yes," Lawrence nodded. "We have done that *now*. By chance or design, who knows? But we could not do it then. And we could not *promise* to do it ever. These things have just happened to us when it was time. I never promised Fiona this life, stability, children, anything. Nor did she ask me to. That is why I am lucky, you know." He smoked for a few moments. "Think, Allison, what has Robert promised you?"

"I don't know," I said. "Nothing, really. Everything *has* just happened. It just happened, I guess."

"Yes," Lawrence said softly, looking straight at me. "I suppose it has."

I knew then that Lawrence knew all about the trouble Robert and I had had, that Robert had written to him or talked to him about the difficult years, how unsure we both were, how painful it seemed to be together lately. He knew, too, even before I told him, that I envied his strong marriage, the way he and Fiona seemed to melt into each other with no effort and yet remain apart. How she could scold him without his turning on her, how he could tease her and she would just smile at him? Lawrence was just perverse enough to let me envy them and their outwardly perfect marriage, too; he would reveal nothing of his true nature, all the while knowing the truth about Robert and me.

Lawrence was happy just to let me bask in my vision of Fiona and him and the solid marriage that radiated its energy around them. He would give up nothing of whatever truths lay underneath. But I knew now, after so much time with them, that if it really was true that Lawrence and Fiona cheated death, as I had thought when I first met them, it was due only to Fiona; she pulled her husband out of the abyss and hoisted him up beside her. She was the strong one. Lawrence may not have made any promises to her, but she had clearly made them to him.

And I suddenly knew that I was wrong about Robert not promising me anything. Lawrence was wrong about his friend, too. If anything, Lawrence and I were the ones alike, the kindred souls, the difficult partners in our marriages, the ones who gave too little, asked for too much, elicited no promises we could not handle, and promised nothing much back. We were the ones always ready to hurl ourselves over the edge. Our crucial difference was that he was willing to let someone he loved talk him out of death and I had not yet given up that much control over my own fate.

I was well aware, too, that one day it was possible Lawrence and I might even touch with grace, passion, and tenderness, if given just half a chance. He might even, were he feeling truly brave, let me think he had made the first move. He might even really make it. It would not be unexpected. Lawrence and I were clearly the weak partners, the ones constantly falling, causing those who loved us most to hurry back and help us up. We could talk and talk, but Fiona and Robert were the people of action. And someday they might find Lawrence and me just too difficult to endure.

In the kitchen window I could see Robert and Fiona sharing the dishwashing; he had his hands in the soapy water and she leaned up against the counter, her hands clutching a soggy dishtowel to her ever-increasing belly. I watched them and wondered if I could finish out the month's vacation and go back to America and remember all that I had learned. Could I think objectively about mismatched love without it hurting? Could I imagine how it would feel to be with another man, what I would do if Robert left me, and if I could ever finally leave him, without sinking into the despair of it? I suppose I could. I suppose I could wonder and wonder until I exploded with confusion, missed connections, decisions put off. I could think and wonder until I finally self-destructed.

Lawrence's knowledge of my inner life embarrassed me but also made me feel strong and wise. His pain was yet to come. I had lived with mine so long I hardly noticed it. But wasn't it possible, probable perhaps, that even Fiona would tire one day of trying to talk her husband away from the edge? And wouldn't there come the inevitable day when he would lie next to his wife and really wish to be elsewhere? Wouldn't they, one day, have to make a journey of their own, their own salvage trip? Was it possible that even they might some day self-destruct from all the wondering? And wouldn't we all then just have to put their pieces back together, too?

Shouldn't Robert and I then, before things completely broke apart, before the shattering was too awesome, set the glue, today, when our rough edges could still be mended with only a few ragged seams showing? Wasn't that so much easier than trying to gather up a thousand tiny shards that had hurled themselves into love's universe?

Lawrence and I watched together as Robert tossed soapsuds at Fiona and the two of them began to laugh. I could feel Lawrence close to me, I could almost feel his hand on the back of my neck, I could imagine him that clearly. But I knew, even as I felt the scorch of that imaginary touch, that there was no real possibility that I could siphon life from him. He had no extra to give. I was going to have to siphon it from Robert, swallow my pride, and take what he was offering me.

Suddenly, Fiona began to sing with the music that wafted out the kitchen window, and she and her huge and wonderful belly danced clumsily around the room. After a moment Robert dried his hands on the damp towel and took Fiona's hand, twirling her in her dance. It was just at that moment that I suggested to Lawrence that we go in and join them.

Nor Hall

APHRODITE IN AVIGNON

Every other summer the Roy Hart Theatre's off-shoot, Pantheatre, hosts a Myth and Theatre conference in Southern France for actors, dancers, and archetypal psychologists. The last one was on Dionysus, this one on Aphrodite. Some of us give papers (James Hillman, Ginette Paris, Charles Boer, *et moi*) while others perform (Enrique Pardo, Linda Wise, Dominique Dupuy, Venice Manley, Liza Mayer, Pascale Ben, etc.). We spend two weeks in Villeneuve Les Avignon with fifty or so participants from Europe and the Americas talking, moving, doing voice work, attending performances, eating, drinking, and watching the stars.

This is the first place I have ever given a lecture in a dress with an open neckline. The women are different here: they are round where we are angular, soft and seamless where we are hard, squared, and pressed. Their tops and skirts roll over, flow and tie with a kind of allowance for the body's fluidity. Like Sonja, made of melons. Even the thinnest women assign themselves to Aphrodite's care, enchancing their curves with clothing, exposing shoulders and delineating hips with draping fabric—drawn by a hand that prefers the cursive *p's* and *q's,* with its long loops and opulent rounds. Their ease somehow relieves me of having to cover up the blush of anxiety that inevitably blossoms under public scrutiny.

Lauren and I are lying on our backs halfway up the hill of Fort St. André. Occasional headlights of other midnight starwatchers play across our prone bodies. It is August 1993, night of the shooting stars, and we are counting. When a car passes we hold up our hands to show eight fingers.

"Combien avez-vous vu?" I can understand French spoken in the dark at 1:00 A.M. when I am exhausted and happy on a starlit hill. "How many have you seen?" Pebbles, brittle weeds, and ancient crustacean casings poke into our skin through thin towels. Lauren says we are resting on a mountain of shells (a comment our Venusian patroness would like). When we reluctantly head back down the hill, the boys who had been circling us with curiosity in the dark, call out: "Mama?" "Cherie?" Their interest in trying to figure out who we are makes Lauren's step even lighter.

Somewhere deep inside the Fort there is a second-floor room of ancient stone painted red. I could probably find it in the blackness if it were lit by torches again. The Italian theatre company, directed by an avant-garde brother-sister pair, has left these signature red rooms in their hit-and-run wake around Europe. Coming upon it unawares would have felt even more disturbing. Was this done by descendents of a cult at Catal Huyuk? from Pompeii? A tribe of wandering moon sisters? (It's a mystery why the French Ministry of Culture gave permission for painting these twelfth century ruins red, especially when this troupe is considered somewhat ideologically dangerous and has to be back in Italy within forty-eight hours.) They made us sit on primitive benches behind a wire-mesh fence that separated us from the two chained mastiffs, huge as horses, and three clay-daubed actors bathed in the spectral light of a convincing Underworld. There was supposed to be a huge snake dripping from the ceiling that night, but she was indisposed due to traveling in the close heat of the Societas Raffaello Sanzio Company mini-van, non-stop from Cesana to Avignon. When the dog pissed on stage (shortly after the other one had been humping the character Gilgamesh), my translator got up and pressed her way past the tight line of knees to get out. Then, when the event was signaled *fini* by the slow turning of a mirror toward us, we rose to exit and found our silent way, processing out the same way we'd come in. In the black archway of Fort St. André, framing a beautiful moonlit scene of the Papal palace below, we saw the furious orange-red dots of the translator and several others who had left in disgust. People gathered in dark clumps to exhale their astonishment.

Pascale told me the next evening's performance was more tender. The recuperated python was in it—climbing a rope to the rafters, and the dogs merely trailed each other. Charles, who went both nights, has been teaching mythology for twenty-six years and says it's the first time he has seen the Underworld.

✧ ✧ ✧

A fine mosaic of Provencal crumbs decorates the patio stones. Remnants of last night's bread, goat cheese, black olives, red tomatoes. I am sitting with my manuscript in the sun before the girls wake up and open their yellow shutters. Roger is in town for his morning instructional with Mme. Jacqueline. Our apartment is a renovated cell in a Carthusian abbey situated directly on the St. Jean cloister below the Fort. (Joan of Arc was here.) I wanted to be a monk once. I studied the Rules of various orders and designed imaginary communes and now, here, the French government has accomplished it for me, transforming spare cells into private flats for visiting artists. Behind every ancient door is a surprise—wine bottle size pass-throughs at waist height, confessionals, an original privy (not to be used), niches for icons no longer there. The thick-walled rooms are constructed for airy openness and complete privacy. Opening all the upstairs casement windows gives access only to an expanse of blue and a solitary bee. In my courtyard garden I am protected by a high stone wall. One of the brothers could leave breakfast in the cubicle while I illuminate my manuscript in this sunny scriptorium. Paradise for an introvert. Sightlines are blocked, but sounds travel freely. Quietly ecstatic, I am "rimed-round with sound"(R. Duncan). Voice work is going on in various studios hidden in turrets and naves, singular warm-ups rather than any kind of chorus. A low-pitched siren repeats its rise to a sharp stop, over and over. Someone else practices a chirp at the back of the nasal cavity, over and over, vying with cicadas. Sounds float through the doors of the Chapel of the Martyred Deacons, down the cloistered walkways—strange and wonderful extensions of the human voice. A magical, crystalline quality in the air transports me. I am running past the practice shacks at Chautauqua on an early August morning. I am on the beach in northern Bali at sunrise when the Buddhist's slow groaning chant rose up from behind the green wall. My heart leaps like the baby dolphin in the background of that memory. It is like a tiny black comma connecting that shoreline to this one in the lecture spread out on the table before me, where I labor over the scene of Love's birth on the pink sands of Cyprus.

When the girls are up, we take a sheet off each of their beds and gather a bunch of dried silk roses. Deirdre's hair is long and loose. She looks the part of the classical nymph. Whether or not she wants it yet, she comes by this role today by virtue of being my daughter. We are going to Aphrodite's garden studio set up by Diana, the photographer, who has issued the invitation: Come have your aphroditic fantasy photographed. I knew instantly what mine was. It was not going to be a life-imitating-art adaptation of a Jeff Koons piece with my husband (very briefly considered), but rather a tableau of my desire to found "Sappho's School for Young Girls."

> She will walk
> among us like a mother with
> all her daughters around her
> when she comes home from exile. (frag. 43)

I took only a sheer gold scarf to wear in some immortal fashion in Diana's garden which was groomed perfectly by the ghost of a romantic monk: a stone bench against the rock wall tinged with the natural greens and golds of age, rose bushes arcing down to the ground offering up pink cups with bronze interiors for our use. After hearing my fantasy, which was further warmed by my attraction to her (another goddess in our midst, as if she'd just traded in her archer's bow and hound for this camera belt and bag), she followed us around the garden, taking her orders from the ten o'clock sun. We took a variety of positions with limbs overlapping, heads turned, eyes locked, breasts forward, feet poised, ready for the epiphany of the goddess who comes to those who cultivate the Muse in her honor. "Queen, Cyprian!/Fill our gold cups with love. . . ." (frag. 37)

A week later, in a postcard shop in Paris, I saw her eyes looking out at me from the wall of images. Yes, it said so on the back—it was a portrait of the photographer and her sister in black and white but with eyes that appeared to be as green as the sea. They stood facing the camera in their ivory eloquence, each with one hand on the breast of the other.

The outside of the sanctuary was intact, but as soon as we passed through the massive carved doors into the cavernous interior, it was as if the hand of God had raised the roof to the stratosphere. The roof was gone. We looked straight up into the blue-black sky. The back wall of the chancel was gone too. Instead of an altar there were fallen stones and a lovely, lone tree growing up in the far cloister garden. Dozens of us carried candles and hummed a low reverberating tone, becoming candidates ("dressed in white") of the initiation we pretended. A gigantic shadow belonging to Shakmah, the African priestess from Philadelphia, loomed up to greet us. I wondered where Deirdre was in the line and how she was responding to Shakmah's invocation—asking the deity of Love to appear in this closely guarded sanctuary of the Popes. Innocent VI lay buried to the right. What would be raised (or buried?) in a Catholic girl's heart on a night like this in Southern France. But suddenly the room was shaken, if monumental stones can be so moved, by sound. We were immediately elsewhere. "Shuh-kuh/shuh-kuh/shuh/kuh." The ceremonial priestess moves her royal body down the center aisle in an exquisitely slow shoulder-rolling dance, black fire in her eyes, elbows moving like huge, archaic butterflies stirring up an awesome passion. Her presence is overwhelming. I am holding my breath, feeling a pulse that belongs to Vodun. Zora Neal Hurston's description of the Haitian night ceremonies scrolls through my brain. Fascination roots my feet to the holy stones even as her music moves my torso. She and her attendant are dueling spiritually with erotic energy. The young one is like the biblical Shulamite, singing a heart-stopping *Sanctus Domine* with her hair in endless braids down her white silk chemise, her arms raised to the sky, with her voice following. Shakmah's voice weights the high trill of praise and the chant of "shuh-kuh" crescendoes: "shuh-kuh/shuh-kuh/She-comes!"

Outside, milling about on the cobblestones, eating the luscious peaches of communion, still holding our burnt-down candles, everyone is in love. The tower of Babel's trend reversed. We're all speaking different tongues (Swedish, Italian, Spanish, Dutch, German, English, French, etc.), expressing a similar wonder, and unwilling to leave this radiant company.

Early on a sun-washed morning we wander the main street, stopping in the flower shop. Eva is there before us, considering what flowers she will take to someone as a way of saying good-bye. Her presence is suddenly even more evocative of the golden goddess here, surrounded by the greens and purples and yellow-golds of a Provencal tribute to summer, than it was on the stage of her lecture, surrounded by Aphrodite's projected image. She and Deirdre are deep into conversation about girlhood. About having children and writing biographies in which they imagined their ebullient futures. Laughter of mutual obsession fills the fragrant shop. They embrace. Strands of hair—champagne and chestnut—interlace. Our arms are full of flowers.

✧ ✧ ✧

"Sur le pont, d'Avignon . . ."

Only half of the bridge remains, flung out across the river toward nothing. The boat slides into port, stopping short of the famous structure. Everyone is singing and shouting in general *hilaritas*. Why do I only find myself in these singing groups of friends when I travel? (In Greece last summer—how the "Dreamers" poured their lungs out into the orange sunset over the isle of Andros. Or in Mexico this winter—how I sang to the stars, songs from Carmen, floating in the hacienda pool with the other women.) Traveling activates some hinter-lobe designed for melody and association. Six moons ago we chugged past another half-remaining bridge in the diesel-powered U.N. boat on the Mekong. It spawned part of the river like the skeleton of a forgotten hope, reaching from Phnom Penh toward the illusion of safety. And two moons ago, the music of Bob Dylan in concert on Lykobettos Hill in Athens. I danced that night on the hill that lies in direct geomythic connection to Delphi and St. Michel—flinging myself out toward everything that I loved, to make a bridge, to meet my life more than halfway.

Last night it was my sixteen year old who went out dancing.

I sat under the lemon tree in the restaurant garden and felt the tectonic plates of my psyche begin their slow shift. I am only forty-five, but I felt tired. Today we packed up, said farewell to our dear abbey, La Chartreuse, and took the silver train to Paris. We unpacked in a jewel of a hotel on Ile St. Louis, once an old ball court, exactly as engraved in the *History of Theatre* book in the chapter that describes the invention of limelight. Actors came off the streets into these long, dark, high-ceilinged ball courts to try their dramatic potential. Once the spotlight came into play, the distance that had grown up between the actor and the audience suddenly closed and the content took a dramatic turn inward. Our room at Jeu de Paume is in the renovated rafters directly over the spotlit stage. From this third floor vantage we can look down at what is now an elegant dining room. In the morning we draw the girls to one of these tables to plot our day. They have already been out to scout a shop that shows Tin-Tin paraphernalia and tattoos in the window.

Parisians are returning to their city just as we prepare to leave. This is the first trip in years that finds me not particularly willing to go home. A jovial cab driver takes us past all the other places we could visit if we had time and talks about his daughter's apartment in Massachusetts at the same time Roger tells him about my grandfather having this apartment in Paris. Seven bedrooms! Seven baths! I can hear my mother as we pull up to the American Church on the Quai d' Orsay. Grandfather Leiper had this pulpit for one glorious summer in 1932 when his daughter turned sixteen. The image I carry closest to my heart is not of him preaching from this rich, mahogany lectern, but of her celebrating her birthday, dancing in the streets, coming-of-age with all of Paris turned out to revel in the fall of the old Bastille.

Persis Knobbe

WHEN I SPEAK FRENCH

We were part of the audience rushing from the Drury Lane Theatre to the Underground when my foot caught on a cobblestone. I was airborne for a moment before I hit a parked car with my shoulder and cheek, finally landing on the pavement beside one lens of my glasses. A young couple, seeing my fall, broke off from the group and came over to me. Fair and tall, at least from my vantage point, they loomed like kindly British giants in evening dress.

"Are you hurt?" the woman asked as she bent to me.

Simultaneously Ben broke through and asked, "Are you okay?"

"Oh, she has someone with her." The woman looked up at her escort who extended his hand and pulled her back to giantdom.

Must you go, I wanted to ask, as if they could stay to tea and scones.

"You're going to have a black eye," Ben said. His eyes, dark and ringed with soft circles even when he slept well, looked worse than mine. I slid easily into the time change when we went to London, but Ben needed a few days to adjust. We should have skipped the Drury Lane musical (Ben called it the Dreary Lane musical) and taken a walk to re-circulate our jet-lagged blood.

I hoped I hadn't broken anything, not at the start of a vacation. My wrist, that might be a problem. I had tried not to land on it. I moved my hand and felt no pain.

"God, am I lucky," I said as Ben brought me slowly to my feet.

"See how you wake up tomorrow morning." Ben sounded grouchy. He would be unbearable until he caught up on sleep. By the time he did, we would be in France, one hour further from California time.

✧ ✧ ✧

On the train to Marseilles we saw a man who looked exactly like Michael Redgrave. He was the only man in the car wearing a tie, tall, with good bones, a bit thin but he would photograph well. "Is Michael Redgrave still alive?" Ben wanted to know.

"No," I remembered, "he died a few years ago." The death of an actor is hard to accept. At the end of a play the actors resurrect and bow. And film stars, so alive on the big screen, seem eternal. This man, from a distance, had something called star quality, something that drew your attention. Apparently he drew Ben's. There was my husband, on his way to the bar, stopping to talk with him.

When Ben returned, he said the man and his wife were also on their way to Avignon. They had driven down from Kent and spent the previous night in London. Their names were Phillip and Vera, and very shortly we were seated opposite them at the only table in the car. Phillip had waved us over when the couple facing them got off the train at Lyon. "He always gets the place with the table," Vera said. She tapped her husband's knee. "These long legs need plenty of space." I noticed a deck of cards in the middle of the table and wondered if they were hoping for a game.

Phillip leaned across the table to me. "Only an American would have opened a conversation as your husband did. He said, 'The late Mr. Redgrave, I presume.'"

"But that's what we like about Americans," Vera said. "They're not shy; they cut straight into our reserve."

She was the picture of British reserve in her silk shirtwaist dress, everything in place: her straight spine, her cream-colored hair and pearls, the precise match of mauve in dress, shoes, and belt. "We're throwbacks, Phillip and I, and eccentrics as well." Throwbacks, maybe. Eccentrics? I saw nothing eccentric. Did she laugh too much? No more than the rest of us.

We hit it off, no question, even though Ben and I didn't play bridge. Phillip was keen on taking Vera to Avignon. He would show Vera the pension where he and his first wife had spent their honeymoon thirty-five years ago and where, one night, they had been kicked out of their rooms.

"Booted out," Phillip said, "because we were caught dining at another hotel. A crime, don't you know." His lips barely moved in a glottal stop of a laugh. "It was just what the marriage needed, a sense of danger, very promising." He sighed but not because they lived dangerously. They led "very proper church-going lives, after all."

"Fairly proper," Vera corrected. Vera and her first husband had been close friends of Phillip and his wife, lived in the neighboring counties of

Kent and Sussex, traveled together. After both spouses died, Vera and Phillip (the leftovers, she called them) decided to marry. Vera and I were waiting our turns for the bathroom in the smoke-filled platform when she told me how Phillip had proposed. "He asked me if I wanted 'to continue' and I thought that was a lovely way of putting it."

What was she saying? Was it a marriage of convenience? Or had they been lovers? They were so nice to each other. His food quirks, her energies; nothing drove them crazy. I was completely charmed by the pair; it was like traveling with Masterpiece Theatre.

Ben said he knew I was a Francophile, now it appeared I was also an Anglophile. He accused me of changing my philes midstream.

"Nothing of the sort, my dear." I admitted I was a chameleon, an involuntary one, when there was an accent present. Put me with Southern speech, of which I'm not overly fond, and my *I's* become *Ahs.* I was not "speaking British," as he accused, just toning down my American accent. I liked the way I sounded, crisper than my real self.

They suggested the four of us rent a car in Avignon, proceed to Arles, Nimes, Orange, then down to Aix-en-Provence. We would follow the tracks of the Romans, and, before them, remnants of the Greeks and Celts. I was surprised when Ben said yes. We had never "hitched up" with another couple for travels, as our parents did, the women walking ahead, the men joking, trailing behind, everyone oblivious to the scene at hand. What worried Phillip about the arrangement was the age difference; that they would cramp our style. He didn't want to hold us back because of Vera. Her energies were limited, he said, when she was out of earshot. She couldn't walk for hours, as he was sure we could.

He was wrong there, I told him. Once I could spend a whole day following curvy streets to the top in the *villages perches.* The only reason to stop was because I got hungry. I've slowed down a bit recently. We'd be fine together. "We'll take more time to do less," Phillip said, "and we'll be in good company, *vive la compagnie.*"

"You brought it up deliberately," Ben said, after an evening spent with Phillip guiding us through a map of Provence while Vera read aloud from the Michelin.

"What, what?"

"The walk in London—to the East End." At dinner I had mentioned that Ben and I were going on a guided walk to the old Jewish quarter when we returned to London. "You wanted to let them know."

"Maybe."

"Is that called a preemptive strike?" He smiled at me the way he does when issues recur, a forebearing smile.

I thought it was a good idea to let them know, simple and straight. We would be with Phillip and Vera, much of the time confined in a rental car, for a week. I didn't want to be in the middle of the Pope's palace in Avignon when they suddenly learned we were Jewish. "I was thinking of everyone's comfort, theirs as much as ours."

Ben thought I was crazy, a Woody Allen Jew. But we have been at dinners in London where polite, anti-Semitic remarks float across the table like salt being passed. ("He's an old Jew, what did you expect from him, mercy?") It would be naive to call someone on it. It's the kind of European anti-Semitism you take for granted; part of their lives, part of their literature, from Anthony Trollope to T. S. Eliot.

"You've never done that before," Ben said.

I smiled, remembering Phillip's response. "What day is the walk?" Phillip had asked. "Maybe we can join you, I don't know that part of London."

We traveled well together, sometimes a foursome, sometimes ones or twos, tourists doing museums, churches, plopping on benches and people-watching, sitting on the banks of the Rhone. Phillip often led, calling back to us in French, *"Attention!"* to alert us to small dangers. He led even when following, tapping my shoulder and pointing back to something I may have missed, human bones under glass in a church alcove or a pair of walnut entry doors. I was a collector of doors; I bagged them for my camera as if they were wildlife. The outer doors in Arles had the finish of a fine armoire, maybe the one that led to Narnia, C. S. Lewis's magic kingdom.

"Two Old Ladies Locked in the Loo" became a theme song for Vera and me. One night after dinner we became prisoners of the W. C. until I saw that you had to *turn* the mechanism, not slide it, as we had both been struggling to do. We emerged at the same time from our separate cabinets and leaned against one another in helpless laughter. She had a great laugh, I told her, pronouncing the word somewhere between *laff* and *lahff.*

Ben had a good ear: I *was* speaking a different language, not British English by a long shot, but using less American slang, speaking more carefully, referring to the *W. C.* for the toilet or the *indicator* for the turn signal. I alternated between talking French with shopkeepers and waiters and then International English with Phillip and Vera. I was happier out of my own language. When I spoke French, I left something of myself behind, weightiness that was lost in translation. I felt light, unburdened, on holiday.

And now, spending hours with Phillip and Vera, picking up their intonation and a few idioms, I felt crisp and Brit. until the black Renault cut us off on our way to Nimes and I lost my new English. The small car swerved in front of us, barely missing our fender. I had been absorbed in reading the road signs and didn't notice the flash of black until the others gasped. Then my own response came, belated and exacerbated by theirs. *"Oy gevalt!"* I yelled. I didn't know where it came from. It has never been one of my expressions. I tried to remember what I said in moments of stress: *Oh God* or *Jesus Christopher* or a lesser-value four-letter word. *Oy gevalt* was positively elemental, out of the depths.

Funny thing, Phillip and Vera didn't seem to have heard it. "Close one," he said. "Dreadful, these drivers," she said. I waited for Ben to burst into laughter, once it was clear we were out of danger. Or was it possible, in his concentration on the road, that Ben didn't hear? He would have reacted if he had. Clearly, I was the only one who heard. I leaned into the back seat, my face flushed. I had broken out into the language known as *mama-lochshen,* mother's noodles, Yiddish.

We returned late from Nimes and I sat for a moment in the hotel lobby before going up to our room, hoping the chest pains would go away. Not now, I thought, not here. It couldn't be a heart attack, I insisted, but Ben wanted a professional opinion. Doctors still make house calls in France and one was on her way within minutes. Fatigue, I told her as I went through my list of symptoms in addition to the chest pains: pounding heart, shallow breathing, tingling in my hands. Perhaps a belated reaction to the fall I had in London.

She listened closely to my heartbeat, took my blood pressure, checked my pulse. *"Ca va,"* she said, "okay."

"You mean I can just go on with the trip?" She smiled with pursed lips, a tolerant smile. *"Quel chance!"* I said, moving quickly from new death to new life. I had described all my symptoms in French. Amazing, I congratulated myself, how my French had improved. Then the thought: if I can think about my French, I can't be dying.

"Oui, d'accord," the doctor said, laughing when I told her about not

dying. She inhaled on the *oui* as Frenchwomen do, producing a soft, emphysematic sound. My malady, she said, was caused by heat, exhaustion, and anxiety. "Do not run the marathon of the tourists," she advised, "be a little more tranquil." She gave me a note advising me to see my doctor at home about a condition that calls itself Panic Disorder.

"Bizarre," I said. What did I have to be panicky about?

✧ ✧ ✧

"He likes you," Ben said.

"I know."

Phillip. In the car, in restaurants, it seemed that everything he said was directed toward me. His somber face changed when I entered a room even as he continued speaking to Vera. Any excuse to tap my shoulder, touch my hand, lean across me to talk to Ben, again his hand on my shoulder. Vera often on one side, he escorted me across streets, bridges, waterways, into the car, the café, the hotel. His hand beneath my elbow was a formality, his touch too light to bear any real weight.

"More wine?" Phillip was always asking me. See to Vera, I wanted to reply. But Vera was not overly fond of wine. Phillip and I were the principal drinkers, the savorers. Ben liked a good wine but he didn't sip and stare ecstatically into space as Phillip and I did in a garage/winery near Sisteron. Phillip's attentions to me were mostly shared enjoyment, I told Ben. The personal aspect was minor, nothing that kept any of us from the pleasure of the moment. *Quite,* I could hear Phillip saying.

"I think I died and went to heaven," I said, eating up, drinking in, *la vie de Provence.* I said it in a *boulangerie* in Arles, breaking into my long loaf of bread before I was out the door, and at the warm water fountain on the Cours Mirabeau in Aix. *Died and went to heaven.* That was my mother's line. It's possible she said it before she died. In her own home she once kept Kosher but when she traveled she ate the food of the region with a gusto that made my father laugh out loud. He would hold his fork in midair and watch her. After a dinner of veal and *risotto* in Florence, her favorite city, she and my father took a slow walk and, when the hotel elevator didn't work, climbed the stairs to their room. She sat on the edge of the bed to catch her breath, collapsed, and died.

"Enough to give anyone Panic Disorder," I said to Ben, remembering the details as they were told to me by my father. Ben and I were having breakfast in our room, embellishing the complimentary roll and croissant with the peaches and strawberries we bought at yesterday's outdoor market. Ben asked me how I was feeling.

"Must be a strain," he said, "playing a role. Sustaining it. Doesn't it wear you down?" He was sitting on the edge of the bed, looking less tired than he did in London, like a man who had completed two thirds of his vacation. I was about to reach for his hand and tell him how good he looked before he accused me of playing a role. Now I felt like popping him one. "I feel fine," I said.

He went on, "Something happens to you when you get over here. You want to blend in with the scene. You don't want to be taken for American—not a Jewish-American—only one generation removed from *Oy Gevalt.*"

So he had heard. Oy. But I am on holiday. Why shouldn't I have a vacation from myself?

There was no recurrence of the symptoms I had that night in Avignon but Ben watched me. He watched Phillip watching me as well. Ben seemed to be amused but I wasn't sure. He was taking a back seat, literally, often letting Phillip do the driving. Letting an Englishman drive in France was not a good idea. Phillip over-compensated, just as we did when driving on the wrong side of the road in England, staying too close to the right, hitting the curbs with annoying frequency.

Ben took the wheel again in Nimes, after which he and I alternated as drivers, but Phillip led us the rest of the time, playing host, running interference in crowds, seating us in restaurants. When Ben walked into a restaurant, he needed time to look around. Phillip pulled out the chairs. In all fairness, Ben was making an effort to charm Vera, listening to her carefully, making her laugh with stories of his *faux pas* in French, but she wasn't buying. She sat waiting for the return of Phillip's attention in her soft shirtwaist, playing with the watch fob she wore every day. An emerald at one diagonal, a small diamond at the other, it dangled at the end of a long chain, a gift from her first husband. She laughed politely at Ben, occasionally patting his hand. Laughter was Vera's form of communication. The French understood her modulations perfectly.

"Well, only a few days to go," I said to Ben. I was beginning to tire of being a foursome, never having fully adjusted to being a twosome. When you're down to your last set of clean underwear, travel becomes a performance—with an audience that never goes home. The presence of Phillip in the audience didn't help.

"There's nothing to it really. It's only because I'm younger," I assured my husband. "That's my sole attraction."

Ben agreed.

"To poor, smitten Phillip," Ben said, raising his glass at a Vietnamese restaurant in Aix-en-Provence. Phillip and Vera did not fancy Asian food so Ben and I had a summery night to ourselves. We dined *en plein air,* surrounded by market umbrellas, lighted plane trees, and the most amazing quiet, remarkable because not far from us was a café filled with beer-drinking university students whose shouts evaporated into the night air of Aix. There was no need, I said, to introduce Phillip into the conversation.

"He almost killed himself for you today," Ben said. We had driven up in the late afternoon to the Pont du Gard and looked down, surprised to see a beach scene below us, the French spread out on towels, picnicking and swimming. Ben glanced up at the arches of the bridge and said "Nice frame for a swimming hole." I didn't do much looking up and down, myself; vertigo teased at me. In America we would have put up barriers on the Pont du Gard and done something about that open space at the division of the bridge. Phillip, long legs scissored, leaped from one side to the other and came rather close to the edge. As Vera scolded, he grinned at me.

"All right," I felt the tension in my neck when I turned my head to Ben. "What do you want me to do about Phillip? I'm not thrilled, myself. Two more days. What can I do?"

"You could watch yourself."

Infuriating. The woman deliberately enticing. "What exactly am I doing?"

"You play to the crowd. The wide smile." He sang, "'The way you wear your hat . . .'" When I didn't smile, he said, "You know how you look when you laugh or when you turn your head all of a sudden. There are things you do that photograph very well. The actress that you almost were likes to spark her audience. Dim the lights, that's all. A star was born, a star must fade."

"Thanks."

The day before we left, Phillip called to ask if he could come to our room to settle accounts. We had tried to divide finances as we went along but there were lapses.

"Why don't you go to *his* room?" I asked Ben.

"Vera is resting."

Vera. Ben didn't know about my conversation with her. It had been pleasant, embarrassing only in retrospect. "I know you understand," she said. We were sitting on a park bench where we had watched the French playing *boules* earlier in the day, admiring the slow wind-up and precise path of the metal ball. The idea was to send the ball as close as possible to the jack without hitting it.

"Phillip loves to play the dashing young man. Poor love, his skin!" She let out a breath of a laugh. "He's shaving every day, for your benefit, of course. When he's home, it's every second day. He's sensitive to the razor, he says. But here—love soothes all."

She spoke as if we were intimate friends, in this together. It made me wonder if Phillip had established a pattern to which Vera had resigned herself. Now Phillip was coming to our room. I opened our suitcases and began packing, I didn't know how to act with him, especially in Ben's presence. I had taken measures to "dim the lights": I quickly extended my hand when we met; Phillip had begun the French custom of the double kiss. I tried to keep my mouth closed when I smiled.

"I think I'll just be out," I said. I left the room before Ben could respond and was going down the hall when Phillip emerged from the elevator.

Opening his arms to me, he said, "Voila!"

I put my hand straight out in front of me with what I hoped was a friendly smile.

He took my hand. Was he going to kiss it? He held it as he spoke, smiling reproachfully. "You don't have to avoid me, my dear."

I asked the hotel carpeting to swallow me up.

He walked me back to the elevator. "It's been lovely," he said.

Isn't the next line: *Let's not spoil it,* not that there was any *it* to it? Then his posture, the pull of his neck from his shoulders, the concentration in his eyes made me feel small.

When we reached the elevator, he said, "You have a lovely smile. Once more? May I see it? Ah yes, exactly."

It was hot the day Ben and I did the East End walk, eighty degrees in London. In Kent also. Vera called to say they wouldn't join us. Phillip was working in the garden in this heat, imagine. She had hoped we'd visit them before we left. The countryside was lovely, covered with apple blossoms. Then she did want us to come. When the invitation was first extended, I wondered if they were pretending to invite us and we were pretending to accept. I knew, as Vera and I spoke about arrangements, train schedules to Kent, that we wouldn't go, that we were saying goodbye. Vera and I would correspond for a bit and send Christmas cards forever.

Phillip and I had already wound things up in Avignon. We stayed and talked near the elevator, watching it go up and down.

"We began so well," he said, "the four of us. Then we paired off rather oddly, perhaps, because you and I shared interests."

"A taste for wine."

"A taste for each other."

He must have seen that I was startled but he went on, "And then you dismissed me. I was not sure what purpose I had served. Do you tell your friends everything? Was I your summer anecdote? Conversation for your morning jog?"

"I don't know what to say."

"Poor girl, your back is to the wall. Careful." I had literally backed myself to the elevator wall. He glanced at the numbers above the doors. "It looks like the elevator is no longer marching. You'll have to take the stairs."

I didn't move. "What do you expect from me, Phillip? Here we are about to leave."

"Nothing. I am being ridiculous, Vera would say vain. That's what it is at my age, vanity."

I couldn't leave him with that twisted look on his face. "A man who looks like Michael Redgrave is entitled to be vain," I said, lifting my face to kiss him, bridging the distance between his height and my own. I trusted Phillip. He would not, as Vera might put it, take advantage of the situation. Vera would have been right. Phillip was perfect: tender, barely parting my lips, placing me at a slight tilt as if for the camera. It reminded me of the way my father dipped my mother after a slow dance. Then, tears in my eyes, ham that I am, I turned to the *sortie* and walked down four flights of stairs. I had no idea of where I was going but I knew when to make my exit.

Judith Barrington

WORLDS APART

I celebrated my twentieth birthday on July 7, 1964, with a sumptuous French lunch at an open-air restaurant somewhere in the middle of the windswept plain south of Narbonne, accompanied by a good-looking hitchhiker named Tony. I unloaded a large pile of gifts from the trunk of my newly-inherited Triumph Herald—the convertible my mother had always coveted and had been able to enjoy for a couple of years before her death six months earlier. As I opened the parcels at the café table, Tony toasted me with champagne and sang a full round of the birthday song between each present. Hot gusts of wind snatched the wrapping paper and tossed it away across the barren landscape until it caught on the spike of prickly pear, or flapped against the twisted trunk of one lone olive tree, bent double by years of *mistral*.

After lunch, sleepy and hot, we drove on toward the Spanish border, the hot wind whipping round the windshield, my silk scarf flapping wildly. As we sped across the parched plain, I seemed to float above, looking down at myself as if I were a character in a movie driving this open-top forest-green Triumph Herald—a potent symbol of my mother, whose frustrated dreams and longing for adventure had all become focused on having a convertible of her own. My father had, for years, made fun of this dream. He said that convertibles were impractical, especially in England, where you could rarely have the top down, and where the canvas roof inevitably leaked in the winter. I thought he would never give in, but when I was sixteen my mother prevailed. She got her convertible.

Three years later my parents were dead and I had the car. My father, too, had had a long-frustrated dream: a cruise. Like my mother, he had held fast to his own vision of freedom and adventure, while she refused to cooperate, being prone to seasickness and terrified of the ocean. But once again, the dream finally won out, though I don't know how he brought her round, and it was his Christmas cruise that had killed them both when their cruise ship, *Lakonia*, caught fire. Although some nine hundred people had survived, my parents were among the hundred who stayed on board the burning ship after all the lifeboats had been launched in a panic—many leaving half empty—and eventually climbed down a ladder into the sea. Their bodies had been picked up by one of the rescue ships.

So here I was, a dashing figure in my little sports car. Only I knew its history. And I wasn't telling. I had barely shed a tear in the six months since my parents' deaths. I had stopped menstruating. I had drunk a lot of whisky. I was heading south with a suitcase full of brand new beachwear, determined to be glamorous. Grief was something I didn't understand and had no intention of indulging.

I had dragged along the birthday gifts as reminders—as a rather desperate way of keeping a foothold in my other world. There were records and bottles of perfume and hand cream from my London friends, with whom I had partied, shaking the floors of shared flats to the beat of the Beatles, and from at least one old school friend. There were books from my brother and sister, and drawings and specially-made cards from my niece and nephews. I wasn't afraid to go off alone on this adventure—at least I wasn't aware of being afraid—but I did seem very determined to stay in touch with all the compartments of my life.

There was at least one part of my life I'd have liked to leave behind, but instead I felt compelled to drag it along too. Many times over the past six months, I had driven this green car very fast for ten or eleven hours through the darkness, winding along beside roaring Welsh rivers, to spend a night with the woman I had gone to for comfort when my parents died—the woman who had offered more that I had bargained for. Somewhere among the presents was her offering—the offering of a lover: an elegantly wrapped copy of *Spoon River*, and a note that quoted Yeats's poem beginning "Had I the heavens' embroidered cloth . . ." Most of the time this part of my life remained hidden even from me. But I brought it along too, a set of gift-wrapped, guilty pleasures I couldn't get rid of.

For a few years now I had been struggling in my relationships with men. The fact was I was good-looking enough to attract their interest, but I had no idea how to talk to them. And, although I saw quite clearly that I was supposed to be fascinated, I really wasn't. Since the unmentionable love affair had started six months ago, I had renewed my efforts vigorously. I hadn't yet approached the terrifying thought that I might be more emotionally or sexually tuned in to women, but there was beginning to be a touch of desperation in the energy I directed at men.

This did not mean I couldn't like them. Tony, for example, was very likable, and easy for me to get along with since he didn't try to sleep with me. He had been hitching a ride in the middle of Montauban as I drove by with the top down. When I found myself stopped by a red light next to him, he asked very politely if I was going south. "Yes," I said coldly, not inviting him in.

"Would you consider giving me a lift?" he said, in a north country British accent, with no hint of a come-on. "I'd really be very grateful."

"All right then," I said ungraciously, and he swung his small suitcase into the back seat and hopped over the door to sit beside me. That night we found a cheap hotel and took two single rooms with no discussion. After dinner, which Tony paid for, he excused himself, pausing only to ask, "Is it all right for me to ride with you tomorrow as far as the frontier?" By then I had learned to appreciate his droll jokes and his descriptions of life on his father's farm, and anyway I wanted someone to celebrate my birthday with. I said I'd be glad of his company, and it was true.

I was on my way to Spain, where I had a job waiting for me—or so I believed. I had to admit that the hiring had been a bit unusual: I had been introduced to Arturo by a man I worked for as a temporary secretary. He told me that Arturo was the son-in-law of one of the richest men in Spain, Miguel Mateu, whose interests included a wine company called Perelada, where they lived now and again—when they were not in Barcelona or Madrid, or at their villa on the beach, or some other part of the world. Arturo was running the wine business and wanted someone to take charge of the hoards of tourists who stopped by, wanting to visit the castle and the wine cellars. He thought Perelada, like many French vineyards, could use its history to advantage. My fairly adequate Spanish, together with my boss's recommendation, got me the job.

Arturo had pressed some large bills into my hand at the end of our lunch meeting and asked, "When can you be there?"

"First week in July," I had replied, pocketing the money.

Now, as Tony and I gasped at the breathtaking views that unfolded, I wondered again if I had been foolish to set off for Perelada with so little knowledge of what my life would be like there. Climbing toward Cérbère and the coastal frontier post, we stopped high up over the turquoise sea and gazed south into Spain, past Port Bou to a huge rocky headland that jutted out with a small fishing village nestled in its armpit—a village that would turn out to be Puerto de la Selva, and which I would come to know well. The headland was bare of trees, except for a few small olive groves, and loomed magnificently against the deep blue sky. Standing on the French side of the border, we imagined everything changing just a few miles down the road, even though the rocky landscape looked very similar to the north and to the south, and even though we knew the Catalan region spanned the frontier and we would hear the same language down there as we had been hearing here in France for the past several hours.

"I'll be leaving you at the frontier," Tony said after a long, companionable silence, and I found myself a little sad for a moment. I was just getting used to him.

"Okay," I said casually. He was only a hitchhiker after all. Then, watching the sun sparkle on the waves below, I added, "Send a postcard if you like."

"I will," he said, smiling. But he never did.

I had never seriously doubted the existence of Perelada, or that I would create a job for myself there. Still it was reassuring to become acquainted with its physical reality: to search out the Perelada shop in Figueras, the small market town where I settled myself into an old-fashioned hotel, and then to drive the five miles to Perelada village.

The houses of Perelada covered a perfectly conical hill that rose out of the flat Ampurdan plain, and was crowned by the church. As you approached the village on the narrow winding road that wound between tall walls of sugar cane and corn, the distant Pyrennees fell in a backdrop of craggy steps from their grandiose, indigo heights to the ocean. In certain kinds of light, Perelada stood up from the plain, as three-dimensional as a cardboard cutout. The fields were fertile, producing crops and animals that ended up at the weekly market in Figueras, and, on the lower slopes that climbed away from the plain, miles of cooperatively owned vineyards produced the fruit that fueled Perelada's industry. Once you left the flats, however, and climbed into the higher land that ran between the plain and the rugged coastline, farms and vineyards gave way to rolling hills, dotted with sage bushes and occasional cork or olive trees. It was a landscape of tortoises and prickly pears, alive with crickets, and criss-crossed with arroyos that carried water only during flash floods. I quickly grew to love the wrinkled rocks, the smell of the hot earth, and the heat that rose from the impenetrable ground, as if someone in the underworld was always cooking.

My new life took on an immediate reality, as I shook the hands of the wine-cellar technicians, truck drivers, dispatch clerks, labelers, packers, mechanics, and was introduced to the wine-bar waitresses, Rosé and Maria. It took on additional layers of reality—and complexity—when I met the Mateu family and their numerous servants at the castle. For the first few days, I wondered if I would ever remember who was who, but, as always happens, names gradually started to attach themselves to particular pairs of brown eyes and certain styles of black hair; people's jobs separated themselves out, bottlers from packers, loaders from mechanics, until I even began to know which truck driver was married to which labeler.

Once I figured out what my job entailed, I realized that the greatest skill I would need in my work was an ability to juggle the old feudal world, and those who believed in it, with the new capitalists, who believed in progress. I was public relations person, interpreter, guide to large tour groups, and host to the important wine merchants who came over from England. On the one hand, I was required to pacify "the old lady," the autocratic matriarch of the Mateu family, whose presence in the castle cast a pall over the entire village, and on the other, I had to wine and dine businessmen, whose holidays were in part geared to cementing their relationship with the wine company. In spite of the confusion, I enjoyed feeling important as I advised the businessmen's wives on water-skiing, shopping, and where to eat dinner, and I was glad to be constantly busy as I negotiated with tour companies to put Perelada on their itineraries and led huge busloads of British, French, German, Dutch, Belgian, Italian, Swedish, Swiss, and Austrian tourists around wine cellars.

The most difficult of these worlds to negotiate was "the family." The old lady approached being a caricature of the aristocrat, staring haughtily at me down her hooked nose, but there was nothing funny about her. She scared me to death. She made no bones of her disapproval, particularly when I started bringing tourists around the castle grounds. She sent Pedro, the major domo, to tell me that it was "not a convenient time" on several occasions before I realized that no time would ever be convenient. Taking the line of least resistance, I held off on taking the bus tours inside the castle walls until the family was away, limiting regular visits to the wine cellars and bottling plant. But the "special" visitors—those importers of Perelada wine I was paid to give special attention—demanded a look at the castle. I trod a wary path with them, leading the way around the gardens farthest from the family's windows, and showing them the old Carmelite convent with its cloisters and chapel, which was separate from the castle, along with the magnificent library, which was housed in the convent.

When invited for *merienda* in the castle drawing room, I would balance my fine china plate on my knee, trying to cut tomato-soaked bread with a gold knife inlaid with the Perelada coat-of-arms, and weighing up the relative merits of speaking with my mouth full or requiring the old lady to wait for an answer to one of her probing questions. I would balance the spontaneity of my remarks with the approval I needed from Señora Mateu to meet the actual needs of my job. I weighed my desire to be myself in conversation with Carmen, the twenty-eight-year-old Mateu daughter, against the need for formality that precluded virtually everything I could think of to say.

When hanging around in the office at Las Cavas, as the wine production plant was called, I had to be very careful how I spoke about the family. The dispatch clerks, my office mates, clearly resented the social invitations that I received from the Mateus, while I had a hard time understanding the unique blend of adoration and disparagement that characterized their attitudes towards their patrons. The feudal system, which was very much alive in Peralada, meant that all the inhabitants of the village depended on the Mateus for their living. Like good feudal landlords, the family treated its dependents benignly, thus eliciting a potent brew of gratitude and resentment. Although I was clearly not one of them, I enjoyed a certain access to the family, which disturbed the guys in the office, who knew that everybody ultimately belonged in one camp or the other.

Walking back from tea at the castle, across the road and up the driveway to my office at Las Cavas, I would effect a lightning change of personality. From the cautiously sophisticated young woman, balancing her plate and her remarks in the drawing room, I transformed myself into a hearty co-worker, who breezed into the office, slapping Tomás on the back, and cracked a joke about his pile of unfinished work.

Visitors, who were my clients, would elicit other behaviors that suited the temperament or profession of the individual. Visitors on holiday, for example, required a different style from those who were on business. If I could have changed my outfits several times a day, I would have whisked from a stylish beach dress or bright cotton pants to a navy linen suit. Instead, I displayed my willingness to adapt by my manner: cool but friendly to the holidaymakers, with a good supply of jokes about tourists (which made them feel singled out as exceptions); businesslike and knowledgeable with the wine merchants.

Sometimes I was disconcerted when these worlds overlapped. I might, for example, take a busload of visitors down to the wine-tasting bar after handing each one a voucher that could be exchanged for a free glass of champagne. Bursting into the little bar at the head of my noisy crowd, entrenched in my popular pose of beach-bum-cum-jaded-world-traveler, I might spot a family seated at one of the tables. When the man turned out to be one of the English businessmen I had met with a few days earlier to discuss his wine imports, I would remember the persona I had presented on that occasion and feel momentarily fragmented. Who was I supposed to be today? That was always the question.

Travel in those days was still primarily romance to me. In spite of the many holidays I had shared with my parents in Caldetas, further down the coast, when I arrived in Figueras I knew little about Spain and less still about its politics. In Caldetas, the poverty, the danger of typhoid from the open sewers that ran down to the beaches, and the *guardias* who clearly engendered terror in ordinary people, all had disappeared behind the charm that had seduced my teenage self along with the music, the sunshine, and the brilliant landscape. I had barely known what Franco stood for, and certainly had no opinions about him.

Looking back, it's hard to know if my parents thought about it either. They never discussed politics, though I knew they voted Conservative in general elections back home. Still, there must have been at least one discussion of Franco's government since my mother once made the caustic comment that "at least he's built some decent roads and got the telephones working." Now in Figueras, thinking about fascism for the first time, my mother's approval of Franco's roads seemed to reveal an appalling lack of sensitivity. Later, however, I thought it more likely that she had simply been reaching for anything positive she could find among the massive changes she encountered in "her" Spain. She hated the invasion of tourists, but could applaud the absence of potholes in the roads; she loathed the modern hotels that disfigured the wild coast, yet somehow felt glad to nod approval at the telephones that linked them to the outside world.

Living and working in Figueras, however, I couldn't help thinking she had exaggerated this improvement in telephones when I discovered it often took three days to place a call to England. The locals knew it was quicker to drive the four hundred miles to Madrid than to wait for a phone connection. How bad could the telephones have been back in the thirties, in my mother's golden era, if she had found this state of affairs to Franco's credit? It made sense only when I realized how desperately she had missed the Spain she and my father had inhabited as a young couple, until the Civil War drove them back to England, and how much she needed to like it after her long absence.

As I carved out a daily life in Figueras, I wanted to ask my mother what she had meant about the roads and phones; I wanted my father to explain why he had left for good in 1936, while his friend Freddie continued as a business man in Barcelona. Was there some political explanation? Could my father have been someone who wouldn't do what it took to coexist with Franco? I wanted to argue with them, to declare that if I had been born earlier I would have fought with the brigades or driven an ambulance. I needed to witness their parental shock.

The Hotel Paris, where I lived, was right on the central square of Figueras, a sprawling little town just off the main highway from France to Barcelona. The square, always referred to as the *rambla*, was a long, rectangular patch of concrete, raised three steps' height from the sidewalks that surrounded it, and shaded on all sides by tall elms. Ornate iron benches, covered with layers of bird shit that only disappeared after a rainstorm, surrounded the open area, where hundreds of people strolled up and down before dinner. Old people sat on the benches chattering even more loudly than the birds that clustered in the branches above, fighting over the best roosting spots. Small children, dressed up in ruffled shirts or dresses and shiny patent leather shoes, dashed among the stroller's legs or jumped rope in front of their doting grandmothers.

Traffic rushed along the road that surrounded the *rambla*, while on two sides of the outer perimeter of this road cafés sprawled across the broad sidewalks, vying for the customers who wandered past the white plastic chairs and tables of the Café Luna and the red and white checked tablecloths of the Madrigal. The waiters, all immaculate in their black and white, with starched napkins tucked around their waists to form short aprons, greeted each passerby with resignation, knowing only too well that people rarely abandoned their regular spots. Tourists, however, brought them to life and they would bow and smile their invitations at the French and English families who stopped off on their way to the coast.

The Hotel Paris was nestled in among these cafés, its dining room on the second floor looking out onto the *rambla*, while my room, on the fourth floor at the back, looked down on one of the narrow streets that led to the market square, just a couple of blocks away. Opposite my window, with its tiny balcony and iron grille, a whole block of similar windows and balconies displayed geraniums, washing lines, and a variety of wooden shutters, some with peeling gray paint, others newly varnished. The old lady across the way always waved her finger at me and winked after the time my underwear blew off my balcony and ended up being presented by her grandchildren to Señor Fernando, the tiny, rotund, hotel manager.

Life in Figueras comprised not just all the various pieces of my job in Perelada, but a multi-faceted social life as well. My nightlife mostly took place in Rosas or Cadaquez, which were nearby beach resorts. There I danced at discos until four in the morning, drank like a trooper, drove my car over mountain roads at ninety, and had unrewarding sex with virtual strangers on the beach, watching out for the *guardias* who paroled to limit such activity.

Sometimes a love-struck waiter I had picked up at a disco or a hopeful student I had chatted with over a brandy or two would show up in Figueras. They would come to my hotel, where Señor Fernando gravely asked their names and sent a maid to fetch me if I was up in my room. Señor Fernando once ventured to warn me about one of these admirers, telling me in a confidential voice that he was a *no buen chico*. I probably knew this already, but I wasn't interested in good boys. I thanked Señor Fernando for his warning and told the not-good-boy to go away, which is probably what I would have done anyway, since I didn't like my night life pursuing me into Figueras.

Off-duty, I lived in an entirely Spanish world. I knew only Spaniards—though they would have hated me to call them that, since Catalan nationalism was at a militant high. I hung out with the young Catalan men at a café in the *rambla* and had friends and acquaintances all over town, from Emilia in her dusty store with its sacks spilling out lentils and chick peas to Enriqué, the head waiter at the fancy Hotel Duran. I shopped in the market, discussed the weather with the old men who sat all day at the Café Luna, and had my car, my hair, and my sandals fixed by nearby neighbors. I was the only foreigner in town.

From time to time, however, just as I began to sink deep into life in Figueras, representatives of my old life would show up, propelling me into a state of conflict. Marian, my friend at the BBC, where I had been working when my parents died, arrived, wanting to spend some of her vacation with me. I gave her a tour of Peralada, shared my tiny bed with her, and found her a room at a congenial *pensión* in Rosas, where I joined her from time to time for swimming and sunbathing. My Catalan friends, the boys I hung out with at the café, were very interested in her and angled for invitations to accompany us both to the beach or out to dinner, but I found myself reluctant to let them in on this piece of my other world. Or was it the other way around? Perhaps it was them I wanted to keep safely to myself—safely separate.

Then the daughter of a close friend of my mother's turned up. Not looking for a traditional beach holiday like Marian, Heather was a flamboyant character who had somehow finagled an invitation to stay at Salvador Dali's house in Port Lligat. I was supposed to deliver her there, pick her up a few days later, and drive her to Perpignan Airport. Not assertive enough to extract even an introduction to the great man in return for my services, I did as she asked, picking her up on the appointed day to discover that she was returning to England with a five-foot statue in tow. It barely fit into the back of my open car, but I managed to get the two of them to the airport, only to find that Heather needed a huge loan to pay for the statue's transportation. Ruefully smiling at my gullibility, I drove back to Figueras from the airport feeling suddenly quite bereft. But later that night, sitting at the café with the boys, I told them the story, sparing Heather none of the mockery we all heaped on foolish foreign tourists. As we laughed together at Heather's antics, my sense of abandonment gradually dispersed, and once again I sank into the illusion of belonging.

It was different, though, when my mother's old friend, Germaine, came to Spain. For one thing, she never came to Figueras, so my two worlds weren't forced into a direct collision. Instead, she returned year after year, with her friend Mary, to Caldetas, where my parents and I had often vacationed with Germaine's large family a few years earlier. These days she complained bitterly about the new freeway, the crowds, and the ugly buildings that were sprouting up the hillside. Gone were the days of her *pensión* next to the level-crossing; now she and Mary installed themselves at the Hotel Colon, that grand old edifice on the seafront, where the usual clientele of businessmen and retired British and German couples was interspersed with very old, apparently very rich, regulars. There was the ninety-year-old who sat at her special table overlooking the beach, peering critically at the label on her bottle of wine over an enormous hooked nose. And there were old men too, carrying polished canes, one even wearing spats: Germans, Spaniards from Madrid, and an occasional Italian, all regulars for who knows how many years?

I would drive down from Figueras to spend Sundays with Germaine and Mary two or three times during their vacation. Being with them was a kind of time-out that I needed. We sat under their striped umbrella by the rocky breakwater, where a huge group of us, including my parents, had once dominated the long, gravelly beach, Germaine would say in her French accent, "Foufou is doing so well, you know. She's running the Mexican tourist office all by herself now! My dear Mona is so proud of her. Me too, of course. Your poor dear mother would have been . . ." But here her voice would trail away as it always did when she mentioned my poor dear mother.

There on the hot sand, I could almost hear my mother's musical laugh emerging from the shouts of ball players and the screams of children, and I always expected to turn and see Mona with her enigmatic smile, or my father sitting up hugging his knees, while we all joked and made plans. There, the past and the present coincided more than they collided, as, on that familiar patch of sand, I talked to Germaine, first about my job at Perelada and then, in an easy transition, about the old days when we had bowled in the park until the early hours of the morning. Later, relaxed by the day's sun and a tepid shower, I would stay on at the Hotel Colon for dinner with Germaine and Mary, the rest of the old group fading until they became just ghosts. The three of us would eat quietly in the vast, formal dining room, overlooking the oily sea, while behind the hotel, thousands of sparrows jostled noisily for a place to roost in the plane trees. Under their canopy, in the cool dark, my mother's green car waited to take me back to my new life.

Anita Skeen

CLOSED AT DUSK

When I awoke today and peered through the slit I always leave in my flowered drapes so that morning will pry its way into the room as soon as possible, I noticed the way the light falls on the black iron gate at the top of the stairs outside my window and the way it spills over onto the edges of the concrete steps that curve down to my underground door. This London flat is so different from my Michigan house on its acre of green grass, but it has its own beauty, and this morning there was something very sensual and nostalgic about it. I wanted to take a photo, but by the time I roused myself from bed and got around to actually beginning to do something about it, the light had gone and the mood had changed. How light creates those moods is a phenomenal thing, isn't it? I think particularly of New Mexico, of Abiquiu, of the way the light tumbles onto those red mesas and wheat-colored hills, tumbles off the precipice at Chimney Rock, fills up the vast opening of Echo Amphitheater. It does the same thing here, in the heart of London, on my old concrete stairs and decaying iron gate. How the light washes the whole scene with some magic liquid and transforms it. I think of the incredible watercolors of Hannah Creighton, how the light gives such depth and richness to those paintings, how it seems she must have a tube labeled Light that she paints across the picture when she's almost finished and, suddenly, the painting breathes, comes alive.

Last night, in some part of my dream, a man had seen a watercolor that I'd painted of a forest in autumn and put an ad in a newspaper saying how moved he was by the painting and that he wanted to meet the artist. Someone saw the ad and told me, I believe it was Jeanine Hathaway, my Wichita poet pal, and arranged for us to meet. He wanted to buy the painting, offered me a lot of money, but I wouldn't sell. I kept looking at the painting and asking myself, "What does he see that makes the painting that wonderful for him?" I couldn't see it. I saw tree trunks (I will admit that I felt I could reach out and touch the bark), limbs extending over water, leaves patterning into collages of color. The painting seemed, in my dream, impressionistic rather than real. Why wouldn't I sell? The feeling that I could never paint it again, that I could never produce as good a work the second time, that I could never find my way back to those same impressions. That's what I often feel with writing, that I'll never be able to duplicate the impressions.

I think I must have known very early on that I was different from people around me, not just my family, but even my close friends. That's probably one of the reasons I spent so much time in the woods alone, reading voraciously. The reading led to writing. I could see the internal workings of the characters' minds on the pages, and I wanted to see my own. What was I thinking about my friends wanting boyfriends, about my grandmother's illness, about my baby brother? I had to write it down to know what was there, to know what it was that was making me feel the way I did, to feel less the way I did by writing it down. Margaret Atwood has a poem called "The Page" where she talks about the dangers of the blank page and the tools you must take with you for survival when you enter the blank page. The blank page is terrifying, I agree, though not because of what lies below or within the surface of the page, but because of what lies below the surface or within you.

The act of writing may be like that morning light that creeps down my staircase: it reveals oddities and eccentricities in the surface to which normally I pay no attention. It shows me something necessary that I might have missed if I had not taken a few extra moments to look carefully.

If I believed in omens or signs, or that coincidence is not really coincidence but a message delivered in some inexplicable way, I would believe that I waited to read *The Joy Luck Club*, a book I've had for over a year and one I will teach this term in my Twentieth Century American Literature course, until it would help me deal with the anguish of the visit I just had with my parents. I took the book with me on the train to Scotland to read while we traveled, but didn't begin reading until one night in Aberdeen when I felt I had to withdraw from the small space we were cramped into, the snapping my folks were doing at each other, the isolation and loneliness I felt in a foreign territory. When I began the book, I was distressed that I would be teaching it rather than *The*

Woman Warrior, which I thought was technically, thematically, and structurally superior to *The Joy Luck Club*. Having finished that book only moments ago, I still believe that to be true. But the theme in *The Joy Luck Club* strikes home now: mothers and daughters do not appreciate each other until it is too late. They are ashamed of each other for behaviors they can never understand. They expect behaviors from each other that are impossible because of differences in circumstances or generations. They do not ask the right questions, or the important questions, of each other until it is too late. June Woo, the central narrator of the tale, writes about her mother, "I didn't know what to do or say. In a manner of seconds, it seemed, I had gone from being angered by her strength, to being amazed by her innocence, and then frightened by her vulnerability. And now I felt numb, strangely weak, as if someone had unplugged me and the current running through me had stopped." This is what I experienced with both my folks during the twelve days of their visit to me in England. I don't know how to sort through it all, how to make some kind of sense of it that allows me to go on to the next step of my relationship with them, except by writing. They seemed more fragile, physically and psychologically, than I was prepared for. They will not live forever, nor will I. I would like for there to be peace at that final parting. I would like us not to be disappointed in the lives we have lived with each other.

There could be a hundred stories written from the events and interactions of the last twelve days, a hundred pieces of fiction, but how many pieces of truth? My truth and theirs is not the same, not about the vacation experience, not about our relationship, not about the world. They will go home, I think, and say they had a great time. They got to see Buckingham Palace, the Tower of London, Covent Garden, Harrod's, and all the places we toured in Scotland. My father got to see the Kirkton of Skene near Aberdeen, the village he is sure his ancestors came from generations ago, before they settled in the hard-rock mountains of West Virginia. They will talk about how they couldn't understand the odd accents; how people never finish their words or run them all together; how they couldn't eat the strange food because they were never sure what was in it; how they couldn't understand why buses with double decks don't tip over or why the British don't use ice in their drinks. Weird, they will say. Very weird. Why don't they do it our way? They will say the weather was remarkably good, that they probably walked eighty miles in the ten days we toured, that there were more steps in London than grains of sand by their ocean at home. They will say they had a great time, the experience of a lifetime.

I have said that these were among the hardest twelve days of my life. From the moment I arrived at Heathrow Airport to collect them and realized that I would have to scout through a thousand faces, all in search of someone I should have known I would be searching the whole time they were here: for the quickest routes, for the best sights, for the right words, for the invisible genetic link that means we have something in common, some ancient and ancestral reason for belonging to the same clan. I couldn't find that slender thread, that nicked gene. I still feel the anxiety like a knot at the back of my neck, the stress in my inability to sleep, the frustration in the fact that I feel paralyzed by the experience. Writing about it is a kind of stretching, a physical and emotional therapy that loosens the muscles of the heart. I exhausted my emotional limits, from anger to grief, from amazement to despair. I cannot say from sadness to joy, for, honestly, though I felt great sadness at times, I felt little joy.

My father's hearing loss is even more apparent than it was the last time I saw him. When he's spoken to by a waitress, a taxi driver, a sales clerk, he looks at my mother and expects her to answer. Which she does. Then it's okay. He refuses to wear a hearing aid and turns up the volume of the television so loud it's impossible to think about anything, even what's on the TV He seems totally absorbed in what he wants and needs. That seems new to me, though perhaps I've just ignored it before. We had terrible meals most of the places we traveled because he wouldn't eat anything new. In Aberdeen and in Edinburgh we ate cheese sandwiches and spaghetti. When he couldn't find an American restaurant (we ate at Chi Chi's twice in London), he ate someplace where he could get a burger and fries. Two nights in a row I had french fries and coke because he wanted to eat at McDonald's and there was not much on the menu for a vegetarian.

My mother is complicitous in this because she gives in and does what he wants. Her long-suffering and self-sacrifice make me just want to shake her and say, "Stand up for what you want for a change, will you? Stop doing what's best (you say) for everyone else." She wants someone else to have the best bed, the best seat at the table, the heaviest jacket (because it's so cold), the biggest piece of dessert. She will buy presents for everyone but herself and buy the two sweaters she does take home for herself at the Charity Shop. She will wash the dishes, hem the trousers, do the laundry, and keep right on doing things for everyone else. She has made my father helpless, and he's let her. She keeps both passports because she's afraid he'll lose his. She reads him the menu and tells him what he'd like; she tells him what clothes to wear so he won't catch cold, what shoes would be best for his feet today, what books he'd like to read when we browse in the bookstore. And, as you would expect, periodically he explodes and tells her, not in so many words, to leave him alone. He's hateful when he does it. My mother shrugs it off and keeps right on doing what she was doing before. And he goes right back to doing what she tells him. She treats us like children. Must she be so necessary, so essential, the way a parent is to a child? Does she think we can't see if it's raining outside when she tells us to put up the umbrella? Does she think I am hungry every time she is?

After they had been here only a few days, my mother told me she thought my father was having serious trouble remembering things. I thought he had just quit listening to her because she talks at him all the time. I told her he wasn't listening, not that he didn't remember. I think I was wrong. Our first full day in Edinburgh he decided to take the bus out to St. Andrews to play golf. The woman at our B & B told him how to get to the bus station, but I wasn't sure he understood her, or that if he got lost along the way he would be able to hear/understand the directions given in a strong Scottish accent. So I suggested that Mother and I go with him on our walk downtown past the bus station. When we got there, he misunderstood what the man at the desk said about the time and the fare and would not acknowledge that he'd misunderstood. The fare was six pounds, but the trip took almost two hours. I knew he had his heart set on playing golf at St. Andrews, and I encouraged him to go even if he only got to play nine holes because of getting a late start. He looked defeated. We sat down to talk about it, and he decided four hours of bus travel was too much. He seemed like a little boy who's just been told he can't go to the ballgame with his best pals because he doesn't have enough money. Mother said later, and I think it was true, he wasn't sure he could get there and back on his own. So, he stuck the bus schedule and all the information he'd written down in his back pocket. Two days later, in Aberdeen, when we were getting ready to leave our room in the B & B in the morning, he reached in his pocket, pulled out the schedule, and said in his accusatory tone, "What's this? How did this get in my pocket?"

"That's the bus schedule to St. Andrews," I said.

"Bus schedule to St. Andrews?" he said. "I walked there. What'd you mean?"

"No, Daddy," I said, "not the Royal Aberdeen," where he played golf just yesterday, "but St. Andrews, in Edinburgh, remember?"

He looked at me like I was totally mad.

"Remember, we went to the bus station and the ride back was too long, and you decided not to go?"

He unfolded and refolded the schedule, squinting as though the print were too fine or the words Celtic and bizarre.

"That was here," he said.

"No. That was in Edinburgh."

He looked across the room, not at the painting on the wall, or even the wall, but some place beyond the wall, some place beyond memory.

"Oh, yeah," he said a moment later. "St. Andrews, right." And it did appear that something had finally clicked. But it took a long, long time.

Throughout the trip, he seemed to make up information as he went along. Now, granted, it is difficult for Americans to remember that James VI of Scotland became James I of England, that there were numerous Georges, and one was King at the time of the American revolution and another one was married to Queen Mary and so on, but to hear him tell British history was like waking up in the middle of a Monty Python movie and not being able to escape from the script. Kessington Castle (Kensington Palace) was where Prince Phillip lived, and Westminster Cathedral was built to commemorate the Battle of Britain. (We strolled by Westminster Abbey on a Sunday morning right after the service commemorating the fiftieth anniversary of the Battle of Britain let out. Prince Phillip was in attendance.) John Knox was beheaded along with Sir Walter Raleigh in Edinburgh Castle and his ancestor, John Skene, was knighted by Charles II of Scotland. Trying to straighten it out did no good at all. Buildings migrated from city to city, monarchs rose and fell in astounding historical order, and somehow all of it had something to do with the Second World War. Spellings took on strange pronunciations. It made me dizzy. I know part of that behavior is his being seventy-five years old, but his mental capacities seem remarkably dimmed. He read aloud like an elementary school child sounding out the words, and he seemed never to be quite able to get the directions to the hotel straight. In London, we walked past the sign that said Westminster Hotel probably twenty times during their stay, and when he and mother were ready to leave, Mother said something to him about the Westminster Hotel, and he asked her how she knew the name of it and why she expected him to. Several times he went off on his own, and I was worried that he wouldn't be able to find us. We were to meet him in Aberdeen at the Marks and Spencer Department Store after he played golf, and I happened to run into him, or he saw me, actually, in a mall one street over from Marks and Spencer about an hour after our scheduled meeting time. He was waiting for us at Burger King. He thought the entire mall was the Marks and Spencer Store, though nowhere was the name Marks and Spencer in evidence. The longer he traveled, the more worried I became that if we got separated he wouldn't know how to ask directions to where we would be. In some ways, I felt like I had two children on a vacation. I had to keep them together, be sure we got where we were going, be sure they had their train and subway tickets, try to keep them from fighting, and find some place they could/would eat. It was absolutely exhausting.

My mother's anxiety about the world seems to have reached epidemic proportions. She was afraid to go off and leave extra money in my flat, worried about passports being stolen, and when news came of a train wreck in Louisiana, she was sure it was an act of terrorism and that someone had blown up the bridge. She didn't want to pay for the night's lodging at the B & B's with a Mastercard because she was afraid the proprietors would steal her number and use it again. I could see how uncomfortable she was on a train car where many of the riders spoke a language other than English, and when we went to the theater in Edinburgh, she was too afraid to walk from the theater to the B & B at night, though there were many people out on the street. We had to call a taxi. I wanted to go one night on the "Ghost Walk" in Edinburgh, up the alleys and down the narrow streets on a guided tour where the town's spooky and macabre history was explained to the walkers. She was sure it wasn't safe, that I shouldn't go alone, and it was just easier not to go rather than to have to deal with all her distrust of the situation.

Now that I have sent them back home, am relieved of my responsibilities, and am recovering my space and my life, why do I continue to be so disturbed by the shadows of the visit? They have visited me in the past when I thought I would pull out my hair before they left. What is different this time? Since I don't see them regularly (sometimes six months or more passes between visits), I suppose it seems more dramatic each time, as the aging process takes hold of them in their later years. They are looking old, and they are behaving like old people. By deduction, that means I am getting older, too, and perhaps mortality flashes in garish neon letters on some back street of my brain when I'm with them. They are people who, all through my childhood, could do everything. Mother worked as a legal secretary, cooked the meals, sewed our clothes, painted the house, made the curtains, planted the garden. Daddy did the plumbing, fixed the car, built the stone wall, bricked the house. Their motto wasn't, "If you can do it yourself, don't hire it done." Their motto was, "Of course you can do it yourself." Perhaps that's one of the reasons I feel I can't do anything right. They always were able to do it better. Now I see that there are many things they can't do any more.

I think sewing is getting more difficult for my mother, and the results are not as perfect as they once were. Daddy doesn't have the stamina to do the kind of work he once did, and he's not willing to admit it. In the midst of my anger at them about irrational or xenophobic behavior, suddenly I see their vulnerability. The world is speeding by them—computers, automatic bank tellers, camcorders—and they can't keep up. We're living in the Information Age and they've hardly dealt with the Industrial Revolution.

When I see my father's confusion over a piece of paper he finds in his pocket that he doesn't recognize, or my mother's anxiety about who might steal her luggage on the train, it breaks my heart. I suppose we always believe, as long as our parents are living, that they will be here to take care of us in the event of unforeseen disaster. When we realize that we have to start taking care of them, that their aging and deterioration is our unforeseen disaster, the world flips upside down and that last security rope we so cavalierly tossed over the summit frays and snaps before our eyes.

Someone in one of my classes yesterday quoted Cocteau as having said that good writers do not long to be famous, they long to be believed. I like that. I *believe* it, too.

My friend M.T., an artist I met last year at the Virginia Center for the Arts, where we were both in residence for several months, arrived about noon today. She was suffering a bit of jet lag, so we talked awhile, had a cheese, bread, and apple lunch here in my flat, then she napped awhile before we struck out to find Highgate Cemetery. She is the same age as my mother, and I wondered about how well she would do with an excursion so soon after her flight. But she is an experienced foreign traveler, on her way to a show in Germany that includes some of her work. What I liked about her so much when we first met was her curiosity about the world, her wry sense of humor, her willingness to take risks and explore the unknown.

I thought *she* knew how to get to Highgate Cemetery, as she's spent time in London in the past, and she thought *I* knew how to get there, so by the time we really did figure out that neither of us knew where we were going and got underway, it was 3:30 in the afternoon. We took the tube to Highgate Station, then walked in the direction people told us to go, until we started getting contradictory information. We had to retrace our path several times. But it was a beautiful autumn day. Yellow, orange, and red leaves snuggled in the gutters and against the railings, and the light was that thin, late afternoon, October sunlight that settles on everything like dust. I had my camera, so I tried to record some of it. We walked through Waterloo Park, and just as we arrived at the Cemetery gates, at 4:55, the little ladies who were the guides and gatekeepers snapped them shut and left us standing like eager puppies on the outside.

"Closed at Dusk" the sign on the gates proclaimed.

"Please," we pleaded, "we've come a long way!"

"Our feet hurt," they replied. "Try standing all day."

Clang.

That quickly. That fast. That was it.

M.T. consumed more than three days worth of energy in the three days she was here. I felt I was still recovering from her visit until yesterday. I felt trapped again, as I did when my parents visited. Having another person in the same space, the same room I'm in, all the time, is like slow suffocation. That person seems to be hoarding all the air and totally unaware of it. I get more and more frantic to get out. We did hike back to Highgate Cemetery on Monday, went on a tour, and took lots of pictures. I saw the grave of Karl Marx, and I couldn't find the grave of George Eliot. The surprise was stumbling across the grave, or mausoleum, of Radclyffe Hall, the British poet and novelist who upset the British literary apple cart in 1928 with the publication of her novel, *The Well of Loneliness*, a largely autobiographical work that attempted to deal openly with lesbian identity in the genre of the novel. Despite the support of many writers, including Virginia Woolf, the novel was prosecuted for obscenity.

There were flowers strewn around the entrance. The guide told us that October 7 was the anniversary of her death and a group had come with the flowers last week. M.T. did not know who Hall was, nor did it appear that most of the people on the tour did. But there were two other women, a couple, I thought, even before this, who stayed behind, as I did, to click the shutter and pause for more than a moment. We gave each other a knowing look. What kind of signals do lesbians give each other? I knew they were lesbians about five minutes into the tour. Perhaps it isn't what we say (they did not speak English, but a language that sounded very Nordic, very frozen) but how we speak to one another—the inflections I heard exchanged between them, the easy familiarity, the comfort of being connected by love rather than blood.

That afternoon, in the rain, M.T. and I went to Dennis Seavers's house for "the tour." This is impossible to describe. The house, room by room, is a reconstruction of other eras. The visitors drop in on an imaginary family, the rooms arranged as though currently inhabited, as though the tenants had just stepped off into another room as the viewer enters, food still on the table, lamps still burning. The periods begin with the Huguenots and end in the reign of Queen Victoria. Walking into each room is like walking into a still life of the period. It's an ambiance he's created, a whole sense of an historical moment in one small room. The tour was one of the most fascinating journeys I've ever taken. I thought about the boxes that M. T. constructs as part of her art, whole worlds, often fairly surrealistic, preserved in the moment of the wooden frame. I felt as though we had just stepped in, and out, of a Seaver box.

The next day, I met M. T. at the Tate Gallery after I left Roehampton. I was exhausted from teaching all day by the time we met. We spent about two hours wandering through the galleries. I was somewhat disappointed, but I followed M. T. around rather than seeking out where I might have gone alone. We did see the work of the Pre-Raphaelites, which I enjoyed a great deal despite their religious motifs, and I saw the first work I'd ever seen by Vanessa Bell, Virginia Woolf's sister. How coincidental to come across these now as I find myself being immersed in Woolf's writing and life. But, overall, I much prefer the Art Gallery of Ontario, my favorite of all art houses, partly because of the Henry Moore sculptures in residence there as well as the stark and startling works of The Group of Seven.

We ate dinner at the Whitely Center, M. T. eating more slowly than the most finicky of cats. I thought I would fall asleep in my rice. Afterwards, we returned to my flat, loaded up her suitcases, and I took her, in the pouring rain, to the B & B out near the airport where she was to stay because of the early departure of her flight the next day for Vienna. When I finally left her in the care of the proprietor, it was 9:30 P.M., I had an hour train ride home and preparation yet to do for my classes the next day. Plus, I was soaked to the bone. As I walked from the B & B back to the tube station, neon lights flashing and reflecting in the deep puddles everywhere, the sound of traffic whooshing by, I felt ecstatic to be alone again, to be out in the rain-aroma night, to be independent and free. M. T. had asked me if I were afraid to walk back to the tube station alone. It had never occurred to me to be frightened. I realized, riding the nearly empty train back to Bayswater, that I'd been on ten different trains and buses that day. No wonder I was exhausted and asleep in my seat.

The rest of the week remains a blur of students, lectures, papers handed in, papers handed back. I finally was given an office at Froebel College, on the top floor, on the north side, in what, temperature-wise, feels like the heart of a glacier. I understand that, when this building was the manor house, the offices that now house the English Department were the servants' quarters. Hmmm. Not much appears to have changed.

Last night I curled up in bed with *The Sun Also Rises*, which I teach on Wednesday. Last week it was the slaughterhouse of *The Jungle*, this week it's bullfights in Hemingway. Next week it will be hit-and-run in *The Great Gatsby*. American literature seems to be littered with corpses. How long do I have to wait to get to a woman author? The whole British educational system seems very male, very hierarchical. I need to draw up an alternative book list of works of American literature to give my students, one that wasn't developed by a committee consisting of an Australian, an Irishman, a Bosnian, and a Turk.

Today, Sunday, and *The Times* and *The Observer*. Reading them has become my favorite weekly activity before I start on all the papers I have to mark today for my Romance and Epic class. The process of grading has become a task I can't bear, and I put it off until the last possible minute. I vowed, on Tuesday, to grade ten papers a day, to space them out. So, when do I begin? Sunday afternoon. Sometimes I feel that teaching will kill me. Other times, I know it will. That one day, I'll pick up my millionth paper, put my pen on the first sentence, or sentence fragment, with two misspelled words, and something will snap. A tiny little IRA bomb will go off in my brain, blow out all the shop windows, leave rubble scattered in the street. Inside my head this little voice keeps whispering, "You can't do it. You can't read one more paper. You can not do it." But somehow, I do. When will I not be able to? I wonder. When will it finally happen?

I've begun reading the letters of Vita Sackville-West to Virginia Woolf. I read the Hemingway novel and then, as a reward, I allowed myself to read the introduction to the letters. Then I read "Sir Orfeo" and "Emare" for class tomorrow, then read forty more pages of Sackville-West. Now that I've graded twenty some papers, I'm ready to stop and read more of what I want to read. I continue to be enthralled with their correspondence—the wit, the candor, the literary world they inhabited, the magic and grandeur of their lives. They seem both real and like icons at the same time. Did they have any idea how many people would read this private correspondence, this exchange between intimates? What would they say about it? Vita, I think, would laugh. Virginia . . . I don't know,

Virginia might be disturbed. Almost makes one afraid to put pen to paper on the off-chance that, unfortunately, one might become famous.

I went down to Picadilly Circus yesterday to see *Orlando*. Six pounds (nine dollars! outrageous!), and the crowds of people on the streets make me not want to go far from the Bayswater area on weekends. I enjoyed the film, although if the viewer didn't know the relationship between Woolf and Sackville-West, the film might be very puzzling, but a visual treat, in any event. Nigel Nicholson, Vita's son, calls the novel "the longest love letter in history." I like that, that love letters do not have to be letters, per se, but can be novels, essays, memoirs. I like the blurring of genre lines. Perhaps that's one of the reasons I like Woolf so much. She blurs genre lines in her writing and gender lines in her life.

I feel like all this is about to become meaningful both for me personally and for my writing when finally I sort through it. Did I come to London to learn something about/from Virginia Woolf? It seems that way. I remember Frank Baldanza who taught my Twentieth Century British Literature class in graduate school, who was obsessed with Woolf and the Bloomsbury Group. Uncle Frank, what would you say now if you see the young student, who kept falling asleep in class as you extolled the brilliance ofVirginia Woolf, wandering wide-eyed through Bloomsbury and joyful among the pages of *The Waves*?

This morning, as I walked to the Bayswater Station in an almost invisible mist, I was startled by a taxi speeding through a flurry of pigeons: black blur of taxi and spinning wheels, white and gray wings flapping, a rising of tatters and flutters in the air, then the taxi vanished, and the heavy pigeon bodies thumped back down to the blacktop. It was a startling moment in the sleepy world of morning, the black and white world before the colors of the day bleed through. Just recalling it makes me want to write about it. But there's no time. I have to think about Lear and Gatsby, about how tragedy works its way into the lives of us all, the king and the garage mechanic, the dutiful daughter and the boy who works to have it all, how astounded we remain, despite all we know of history and literature, when it happens to us.

There are disruptions here on the subway daily because of the IRA bombings in Belfast on Saturday that killed ten people, the three retaliatory murders, and the three bombs that were discovered this week at outlying British Rail stations. Cathy was late to work this morning because of a "security alert" at Waterloo. I heard on the news tonight that the Central Line is shut down and the District Line between High Street Kensington and Victoria. This morning, when I waited in the Bayswater Station there was a guard pacing the platform obviously looking for that one thing out of place. Funny, I worry more about delayed and canceled trains than bombs blowing us all to smithereens. Probably shows my naiveté and unfamiliarity with the situation here. One always thinks the bomb will go off somewhere else, that the hoodlum's bullet will gun down the other guy. That's probably what keeps us all from living in constant fear. The number of things that could kill any one of us on any given day is astronomical. It could just as easily be a bomb as a speeding car, a plane dropping out of the sky as food poisoning. When do we finally believe that it's happening to us? At that last minute? No, I imagine, not even then. Not to us. Not to me.

Faylene De Vries

"AND HOW'S THE MISSUS?"

"The curtains didn't fade!" I exclaim, perhaps more intensely than such an observation merits, as I walk into the cottage kitchen for the first time in nine months. I am about to begin my fourth summer in rural Ireland, my third as the new spouse of a divorced man the locals revere as their poet-in-residence even though his nationality and lineage are non-Irish.

"Yeah, I noticed," returns Gaylord, the older of my two stepsons, who, having arrived ten days earlier, is eager to report how the cottage has fared during our absence.

"Must be some synthetic fibers in the material," I mutter while my mind retreats into the past. I recall last year's arrival and my disappointment at the discovery of significant sun-fade to the living room drapes. My first attempt to establish my identity in the cottage, they were symbols even before they were stitched, their deep red weave replacing the dull pink brocade chosen by the cottage's former mistress. But as I aroused uneasy curiosity from the community, the drapes had intruded on the cottage. They had been too bright, as I had been naive about my new role.

Eager to explore my new home during that first summer of our marriage, I wanted the hired car to rush the thirty-five miles from Shannon Airport to the cottage. The sun, like a clichéd blessing, welcomed us. Everything seemed brighter, as if all colors had found a new prism through which to filter. Each blade of grass appeared distinct. I felt in my prime; like properly aged wine, my new life was ready for tasting and savoring. "There's the Crimson Flash. Gerry's driving it out of the garage now." Lincoln's gentle voice, raised a bit in excitement, had interrupted my reverie. The Crimson Flash was Lincoln's '64 Volkswagen resprayed a bright red. Each year in advance of our arrival, Lincoln mailed the key to Gerry Whelan, the local miracle mechanic, who brought the car back to life. Seeing it dart out toward the Kilmara Road just as we arrived in the taxi only furthered the summer's favorable signs. Gerry's hearty "Welcome home," spoken to Lincoln, affirmed them more. To be viewed as a native and not just a tourist was the missing ingredient all my other jaunts to foreign places had lacked. Officially, this was already true. As Lincoln's spouse, I also had claim to his status of residency. I was positive the same would soon be mine socially.

In the next few days, I was to hear the "welcome home" greeting many times. I heard it, but was not its recipient. The words, warm and familiar, were for Lincoln; looks, curious and suspicious, were reserved for me. I felt assaulted by the Small Town Look. The Look of Bidsie Mac, former publican turned full-time gossip, cornered me out of the edges of her greeting to Lincoln. Nell Ryan's Look was less steady. The spouse of the man who had played a major role in many of Lincoln's stories about Ireland, I had been eager to meet her, somehow sure we would become instant friends. I had not foreseen the Look. Up and down, down and up it went until I was sure there couldn't possibly be any more stocking runs or makeup smears to discover. Besides, since I was wearing neither, I was sure the Look was uncovering far more serious faults, piercing my thin skin to expose my Protestant upbringing and my feminist views. My expectations for the summer—now becoming illusions—faded as rainy days replaced the sunshine of our arrival.

The uneasiness I then felt meeting Lincoln's friends and acquaintances transferred into more mundane activities. Marketing in the small shops of Carrigfeale and Kilmara soon became more of a chore than living out a fantasy. On two previous trips to Europe, some years before my marriage, I had always been charmed by the small shop approach to marketing. Indeed, my favorite entertainment on my low-budget backpack tours was to "prepare" dinner. This involved several different shops: the dairy for cheese or yogurt, the green grocer for fresh fruit, the bakery for bread or an extravagant-looking pastry. I never missed shopping from the oversupplied shelves of U.S. supermarkets to the Muzak tune of *buy, buy, buy.* Now I'd put these delightful memories to use for my family. Naive, I overlooked the tourist's acceptance of infrequent overcharging or amused looks of shopkeepers at the foreigner's fumbles. After all, the mistakes are usually all forgotten as the next day's miles separate the event from the place. Once again, I was not prepared for the lack of freedom my new situation presented me. If I shopped alone, I often paid more than if Lincoln were accompanying me. If I ordered a pound of mince meat from the local butcher or a half pound of Irish cheddar from the supermarket clerk, I would be sure to receive more than I requested. But worse than the inflated prices and measurements were the smirks that seemed to curl up from the lips of clerks, those patronizing looks of amusement reserved for speakers with strange accents. Such assumed treatment leads to disquieting consequences. I began to feel as if forces larger than I were puppeting me about and that even the shopkeepers knew better how to organize my life than I did.

As if to verify my fears, my next errand occasioned advice giving. Having agreed to pick up Lincoln's jacket and trousers at O'Donoghue's Drycleaning, I handed the claim ticket to Mr. O'Donoghue, the more than somewhat splenic-looking senior proprietor. His bewildered Look once again reminded me that business in most rural establishments is seldom complete without documentation of the customer's identity. My ticket number was insufficient and my face too unfamiliar. I filled in the gap, "Ramsey's the name," willing, for the moment, to compromise my own name for the sake of convention. Certain Mr. O'Donoghue would recognize the family name, but not me, of course, I braced for the inevitable. Trying to stay on the offense, I murmured, "We live over in Kilnadoon." I had quickly learned that for many Irish, place can be a more important factor of identity than name. Relieved, I saw bewilderment give way to recognition and hoped he would now fetch the cleaning and allow me to be on my way. But just in the time it takes to adjust his glasses upon the bridge of his nose, he decided "Mrs. Ramsey" had taken a different shape. "But you're not . . ." "No, there's been a divorce," I mumbled, irritated at myself for allowing him to be so personal. I knew then I was in too deep to get out without a full confession. Recognition gave way to disapproval. "And where are the children?" he asked. Too aghast to answer, I listened as he instructed me in the merits of children being with their mothers, making it quite obvious that stepmothers are inferior imposters to maternity.

That feeling climaxed on a Sunday afternoon a few weeks after our arrival. The chaos I was experiencing outside the home was in no way diminished in the cottage. The irritations we faced there could fill a dozen more essays: a coal-burning winter tenant had left the cottage smudged and grit ridden; the refrigerator wouldn't work and the Dublin repair person wouldn't be in the area for three weeks; the Crimson Flash's perky welcome proved false, and her starting ability became a question of maybe; and, worst of all, our water tank with the summer's supply of water had sprung a leak. The consequences were hilarious experiments with the domino theory. The broken refrigerator necessitated daily trips into town for perishables, but if the car didn't work, we'd have to take bicycles. But, if we cycled, we wouldn't obtain water from the town pump, and, if we didn't have water, we couldn't clean the house, and we were already washing the dishes only once a day. And the rain dripped and splashed and pelted, creating mud carpets and hostile temperaments. But if it didn't rain, the rain barrel would empty and personal hygiene might be as limited as our dishwashing. Perhaps now my furrowed brow and silent high-pitched scream can be understood that Sunday afternoon. Having just finished off the larder's provisions with the mid-day meal, I poured the last of our water supply into the sink to wash the dishes. Lincoln and Gaylord prepared to go into town, collecting our three plastic five-gallon and two one-gallon containers for water. Taking precaution, Lincoln had parked the car at the top of a hill on the main road. He and Gaylord would hike the neighbors' fields to get to it. In his usual sensitive way, Lincoln had noted my near hysteria and announced on departure, "We'll bring you back a surprise from town." Now if anything brings on a Pavlovian response from me, the word *surprise* does. I didn't mind the giant mound of dishes four people make over three meals as much then. Instead of caked-on-Alpen cereal bowls and butter-smeared plates, I imagined bars of Cadbury Whole Nuts or bottles of Bulmer's Cider or better still one of A Winter's Tale. The glasses and flatware barely finished, the stomp stomp of Gaylord's gait startled me.

"Surprise! Here's your surprise!" his teenage eyes grinning as he presented me with a very clumsy package wrapped in grease-marked newspaper. My dripping hands reached toward the object, my knees weakening with the dread that anticipates one of Lincoln's rare, hard-to-understand-the-humor-of practical jokes. Seeing the contents sent that dread shooting up and out my vocal cords as, "What the hell is this piece of junk?" My hand had gone rigid around a long narrow piece of rounded metal topped with a plastic knob. The gear shift handle had snapped off before Crimson's stubborn battery could be coaxed into starting the engine. Gaylord's and Lincoln's usually infectious laughters did not move me. In a moment of rare affinity with Queen Victoria, Faylene was not amused.

I am amused now. Now is 1989, eight years from the time of the above events. Oh, the nameless reference to married women still sends my eyebrow arching, but the hysterical newcomer described above really makes me laugh. Along with the newly installed water scheme, the new refrigerator, and the newer Ford Escort, that newcomer has been replaced by a much more complacent cottage dweller. I would not say the change has been easy or painless—rather like a strenuous uphill climb on a one-speed bicycle. The hill seems unending as you pedal up; the leg muscles shout at you to give up and get off the bike; your heart warns of bursting veins. In fact, I was in the middle of just such a ride during that summer six years ago when my stepson Andrew challenged my self-pity. We had just left Carrigfeale, where once again my request for one pound of mince had been answered by one and a half pounds. Stuffing the too large package into my knapsack and the little left from our too small budget back into my wallet, I muttered as I pushed against the hill ascending away from the town, "When are these people ever going to accept me?" Always very patient with me (he would go up and down hills twice while I huffed my way up once), Andrew suggested, "Why don't you give them time to know you?" Why didn't I, indeed? From that moment on, I responded *to* my new world rather than expecting it to respond to me.

That resolution was tested at the beginning of the very next summer. Lincoln and I happened to arrive from the States on a Tuesday, which is Market Day in Carrigfeale. Although not as grand as in the past, Market Day still attracts many additional vendors to the town square, and shoppers flock to the town to take advantage of the extra choices and frequently better bargains. Local producers offer vegetables and plants at keener prices, while mobile drapers and ironmongers compete favorably with local merchants. Since many of the vendors return week after week, one can also establish a rapport with them similar to that shared with a local merchant. Lincoln and I had developed such a relationship with a certain brother and sister partnership the summer before. Each Tuesday we'd look for the two selling vegetables in front of their olive green van. We could always count on getting the best carrots from them. Now twelve months later, we decided to explore the market before even going to the cottage. "Look," I noticed, nudging Lincoln. "There's the Carrot Team." As we walked across the street to make our purchase, the brother looked up, spotted me, and nodded. I smiled in return, but determined to have fewer expectations than the first summer, I prepared only to do business. However, before I could request my two pounds of carrots, the young man greeted me, "Welcome home, Missus."

Faylene De Vries

VIEWS FROM THE KITCHEN

Two windows open our Kilnadoon kitchen to light: the only room—except for Lincoln's study—which has the extravagance of two views. Perhaps this design is the basis for the habits I associate with each window. The larger two-paned one, facing toward Moher Bay, assists me in very practical ways beginning with my initial glimpse of the day. Stumbling from the bedroom, I lift the multi-colored café curtains and check on the weather, reporting my findings to Lincoln who may or may not have followed me. If he has, he will join me at the window where we'll discuss what size fire is needed and, if it is summer, whether or not our neighbors will be able to save hay that day. On some days the left side of the lower pane rattles and clacks. Then, we are surely warned of a great County Clare rainstorm complete with strong sea winds and lashings of rain.

No matter what the window may report or forecast, our supply of turf, squatting just outside the window, reassures us that we can challenge any weather. Around mid-day, I'll carry in buckets of the hard black bricks to replenish the turf basket beside the kitchen's Stanley, our solid fuel range. Just beyond the stand of turf and behind the stone wall and whitethorn trees, I can see our neighbor Gussie's fields and his house above them. Sometime during the morning, the window will alert me, almost unconsciously, of Gussie's routine movements. Gussie, a bachelor, lives on his own and has experienced ill health these last few years. If, when it's time for the one o'clock news, I sense a slight uneasiness in myself, Gussie has probably not yet made his appearance, or I missed him. Then, until Gussie himself or his voice makes itself evident, my third eye scarcely leaves the window.

The clothesline is also visible through this window, and once the wash is hung out, the window helps me keep vigilance on any sudden cloudburst or invading bullock which may threaten the drying clothes. Since both panes will open, the window becomes a tool for carrying out several other household chores. The bottom one gets shoved up any time I want to throw out used tea leaves (the flowers below thrive on them) or desire the aid of a breeze to dry a just-mopped floor (it's cheaper than an electric fire). Lowering the top pane will cool the cook when the range is needed at full blast to cook a meal.

Generally, Lincoln and I can only afford to spend summers at the cottage. However, twice in the last ten years, we've managed to leave our teaching positions for longer stays here. During those times, this western window serves as an entertaining observer of the passing seasons. In winter, no blackberry vines camouflage the stone wall between our garden and Gussie's field. The wall's stark grayness reflects light off the branches of the bare thorn trees, bristling with the wintry gales. Then, just as a whisper of green murmurs over the branches, the birds sing us into spring. Jackdaws, pied wagtails, rooks, robins, magpies, and finches announce their frantic hurry to nest. Beaks full of twigs, straw, or string scavenged from the fields, they make no secret of their business. One sizable jackdaw impressed and amused us all through one day's lunch as it attempted to get airborne with an even more sizable twig. Not willing to give up, it fluttered from the ground to the top of the stone wall; then it took an awkward, but successful, sideways flight to a whitethorn branch before flapping up to the rooftop and out of sight. I could only imagine that its frustration must have been increased by understanding that to release even one epithetic "caw" would have eliminated any chance for success. A few days later, however, the jackdaw's triumph was our dismay. We suddenly realized the destination of that monstrous twig when Lincoln tried to light a fire in the sitting-room and was answered only by choking smoke coming from the fireplace. What the chimney sweep removed transformed my dismay back to respect.

We recognize spring is giving way to summer when our morning muesli is accompanied by the pecking rhythm of the birds breakfasting on the seeds and bugs embedded in the turf pile. We hold on to this view as long as possible repressing any thought of fall responsibilities. However, this window will not let us ignore the migrating birds. For some reason, our cottage seems to be an official rest stop. A flock will land briefly in the trees, on the power and clotheslines, or on the roof before whooshing off again. The noise a flock's take-off can make haunts me. Its intensity somehow shivers loneliness into my landscape as if someone dear were deserting me. On those days, the window reminds me that I must pack my summer into boxes for the attic and unpack my textbooks and teaching habits for school. With the birds, I must migrate to my winter feeding ground where the kitchen takes second place to the classroom.

As in many country cottages, our kitchen is the center of the house, able to shift its function to need. At different times, therefore, it also serves as the dining room, the laundry room, a dressing room, or the receiving room. That is primarily true because the kitchen maintains the warmest fire. Although a Waterford Stanley range has replaced the traditional hearth of postcards, the fire's importance has in no way diminished. It not only provides heat, but it also boils the potatoes, bakes the custard, warms the bath water, and fights mildew. Without central heating, I quickly understood how all those clichés about hearth and home and heart came into being. My own vision of my childhood "home" in rural Washington State is not the town dwelling we moved to when I was eleven. Instead, the kitchen of our previous farmhouse supplies most of my memories: the combination range, a strange invention that burned wood on one side and provided electrical cooking elements on the other; the low rocking chair beside the range, in which my father switched a linesman's climbers for farmer's rubber boots; the small mirror on the opposite wall before which Dad shaved and my older sisters pinned their curls; the sewing machine from which Mom shaped yards of material into Easter outfits, living room curtains, and wedding dresses; the long kitchen table Mom and my sisters covered each Saturday with chocolate cakes, boysenberry pies, and cinnamon rolls and at which Uncle Harve intoned a sermon-length grace while Mom's Sunday fried chicken and gravy cooled; the old metal washtub that became a kitchen bathtub when winter Northeasters sent the bathroom temperature below freezing; the kitchen sink where my sisters washed dinner dishes and sobbed over yet another tragic love story on the "forbidden" *Lux Radio Theatre* while Mom and Dad were out milking. In a similar way, our Kilnadoon kitchen was the first place I felt "at home" in Ireland. Here Lincoln and his boys welcomed me with homemade signs and my first cups of Irish tea. Here Gaylord kept an all night vigil over Collette, the family's beloved sheepdog, after she had been kicked by a horse. Here, with Gussie's guidance, I cooked my first goose dinner on the Stanley. Here Gay Byrne and Marian Finucane introduced me to the Ireland of R.T.E's *Radio One.* Here I realized the value of my teaching profession. Here I dreamed of changing careers or, even riskier, putting my thoughts to paper.

These dreams occur most often when I stand before the kitchen's other view. Far less practical than the two-paned one, the kitchen's second window, with its small panes rimmed in glossy black, faces the road with a more traditional appearance. Opened only for repainting or thorough cleaning, the window sits behind the kitchen work table and, therefore, makes a perfect spot for daydreaming. As I chop onions or knead pizza dough, I memorize the features of the landscape, depositing them in my memory's eye bank for homesickness cures when I'm in New Whatcom, Washington. Just outside the window the ground slopes down to that swampy area resting just inside the stone wall separating our front yard from the road. In the middle stands a line of lily plants whose yellow blooms usually remain long enough to welcome us back in June. To the left of them stands a crabapple tree strangely shaped by prevailing winds and the county's hedge-trimming machines. I have yet to see an apple on it, but would be fiercely annoyed if the tree were removed. When our neighbor Beth's donkey is in residence, I will frequently see her take shelter from the rainstorm of the moment under the crabapple's protective branches. I know how she may feel, for I need only gaze out this window and whatever is wrong will almost be right again. For that to happen, I will have to look over the crabapple tree and across the road to Martin O'Connell's fields. Curving up the gentle hills, these fields are quilts on which I patchwork my dreams. Some days the fields just shimmer in their various greens cut across by the grays of the stone walls. That will kindle languid daydreaming into fervent inspirations. My lunchtime chatter will feed Lincoln's slightly amused attention with new business schemes, best-selling plot lines, cottage improvements, a reply to deconstructionism, and world peace plans. On other days, the window displays machines and men harvesting tender shoots for silage. Flocks of seabirds and crows soon arrive on the scene, swirling and gliding before gleaning the tasty seeds left behind. Then the cows, black and white Friesens (the Irish name for Holsteins), take over, chewing the new grass with a delight similar to what I reserve for strawberries with fresh cream. I stand, hot cup of tea at chin height, drifting through the steam into the reflection those hills now urge. Last week's schemes and plans require second thoughts. I need to select what is best and make it workable. The best prevention of cynicism must be to make sure the ideal produces results. Therefore, planning world peace revises into a unit introducing contemporary Irish authors to Kulshan College's students in Lit. 131; adding a room on to the cottage becomes uncovering and refinishing the wooden floor in the sitting-room; developing a chain of ice cream parlors in the west of Ireland evolves into proposing a one-quarter sabbatical leave from teaching; purpling prose for a potboiler changes into writing a collection of essays. Feeling energized, I arouse from reverie and realize the view has also renewed itself. As if some agreement had been reached, every single cow is lying down while another flock of birds takes its turn pecking at the grass. With surprising tolerance, the cows allow the flock so near I expect at least one trusting bird to hop right on a cow's back. Although that doesn't happen, I do feel a natural benediction granted to my dreams.

To suggest that some of my dreams are being realized in a kitchen makes me feel, well, vulnerable—to say the least. I cower, sensing all my feminist friends crying "Betrayal!" Lowering myself to defensiveness, I'll quickly remind you that I'm the daughter who hates housework and show you my dusty, cluttered house as credentials. If needed, I'll even brandish my marriage contract that clearly reveals our belief that marriage is a partnership by stating that I am not solely responsible for household chores as Lincoln is not expected to provide all the finances. In fact, I've been fighting this essay myself for two years. At that time, Lincoln and I were enjoying a seven-month stay at the cottage. Lincoln had been granted a sabbatical to write a book, and I chose, negotiating an agreement with him, to take a two-quarter leave without pay. Having never "not worked" since leaving the university, I wanted to experience the luxury of responsibility-free days. Fortunately, our circumstances, finances, and a then strong U.S. dollar made that desire a reality. Never bored, I filled my days with activities from my long "things to do when I have time" list. I tried to bake bread; I read a whole novel at one sitting; I explored the canon of Henry James; I took long walks with my wildflower guidebook in hand; I added more items to my list; I even cleaned house. To be truthful, this essay surfaced during an afternoon mopping spree. Down on all fours, grinding my bony knees against the tiled cement, I was also listening to an R.T.E interview with Marilyn French, whose *The Woman's Room* had been receiving attention in Ireland. As I was caught up in that discussion, the drudgery of the task seemed less oppressive, since I was reminded that women's work is also done outside the kitchen. However, that transformation is only possible if I, the kitchen worker, also have access to that outside world. I am happy in my Kilnadoon kitchen because I am not trapped here. My identity is not shaped in its confines. I can look beyond the windows into a classroom where I find satisfaction (most of the time) developing basic skills and, even more, challenging my students to think beyond stereotypes. At the same time, I assert that I teach better and enjoy it more because of my kitchen's reflection.

Luckily for me, two windows open our Kilnadoon kitchen to light.

Deena Linett

NORTHBOUND

We make landfall in a northern harbor facing a city
studded with dark fortresses, Oslo or Helsinki, civic
buildings shining white and yellow in thin skins of sun.

I had imagined this for a very long time: perhaps twenty years. It was last year, and my first trip to Europe (if you don't count a week in London, which I don't). I knew the buildings would be largely unadorned, massive, and stone, but the broad open harbors felt like nothing in America, nothing I had ever seen. I could not have imagined their wide embrace, the blocky low profiles of cities you approach by water.

I don't tend to prepare for a new place by reading travel books. I want—but without the customary sense of suddenness—to be surprised. I want the experience to unfold as I move through it. One has expectations, anyhow. Mine were amorphous, feelings for and intimations toward, like the mist I soon would see on the Sognefjord, and in the Oslofjorden, a sense of coming pleasure. I bought a Swedish phrase-book and practiced saying *Tack så mycket* and *Manga tack,* working at the accent—on the first syllables (this gives Swedish its singing feel to American ears). I expected a sense of northernness, a sense that I would be farther north, and east, than I had ever imagined. I was captivated by the idea that the cities faced morning, where the sun comes from.

Streaming out of the austere blue sluice farther north,
  shot through
with brilliants like little icy dazzles in the snow, the air is
  polished

to a silver sheen. Here is the light we need for a time
when naturally we gravitate toward cities and the gritty
real,
the time for islands having passed.

The "islands" come from the particulars of my history; I grew up on the Gulf Coast of Florida, and the islands I was thinking of are tropical, easy islands, not islands bound by ice, wrapped in darkness. Stockholm, whose name means "tree-island" is of course built on many islands.

In photographs of fjords it isn't possible to see
deep passageways behind the walls of rock
spotted here and there with lichen, streaked
with frozen water, and greened between the waterfalls
by stands of trees. The mother of the Earth
is here: these are her strands of silver hair. Luminous
mist clings to the rock in the mornings, climbs
to hover above the fingers of the sea. Here,
beyond memory and speech, where fairies live
and trolls are born, a sound unrolls like smoke, and gathers,
wraps our heads and shoulders in its shawl: echo
of the low insistent foghorn's call.

For half a day I stood on deck on a ferry on the Sognefjord, the deepest and longest of Norway's waterways. I don't think it's possible to render the complex foldings of the fjords: in every direction, passageways of deep waters, dark and clear, like mirrors when you're dreaming. While our boat made its way through the perfect green stillness between huge steep mountains made of rock, there was the sense that if we could just go that way, or that, we would see something marvelous, some other combination of water-stone-and-sky. Waterfalls stream down the perpendicular dark stone faces as if a Spirit wept.

The clouds were massed silver—lit here and there as if by an inventive stage-manager—and lowering grays. In the fjords there are more shades of gray than can be imagined: the water and sky and rock and clouds and birds. The hills and mist; light-washed, worn-to-silver wooden houses cling to the sides of hills so steep the only access is by boat and rope. When you look up, cloudforms appear above the rocky walls of the fjords; they reappear in the still waters.

Before we leave the vessel this last time
the harbormaster comes aboard
and ticks his pen against the manifest, eager
to be off; he has other things to do. In the hold
a bar of chocolate and an orange, precious
little of importance to anyone but us, books and stones,
a pierced blue bowl. Weight of invisible cargo,
winds pressing water into walls of thick green glass,
and memories of stops at savage ports, keep the craft low
in the water, but she's sturdy, and she holds.

A Jew, I am drawn to the sacred, so I went to cathedrals in Copenhagen, Oslo, Uppsala, Stockholm. What I saw surprised me. Much more ornament than I imagined Protestant northerners to have needed, or to have had the taste for: ebony encrusted with mother-of-pearl, massive baroque statues of St. George slaying equally massive and fully articulated dragons, brilliant gold altars and chandeliers, interiors dyed red and blue as light poured in through windows of stained Swedish glass.

In Mora, Sweden, I happened on a small village church which looked like the simple Protestant churches I'd expected: unornamented cool gray stone walls; light wood, some of it painted pink, edged the stone here and there with quiet color. The windows, high up, were stained glass and very beautiful, but everything at human level was plain; all the work that spoke of beauty was up, toward God. I left a small donation and a note of thanks at the table where one could buy a booklet about the church. St. Olaf brought Christianity to Sweden in the eleventh century, but it was not a choice, not a gift.

In the cool ornate interiors of cathedrals near water, Olaf
the Holy stands on the backs of shivering pagans crumpled
underneath his weight like piles of clothes. Christ has come
and they must choose him. Jews walk the cobbles
selling little silver herring fish from baskets, and time,
like the sea, foamy and beautiful, bears us up. In the light
from windows in small shops along the quay, artisans bend
to fix watches and sew linings into coats. All along the
  corridors of water
you can hear the crooning skalds sing kennings to the sea.

A tour guide told me to save my money and not go inside the stave church at Borgund, but I needed to go into it. Only twenty-six of these wooden churches remain in Norway. They are Christian, but Viking ornamentation marks the tops of exterior peaks. Oddly, their belltowers are separate, built beside them, lower than the churches, handsome structures on the hilly ground. Going into the stave church was one of the most important things I did in Norway.

In the dark stave church built a thousand years ago,
you can smell woodsmoke that has curled into the walls
and frame, the tarry scent as fresh as sky. Spirits
of the dead flicker like firelight, dancers
humbling themselves before the new god. High
on blond wood pillars faces bless the red-washed altar
where a little gold and blue remain. Stars
are visible through small high windows to the night-blue sky,
and farmers in their layers of felt and wool huddle for hours
in the permanent dark in cold beyond imagining,
their backs to the north where evil and the wind come from,
asking, as we do. Please remember in honor my dear dead
brother,
the runes outside the Uppsala Cathedral say.

I saw those runes. At the Cathedral in Uppsala, which was consecrated in 1435 and begun long before that, the medieval stone soars, and as you walk through, you can imagine being there five hundred years ago—except that how can we imagine those times truly? The only source of light was candles, and what seemed no end to crushing cold.

The day I was there a group of young folk-dancers practiced for an evening performance on the wide stone plaza in front of the main entrance, but before I went inside, I had to go around the corner to see the runes, which looked as one imagines runes to look. I was surprised by the government's having provided translations, one of which said something close to what I have above. Standing there in Uppsala, I was reminded of a stone slab at the Art Institute in Chicago, where inscriptions in an Ur-language just being decoded tell the love of an ancient king: he dedicated a building to his wife with words very like these.

I suppose one of the reasons one writes—poems, journals—is that they provide access to states of mind and feelings one is not aware of at the time. ("We had the experience but missed the meaning," Eliot says in "The Dry Salvages.") Or, one is about to learn something, cannot yet say it, but can express it, wrapped in the velvety folds of metaphor. Perhaps the saying of it, even badly, even disguised, makes a later, clearer saying, possible.

Now we have come to where the truth is dark and cold, clear
as water, almost sweet. Roofs of gunmetal blue slates gleam
in their light wash of gold light as you follow the winding road
down from Holmenkollen to the city, walk familiar foreign
  streets.
You know you have come near the Resistance Museum
when passers-by won't meet your eyes, and the immured cries
of the suffering dead seep from shadows of blue trees and
  crevices in buildings,
clatter in the leaves, and mutter softly from the stones.

There is something of relief in facing unknown or unacknowledged parts of ourselves, I think. But we are physical beings located in the physical, and so always the recognitions must be specific to some place, a place with a name and history; a place it is possible to return to. That place, with its local particularities, is important: something of the color of light on stone, the slant of hill or twist of tree, the geometry of a window, has perhaps made recognition possible that could not occur elsewhere.

Behind its cloak of clouds, the sun's a copper burnish on the sky.
You climb the hills to Akershus and go inside. You can't resist.
Here are the narrow passageways between cages. Here
are toilets in barracks lit with blue light. Bare stone
floors and walls, and no mirrors. So cold
you must look up to check: are these rooms open to the sky?
You drag your hand along the walls as you walk the cobbled paths,
as if it were possible to console them. Soldiers' boots pound
our own heart's rhythms. We know them by their radiant chains,
their sounding presence in the still icy night, in the rain.

At the Akershus, a fortress dating from the fourteenth century high on a hill above the harbor, cobbled walkways, stone half-timbered buildings mark the way up to the castle. All are medieval in feel, even the small buildings added much later. I looked for vistas that would have been unchanged since the thirties, thinking of the Occupation, the Norwegian Resistance fighters on skis here, in Telemark, and farther north, thinking of people I know whose arms are tattooed, whose spirits have been marked by war's unspeakable sufferings. Here's how language fails: to Americans the Occupation in Norway is a concept. To Norwegians it means not a period of time, not an abstraction, but their personal history: every day for years. Every minute of every hour of each and every day—for years. In the darkness of winters and in the sunlit and desolate summers.

To walk there fifty years later, alone, on a day in late summer when light rain fell, was to walk in a timeless place. Though the lawn was uncannily green, and there were no wounded, no cries, no shell-holes in the ground, all the buildings intact, I heard it anyway, the weeping. How could one not?

Perhaps a writer can experience events fully only by writing about them. Paradoxically, experience, whose nature is flux, is shaped by stopping it in language, because language, with its requirements of grammar and structure, with its inherent sense of audience, requires limiting and defining—naming—that which has been unnamable. This compassing—saying this is *this* and not *that*—makes knowing possible, and knowing is a social act: it takes place in a context. There is an *I* who is writing, an *I* discovering; but as something written comes into being, it requires that what I am beginning to know be made available to you: it is always necessary that there be a you.

But a poem is a distillation of, and metaphor for, experience; it is not the experience, and in its re-creation and recollection, it fails to tell the whole. Or that's not its task. What I left out: the sense of being at home in a strange place; the presence, everywhere, of water nearby. The longboats taking Swedes to church that I saw on a Sunday morning on a sliver of stream, barely glimpsed in the deep green of a forest. Overnight cruises from Copenhagen to Oslo and from Stockholm to Helsinki. Lightning and a powerful storm one night didn't even rock the ship where I slept easily. When the next day I went to an SAS office to confirm a ticket, the reservations agent asked if I'd been frightened: "You were in that big storm on the Skagerak last night." "Oh," I said, "but I was sailing with the Vikings!"

In fact it was a very different trip from Stockholm to Helsinki, where at dinner people pushed and shoved at me—I suppose I was in the wrong line. Beautiful and elegantly dressed young Swedish women elbowed me; it was deliberate, physical. They may have thought I was a native, being difficult (on the street in Oslo twice people had asked me directions in Norwegian). Safe in my stateroom late that night, I knew: if this ship goes down, they are the ones who will be on the lifeboats.

I left out: the Fram Museum with its restored Fram, the first "Polar Vessel to go farthest north and farthest south." The Fram, a ship small enough to be believable, makes Polar expeditions convincing—moving—to a modern mind. In addition to the ship itself, massive taxidermied musk-ox and polar bear, colored sketches of the Northern Lights by Fridtjof Nansen, and artifacts from the journey. Before I saw these watercolors and colored-pencil sketches, it had never occurred to me that until cameras, artists' renderings were the only images we had of explorers' visits to new places.

Early photographs of the ship trapped in pack ice, tilted and nearly overcome, saved only by the design of her keel and the intelligence of her captain, Otto Sverdrup, are surprising in their power, a century after she first drifted north to test Nansen's theories of Arctic currents (1893-1896). On this same ship Amundsen sailed to the South Pole nearly ten years later. Out in front of the museum, a boat called Gja, the vessel Amundsen outfitted for his first attempts to find the Northwest Passage (1905); during this voyage the magnetic North Pole was located and charted. On these early modern voyages explorers first mapped the northern coastline of Norway and many islands in the Arctic Ocean.

I left out: the crushed brown-paper skin in the vee of her blouse of the elegant woman in her eighties from New Orleans whose husband called me "honey," and whose accents I recognized as being from the bayou country south of there. She drank Scotch and gossiped as if she didn't know that every day was a gift, but she did know: he was nearly ninety, and I saw the way she waited on him.

In an Italian restaurant near the hotel in Stockholm, when she ordered, the waitress's eyes flew wide, though her face remained still in a perfection of politeness. "An accent from the American South," I said—I had to say.

I left out: the beauty of the moon-swept Hardanger Plateau in Norway, up above the timberline where stunted trees, twisted and tortured-looking little birches and a few crippled pines give way to vast expanse where nothing grows, rock-strewn moraine, a few cairns built by hikers, an occasional thatched travel-hut, a temporary marker on the permafrost.

I left out: my surge of pleasure as the ship drew into Helsinki a little after dawn on a rain-swept day that lightened later, but retained the gray I'd come to understand as north. It seemed for those few moments on that boat that I was coming back to someplace I had been before, though I couldn't speak the language—or even make out most of it from reading. I want to know how it can be that going north, when one has dreaded cold, is coming home.

I left out: the massive yellow ice-breaker waiting in the harbor at Helsinki in August. The World War II bunker in the garden of the hotel at Stalheim. I walked into its cool yellow light and looked down into the deep valley—the Stalheimskleiven is the deepest gorge in Europe—and across scrub and stony hills to horizons on three sides, imagining boys on watch in the dark, through silent frosty nights.

All travel memoirs must be cross-hatched with what has been left out, not well-enough remembered, does not suit. My first trip out of North America took me to Peru; I carried not a camera, but a notebook, and a novel grew out of those notes. In Helsinki, at the Suomen Kansallismuseo, the Finnish National Museum, I spent a good deal of time in the basement, looking at the mannequins in ancient Finnish clothes. Blond life-size dolls with faces from central Asia wore beautifully embroidered woolen dresses, trousers, and tunics of bright red or blue; ornamented boots made of skins and colored felt had been sewn and beaded. I couldn't imagine the cold. That people have flourished, made architecture and music and inventive food, grown flowers, and praised creation in places so far north humbles one used to the comforts of North America, its wealth and its ease. What I saw was in many ways beyond language, though it can be pointed to, aimed at, if not named.

Endurance, yes, but more: pleasure in detail, the constancy of making, whether it's the stirring of a soup, the hammering of tin, the sewing of a coverlet. I need to remember—I needed to learn—that life flourishes in the cold, in places we cannot imagine and have never been. People live out their lives there, loving and singing. They tell their times with stories, things they cherish, countless human ordinary things we think we know, but do not know until we see.

An old part of me believed that travel is a pure extravagance, perhaps my medieval self, which found its resonance in medieval structures. What I learned is what everybody else seems always to have known: seeing is a powerful and irreducible way of knowing and being, and it changes us. Deep feeling is an indication of something needed, not a frippery and not a frill. Travel is perhaps like art: it nourishes the parts of us we didn't know were longing. What I experienced in Scandinavia is beyond saying; I wrap it close around me like a wool embroidered shawl.

About the Authors

Barbara Abel has received a University of Wisconsin-Madison Vilas Essay Award, a Loft Creative Nonfiction Award, and a Lake Superior Regional Writers Award in poetry. Her poems have been included in several publications, including *The Nebraska Review* and *Kalliope.*

Judith Azrael has a collection of her poetry, *Twelve Black Horses,* published by Salmon Run Press.

Helen Barolini was born and grew up in Syracuse, New York. After graduation from Syracuse University she traveled in Europe writing a series of articles for the *Syracuse Herald Journal.* She spent much of her married life in Italy, and her seven published books, including *Chiaroscuro: Essays of Identity,* reflect her dual background. Her first book, the novel *Umbertina,* was completed with the help of a grant from the National Endowment for the Arts, and was followed by *The Dream Book: An Anthology of Writings by Italian American Women,* which received an American Book Award. She has been a Fellow at Yaddo and the McDowell Colony, a Writer-in-Residence at Elmira College's Quarry Farm, and a resident writer at the Rockefeller Foundation's Bellagio Center in Italy.

Judith Barrington is a poet from England who has lived in the U.S. since 1976. She is the author of two collections of poems, *Trying to be an Honest Woman* (1985) and *History and Geography* (1989), both published by Eighth Mountain Press. She is the founder of The Flight of the Mind, an annual summer writing workshop for women writers, and she teaches in the Arts Education Program in Oregon, Washington, and Utah. From 1964 to 1966, she spent most of her time in Cataluna, working for a wine company based in a castle near the French/Spanish border. She has also been a secretary at the B.B.C., a public relations executive, a furniture mover, and the director of a heating and ventilating company. She now lives in Portland, Oregon, with her woman partner of twelve years.

Michelle Blair holds a Master of Fine Arts from Columbia University's graduate writing program. She has published fiction and nonfiction in a number of small literary journals and anthologies. She has been an instructor of writing and literature on the college level for many years and is on the verge of becoming a full-time high school teacher. Her most recent travels have taken her across Canada, where the province of Saskatchewan captured her heart, and, to the north, where, in a canoe on a lake at the edge of the boreal forest, she saw her first northern lights, so magnificent they brought tears to her eyes.

Laurel Berger lived in Madrid from 1985-94. Her writing has appeared in numerous publications, including *The New York Times, Artnews,* the *Independent on Sunday,* and *Time Out.* She lives in Sag Harbor, New York, and is working on her first novel.

Leslie Brody's memoir *The Magpie's Dream* will be published in the fall of 1998. She lives and teaches in Connecticut.

Kelly Cherry's memoir about the Soviet Union, *The Exiled Heart,* was published by Louisiana State University Press in 1991. Other recent books include *Death and Transformation* (Louisiana State University Press, 1997), and a collection of essays, *Writing the World* (University of Missouri Press, 1995). The original version of Imant Kalnin's Fourth Symphony, using Cherry's "Lyric Circle" as the text for the final movement, received its world premiere by the Detroit Symphony Orchestra, conducted by Neeme Järvi, in 1997.

Sharon Chmielarz has had two books of poetry published by New Rivers Press: *Different Arrangements* and *But I Won't Go Out in a Boat.* More recently she has been working on a manuscript of poems dealing with the life of Maria Anna "Nannerl" Mozart. After thirty years of public school teaching, she is writing full-time. After visiting Italy recently, and not just imagining it, she would describe the country as *la bella paesa.*

Faylene De Vries, a native of Washington state, presently resides in Ireland. She taught English at Skagit Valley College in Mount Vernon, Washington. Her work has appeared in Irish, English, Australian, and American journals, including *Books Ireland, Staple, Famous Reporter,* and *Rosebud.*

Wendy Erd lives in Homer, Alaska, where she and her husband have spent the last twelve years as commercial salmon fishermen. She has received local and statewide awards for both her poetry and nonfiction. Her most recent work has appeared in *Alaska Quarterly Review.*

Currently, she has retired her nets and returned to Vietnam to teach English in Hanoi.

Mary Ellen Fieweger is a writer, translator, and lecturer who has lived in Ecuador for twenty years. Her creative essays have appeared in *Tamaqua* and *Cream City Review,* and in local publications including *La Palabra Suelta* and *La Liebre Ilustrada*. She translated selections appearing in *Water Lilies: An Anthology of Spanish Women Writers from the Fifteenth through the Nineteenth Century* (University of Minnesota Press) and the works in *Diez Cuentistas Ecuatorianos/Ten Stories from Ecuador* (Ediciónes Libri Mundi), a bilingual anthology. In 1996, her translation of *Sueño de Lobos (Wolves' Dream),* a novel by Abdón Ubidia, was published by the Latin American Literary Review Press.

Vicki Goldsmith teaches women's studies, Advanced Placement Literature and Composition, Theory of Knowledge, and at-risk freshmen at Roosevelt High School in Des Moines, Iowa. In 1995, she received a fellowship from the National Endowment for the Humanities to study Greek mythology and religion. Her project is currently being profiled in a collection written by the director of the Council on Basic Education.

Pamela Gullard has won a PEN Syndicated Fiction Project Award and an H. G. Roberts Award for fiction. Her stories have appeared in *The Iowa Review, Mademoiselle,* and in her collection, *Breathe at Every Other Stroke* (Henry Holt, 1996). She teaches writing classes at Writers Connection in San Jose, and lives in Menlo Park, California, with her husband and two sons.

Nor Hall brings an interdisciplinary approach to her work in psychotherapy. Combining interests in mythology, poetry, and theater, she collaborates with artists in various media on projects exploring the psyche's penchant for art. She maintains a private practice, leads workshops, and sits on the advisory board for *Spring: A Journal of Archetype and Culture.* Her books include *The Moon and the Virgin: Reflections on the Archetypal Feminine, Those Women,* and *Broodmales.*

Danielle D'Ottavio Harned's work has appeared in *Kansas Quarterly, Aphrodite Gone Berzerk, The Machineel Journal, Perimeter of Light* (Iris Editions) and *L'Overture.* She was awarded first place in the Hackney Literary Awards, was a resident at The MacDowell Colony, and a Fellow at the Alden B. Dow Creativity Center.

Persis Knobbe, who writes in Marin County, California, is working on a collection tentatively titled *The Morris Stories.* Her stories have been published in *American Fiction, Volume Three* and in *Nice Jewish Girls,* a Penguin/Plume anthology. Her short story, "Here I Am," is included in an international collection published by the Jewish Publication Society.

Marilyn Krysl is the author of five books of poetry and two books of two stories, including *What We Have to Live With* (Teal Press, 1989), which was awarded the 1990 Mountains and Plains Booksellers' Association Poetry Award, and *Mozart, Westmoreland, and Me* (Thunder's Mouth Press, 1985), which won the University of Colorado Faculty Book Prize in 1986. She is a past director of the Creative Writing Program at the University of Colorado, Boulder, and has served as Artist-in-Residence at the University of Colorado School of Nursing's Center for Human Caring.

Diane Lefer is the author of the short story collection, *The Circles I Move In.* She lives in Southern California, where she teaches in the Writers' Program at UCLA Extension and also works with endangered baboons.

Michelle Dominique Leigh is a writer and illustrator who has lived and worked in Europe, Africa, Asia, and North and South America.

Joan Lindgren, a translator of contemporary Latin American poetry, has made many trips to the Southern Cone of that part of the world. Her translations, essays on poetry, original poems, and prose pieces have been published widely in magazines and anthologies, including *Latin American Literary Review, Seneca Review,* and *Two Worlds Walking,* (New Rivers Press). Most recently, she edited and translated an anthology of the work of Juan Gelman entitled *Unthinkable Tenderness* (University of California Press). Gelman, father of one of Argentina's Disappeared, has just been awarded the National Poetry Prize of his country. Lindgren's work with the families of the Disappeared will be documented in *Translating Argentina.*

Deena Linett grew up on the Gulf coast of Florida and teaches writing and literature at Montclair State University in New Jersey. The author of two prize-winning novels, she has twice been a Yaddo Fellow. She is currently at work on essays about Scotland and a trip to Montana with her grown daughter.

Leza Lowitz is editor of the anthologies of contemporary Japanese women's poetry, *A Long Rainy Season* and *Other Side River* (Stone Bridge Press, 1994, 1995), author of *Old Ways to Fold New Paper* (Wandering Mind, 1996), and co-author of the script *Milk* (Fischerfilm, Vienna 1997). She lived in Japan from 1990 to 1994, where she was a freelance writer for the *Japan Times* and *Art in America* and taught writing at Tokyo University. She currently lives on the other side of the Pacific in a small village on the northern California coast.

Margaret Todd Maitland is currently at work on a collection of essays entitled *The Dome of Creation*. The managing editor of the *Hungry Mind Review,* she lives in Saint Paul, Minnesota, with her husband, poet Dan Bachhuber, and their son.

Elizabeth Mills is senior editor and director of development of the *Southwest Review.*

Kathleen Moore's first job after college was teaching English in a small village in Ethiopia. Since then, she has worked in a Job Corps Center, raised a son, gone to graduate school, and worked for various city and county government agencies. She is once again teaching English as a Second Language and is a co-founder of WISE (Women's International Self-reliance Enterprise), an organization that helps immigrant women find support and resources. Some of her writing has appeared in *The Single Mother's Companion* (Seal Press), *26 Minnesota Writers* (Nodin Press), and *Women Celebrate: Breaking Silence into Joy* (forthcoming).

Rhiannon Paine's contributions to *An Inn Near Kyoto* come from her book *Too Late for the Festival: An American Salary-Woman in Japan.* When she got home from Tokyo, Rhiannon followed her boss Ron Tamura's advice and used her savings to buy a Victorian cottage in Healdsburg, California, where she has lived ever since. When she is not doing technical writing, creative writing, or Scottish country dancing, she spends her spare time trying to find the whereabouts of her friend Yas (who left YHP many years ago) and Burt, the Australian frilled lizard.

Ann Pancake's work has appeared in *Virginia Quarterly Review, Chattahoochee Review, Antietam Review,* and other journals and magazines. In 1996, she received a fellowship from the National Endowment for the Arts for her fiction.

Edith Pearlman is the winner of the 1996 Drue Heinz Prize for Literature. *Vaquita,* a collection of her short stories, was published in 1996 by University of Pittsburgh Press. Recently, her work has appeared or is forthcoming in *Antioch Review, Ascent, Kalliope, Palo Alto Review, Paris Review, Santa Barbara Review, Widener Review, Smithsonian, Hope,* and the anthology *An Intricate Weave.*

Simone Poirier-Bures teaches writing at Virginia Tech and is also the author of *Candyman* (Oberon, 1994), a novel about a French Acadian family set in her native Nova Scotia. Her fiction and prose have appeared in more than two dozen journals and anthologies in the United States and Canada.

Judy Rosen has worked for the U.S. Forest Service and National Park Service for the last eighteen years as ranger, environmental educator, planner, and exhibit designer. Her assignments have included stints in Denali and Katmai national parks and preserves in Alaska, Padre Island National Seashore, Texas, Canyon de Chelly National monument, Arizona, Medicine Bow National Forest, Wyoming, and Rocky Mountain National Park, Colorado. Her interest in natural and cultural heritage has led to extended visits of parks and forests in Asia, Europe, Central and South America, and Australia—where she served as a ranger/consultant for the Queensland National Parks and Wildlife Service. She works part-time for the U.S. Forest Service planning and designing exhibits for national forests throughout the Rocky Mountains. She lives with her husband and two sons in a log cabin in Estes Park, Colorado.

Andrea Benton Rushing is Professor of English and Black Studies at Amherst College in Amherst, Massachusetts. She is also the co-editor of *Women in Africa and the African Diaspora* and the author of numerous articles and reviews published in academic journals and collections. Her current work-in-progress is *Speaking in Tongues: The Language of Yoruba Women's Attire.* Her exhibit of cloth, jewelry, and color photographs, entitled "A Language of Their Own: Yoruba Women's Attire," has been shown at a number of colleges and universities. She has traveled extensively in the Caribbean and has made several extended visits to Nigeria.

Lee Sharkey directs the Women's Studies Program at the University of Maine at Farmington. *To A Vanished World,* a poem sequence in response to Roman Vishniac's photographs of Eastern European Jewry in the years just prior to the Holocaust, was published by Puckerbrush Press. She is an editor of the *Beloit Poetry Journal* and the winner of *Zone 3*'s 1996 Rainmaker Award for poetry. Her poems, essays, and translations from the Russian have been published in *Cream City Review, Poet Lore, The River Review, Southern Humanities Review, Willow Springs,* and elsewhere.

Joan Silber is the author of the novels *Household Words* (Viking/Penguin, 1980), which won the PEN Hemingway Award, and *In the City* (Viking/Penguin, 1987). Her short fiction has appeared in *The New Yorker, The Voice Literary Supplement, The Paris Review, Boulevard, Witness, Michigan Quarterly Review,* and other magazines. She recently completed a story collection, *Now I Have a Different Life*, and is currently at work on a novel. She teaches at Sarah Lawrence College, the Warren Wilson M.F.A. Program, and the 92nd Street Y.

Anita Skeen is Professor of English at Michigan State University, where she teaches Women's Studies, Canadian Studies, and Creative Writing. She is the author of two volumes of poetry, *Each Hand a Map* and *Portraits.* She is currently completing a new volume of poetry and a first novel.

Lisa Solod has had stories published in many literary magazines, including *The American Voice, Parting Gifts,* and *Good Stories.* The recipient of several fellowships to the Virginia Center for Creative Arts, she lives and writes in Virginia.

Carol Spindel teaches creative nonfiction at the University of Illinois at Urbana-Champaign and at summer workshops in places ranging from the University of Iowa to Paris. Her short essays are a regular feature on her local NPR station AM 580. Her most recent book is *Dancing at Halftime.* She has returned to Kalikaha many times since 1981 with her husband, Tom Bassett, and their two children.

Nadja Tesich was born in Yugoslavia. She is a filmmaker, playwright, novelist, and short story writer. Her short stories and essays have appeared in many magazines and anthologies. Her novel *Native Land* was published in 1997. New Rivers Press published her first novel, *Shadow Partisan*, in 1989.

Sarah Ventres was born, and spent the first twenty-five years of her life, in Evanston, Illinois. Following graduation from Northwestern University with a B.S. in history, she worked for *Vogue Magazine.* Most of her second twenty-five years were spent in Minneapolis, Minnesota, as a mother, homemaker, and dedicated volunteer. So far, her third quarter-century has been filled with returning to the work force, earning an M.B.A. at University of Saint Thomas in Saint Paul, Minnesota, and taking early retirement in order to serve in the Peace Corps. Assigned to Haiti, she served as administrator of a government outpatient clinic in a burgeoning slum in Cap Haitien. She now lives in Santa Fe, New Mexico, where she is trying to set aside time each day for writing.

Nancy Von Rosk is a doctoral candidate at the University of New Hampshire, where she teaches courses in writing and American Literature. She taught English at the Casablanca American School from 1990 to 1992 and traveled extensively throughout Morocco during those years. Her most recent traveling adventure was a trek through the Indian Himalayas. Originally from Long Island, New York, she now lives in Portsmouth, New Hampshire, with her husband and soon-to-be baby.

Sondra Zeidenstein is a poet, editor, and publisher of Chicory Blue Press, a small literary press focusing on writing by women past sixty. The latest publication of the press is *The Crimson Edge: Older Women Writing,* an anthology of writing by seven women whose average age is seventy-three. A selection of her recent poems is included in *Passionate Lives,* edited by Elizabeth Claman (Queen of Swords Press, 1997).